CRITICAL EDUCATION AGAINST GLOBAL CAPITALISM

Karl Marx and Revolutionary Critical Education

Paula Allman

Foreword by
Peter McLaren

Critical Studies in Education and Culture Series
Edited by Henry A. Giroux

Bergin & Garvey
Westport, Connecticut • London

Library of Congress Cataloging-in-Publication Data

Allman, Paula.
  Critical education against global capitalism : Karl Marx and revolutionary critical
education / Paula Allman ; foreword by Peter McLaren.
      p. cm. — (Critical studies in education and culture series, ISSN 1064–8615)
  Includes bibliographical references and index.
  ISBN 0–89789–743–9 (alk. paper)
  1. Capitalism.   2. Marxian economics.   I. Title.   II. Series.
  HB501 .A553   2001
  330. 12'2—dc21   00–064211

British Library Cataloguing in Publication Data is available.

Library of Congress Catalog Card Number: 00–064211
ISBN: 0–89789–743–9
ISSN: 1064–8615

First published in 2001

Bergin & Garvey, 88 Post Road West, Westport, CT 06881
An imprint of Greenwood Publishing Group, Inc.
www.greenwood.com

Printed in the United States of America

The paper used in this book complies with the
Permanent Paper Standard issued by the National
Information Standards Organization (Z39.48–1984).

10 9 8 7 6 5 4 3 2 1

For Chris
and Danielle, Brett, Branden and Jim

Contents

Series Foreword

Educational reform has fallen upon hard times. The traditional assumption that schooling is fundamentally tied to the imperatives of citizenship designed to educate students to exercise civic leadership and public service has been eroded. The schools are now the key institution for producing professional, technically trained, credentialized workers for whom the demands of citizenship are subordinated to the vicissitudes of the marketplace and the commercial public sphere. Given the current corporate and right-wing assault on public and higher education, coupled with the emergence of a moral and political climate that has shifted to a new Social Darwinism, the issues that framed the democratic meaning, purpose, and use to which education might aspire have been displaced by more vocational and narrowly ideological considerations.

The war waged against the possibilities of an education wedded to the precepts of a real democracy is not merely ideological. Against the backdrop of reduced funding for public schooling, the call for privatization, vouchers, cultural uniformity, and choice, there are the often ignored larger social realities of material power and oppression. On the national level, there has been a vast resurgence of racism. This is evident in the passing of anti-immigration laws such as Proposition 187 in California, the dismantling of the welfare state, the demonization of black youth that is taking place in the popular media, and the remarkable attention provided by the media to forms of race talk that argue for the intellectual inferiority of blacks or dismiss calls for racial justice as simply a holdover from the "morally bankrupt" legacy of the 1960s.

Poverty is on the rise among children in the United States, with 20% of all children under the age of eighteen living below the poverty line. Unemployment is growing at an alarming rate for poor youth of color, especially in the urban centers. While black youth are policed and disciplined in and out of the nation's schools, conservative and liberal educators define education through the ethically limp discourses of privatization, national standards, and global competitiveness.

Many writers in the critical education tradition have attempted to challenge the right-wing fundamentalism behind educational and social reform in both the United States and abroad while simultaneously providing ethical signposts for a public discourse about education and democracy that is both prophetic and transformative. Eschewing traditional categories, a diverse number of critical theorists and educators have successfully exposed the political and ethical implications of the cynicism and despair that has become endemic to the discourse of schooling and civic life. In its place, such educators strive to provide a language of hope that inextricably links the struggle over schooling to understanding and transforming our present social and cultural dangers.

At the risk of overgeneralizing, both cultural studies theorists and critical educators have emphasized the importance of understanding theory as the grounded basis for "intervening into contexts and power in order to enable people to act more strategically in ways that may change their context for the better."[1] Moreover, theorists in both fields have argued for the primacy of the political by calling for and struggling to produce critical public spaces, regardless of how fleeting they may be, in which "popular cultural resistance is explored as a form of political resistance."[2] Such writers have analyzed the challenges that teachers will have to face in redefining a new mission for education, one that is linked to honoring the experiences, concerns, and diverse histories and languages that give expression to the multiple narratives that engage and challenge the legacy of democracy.

Equally significant is the insight of recent critical educational work that connects the politics of difference with concrete strategies for addressing the crucial relationships between schooling and the economy, and citizenship and the politics of meaning in communities of multicultural, multiracial, and multilingual schools.

Critical Studies in Education and Culture attempts to address and demonstrate how scholars working in the fields of cultural studies and the critical pedagogy might join together in a radical project and practice informed by theoretically rigorous discourses that affirm the critical but refuse the cynical, and establish hope as central to a critical pedagogical and political practice but eschew a romantic utopianism. Central to such a project is the issue of how pedagogy might provide cultural studies theorists and educators with an opportunity to engage in pedagogical practices that are not only transdisciplinary, transgressive, and oppositional, but also connected to a wider project designed to further racial, economic, and political democracy.[3] By taking seriously the relations between culture and power, we further the possibilities of resistance, struggle, and change.

Critical Studies in Education and Culture is committed to publishing work that opens a narrative space that affirms the contextual and the specific while simultaneously recognizing the ways in which such spaces are shot through with issues of power. The series attempts to continue an important legacy of theoretical work in cultural studies in which related debates on pedagogy are understood and addressed within the larger context of social responsibility, civic courage, and the reconstruction of democratic public life. We must keep in mind Raymond Williams's insight that the "deepest impulse (informing cultural politics) is the desire to make learning part of the process of social change itself."[4] Education as a cultural pedagogical practice takes place across multiple sites, which include not only schools and universities but also the mass media, popular culture, and other public spheres, and signals how within diverse contexts, education makes us both subjects of and subject to relations of power.

This series challenges the current return to the primacy of market values and simultaneous retreat from politics so evident in the recent work of educational theorists, legislators, and policy analysts. Professional relegitimation in a troubled time seems to be the order of the day as an increasing number of academics both refuse to recognize public and higher education as critical public spheres and offer little or no resistance to the ongoing vocationalization of schooling, the continuing evisceration of the intellectual labor force, and the current assaults on the working poor, the elderly, and women and children.[5]

Emphasizing the centrality of politics, culture, and power, *Critical Studies in Education and Culture* deals with pedagogical issues that contribute in imaginative and transformative ways to our understanding of how critical knowledge, democratic values, and social practices can provide a basis for teachers, students, and other cultural workers to redefine their role as engaged and public intellectuals. Each volume attempts to rethink the relationship between language and experience, pedagogy and human agency, and ethics and social responsibility as part of a larger project for engaging and deepening the prospects of democratic schooling in a multiracial and multicultural society. *Critical Studies in Education and Culture* takes on the responsibility of witnessing and addressing the most pressing problems of public schooling and civic life, and engages culture as a crucial site and strategic force for productive social change.

Henry A. Giroux

NOTES

1. Lawrence Grossberg, "Toward a Genealogy of the State of Cultural Studies," in Gary Nelson and Dilip Pararneshwar Gaonkar (Eds.), *Disciplinarity and Dissent in Cultural Studies* (New York: Routledge, 1996), 143.

2. David Bailey and Stuart Hall, "The Vertigo of Displacement," *Ten 8,* 2:3 (1992), 19.

3. My notion of transdisciplinary comes from Mas'ud Zavarzadeh and Donald Morton, "Theory, Pedagogy, Politics: The Crisis of the 'Subject' in the Humanities," in Mas'ud Zavarzadeh and Donald Morton (Eds.), *Theory-Pedagogy-Politics: Texts for Change* (Urbana,

IL: University of Illinois Press, 1992), p. 10. At issue here is neither ignoring the boundaries of discipline-based knowledge nor simply fusing different disciplines, but creating theoretical paradigms, questions and knowledge that cannot be taken up within the policed boundaries of the existing disciplines.

4. Raymond Williams, "Adult Education and Social Change," in *What I Came to Say* (London: Hutchinson-Radus, 1989), p. 158.

5. The term "professional legitimation" comes from a personal correspondence with Professor Jeff Williams of East Carolina University.

Foreword

In her important new book, *Critical Education against Global Capitalism*, Paula Allman raises a series of crucial questions for the future of educational criticism: How has capitalism managed to become fully internationalized and in the process so completely naturalized that we continue to live within the belly of this beast without prodding it to vomit us up, let alone clawing our way directly through its guts? How are we implicated in this Frankensteinian creation, and why do we continue to obey its illogical and predatory demands? How does capital and the unending limits to its ratio of exploitation continue to expand and, in the Gramscian sense, to "win the consent" of wider communities of the oppressed? How does the material production of the objective world get confused in current educational theorizing with the materiality of discourse, thereby camouflaging the role of social power in maintaining the social division of labor and concealing the socio-historical relations within which discourses, themselves, are produced? How does such a confusion ultimately serve to underwrite a market-driven social order grounded in the exploitation of the direct producers?

In answering these questions and a host of others, and in challenging the radical ahistoricity and anti-materialism of contemporary theories of education, Allman argues for a materialist praxis geared toward a global transformation. She does this through the pages of a book that is at once an impassioned indictment of the barbaric nature of capitalism and at the same time a celebration of the catalyzing power of revolutionary praxis.

When I first read through the manuscript of this book, I was gripped by a feeling that its publication would mark an important moment in the history of critical pedagogy. After several readings, I feel even more assured that this is indeed the case. It is a book whose time has come. This statement might strike some education pundits as absurd, given that Allman's text reaches back for its moorings into a history of Marxist criticism that some have condemned as hopelessly irrelevant to these "new times." Nothing could be further from the truth. In this case, "going back" to Marx is a singularly progressive move and represents a giant step forward for educational criticism. What is "absurd" is continuing along the same rudderless path of educational criticism whose post-modern meanderings have led us back into the jaws of capital once again, after thrilling diversions and James Bond-like adventures with the postmodern theorists. And there is nobody more qualified as a guide in this endeavor than Paula Allman. She has been at the forefront of Marxist criticism for years, and her work in the area of revolutionary pedagogy has helped illuminate the work of Gramsci and Freire for generations of educators. She is part of a bold new group of Marxist educationalists in Britain—Glenn Rikowksi, Mike Cole, Dave Hill, Andy Green and others—who are taking Marxist educational theory to new heights and reshaping current debates over educational policy. That I have been given the opportunity of writing the introduction to another of her Greenwood Press books is, for me, a special honor. The reason is simple: I consider Paula Allman to be one of the best critical educational scholars on the planet. For those readers unfamiliar with her work, the evidence for my assessment should be clear after reading *Critical Education against Global Capitalism*.

If there is an educator who lives and breathes the dialectic, it is Paula Allman. For Allman, it is absolutely crucial that current capitalist social relations, with their irreducible structural tendency to overcapacity, be dialectically grasped and understood. In making this assertion, she takes Marx's historical materialist critique as her mode of theoretical and political engagement. She works from a tradition of reading Marx dialectically (i.e., reading Marx's dialectical critique of capitalism dialectically), a reading that permits her to map the movement and development of the material reality of capitalism. In short, hers is a reciprocal reading that is neither reductive nor teleological nor one that occupies a historical space of irreversible closure. It is, in other words, a decidedly open reading of Marx as well as of capitalism. Only by employing such a critique, maintains Allman, is it possible to identify the myriad roles that capital plays in our lives and to explain the differential educational practices and outcomes that are endemic to capitalist social relations. That is, only by employing historical materialist analysis is it possible to analyze schooling practices from the perspective of the underlying system of exploitation that deploys them. Historical materialist critique makes it aggressively possible to read the world of global capitalism critically, to rudely undress the dialectical unfolding of its essence and to lay bare the way it has been internalized and integrated into the labyrinthine dimensions of our everyday subjective awareness.

Allman uses Marx and his primary texts as the key to understanding the workings of contemporary capitalist formations, employing his insights as a solvent to dislodge the crusted-over mystifications and misunderstandings that, over the years, have clouded our ability to map the complex workings of capital's internal mechanisms, especially the glacial shifts that mark capitalist social relations over the last half-century. The result is a pristine, unvarnished reading of Marx, essential to understanding the ways in which the law of value has insinuated itself into the furthest extremities of our social universe. In keeping with Marx's central insight, Allman asserts that the most fundamental social relations are those in which people produce their material world and those in which they circulate, exchange and consume the results of that production.

Drawing upon the work of Marx, Paulo Freire and Antonio Gramsci, Allman has developed a seasoned and sophisticated approach to pedagogy that she calls "revolutionary critical pedagogy," a practice of critique and a critique of practice that, she insists, can enable us to grasp the world-historical catalytic activity of material production and the manifold ways in which the material production of the objective world is linked to the global processes of exploitation based on the laws of motion of capital and the appropriation of surplus labor. This is no small feat, and Paula Allman is one of the few educators today who is up to such a task. This is especially true at this precarious time when the educational Left is itself undergoing something of a crisis, when the nervature of a neo-liberal politics is beginning to root itself in educational policy-making and to camouflage itself under a radical leftist posturing. At a time when—at least in the U.S. context—notable radical education scholars have unburdened themselves of former leftist positions, have ridiculed Marxists as Precambrian economic determinists and have self-servingly dismissed those who call for anti-capitalist struggle as misguided extremists, Allman's book could not come at a more advantageous moment for the Left.

Nobody likes uncomfortable truths, and Allman's book will surely provoke discomfort among some readers and rage among others. Hers is not an abstract desideratum. Its unapologetic and concrete sense-making cuts to the bone. The vagaries and vicissitudes of capitalist domination and the conceptual apparatuses that yield our means of rationalizing it are unceremoniously exposed. Capitalism is revealed as a world-system, an abundant and all-permeating social universe that, in its endless and frenetic drive to expand, cooperates in implacable and irreparable denials of social justice and shameless practices of exploitation. Such is the pervasive reach of capital that no aspects of the human condition are left unrent. Indeed, our very subjectivities are stuck in the "muck" of capital. And the momentum that capitalism has achieved makes it unlikely that it can be derailed without tremendous effort and profound sacrifice.

Allman asserts, following Marx, that living labor creates the value form of wealth that is historically specific to capitalism. In other words, the drive to augment value is what drives the capitalist machine. Allman provides a comprehensive understanding of how capitalism works that enables readers to acquire a profound grasp of the process of the globalization of capital. She does this by exploring the inner dynamics of capitalism, how it raises social productivity to an unfathomable level that does nothing to eliminate scarcity. She also reveals how capitalism's relations of distribution are simply the results of the relation of production, placing a limit on consumption by limiting the "effective" demand of the vast majority of the world's population. She reveals, in turn, how material use-values are only available in the commodity form, and how use-value is internally related and thus inseparable from the exchange-value of the commodity, which is determined by labor-time. The wealth that is constituted by capitalist societies is not the vast array of use-values but—value itself. Capitalism is perhaps best understood as a global quest to produce value.

Allman's exegesis is exhaustlessly—and relentlessly—focused on the texts of Marx. This is unusual for a book whose intended audiences include educators and those involved in educational reform. It has been decades since Marx has been put on the agenda of progressive educators in any serious way. During the 1980s—before the disputatious fragmentation and internal dissolution of North America's education Left—Marx was deputized by some scholars to help capture forms of analysis that could help fathom the latent depths behind the manifest surface of the schooling process, that could reveal the intentions behind received commonsensical norms of bourgeois educational life and the doxa of bureaucratic disciplines that were being appraised to make sense of such life inside classrooms. In those heady days, Marxism contributed to an understanding of the political economy of school tracking and actively challenged the myth of meritocracy. By the time the Soviet Union and the Eastern bloc states collapsed, it was already being argued—even by some on the Left—that Marxism was the veteran of too many revolutionary campaigns, it had been beaten about by the winds of too many wars, had become emptied of whatever potential and promise it once offered as a force for liberation, and in the process had become desiccated beyond rejuvenation. And especially in the face of the irreverent children it had spawned as a result of the unholy relationships it had formed in the bohemian salons of the postmodernists, it was now time to throw Marxism into the philosophical dustbin as a signal contributor to one of history's valiant but failed attempts at achieving social justice for the world's aggrieved populations. For some of the giddy children of such unions caught up in the post-Marxist cult of novelty, Marxism was too passé and anachronistic, sexy only when worn as an ironic, retro style. Instead of joining the postmodernists in exalting the mundane, thematizing dissolution, celebrating creative disequilibrium, or foregrounding the absurdity of everyday existence, Allman brings humanity face to face with its own demons.

Contemporary capitalist relations constitute a crisis-driven pursuit and are exposed by Allman as a resplendent hemorrhaging of the labor–capital relation, where commodities vomited up from the vortex of accumulation are hungrily consumed by tormented creatures—creatures who are deliriously addicted not only to new commercial acquisitions, but to the adrenaline rush of accumulation itself. Here the "essence" of an individual, in Gramsci's sense, is equivalent to the totality of social relations within global capitalist society. Few educators have made the case that individuals are the products of the contradictions within capitalist social relations more boldly and more convincingly than has Allman. It is an assumption that guides the entirety of Allman's text.

Allman's assumption is especially urgent today, given that we exist at a time in which the labor hour has become denser or less porous and contains, to use Allman's words, "more minutes of value-creating labor." The recent degree of density of the labor hour has become the standard that is reflected in the "socially necessary labor-time" that determines the value of a particular commodity. What is most disturbing—yet totally predicable—is that this new degree of density of the labor hour is celebrated by neo-liberal pundits as "progress." Allman notes, following Moishe Postone, that domination occurs through the reduction of socially necessary labor-time (the average time it takes for a laborer of average skill in specific social and historical conditions to produce a particular type of commodity).

The force of value's domination can best be understood, argues Allman, by examining capitalism's totalizing and universalizing tendencies: in other words, by comprehending its specific form of global social domination. After Postone, she argues that while capitalist exploitation through the production of value is abstract, it is also quasi-objective and concrete. In other words, we experience value in concrete or objective forms that are constituted subjectively in human actions and in human feelings, compulsions and emotions. Value is constituted by abstract labor within social relations of production that are objective and personal. This accounts, in part, for the particularly dynamic "hold" that value or abstract labor—the substance of value—has on each and every one of us.

Allman perceptively notes that capital's attempt to relocate its contradictions on a global scale is accompanied by processes of reversal—that is, by a re-location of these contradictions back into national, regional and local contexts (but not always the same contexts from which they originated). She maintains that these reverse processes occur simultaneously (and dialectically) with the homogenizing force of globalization and that such reverse processes also occur unevenly, "moving away from the global arena toward more local venues when the local ground has been prepared for new or renewed efforts at successful capitalist accumulation—when, for example, unemployment or the threat of a jobless future has effectively undermined working-class strength and militancy and thus guaranteed greater docility and "flexibility" within the local labor-force." Such movements, working in conjunction with other "flexible" readjust-ments in capitalist accumulation strategies, make a considerable impact on ideas. Allman cites, as one example, the current postmodernist emphasis on the relativ-ity of truth. Such "ideas" often serve as legitimizing mechanisms within the dominant ideological discourse and give functional ballast to the contradictions that currently proliferate in the world of capitalist social relations. In other words, Allman maintains that "the re-emergence of capitalist crisis during the last quar-ter of the twentieth century affected, and continues to affect, the dominant ideology." Marxist-driven historical materialist analysis is the best way to cap-ture the internal dynamics of this reproductive process.

Throughout *Critical Education against Global Capitalism* Allman insists on a principled and nuanced reading of Marx that is not compromised by common misunderstandings that have blanketed the field of Marxist scholarship for decades, smothering efforts to bring accurate readings of Marx into the light of day. Her own efforts are both conceptually invigorating and compellingly erudite and demand serious study, not least by critical educators themselves. Allman's central thesis is that Marx's efforts were directed at exposing "the inherent and fundamental contradictions of capitalism." She argues that these contradictions are as real today as they were in Marx's time. In making this claim, she mines Marx's notion of the "historical specificity" of capitalist development and capitalism as both a "process" and a "relation" that has preconditions. Capitalism's preconditions become transformed, over time, into complex results. By examining the constituent results of the complex and concrete social totality—the "fertile dungheap" of capitalism's contradictions in which all of us live and labor—Allman argues that it is possible to ascertain dialectically the preconditions and the essence of capitalism. She enjoins readers to dismiss the criticisms of Marxism as essentialist and teleological and to rely not on the perspectives of Marxists but on the writings of Marx himself, writings that constitute a critique of relations specific to capitalism. Allman practices what she preaches. By getting under Marx's theoretical skin, so to speak, and by analyzing the manner in which Marx thinks and explaining how Marx uses specific concepts, Allman is able to provide us with a brilliant exegesis of the three volumes of Marx's *Capital*, revealing the inherent unity of Marx's dialectical conceptualization of capitalism.

The most stubborn and pernicious manifestations of capitalism's contemporary logic is that of neo-liberalism, what Allman describes as "an effective and efficient pedagogue of capitalist truths" and a "tyrannical schoolmaster." She lists neo-liberalism's "valedictorians" as "the 'Third Way' politicians" who quench the thirst that their constituents have for social justice with the "velvet version of neo-liberalism" or "watered-down meanings of fairness, social justice and human rights." This, of course, translates into "business as usual but clothed in the regressively transmuted language of social democracy."

With the aid of dialectical thinking, Allman takes readers into the engine room of Marx's thought and moves gracefully between the pistons of Marx's pounding insights, focusing as she goes on the most essential ingredient of Marx's dialectical conceptualization, the concept of "internal relations," specifically the dialectical contradictions, or the internally related dialectical nature of capitalism itself. She reveals how the value form "moves between and binds all the social relations and habituated practices of capitalism into an interlocking network that constitutes what is often referred to as the social structure of capitalist society."

It is absolutely essential, notes Allman, to understand that the most fundamental problem with capitalism is not in the arena of distribution or consumption, but lies within the social relations of production. Allman's is a dialectical conceptualization of capital that both perceptively uncovers the antagonistic terrain of capital that is inherent in the labor–capital relation itself and thus lays bare the contradiction that lies at the heart of the social relation of production. She informs us that the value form of capital which gives shape to these internal relations or contradictions not only affects the objective conditions within which people labor, but also the terrain of subjectivity itself. This mediative role is far from innocent, and affects our dreams, desires, and beliefs about the meaning and purpose of life. Allman notes, for instance, how capitalists are concerned mainly with how much surplus-value they can realize in the name of their commodities. Life is reduced to acquisition, to accumulation, to the winning and holding of power. Life becomes death, and death becomes life. It is the philosophy of Wall Street's funeral directors presiding over the cremation of democracy.

One of Allman's many important contributions to our understanding of Marx and Marxism occurs when she identifies several fundamental misperceptions that continue to plague socialists and liberal critics of capitalism. Both groups often advocate a fairer distribution of wealth, arguing that the current inequitable distribution that characterizes contemporary capitalist societies results from property relations—in particular, the private ownership of the means of production. It is at this particular juncture that Allman parts company with many of her fellow Marxists. Reading capital in a way that is consistent with Marx's use of the labor theory of value or law of value to explain the laws, tendencies and motions of capitalism and to analyze the historically specific form of wealth in capitalist societies, she identifies—correctly, in my estimation—the real culprit as the internal or dialectical relation that exists between capital and labor within the capitalist production process itself—a social relation in which capitalism is intransigently rooted. This social relation—axiomatic to the production of abstract labor—deals with how already existing value is preserved and new value (in particular, surplus-value) is created. It is this internal dialectical relationship that is mainly responsible for the inequitable and unjust distribution of use-values and the accumulation of capital that makes the fat cats rich at the expense of the poor. It is this relation between capital and labor that sets in train the conditions that make possible the rule of capital by designating production for the market, fostering market relations and competitiveness and producing the historically specific laws and tendencies of capital. True, private property is a factor. But private property, commodities and markets all predate the specific labor–capital relations of production and serve as pre-conditions for it. And once capital develops, they are transformed into the results of that relation. This is why Allman doggedly pursues the abolition of the labor–capital relationship as the means for laying the groundwork for liberation from scarcity. Allman believes that the future of humanity turns on a credible and effective challenge to capital. This book contributes mightily to such a challenge.

Allman also addresses the misconception of historical inevitability. She rejects the existence of a historical and progressive inevitability, arguing against the notion that socialism will grow automatically and inevitably out of the contradictions of capitalism. History does not unfold "according to either its own inherent

teleology or in accord with some external teleological force." She notes that
"Marx was well aware that barbarism was just as likely to be the successor to
capitalism as socialism." In fact, she argues that Marx would not have been
motivated to undertake his vast and world-shaking intellectual project had he not
feared that sophisticated forms of barbarism would be the likely successor to
capitalism.

Allman also criticizes the familiar Marxist insistence that the industrial proletariat be the poster boy for the future of socialism. This is because the future of
socialism means the abolition of the capitalist production process and the value
form of wealth. Nor did Marx argue that socialism would entail only the transfer
of the already existing means of production from private to social ownership.
Allman steadfastly follows Marx in calling for a movement or process leading to
an alternative, socialist society, and from there to a movement leading to a
communist social formation, one that would involve the creation of new social
relations and the transformation of people, processes and objects within these
newly created relations. Such relations would be collective, collaborative and
harmonious ones, in which human beings and the products of their labor would
be transformed for the betterment of humanity and the natural world. Allman is
sincere and passionate in her vision for achieving the full development of human
potential and the full unfolding and enrichment of individuality. Of course, to
advocate communism is a staggering admission today. Yet if there is no alternative but an alternative to capital, then history will surely absolve what in the
minds of many educators would appear as reckless and dangerous advice.

The picture that Allman paints of capitalism disabuses us of any pretensions to
which we may still serenely cling—that it can be reformed and made productive
for the elimination of worldwide scarcity or redeemed for salutary or civilized
ends. In fact, it is functionally deracinating, a social relation that breeds poverty,
racism, sexism and all and every manner of exploitation. In Allman's Marxist
imaginary, capitalism is a traumatic moment, an unhealable wound, a catastro-
phism of seismic proportions. Her reaction is one that is uncommon today, at a
time when capitalism seems as natural as the air that we breathe. But is it
unreasonable? Do we transgress the sacred territory of convention to consider the
case that capitalism persistently correlates with oppression? That it is an irre-
deemable abomination? Or that democracy as it is currently practiced in developed nations is an artificial overlay on more fundamental relations of exploitation
marked by race, gender and class injustices? This is the challenge that Allman
puts before the reader. Throughout *Critical Education against Global Capitalism*, capitalism is presented in all of its fine-grained detail and spine-tingling
horror and forcefully execrated by the author in a relentlessly logical way,
regardless of the discomfort that this logic may present for the reader. In its
synchronization of two agendas—that of illustrating Marx's dialectical understanding of capital and its application in the development of a revolutionary
critical education—it constitutes a challenge to the repressive bourgeois order.
Capital is not an inert thing, or corporate raider dressed in a business suit

preening around Wall Street. It is demarcated by Allman as both a relation and a process that takes place within a specific historical epoch. As a relation and a process it is difficult to identify. What we see are its effects. What we need to understand are its causes.

I agree with Allman that teaching practices that are grounded in a synthesis of Freire, Gramsci and Marx can indeed work in a formal context. Allman's discussion and analysis of her own teaching is highly illuminating. Her perspicacious grasp of Freire is especially welcome, given the often grave misperceptions about Freire's pedagogy that have proliferated over the last several decades, following in the wake of what has been a steady domestication and embourgeoisement of his work. Following in the footsteps of Freire, Allman successfully activated in her classroom a pedagogical site that facilitated the development of critical consciousness, a mode of dialectical engagement with everyday life that disposed her students to reflect upon their own historical experiences. They achieved this through the act of decoding everyday life, and in the process they were liberated to deal critically with their own reality in order to transform it. Students learned that they do not freely choose their lives, that their identities and their objects of consumption are adaptive responses to the way that the capitalist system manipulates the realm of necessity. With a perceptive understanding that Freirean pedagogy is decidedly prescriptive and that Freirean educators are unwaveringly directive, she created the context for her students to name their world and through dialogue to develop the potential to creatively reshape their historical reality. She carefully delineates Freirean pedagogy from its imitators who would turn the teacher into a passive facilitator; she does this by arguing that, after all, is it not prescriptive that we should ask students to "read the world" critically in order to transform it in a way that will foster humanization? Is it not also prescriptive to demand that the world needs transforming and that education should play a critical role in this effort? Furthermore, shouldn't educators use their authority that comes from their own critical reading of the world and their understanding of Freire's philosophy of education? Isn't the most facilitative, non-prescriptive and non-directive form of progressive teaching doubly prescriptive in the sense that it is a prescription for non-prescription as well as for political domestication and adapting successfully to the social universe of capital and the law of value? Of course, Freirean educators direct and prescribe, but in a way redolent of humility and a spirit of mutuality.

Allman recognizes only too well that most critics who decry capitalism complain endlessly about its effects while falling abysmally short of advocating the overall dismantling of the capitalist social relation of production. Regrettably, such critics stubbornly reveal "a general acceptance of the concept of liberal democracy or a resigned acceptance of the common sense notion that this is as democratic as it is possible to be in complex social orders."

Allman advocates the practice of ideology critique, of unpacking the mystifications and lies that comprise the "Achilles' heel" of capitalist hegemony. There currently exist, notes Allman, propitious conditions for challenging the capitalist myth of progress by undressing capitalism as a positive force and revealing the mangled flesh of its underside. Real progress is not something that is irreversible. In fact, under capitalism, progress is likely to be highly reversible. Not surprisingly, notes Allman, do we find the persistence of the idea that we live in a world where there exists more variety and choice for all. And that this is a good thing. In reality, however, only the rich have more choice because their choices are directly linked to their purchasing power. More specifically, those who possess most of the choices in today's capitalist societies are "those with purchasing power, who are ever-needy, multi-needy and ever-ready to shop." What is consistently ignored in this proposition is that millions of people have little or no purchasing power and whatever purchasing power they may have is steadily diminishing under neo-liberalism. What has happened here is that the idea of "having more" has been decoupled from the eradication of scarcity and recoupled to the idea of variety and choice. Allman asks: More choice for whom? And for what purposes? And whose interests will this increased choice serve?

What Allman refers to as "critical/revolutionary praxis" is grounded in Marx's revolutionary theory of consciousness that grasps the internal relations between thought and human practice, or consciousness and material reality. It is aimed at disabusing educators of the misguided idea that liberal democracy can be made to work by holding capital accountable and forcing it to become more responsible or, in words made infamous by George W. Bush, more "compassionate." Hers is a critique dedicated to denaturalizing the terms and categories used to legitimize and promote bourgeois institutions and state apparatuses but also one that links this internal critique of the bourgeois social order to wider social, historical and economic processes. It is an approach that decries attempts merely to revise, delimit or dehierarchize existing power arrangements or challenge their functional effectiveness without challenging the way power is constituted within the social division of labor in the context of the separation between the ruling classes who own the means of production and the working classes who do not. In short, it is a pedagogy as a form of revolutionary praxis, one that links all thought and action to transformative movement, to a movement that breaks through the fetters that constrain our ability to denounce exploitation and to struggle against it. Allman's approach stands in stark political contrast to postmodernist critical practice, which merely reorders the antimony between capital and labor into a perfumed equilibrium and which "mimics the surface movements" that exist within capital's desperate attempt to order, to displace and to temporarily resolve its internal contradictions.

Allman speaks against the "risible utopia" prompted by people who cling to the "ludicrous notion" that "liberal democracy can continue to buffer us from the worst excesses of capitalism and that it can enable us to continue to live as civilized beings regardless of the deepening and expanding of capital's contradictions and the attendant crisis in capitalist social relations." With eloquence and acumen, she attempts to "envision a future beyond the ideologically reinforced horizon of capitalism and its political handmaiden, liberal democracy." While some of the limits to our emancipation are not of our own making, they still can be forcibly challenged. The limits within which we make ourselves can be smashed in the final instance by educative acts of critical consciousness and collective acts of revolutionary struggle. What happens, for instance, when the working class no longer valorizes capital? We need to work toward the direct appropriation by workers of the use-values they produce, thus abolishing the regime of value and of work. Of course, this entails, among other things, the massification of productive forces, with the direct appropriation by workers of their product. Allman still believes that the struggle of the working class—the class that includes all those who are as well as all those who are potentially productive laborers in the production of surplus-value within the labor–capital relation—constitutes an irreducible limit to capitalist development and the seed-bed for internationalist revolutionary alliance-building. Here she looks to a working-class management of its own power that does not require the mediation of a vanguard party since, in Allman's view, the vanguard must be interchangeable with the masses.

Allman advocates a "counter-capitalist, prohumanity form of worldwide to-getherness, or universality." To bring about such an epochal shift in the capitalist social relations that dominate humanity will require us to reject and dismantle "the habituated structure of human social relations that we are all involved in reproducing and sustaining" through our daily grind of "uncritical/reproductive praxis." This, in turn, will require the practice of coherence—that is, the formation of a coherent identity based on developing ideas, values and beliefs that are fundamentally "logical and ethically consistent" and which can help us work through the contradictions of "our multi-layered identities" in order to make sense of the diversity and flux of the contemporary lifeworld. Of course, Allman is aware that the creation of the coherent revolutionary self knows no final closure and is "constantly in the 'making' within a process that involves our constant striving to reach out to and become internally related to every other man, woman and child that inhabits this globe."

Allman follows Marx in calling for a revolutionary praxis leading to an alternative society that would involve the creation of new social relations and the transformation of people, processes and objects within these newly created relations. This will entail a collective, collaborative and critical movement to create new harmonious relations in which we and the products of our labor are transformed for the betterment of humanity and the natural world. Only within such a context can the full unfolding and enrichment of our individual and collective potentialities be made possible.

In the final instance, the struggle to "obliterate capital's horizon" must be an educative one, and Allman places considerable importance on the development of a revolutionary critical pedagogy. For Allman, schools must become theaters for social action, political precincts in which a broad struggle for bringing about a new society can be waged, a society free from exploitation, free from want and from its historical role of training students to be servants of abstract labor. Of

course, the struggle for educational reform is a necessary but insufficient struggle. To create a world outside the social universe of capital means smashing the
totality of interlocking internal relations that keep capital in endless motion.
Saying "no" to capitalism means "living the no" by "struggling to transform it
into an affirmation of humanization." This mandates pushing human possibilities
to their limits in order to achieve what Marx describes as the abolition of "the
existing state of things." Revolution, Allman maintains, requires us to fight the
self-expansion of value and "involves not just the transformation of our social
and economic conditions but also the transformation of ourselves and the way we
relate to one another as social beings."

Allman's vision is a coherent one, as is the praxis that she maps out so
meticulously in the pages that follow. It is a praxis that calls for a radical re-
envisioning of educational theory, the basis of which appears in the chapters
ahead. They may be the most important chapters currently available for the
formation of future educators. Engaging them with coherence will require a
willingness to break with old ideas, the courage to face overwhelming odds and a
determination to follow the path of revolutionary knowledge into uncharted
territory. Allman assures us that with Marx, Freire and Gramsci taking turns at
illuminating the path ahead, our journey will take us into unknown battlefields,
where wars of position will be waged and battles won.

Peter McLaren

Acknowledgments

There are so many people I want to acknowledge but far too little space to express the actual gratitude I feel.

First, my heartfelt thanks to Chris Edwards, the very special person to whom, together with her family, this book is dedicated. She has been my greatest inspiration since we first parted and even more so now, when at last we are together again.

Next, there are the three people whose lives and writings have had such a tremendous impact on my own—Karl Marx, Paulo Freire and Antonio Gramsci. If I can help to pass on to others even a small fraction of the brilliance that they have offered to humankind and the hope their brilliance holds for all of us, then this book, as well as my previous one, are worth every ounce of my effort. In addition to their obvious contributions to my thinking, it is perhaps an irony in the case of Marx and Gramsci, though of course not of Freire, that they also led me to a much deeper and important relationship with God, whose love and wisdom fuel my criticality and my hope and to whom my gratitude is boundless.

I also want to give special thanks to those whose friendship I treasure—those who are a constant source of joy, support and love and who have always put up with me, whatever my distractions—especially Jill Vincent, Maggie and David Richmond, Brenda and David Jackson, Susan and Mary Wallis, Margaret Bauder, Mable Noon, the late Ivan Barker, Hilary, John, Adam and Fran Berridge, Carolyn and also (in loving memory) Wyn Williams, Marion Francis, Gill Goodchild, Rick Heslop, Margaret and David Warsop, Jane and Nigel Howitt, and my lifelong friends from "across the pond": Marylee Searcey, Sandy Haarlow, Sue Dutmers, Helen Farrell and my sister, Ann Aliman Cox.

In addition, I want to acknowledge and offer thanks to those of whom I think as both friends and comrades since we share the same, or similar, political objectives and the same aspirations for humanity's future. Some of these people I have never met in person, and yet, to me, they will always be friends and "comrades of the heart"; others I have had the good fortune to meet and to know personally. But whether in person or through correspondence, the following people have offered me either their support or their critical insights or both, and I thank them all: Debbie Hill, Glenn Rikowski, Ruth Rikowski, Peter Mayo, Peter McLaren, Margaret Ledwith, Henry Giroux, Richard Brosio, John Wallis, Ian Martin, Jane Thompson, Jorge Larrain, Mike Neary, Werner Bonefeld, Peter Preston, Cannel Borg, Dave Hill, Mike Cole, Mike Newman, Griff Foley, Helen Reduntz, Daniel Schugurensky, Tony Benn and the late and very committed and courageous Caroline Benn.

A very special debt of gratitude goes to Peter Mayo, Glenn Rikowski and Peter McLaren. They all read various parts of this book in various stages of its development and offered valuable and, in fact, indispensible comments and suggestions. Peter, Glenn and Peter not only inspire me with their own writings and thinking, but their support and enthusiasm for my work has contributed more than they can ever know toward sustaining my energy, hope and the final results you have before you. So, thanks guys!

I also want to thank and acknowledge Jane Garry and Henry Giroux, my editors, who encouraged me to write this book and whose hard work and commitment made its publication possible. I also extend many thanks to Klara and Eric King for their help and the considerable skill they devoted to the final stages of this project.

Not last, and certainly not least, I want to express a very deeply felt gratitude to all the former students/learning colleagues who shared with me the learning experiences I describe in chapter 6. As I say in that chapter, it would not be fair to single out particular individuals from what was always a collective praxis; however, the support and friendship of these people have extended over many years, and I would like to thank them specifically. Many thanks to Katie Hughes, Lynda Flint-Rooney, Cathy Gibson, Carole Malia, John Conlon, Martin Hoban, Julie Kavanaugh, Anne Rivington, Maria Kennedy, Clara Bueno-Fisher, David Beck, David Billet, Dipollelo Ngatane, Martin Pumphrey and Yoko Watanabe.

Finally, I want to acknowledge my many sisters and brothers across the face of this globe whose unrelenting anguish and dire, inhumane conditions of existence are a constant source of pain in my heart but equally, too, a deep and unyielding source of motivation and inspiration. As Freire—in so many words, and with a few of mine added—would say: I cannot [and will not] be more fully human unless [and until] they are.

CRITICAL EDUCATION
AGAINST GLOBAL CAPITALISM

Introduction

The cruel absurdity of capitalism has spread unrelentingly throughout the global reach of human existence, wreaking havoc and despair everywhere. Abolish it we must, but to do this, first, we need to understand it. This book is about that understanding and also about critical education and the crucial and essential part it has to play in mounting an effective challenge to capitalism. I write with a sense of urgency because there are millions of human beings who desperately await this challenge.

Humanity enters its third millennium engulfed in a world of escalating social divisions, injustice and oppression, with an environment in varying stages of ecological decay. Daily we are bombarded by the schizoid media images of capitalism's extremes. Within the space of a minute, we are confronted with first the ravaged faces and wasted bodies of some of the thousands suffering famine and starvation or the millions living in the world's urban slums and ghettos (millions who find hunger an inescapable fact of life), and then suddenly, before we have time to take in the enormity of their situation, our attention is switched to the gleaming, yet vacuous smile and sumptuously adorned figure of some insatiably extravagant, superwealthy, scandal- and neurosis-prone individual who is one of the select members of the global upper class. Are we meant to ignore the unintentional juxtaposition of these images, the stark and absurd differences they portray, in much the same way that the differences in their real-life circumstances go unquestioned and unheeded daily? Is this part of our conditioning, a conditioning that allows us to tolerate and accept such immoral and illogical contrasts and absorb them unconsciously into our notions of normality and inevitability? How do we accept and live with such absurdity, with the devastation and destruction that capitalism brings with increasing regularity to both humanity and the planet? It makes no logical or ethical sense that this is the human condition at a point in history when human beings have the potential to eliminate scarcity and eradicate every kind of human deprivation, and when we also have the potential to find ways to prevent further ecological damage and possibly even rectify much of the damage that has already occurred. It is not those who live in their privately guarded citadels of wealth who have created this potential: it is the culmination of human ingenuity and endeavor over many centuries. This potential was created by human beings, and it could be used to meet the needs of all human beings while also improving and then sustaining the health of the planet; yet so long as we exist under the domination of capital, human need and environmental health must be denied.

The way out of this labyrinth of devastation and destruction is through a process of revolutionary social transformation aimed at the abolition of the absurdity—the illogical "logic"—of capitalism. Critical education is essential to this process, to its instigation, and also to nourishing its continuing development and expansion. Critical education, of course, is only one of the many components that will be needed to form a movement capable of challenging and then transforming capitalism, but it is the one that is the focus of this book. Without critical education—albeit a particular type of critical education—we will never know exactly what to challenge, nor will we have a clear idea of what must be transformed in order to create a future of social and economic justice for all of humanity.

The process of revolutionary social transformation must begin in the hearts, minds and social relations of people, and in that sense it has already begun. Individuals and groups, in various locations throughout the world, have begun to challenge capitalism. In some cases they are taking on struggles that have existed since the dawn of capitalism; in other cases, challenges have been mounted that are directed specifically at capital's most recent and devastating manifestation, neoliberalism. In response to this growing discontent, we are fed with a steady diet of ideological red herrings designed to garner our acquiescence or at least our resignation. Slogans such as "the death of the subject" and "the end of history" are meant to silence our anxiety and extinguish our hope. We are chastened to be patient and flexible as we enter the "new reality" of the "information age" and the "postmodern" era, carefully herded like sheep toward the one inescapable conclusion that capitalism desperately needs us to draw—the conclusion that "there is no alternative" to capitalism. By explaining how capitalism works, how it grows and develops and what it requires to sustain its growth and development, I intend to reveal the ideological underpinnings of these ideas and also to reveal the necessary role they play in ensuring capital's survival.

I begin from the premise that a socially and economically just and an authentically democratic alternative to capitalism is possible, but that it can only be created by people who understand why capitalism invariably leads to crisis and why of necessity it is driven to produce wealth for a minority and either endemic insecurity or perpetual poverty and scarcity for the vast majority, and by people who also understand why its remedies for environmental destruction must be inextricably linked to profit margins. The future of humanity and the planet depends on these understandings. This is why a global process of critical education—or what in this book I call revolutionary critical education—is required. There have never been more propitious conditions for this type of education because never before has the contradictory and absurd nature of capitalism been so transparent. My argument is that all efforts, large and small, to challenge capitalism must be educational in nature. As Antonio Gramsci (1971) stressed, every social relation formed in the struggle against capitalist hegemony—that is, the economic, social and political forms of domination and manipulated direction it exerts on our lives—must be an educative relation, a reciprocal relation of mutual learning (p. 350). Critical education means different things to different people, but in this book I use it to refer to education that is aimed at preparing people to engage in revolutionary social transformation and that is also, in and of itself, a form of revolutionary social transformation. This is why I frequently qualify and emphasize my meaning of the term by calling it *revolutionary critical education*. I propose an approach to critical education that might serve as a central core within our transformational strategies and struggles; however, it is not my intention to suggest that this is the only approach. It is offered as a point of departure for what I hope will soon be a rapidly developing global dialogue among educators dedicated to a better future for all human beings.

I also begin from the premise that the only way we can unlock the mystery of capitalism and expose the "truth" of capital is through the explanatory power of the writings of Karl Marx. In today's vernacular, Marx "outed" capital well over a century ago, but his explanation has been both ignored and misinterpreted by not only his detractors but also many socialists and even a considerable number of Marxists as well. To continue along these lines can only spell peril and destruction for the lives of millions of human beings. Making one's own way through Marx's economic texts is an extremely rewarding exercise, but also one that is time-consuming and that appears at first sight to be a daunting task. In a previous book (Allman, 1999), I offered an introduction to Marx's ideas that was intended to entice readers to undertake this task and to also render it less daunting by presenting his ideas in a form that would hopefully make his own texts more accessible. That book was also intended to be the type of introduction that would assist those who at present would go no further, yet whose educational work would benefit from an enhanced critical grasp of capitalist reality, thus offering the first steps toward what Paulo Freire would call a "critical reading of the world." In this book, I invite readers to join me in a slightly more arduous journey, one that will take them quite a distance toward "critically reading" the world of *global* capitalism—far enough, in fact, to fully grasp the absurdity of capitalism and the impossibility of humanity's survival if it remains shackled to this inherently crisis-prone and totalizing system of social and economic injustice and domination. Of necessity, therefore, I will be dealing with a level of theory that some consider to be quite difficult; however, I am fairly confident that even readers totally unfamiliar with Marx will not find it onerous or unnecessarily difficult and theoretical. As with my previous book, I do not argue my interpretations against those of other secondary-source authors because my intention is to communicate, as clearly as I can, Marx's ideas and theoretical explanations directly to the reader. I learned from my students long ago that certain texts come across as highly theoretical and therefore inaccessible simply because writers interrupt their conversations with the reader to engage in conversations and debates with other authors. Therefore, what I intend to offer is Marx—or, more precisely, his explanation of capitalism—without interruptions.

The interpretation of Marx's economic texts, presented here, falls within a specific tradition—one based on a dialectical reading of his works. As Milonakis (1997) has noted, this approach—that is, a dialectical "reading" of Marx—is "a long and respectable tradition . . . [however] it has not really emerged as a coherent alternative" to other approaches (p. 303, fn.). Nevertheless, it is a tradition that can be traced back to Marx's lifelong friend and collaborator, Friedrich Engels, who in his own writings on nature (Engels, 1954) may have carried the dialectic further than Marx ever intended—that is, in a mode closer to the dialectic in the writings of the German philosopher G. W. F. Hegel than to Marx's distinctive use of dialectical thinking. Many interpreters of Marx recognize the dialectical nature of his early writings but think that dialectical thinking or conceptualization was something he moved away from or only used in a minor way in his economics. This has led to disastrous consequences for both theory and practice, and it is also puzzling in the extreme since Marx clearly states that dialectical conceptualization is fundamental to his exposition of capitalism (Marx, 1873, p. 102, in Marx, 1867).

One reason why the dialectical tradition is rather loosely composed or lacking in coherence is that many individuals who can be located in this tradition have interpreted Marx in terms more of Hegel's dialectic than of his own. The distinction between the two is important but also elusive, as evidenced by the fact that Engels seemed unaware that he had lapsed into a more methodical and abstract Hegelian approach in his study of nature. And Lenin and Mao, who were, like Engels, clearly materialist thinkers in the manner of Marx, sometimes seem closer to Hegel than Marx in their application of dialectical thinking. Marx acknowledged his debt to Hegel but also clearly demonstrated that he had moved beyond or away from Hegel's philosophical idealism. The important differences between Hegel's and Marx's dialectics pertain mainly to two areas. Hegel's dialectic depicts the movement and development of ideas and how they determine the historical unfolding of the real, or material, world, whereas Marx's dialectic pertains to the movement and development of the material reality of capitalism, movements and developments that result from human beings actively producing their material world and with it their consciousness as well. In other words, according to Hegel, dialectical laws are abstract and divorced from human intention and behavior; whereas for Marx the dialectical movement and unfolding of the material world is concrete and thoroughly human—a result of human agency, or action. For Marx, the dialectic was also a method of presentation, or the manner in which he conceptually presents this movement and development to his readers (Marx, 1873, p. 102, in Marx, 1867). Moreover, Hegel's dialectic is teleological and thus moves or unfolds toward a predetermined end. Marx's dialectic, on the other hand, is open and allows for reciprocity wherein that which determines is also mutually determined or shaped at the same time; and thus there is no outcome that is inevitable or irreversible.

Another factor that leads to the looseness or lack of coherence in the tradition is the fact that many of those who clearly interpret Marx in the dialectical way he intended people to interpret him make no mention of the dialectic and sometimes seem almost unaware that their interpretations adhere to Marx's dialectical understanding of capitalism. This should not be surprising. Marx found his dialectic in the material reality of capitalism. However, in his explanation of capitalism, Marx does not refer specifically to its dialectical nature; he simply presents it. Therefore, it could be that those who make no mention of the dialectic are simply following Marx's lead. It is also entirely possible that they do not mention the dialectic in order to avoid a Hegelian rendering of their interpretations. I fear, however, that if this is their reasoning, they are doing a disservice to Marx. It is my contention that the dialectic is the key to comprehensively understanding his economic texts and thus his full explanation of capitalism; and I present my discussion of his explanation in a way that conforms with and also highlights his dialectical presentation.

Bearing in mind what I have said, I think it is important to identify some of the people who, I think, figure centrally in this tradition. When appropriate in my discussion of Marx's explanation of capitalism, I mention or reference those authors who not only specifically concur with a particular aspect of my explanation but also accentuate it in their own work. In general, those whom I mention have assisted me in deciding which aspects of Marx's writing should be emphasized. It is also important to note that I became aware of this tradition after reading Marx rather than before; therefore, with the exception of the first two people I mention, they did not influence my original interpretation of Marx. It was the writings of Derek Sayer (1983, 1987) and Jorge Larrain (1979, 1983) that encouraged me to undertake my own reading of Marx and that also greatly assisted me in that reading. I would locate their interpretations of Marx within the dialectical tradition, although I am not sure whether either of them would agree. However, some of the earliest members of this tradition would have no reluctance—for example, Rosa Luxemburg, Georg Lukács, Antonio Gramsci and Isaac I. Rubin. And this is probably equally true of some slightly later Marxists— particularly Karel Kosík, C. L. R. James, Raya Dunayevskaya and Roman Rosdolsky. Contemporary Marxists whom I would locate in this tradition and whose interpretations of Marx are similar to some aspect or another of my own include, in addition to Sayer and Larrain, Bertell Ollman, David Harvey, Moishe Postone, Alex Callinicos, Peter Hudis, Christopher Arthur, Tony Smith and Thomas

Sekine. There are also contemporary Marxists whose dialectical interpretation of Marx informs their analyses of history or their contemporary studies of political economy—people such as Ellen Meiksins Wood, the late E. P. Thompson, David McNally, Ben Fine, Dimitris Milonakis and also Werner Bonefeld and John Holloway, as well as other members of the Conference of Socialist Economists who write under the rubric of "Open Marxism." This list is in no way exhaustive. It is simply a list of those who have enhanced my understanding of contemporary capitalism. I include it here simply to position my own analysis within a particular framework and also to acknowledge all of those who have in one way or another either confirmed or assisted some part of my interpretation of Marx or who have shed further light on some specific aspect of the history, development or contemporary nature of capitalism.

Although this book focuses primarily on Marx's theoretical explanation of capitalism and therefore his economics, it is informed throughout by his revolutionary theory of consciousness. This is a theory that Marx had formulated prior to undertaking his empirical studies of capitalism; and it directly underpins almost everything he wrote from 1846 onwards, including his economic texts. Marx's explanation of capitalism is not just an explanation of people's economic relations and behavior. It is equally and importantly about why people tend to think about their material conditions and activities in a certain way—a way that helps to perpetuate and sustain the capitalist system. Marx's focus on consciousness is one of the reasons why his explanation of capitalism is so important for critical educators. Moreover, it is this revolutionary theory of consciousness that also makes critical education such an essential and crucial requirement for all struggles aimed at revolutionary social transformation. I have discussed this theory in considerable detail elsewhere (Allman, 1999) and recap the most important aspects of that discussion in chapter 5 of this text. However, because of this theory's centrality to Marx's thinking and as a consequence to this book, even at this point it is important and necessary to make some introductory comments about its main components. To make these comments, I must use certain concepts whose full meaning will only become clear when I am able to explain them fully in subsequent chapters.

Marx first wrote about his theory of consciousness in a book he coauthored with Engels (Marx and Engels, 1846)—a book that was unfortunately not published until 1932. His theory of consciousness postulates an *inner* connection, or relation, between human practice and conscious thought. As with all of Marx's theoretical formulations, this is not a deterministic relation but, rather, a dialectical one—one involving a reciprocal relation between sensuous human activity and thought, wherein each of the components in the relation mutually shapes and is shaped by the other. In that Marx is postulating an inseparable unity between thought and practice, his revolutionary theory of consciousness is actually a theory of praxis (Allman, 1999). However, it is also a theory that implies two very different forms of praxis, and herein lies its crucial significance for educators.

"Praxis" is a term often used to indicate a sequential linking or application of theory to practice and vice versa. In contrast, Marx's theory of consciousness/ praxis intimately and internally, and thus dialectically, relates all thought and practice. And the implication of this is that we engage in a form of praxis that is uncritical and thus reproductive when we simply enter into the material conditions and relations we find at hand and accept them as natural and inevitable. Even when we sometimes resist our positioning within a certain social relation, we remain locked into an uncritical/reproductive form of praxis so long as our resistance is only aimed at either bettering our position or changing our positioning within the relation. Praxis, on the other hand, can assume a critical and revolutionary form when we become critically aware of the constraining nature of the relation itself and when we then focus on the relation and direct our energies to abolishing it or transforming it. In other words, critical/revolutionary praxis begins when we critically grasp the dialectical, or internally related, nature of our material conditions and social relations and develops in full as we then seek to abolish or transform these conditions and relations, replacing them with ones that can enable us to create a socially and economically just society—a much more humane society in which all people can realize their full potential as human beings. In so doing, we release the critical and creative potential of our consciousness and enhance the development of our critical intellect—our critical understanding of our reality and ourselves.

It is also important to mention at this point that Marx's revolutionary theory of consciousness/praxis contains a negative concept of ideology (Larrain, 1983). "Ideology" or "ideological" refers to any thought, behavior or even symbols that serve to distort our dialectical understanding of reality. It is not a concept of "false consciousness," a notion often incorrectly attributed to Marx. An ideological statement, for example, reflects or refers to aspects of our reality that are real, and in that sense true, but which are only the partial truth, or fragments of something that we cannot fully comprehend unless we can grasp it in its entirety. In this way they distort the truth and thus prevent us from fully comprehending a situation—in other words, they tend to frame our thinking within certain horizons or parameters (Hall, 1982). However, since they refer to or reflect something that is real, even if it is only partial, they normally manage to convince us that the version of reality they portray is the truth of our reality. The ideological forms of consciousness/praxis that arise from capitalist reality actually reflect and thus seem to connect with and make sense of the fragmented way in which we tend to experience capitalist reality—that is, our spatially and temporally disconnected experience of its dialectical nature. This is why they are able to work so powerfully, yet often subtly, as justifications that legitimate the capitalist form of existence. Ideological thinking arises quite naturally from capitalist reality and therefore does not necessarily require a perpetrator. Marx took great pains to show how even many critics of capitalism were often seduced into ideological understandings of their circumstances (see for example, Marx, 1863a, 1863b and 1863c).

I discuss ideology in greater detail in the chapters that follow and also the importance of ideology critique to revolutionary critical education. In offering this brief précis of Marx's theory of consciousness/praxis, I have had to use, as I forewarned, several concepts that are related to his dialectical mode of conceptualizing capitalism. Almost all of the concepts that form some part of his intellectual framework are related to one another—for example, he sometimes uses different concepts in order to beckon us to look at the same phenomenon from yet another angle so that we can form a more complete understanding. It is, therefore, almost impossible to discuss one of his theoretical formulations in isolation from other aspects of the total framework. By the time I return to a more comprehensive discussion of Marx's theory of consciousness/praxis and his negative concept of ideology in chapter 5, these concepts will have been fully explained, and it should therefore be much easier to discern the important implications of this theory for critical education. Hopefully, however, it is already clear that critical/revolutionary praxis is the type of praxis appropriate to critical education and that ideology critique is one aspect of this type of praxis.

Before embarking on the journey that will hopefully lead to a critical understanding of global capitalism, I smooth the way by first explaining some of the conventions I am using and then offering a brief overview of the chapters.

The first convention I want to bring to your attention is one that I find unavoidable but also highly problematical and perplexing. One of the most important and fundamental ideas that we can glean from Marx's explanation of capital is that it is both a process and a relation—a social relation between human beings—and not a thing. Unfortunately if I, or any writer, were to spell this out every time we wanted to say that this process or this relation does something—in other words, every time we wanted to use a noun—our sentences would become extremely cumbersome and awkward. Therefore, the convention is simply to say that capital does such and such; but, of course, this is problematical because it reinforces the tendency to reify capital—that is, to attribute a thing like status to something that is actually a social relation. Even worse, perhaps: it also tends to imbue this "thing" with the intentions and capabilities of a human individual. Whenever I can, I avoid this convention, but as it is sometimes unavoidable, all I can do is urge readers to remember that capital is not a thing. To a certain degree there is a similar problem when we use capitalism as a noun. This can lead to the idea that we are talking about a system that exists as something separate from human beings and their social relations and practices, or, worse still, some sort of a structure—albeit a social structure—that again we imagine as something distinct from human sensuous activity. Again all I can do is to urge readers to conceptualize these terms in a different way—to understand that capitalism is, first and foremost, ourselves—that is, human beings—as we exist and live our lives within a network or web of habituated social relations and practices. Following Marx, I also, at times, use "capital" and "capitalism" interchangeably; however, I do this only when it is appropriate to do so, and often, when I use these terms in this way, it is to imply that they are inseparable—in other words, as I will be explaining, without capitalism there would be no capital.

The second convention is just the opposite in the sense that it is, I think, extremely helpful. It is a convention that I have adopted from Derek Sayer (1987) and one that assisted me greatly in my own study of Marx's writings. When I reference Marx, I use the date that is, according to Sayer, the last date on which he worked on a particular source prior to its initial publication. By using this convention, it is possible to locate Marx's writings within the specific historical context in which they were written. The use of these dates is also important with Marx's work for two other reasons. First, some writers, following Althusser, talk about distinct breaks in Marx's thinking—for example, they distinguish between his philosophical earlier works and his later economic writings in a way that suggests that he actually conceptualized or thought in entirely different ways during these phases of his life. I totally disagree with this interpretation and feel that the best way to argue against the idea of a "break" is for readers always to be able to see just *when* Marx said *what* and thus to be able to trace the continuity in his thought.

The second reason is connected with the fact that some of Marx's important economic texts were never completed—that is, made ready for publication—by Marx, himself. He drafted all of the volumes of *Capital* during the same period, but he spent so much time first preparing Volume 1 (Marx, 1867) for publication and then amending subsequent editions, purportedly to make them more accessible for his intended working-class audience, that the task of doing the same for volumes 2 (Marx, 1878) and 3 (Marx, 1865) was left to his friend and collaborator Engels. The fourth volume, which had been drafted in full by 1863—the three-part text called *Theories of Surplus Value*—was likewise left to Karl Kautsky to publish after Engels's death. The importance of this is that he had fully worked out his complete analysis of capitalism and had committed that analysis to writing, at least in draft form, before he published the first volume. Knowing this should affect the way we understand the relationship between Volume 1 and the others—an understanding that I share in chapter 2. In terms of trying to be helpful, I also frequently cite page numbers in references when I have not quoted directly from the text so that readers can easily locate the idea in the original source and read about it in more depth or check out my interpretation.

The final convention I should mention is also intended to be helpful; however, I realize that some readers might not agree. When I quote Marx, Gramsci and Freire—or, for that matter, any writer for whom I think this is warranted because of their philosophical and political stance on other matters—I alter the implied gender bias of their language by placing a more neutral term in brackets. Sayer (1991), for whom I have the greatest respect, has criticized this practice and has even called it patronizing. He argues that we should not try to cover up or sanitize the language of people who, according to him, saw everything in terms of the social experience of men. I can see his point, but I also think that we might be falling into the danger of overgeneralization in assuming that every writer who used "men" in a philosophical sense to connote humanity should be tarred with the same brush. I am quite sure that at least some of the writers we classify as "modernists" were able to see beyond the narrow horizon of Western civilization and the even narrower experience of only the male members of our species. In other words, it is entirely possible that when they used conventional expressions such as "men" and "mankind," they truly thought in terms of human beings of all genders and all ages. We will never know. I began using this convention not just to sanitize or neutralize their language but for another reason altogether. I found far too many feminist writers and activists dismissing outright the writings of Marx, Gramsci and Freire on the grounds of the male bias in their language. Although there are feminists, like bell hooks (1993), who handle this problem with great wisdom and sympathy, I have always felt it better not to be drawn into the fray and distracted by what I think is an extremely counterproductive and self-defeating position when it comes to the eradication of all forms of human oppression. Therefore, while heeding the points that Sayer has made, on balance, I have decided to stick with the convention of bracketing-out pronouns that might distract readers from these men's valuable contributions to human liberation. I hasten to add that I would use the same convention when quoting, for example, Rosa Luxembourg, or any other great female thinker of the modern era.

You might be heartened to know that this introduction is almost finished; I have only to add a brief overview of the book's contents and also my sincere wish that readers will stay with me through the more difficult bits, especially the perhaps tedious but, I assure you, necessary arithmetic in chapter 3. I should note, since I have raised this point about arithmetic, that an aversion to mathematics was something I had to overcome in order to come to grips with Marx's explanation of capitalism. Because I am fully aware of the struggle this can entail for others like myself who lack confidence in their numeracy skills, I have used the same figures that Marx uses in order to facilitate any crossreferencing that readers may wish to do. I also—and this may be irksome to those of you who are more numerate—tend to spell out the mathematical procedure involved in arriving at the figures I cite. To the more numerate readers, I apologize.

In chapter 1, I begin with a brief sketch of some of the worst and also most ludicrous absurdities that have resulted from the globalization, or full universalization, of capital, and I also offer a brief summary of how various people are interpreting the process of globalization. Then, two relatively lengthy chapters (chapters 2 and 3) are devoted to Marx's dialectical explanation of capitalism. My intention, as I said before, is to offer a fairly comprehensive and detailed account of his explanation, one that takes you far enough to be able to understand, and hopefully to be capable of enabling others to understand, why capitalism is inherently and necessarily a global system. This account also indicates why we are currently experiencing the full impact and suffering the repercussions of capital's inherent need to become, more than ever before, a fully internationalized and integrated system of socioeconomic control and domination—the global system that, as many commentators have suddenly remembered, Marx and Engels (1848) presciently forecast over 150 years ago.

My presentation of Marx's explanation follows the same pattern or format that he uses in his three volumes of *Capital*. This is a pattern that traces the dialectical unfolding of capital's essence, its inherent contradictions, from the simple commodity form to a fully developed capitalist system, and one that in so doing clearly reveals the *raison d'être* of globalization. In other words, I will be following the way in which Marx presented his dialectical conceptualization of capitalism. Many socialists and even some Marxists admit to finding the three volumes of *Capital* difficult to read and understand. In a sense they are right, but this is not Marx's fault, or the reader's, for that matter. In the three volumes of *Capital*, Marx is explaining a very complex system, a system that forms the basis of our concrete reality and that we participate in each day, but one that works according to concrete laws or tendencies that can only be grasped by a mode of conceptualizing that conforms to the inner essence, or underlying contradictions, of the system. This essence cannot be perceived directly because in its pure and simple form it is submerged beneath the immediate, "noisy," frenetic, hustle-bustle of our daily experience of capitalism and the world of ever-proliferating commodities it creates. However, if we use the "key" that Marx left us to unlock the complexity of his explanation and thus the complexity of capitalism—that is, if we use or follow his dialectical mode of conceptualization—the difficulty disappears, and capitalism is left exposed in naked simplicity. All that is required of us is a bit of perseverance in grasping and then using this "key"—a perseverance that I attempt in every way to assist and which, I trust, will come easily to those who have been awakened to the cruelty and absurdity of capitalism.

After discussing Marx's explanation of capitalism, I then go on, in chapter 4, to examine some of the contemporary challenges to capitalism and to explore why, on the basis of Marx's explanation of capital, these challenges cannot possibly be the solution to our problems. Those who clamor for the reform of capitalism are among the challengers. Some of these people think that many of the social democratic reforms and policies that are no longer feasible on a national scale can still be made to work effectively if applied on a global scale. Throughout this book, I stress that capitalism cannot be permanently reformed. We may have to struggle for reforms in order to make life temporarily more palatable, but increasingly it will be difficult to remedy the ills of society by traditional social democratic measures such as governmental interventions of the type inspired by the economic theory of John Maynard Keynes. Keynesian-style interventions in the global economy will run the same course that they did in national economies and probably will do so much more swiftly. The only answer, or beginning of an answer, lies in revolutionary social transformation.

As I also contend that critical education is absolutely fundamental to the process of revolutionary social transformation, the rest of the book—that is, chapters 5, 6 and 7—is devoted to a discussion of critical education. In chapter 5,

I discuss the theory, principles and aims of a particular approach to critical education—the approach I call revolutionary critical education. Chapter 6 is about the experience of trying to apply and also develop this theory as well as its aims and principles—in other words, it describes the critical/revolutionary praxis through which I attempted to apply and also further develop and refine this approach to critical education. And, finally, in chapter 7 I suggest various strategies that critical educators might begin to implement in their own contexts. I also suggest how our strategies might become allied on a global scale. The strategies and the alliance I propose are intended to contribute toward the eventual abolition of capitalism and the beginning of a new and better future for humankind.

I only hope that those who share my commitment to the abolition of capitalism and all other forms of inhumanity and oppression will stay with me until the end and that they will take my discussions and suggestions as they are intended—that is, not as definitive answers but merely as catalysts to the development and proliferation of critical/revolutionary praxis throughout the world.

REFERENCES

Allman, P. (1999). *Revolutionary Social Transformation: Democratic Hopes, Political Possibilities and Critical Education.* Westport, CT: Bergin & Garvey.

Engels, F. (1954). *Dialectics of Nature.* Moscow: Foreign Languages Publishing House.

Gramsci, A. (1971). *Selections from the Prison Notebooks of Antonio Gramsci,* edited and translated by Quinton Hoare and Geoffrey Nowell Smith. London: Lawrence and Wishart.

Hall, S. (1982). "Managing Conflict, Producing Consent." Unit 21, in Block 5: *Conformity, Consensus and Conflict, D102, Social Sciences: A Foundation Course.* Milton Keynes, U.K.: Open University Press.

hooks, b. (1993). "bell hooks Speaking about Paulo Freire—The Man, His Work." In P. McLaren and P. Leonard (Eds.), *Paulo Freire: A Critical Encounter* (pp. 146–154). London: Routledge.

Larrain, J. (1979). *The Concept of Ideology.* London: Hutchinson.

Larrain, J. (1983). *Marxism and Ideology.* London: Macmillan.

Marx, K. (1863a). *Theories of Surplus Value,* Part 1. London: Lawrence & Wishart, 1969.

Marx, K. (1863b). *Theories of Surplus Value,* Part 2. London: Lawrence & Wishart, 1969.

Marx, K. (1863c). *Theories of Surplus Value,* Part 3. London: Lawrence & Wishart, 1972.

Marx, K. (1865). *Capital,* Vol. 3, translated by David Fernbach, Introduction by Ernest Mandel. Harmondsworth, U.K.: Penguin, 1981.

Marx, K. (1867). *Capital,* Vol. 1, translated by Ben Fowkes, Introduction by Ernest Mandel. Harmondsworth, U.K.: Penguin, 1976.

Marx, K. (1873). "Postface to the Second Edition." In *Capital,* Vol. 1, 1967 (pp. 94–103). Harmondsworth, U.K.: Penguin, 1976.

Marx, K. (1878). *Capital*, Vol. 2, translated by David Fernbach, Introduction by Ernest Mandel. Harmondsworth, U.K.: Penguin, 1978.

Marx, K., and Engels, F. (1846). *The German Ideology*. Moscow: Progress, 1976.

Marx, K., and Engels, F. (1848). "The Communist Manifesto." In D. McLellan (Ed.), *Karl Marx: Selected Writings* (pp. 221–247). Oxford: Oxford University Press, 1977.

Milonakis, D. (1997). "The Dynamics of History: Structure and Agency in Historical Evolution." *Science & Society*, 61 (No. 2, Autumn), 302–329.

Sayer, D. (1983). *Marx's Method: Ideology, Science and Critique in "Capital"* (second edition). Brighton: Harvester Press.

Sayer, D. (1987). *The Violence of Abstraction: The Analytical Foundations of Historical Materialism*. Oxford: Basil Blackwell.

Sayer, D. (1991). *Capitalism & Modernity: An Excursus on Marx and Weber*. London: Routledge.

1

Global Capital and the Human Condition: An Absurd Way to Begin a New Millennium

One of the most important functions of those involved in critical education is to problematize reality—to ask probing questions about what is happening and about how we understand and feel about the events that are taking place. This is not a rhetorical exercise, nor one based on naïve curiosity. It derives from the critical curiosity of teachers' and learners' cointentional "act of knowing" reality (Freire, 1974). Teachers or political activists who initiate a process of critical education need to have a certain level of critical understanding before they can effectively engage others in problematizing reality. In this chapter I provide a point of departure for that understanding by first pointing to some of the aspects of contemporary capitalism that have been widely documented and then by discussing the different ways in which this reality—the reality of global capital—is being interpreted. I begin with the types of facts that are frequently cited with reference to the plight of many of the world's children.

WHAT IS HAPPENING—SNAPSHOTS OF ABSURDITY

It is estimated that there are 100 million children living in the streets, for whom home or shelter is, at best, a cardboard box or doorway, and that millions more are living in houses with no running water, electricity or sanitation. Two hundred million children are engaged in the global labor force (Berger, 1998/99)—many working long hours for a pittance in unsafe, unhealthy and often illegal conditions. We know that many are dying needlessly of malnutrition, some as frequently as one every hour in countries that are forced to devote over half of their annual incomes to repaying IMF and World Bank loans (Pilger, 1998). Nor is it only the children of poor countries that suffer. "One in five children in the US live below the poverty line" (Hirschl, 1997, p. 170). These and many other dismal statistics that reveal what for many of the world's children is the sheer horror of being born are often responded to by charity bonanzas. Events like Britain's annual "Red Nose" Day, despite good intentions, raise but a fraction of what poor countries return daily in debt repayments to Western banks (Pilger, 1998).

Perhaps the most frequently reported aspect of contemporary reality is the increasing gap between the very rich and the very poor—the polarization of wealth and poverty. Throughout most of the twentieth century commentators have focused on the division between the developed and the underdeveloped countries of the world or the center and periphery, and while this remains a central focus, the polarization of rich and poor people, both inter- and intra-nationally, is not only more frequently reported but more readily apparent. For example, statistics like the following are frequently cited. There are now 350 people in the world whose assets total one billion or more (U.S.) dollars and who are, therefore, worth more than 45% of the world's population (Harris, 1998/99, p. 29). According to MacGregor (1999, p. 94), who derives her statistics from the 1998 *UN Human Development Report*, the fifteen richest people in the world have assets that exceed the total annual income of sub-Saharan Africa. The same report reveals that the United States has both the highest per capita income of any OECD country and the highest rate of poverty (Mac-Gregor, 1999, p. 94).

Most commentators point not just to the polarization but to the growing distance between the extremes of wealth and poverty. Others have been quick to stress that this is not entirely new, suggesting that the gap is no greater than it was between the new industrial working class and the bourgeoisie in nineteenth-century Britain. Nevertheless, it has been generally assumed that civilization has advanced at least to some degree and that for either ethical or merely pragmatic reasons nation-states would never again permit extreme polarization in their midst. Rightly or wrongly, there has been an assumption that social exclusion would be eliminated as far as possible, if for no other reason than to maintain some basic level of social cohesion. Hutton (1998) has expressed concern that, in certain ways, both extremes, the very rich and the very poor, are becoming marginal to the rest of society. Those at the top of the income/assets league table live in a totally privatized world where they have little need to be concerned about the rest of society. With their wealth becoming less and less dependent upon what the vast majority of their fellow citizens produce and consume and with private security forces protecting them from the escalating violence of society, they can live in rather splendid and luxurious isolation (Hutton, 1998; and also Reich, 1991). The poor also live in isolation, albeit involuntary isolation, having been excluded from the market and as a consequence a society and culture that increasingly gravitate around it.

Revolutions in technology, especially in electronic digitization, have played an important part in many of the changes that have occurred since the end of World War II. A global telecommunications infrastructure has been created that has facilitated the internationalization of production and trade, extending not only the reach of global capitalism and the world market but increasing the velocity of both trade and the turnover time of production and circulation. The impact has been felt especially in the arena of financial capital, where the increasing velocity of trade has led to a proliferation of financial products and the amassing of enormous profits.

The same advances in telecommunications have also facilitated a much greater degree of human communication and have opened up much greater access to information. It is estimated that 122 million people use the Internet (Kundnani, 1998/99, p. 52). This experience and the assumption of its generality create the impression that people have become more integrated than they were previously. While this may be true for some people, it remains a fact that 50% of the world's people have never even used a telephone (Harris, 1998/99, p. 30). From a global perspective, we find not a more highly integrated world but one in which the life experiences of a relatively small percentage of the world's population become further and further removed from the life experiences of the vast majority. The same is true in terms of the global market and capitalist relations of production. While both are more expansive and inclusive than ever before, effectively penetrating the entire globe, millions of people are virtually excluded and deemed excess to capital's requirements as either producers or consumers. As David Harvey (1995) puts it: capitalism is "pulling everyone (and everything that can be exchanged) into its orbit . . . while rendering large segments of the world's population permanently redundant. . . ." (p. 11). The global penetration of capital has been going on for a long time. John Holloway (1995) stresses that "capital moves," especially financial capital, but now with the aid of the electronic superhighway it moves much faster than ever before, compressing geographical space by the reduction of time (Harvey, 1989). Or, as Marx so aptly pointed out over a hundred years ago, capitalism "strives to annihilate . . . space with time" (1858, p. 539).

Remarkable advances have also been made in biotechnology. The potential for increasing food production, preventing, curing and controlling disease and even providing alternative sources of energy that could drive the machinery of the future is amazing; however, the ways in which these advances are currently being employed are both disturbing and imminently dangerous (King, 1997). These advances are seen primarily as information commodities, capable of producing superprofits for the firms who manage to be the first to use or sell them. As a consequence, there is a vicious competitive struggle going on to secure patents on a number of life forms, from the simple seed so fundamental to agricultural production to the genes of human beings. Dan Schiller (1997), drawing on the important findings reported on Kloppenburg's book *First Seed*, published in

1988, says that what the giant transnational pharmaceutical and agricultural corporations want and increasingly demand is "free access to the plant germ-plasm located in the gene-rich equatorial zones while at the same time insisting that international laws of intellectual property be strengthened and harmonized to protect the profits they [make] from the hybrid seed and drugs they [sell] back to these same regions" (p. 115). In other words, they want to protect their profits by patenting and thus monopolizing this knowledge. According to Sivanandan (1998/99), for the most part the big corporations have got just what they were demanding. He says that this was one of the main results of the Uruguay round of GATT in 1994. Corporations were allowed to patent both products and processes based on genetic materials derived from crops and also wild plants found in "Third World" countries and to sell them back to the country of origin, which, according to patent law, could not develop their own equivalent products. King (1997) argues that the discoveries being made in biotechnology are far too important in terms of the consequences for both humanity and the ecosystem to abdicate responsibility for their control and accountability to market forces. Public debate and discussion about the ethical and practical implications of these issues has been almost negligible—far too little and often too late.

When the Berlin Wall fell in 1989, the victory of capitalism and liberal democracy were triumphantly proclaimed. The Cold War was over, and we were promised a lasting peace (not to mention a peace dividend, to which I will come later). Ironically, perhaps, it has been a matter of increasing concern that in the established democracies fewer people are bothering to vote than ever before—politicians who receive the majority of the vote are often being elected by a minority of their citizens. And it is widely known that far too many aspects of our lives are controlled, or at least strongly influenced, by nonelected and unaccountable institutions—quangos within the nation-state and supranational institutions, organizations and agreements such as the IMF, the World Bank, GATT, and so on. Of course, the latter are the creations or collective creations of nation-states (in most cases governments that have been "democratically" elected), but democratic control over these by the citizen is so far removed as to be virtually nonexistent. Habermas (1999) warns that democratic legitimation will be eroded

the more matters are settled through inter-state negotiation, and the more important these decisions are, the more political decisions [will be] withdrawn from the arena of democratic opinion-formation and will-formation—which are exclusively national arenas. [p. 49]

Unemployment and the changing nature of employment are two of the most perplexing problems of contemporary capitalism. New technologies are rapidly reducing national workforces. New jobs are created but not in numbers sufficient to replace those that have been destroyed, and many jobs have been deskilled, either or both manually and intellectually. The general trend seems to be the creation of either high-tech jobs that require considerable skill and or knowledge or low-skill, low-pay jobs and jobs that are often part-time and/or temporary—frequently referred to as contingent jobs. Sally Lerner (1997) raises the question of "whether 'jobless growth,' underemployment and 'contingent' employment will become the norm" in the near future (p. 178). Harris (1998/99, p. 28) reports that by 1995, 60% of all new jobs in the United States were contingent jobs. One thing, however, that people in almost every kind of work share to some extent is a growing sense of insecurity. It's not just cheap, low-skilled labor that has been forced to compete in a global labor market but relatively well-paid, high-skilled labor as well. The high-skilled jobs in Silicon Valley that pay salaries of $60,000 are being performed elsewhere in the world for $12,000 (Davis and Stack, 1997, p. 135). With the exception of company CEOs in large corporations who have become accustomed to 50% bonuses on base annual incomes, to say nothing of a wide range of fringe benefits (Hutton, 1998), the net effect for many people who are fortunate enough to be in employment has been the driving down of wages and salaries and the increasing insecurity of job tenure. From the perspective of those at the bottom, the net effect has been much worse. In the OECD countries, 100 million people are income poor (often referred to as the working poor) and 37 million are unemployed (MacGregor, 1999, p. 94).

One of the most deplorable verities of the contemporary world is the continuing existence of scarcity—hunger, homelessness and all manner of unmet human needs—when technological advances mean that we now have the productive potential that could eliminate most types of scarcity and to do so in ways that need not be detrimental to the environment. The revolutions in electronics (especially digitization) and biotechnology allow for massive increases in productivity using fewer and, most importantly, sustainable levels of natural resources for raw materials and sources of energy (King, 1997; Schiller, 1997). However, as long as goods and services are available only when their price is met, scarcity will continue to exist no matter how anachronistic it has become. After pointing out several examples—such as pharmaceutical companies choosing to develop vaccines for livestock rather than for human beings because people only need inoculating once in a lifetime whereas new populations of cows, pigs and sheep, destined for slaughter, need annual inoculations, thus making farm animals a much more profitable market—King sums up the absurdity of the situation.

Leaving decisions as to whether to produce a product that might save the lives of 20,000 people to investors is socially irrational. Biotechnology was the product of public investment and was almost completely socially developed. Fifty years of taxpayer investment after World War II led to the breakthroughs that are now occurring. The public has already paid for the development of the technology, and its privatization thus represents a form of misappropriation. [p. 153]

King's point applies equally to most other advances in U.S. technology. However, I want to take this argument further by suggesting that if the technological capacity exists, then it is socially irrational to have to choose between improving food production and curing or preventing disease. Moreover, it is socially irresponsible and a gross—indeed, a criminal—infringement of human rights.

Over twenty years ago, Susan George made points similar to King's with reference to "The Green Revolution" that promised a massive increase in agricultural productivity. Her important book, *How The Other Half Dies* (first published in 1976), revealed many startling facts about the conditions that create and sustain world hunger. She called it a process of "planned scarcity"—planned in order to maintain food prices and profitability and thereby the production of food within market relations (George, 1986). Agricultural production in the United States only managed to remain profitable by first becoming large-scale in terms of food production and then becoming larger still by incorporating food production, processing, packaging and often distribution under the umbrella of giant food corporations. For various political and economic reasons, the U.S. government has for a long time considered it important to subsidize agricultural production, as have a number of other governments, primarily in the developed world. The United States has been able to use its surplus production (a direct result of the subsidization) to open the doors of many other countries not only to American commerce but also its power and influence as well (George, 1986).

The full story is a long and complex litany of U.S.-style neoimperialism, which many other nations in the developed world adopted apace once they recovered their productive capacity after World War II. Pilger (1998) recounts incidences of U.S., so-called, "Food for Peace" surpluses being dumped on countries and forcing down local prices to the extent that small farmers are ruined or forced to sell their land to foreign multinational agribusinesses. According to Sivanandan (1998/99), the 1994 GATT agreement prohibited all but the poorest "Third World" countries from imposing import duties on foodstuffs, thereby opening them up to cheap U.S. and European grain exports. The result, he notes, was the "killing off [of] locally produced food such as rice, grain and cassava, etc. (along with the local farmer)" (p. 12). All of this, of course, impacts on and contributes to the increasing polarization of people and nations and the devastation of the lives of millions of the world's children that I mentioned before.

Richard Wilkinson (1998) has argued convincingly that unequal societies produce more mental and physical health problems and, in connection with these, more violence too. The increasing levels of inequality as well as the increasingly insecure position of individuals, firms and even nations are linked to the liberalization or deregulation of trade and finance. Deregulation began in the early 1970s and has continued unabated ever since, accelerating especially in the 1980s under the neoliberal agenda set by Ronald Reagan and Margaret Thatcher and becoming entrenched in the IMF and other supranational institutions that operate in the interest of the international capitalist class (Burbach and Robinson, 1999). According to many commentators, deregulation became necessary in the 1970s in order to facilitate the movement of capital and thus stimulate productivity and profitability, both of which had begun to stagnate for a variety of reasons in the mid- to late 1960s. The resulting flow of financial capital, seeking the most profitable investments, was greatly facilitated by the newly established global telecommunications infrastructure and, in turn, contributed to the further growth and consolidation of that structure. This symbiotic relation also led to a proliferation of financial commodities and increases in the volume of trade as well as the velocity of financial transactions, effectively compressing the time and space involved in these transactions to "zero." Kundnani (1998/99) is one of many writers who cite the amazing statistic that " $1.4 trillion is traded via the global computer network daily" (p. 52). Tickell (1999) says that since the 1970s, derivatives (futures, options, etc.)—a general category of financial products—have become " a ubiquitous feature of business life. . . . [Between 1985 and 1995] the nominal value of derivative contracts [grew by] 2800%" (p. 251).

Deregulation has led to increasing inequality and uncertainty in numerous ways that are not always immediately obvious. It has made it extremely difficult to interpret various statistics that might indicate the overall health of the global economy or of national economies and even various corporations—for example, figures pertaining to corporate profits or national GNP/GDP. In the 1970s and continuing ever since, "asset stripping" became an easy way to restore corporate profitability and a strategy by which corporate raiders like Tiny Roland and James Goldsmith amassed huge fortunes. Politicians—especially Margaret Thatcher, who sold off public assets ostensibly to restore and maintain the "health" of the British economy—applied the same idea in the 1980s on an even larger and more socially irresponsible scale. Deregulation paved the way for "asset stripping," making it much easier for "corporate raiders" or multinational and other large corporate bodies to raise the funds necessary for buying the assets. It has also fostered a situation in which a great deal of economic activity, reflected in corporate profit figures and the growth of national economies, has more to do with the buying and selling of assets and the plethora of financial products than it does with the production of goods and nonfinancial services. As Fine, Lapavitsas and Milonakis (1999) note, since the economic downturn of the early 1970s, the financial system has demonstrated that it can maintain its profitability independently of industrial profitability and accumulation, and they stress that this "disparity of dynamism between industrial and financial accumulation [is] a new development in the history of capitalism" (p. 72). All of this has become a matter of concern to many politicians and economists, adding to the general state of confusion and feelings of helplessness that have been created by the seemingly uncontrollable dynamic of the world market. One of the grimmest consequences, of course, has been the massive job losses that have resulted from the selling off, downsizing and geographical relocation of huge chunks of the manufacturing sector of developed countries.

Relaxation of exchange-rate controls was the first and probably the most consequential act of liberalization/deregulation. It makes almost every nation participating in the world market vulnerable to the vicissitudes of financial speculation. In 1994, Mexico would have been bankrupted by the rapid disinvestment in the peso if it had not been for a rescue package concocted mainly by the

American banks, who also stood to lose if Mexico went "bust" (Harris, 1998/99; Richards, 1997). And a similar round of disinvestment in 1997 was an important factor in bringing about the end of the "Asian Miracle"—the miracle that over recent years has often been held up as proof of capitalism's worldwide success story (Hutton, 1998; Lo, 1999). Rapid investment and disinvestment would, of course, be much more difficult if it were not for deregulation. Harris (1998/99) sums up the vulnerability of many nation-states when he quotes Walter Wriston of Citibank giving a new meaning to the idea of "economic democracy"—a meaning that, Harris notes, excludes 99.9% of the world's population:

It's a system whereby international financiers take a vote on the soundness of each country's fiscal and monetary policies. This giant vote counting machine conducts a running tally on what the world thinks of a government's diplomatic, fiscal and monetary policies and this opinion is immediately reflected in the value the market places on a country's currency. [p. 32]

This type of thinking, having grown out of the period of deregulation, might have reflected the stance of a number of people like Wriston in 1992, but by 1997 George Soros, who had grown very rich by speculating on the world financial market, was warning of the need to regulate the global "free market" (Hobsbawm, 1998). And he was not alone. By the time of their deaths in 1997 and 1998, respectively, both James Goldsmith and Tiny Roland, two of the biggest promoters and strongest bastions of neoliberalism—free markets and deregulation—and two of the most notorious corporate raiders of the 1970s and 1980s, had begun to call for government intervention, warning that it was essential for governments to regain control over the economy (*The Mayfair Set*, BBC2, 8 August 1999). This is not, in fact, a very surprising stance for capitalists to take. Ever since at least the early 1900s, the overall strategy of capitalists has been to adapt the system in ways that allow them to exercise greater control over fluctuations in the market. Often this has involved them leaning on their national governments to persuade them, when persuasion was necessary, to intervene by instituting regulatory measures.

What is perhaps more surprising is that social democratic leaders who currently hold power in several Western governments have made few if any moves to heed these warnings. Larry Elliot, The Financial Editor of the *Guardian* newspaper, speaking on BBC2's *Big Ideas* program on 3 September 1999, said that there was little doubt that the United States would remain the dominant economic power in the world for the foreseeable future because it had the largest and most advanced corporations in the leading sectors of the world economy—a fact he attributed to the U.S. government's investment in defense. In other words, America's longstanding and enormous commitment to defense spending had given U.S. corporations a clear advantage in utilizing "cutting-edge" technology, and therefore, according to Elliot, it was the government's investment in the economy rather than the free market that had made the United States the world's leading economy. There is, however, a fundamental difference between the way in which U.S. defense spending had an unplanned effect on American economic activity and the type of planned intervention now being called for by those who want to see their governments reassert their control over national economies. There is no guarantee that planned intervention in a nation's domestic economy would reap the same advantages at this juncture, when the influence of the world market has become more important. Chris Harman (1996) makes a similar point and argues that investment in defense creates very specific conditions for growth in national economies that do not pertain if investment is focused elsewhere. It is more likely that there is no way to control uncertainty and avoid insecurity in the real world of global capitalism. In chapters 2 and 3, I explain why this is the inescapable truth of capitalism.

No portrayal of the contemporary world, even one as brief as that offered here, can fail to mention culture. Cultural patterns reflect some of the most paradoxical aspects of global capitalism. Simultaneously we find processes that seem to be creating a homogeneous or more uniform world culture, yet also a world of greater heterogeneity or diversity in the form of a heightened awareness of national as well as ethnic identities and differences. Although this seems paradoxical, it makes a great deal of sense, given what has already been mentioned with reference to growing uncertainty and insecurity. When people experience change that threatens their economic security and general well-being, they will often seek the known and familiar havens of cultural practice. Many of those who have little hope of future employment may seek refuge in areas that seem to be the only remaining sources of identity, such as family, ethnicity, nationality and religion. The degree to which the process of differentiation becomes conflictual will depend to some degree on the type of homogenization that is occurring.

Pilger (1998) calls this homogenization "Americanization"—a process that is about promoting worldwide consumerism of "packaged American culture" (p. 69). He depicts it as a shallow culture based on self-aggrandizement and violence that more often than not drowns out the local competition. Harris (1998/99) likens the homogenization process, in which he includes a number of things that would create uniform standards beneficial to trade and commerce, to the nation-building stage of capitalism now being played out on a worldwide basis. He points out that international capitalism requires a world system of uniform standards and that one of the main functions of the IMF has been to eliminate any national variations—cultural as well as organizational and regulatory—that would impede the flow of capital. It is little wonder that we now find, throughout the world and often in the most unlikely places, MacDonald's Golden Arches, Whoppers, Coca-Cola or Pepsi and what some have labeled the Disneyfication of culture. These can be seen as cultural appetizers meant to break down cultural barriers to a steady diet of U.S. commodities. It is little wonder that this type of homogenization or cultural imperialism has encountered various forms of resistance. It is probably one of the many contributory factors that has led to the expression of religious fundamentalism and the growth of ethnic and nationalistic conflict that has become a very real and alarming feature of the contemporary world—a feature that provides some of the rationalization for governments continuing to spend vast sums on defense.

This brings me to a final point about our contemporary reality—a point about one of the most insidious and dangerous threats to humanity's well-being now and in the future—a threat that, far from being new, has been plaguing the world for at least half of the twentieth century and that, contrary to popular opinion, continues to do so with undiminished tenacity. In 1989, President George Bush claimed that the Cold War had come to an end and promised that a "peace dividend" would be forthcoming. However, as we enter a new millennium, it is clear that the "arms race" continues unabated. By 1994, Britain's arms industry had become revitalized, employing one worker in every ten, and the government was spending about 10 billion pounds sterling annually on defense, which is far above the European average (Pilger, 1998, p. 6). Nor has defense spending slowed in the United States, according to Pilger; although we may not hear as much about it, Reagan's Star Wars Program continues under the new acronym, THAAD (Thermonuclear High Altitude Area Defense), and in response the Russians are developing their own system (Pilger, 1998, p. 8). There is little doubt, according to most commentators, that arms production and arms trade will continue to figure centrally in U.S. and U.K. economic and political strategies and will probably remain important to many other countries as well. Both the United States and the United Kingdom sell arms to countries that have appalling human rights records, and both have used arms sales to gain political influence, particularly in the oil-rich Middle East and what were until recently the fastest growing East Asian countries (*The Mayfair Set*, BBC2, 8 August 1999; Harman, 1996). Harman points out that the "bombing of Baghdad is as much a part of the logic of the system [global capitalism] as the Multifibre Trade Agreement . . ." (1996, p. 30). Others have, since then, made the same point about the war in Bosnia.

This brief sketch has pointed to only a few of the most insidious and worrying aspect of our contemporary reality. The explanation I offer for why these things are happening will unfold in my discussion of capitalism in the next two chapters. Here I present a summary of the interpretations others have made.

WHY IS IT HAPPENING?—
A NEW BALL GAME? A NEW STADIUM? OR BOTH?

Globalization is purported to be the dominant force of our times. Ostensibly, it is the unavoidable result of human progress—a process to which people and nations must adapt. In the long term, it is supposed to bring about the best possible results for the majority of people. This is the view, the globalization theory or orthodoxy, that we hear from the media and many politicians. David Held (1998) calls it the "hyperglobalist view" of reality (p. 24). Drawing, in part, on Held's account, the gist of this view goes as follows: Economic processes—

both financial and production—have become globalized. This has come about because multinational and transnational corporations have become the indispensable means for promoting global production, growth and employment and for diffusing technological advances and expanding the distribution of goods and services through the world market. Although multinationals and transnationals often have a specific national base, their strategies for growth and profitability are global. Production is therefore geared primarily toward the global rather than the domestic market. Financial institutions have also become increasingly global, both in size and orientation. Advanced technology and deregulation have accelerated the mobility of capital flows, and the number of financial commodities has expanded dramatically as a consequence, opening up new avenues to profitability and wealth and also facilitating a greater than ever volume of world trade. This has led to nation-states becoming more tightly integrated; therefore, national economies and societies have become much more sensitive to one another. While this means that it is no longer feasible for national governments to pursue independent economic policies, it also has made the likelihood of wars between nations untenable. Even though nation-states may have lost certain powers, they still have an important role to play. Global competition and standards of efficiency may be inescapable, but governments can do a great deal to make their nations more competitive. They will be more competitive if they promote liberal democracy and civic responsibility as well as certain desirable "macro-economic policies aimed at low inflation, balanced budgets, the removal of trade barriers and exchange controls, maximum liberty for capital, minimum regulation of labor markets, privatization and, in general, a streamlined adaptive welfare state to propel citizens into work" (Held, 1998, p. 25). The main obligation that states have toward their citizens is to make sure they are "empowered" to face the challenge of global competition. And this means making sure that they have the proper flexible and adaptable skills and attitudes that will enhance their employability.

As Held points out, the "hyperglobalist view" is neoliberalism writ large, an economic theory of the best way to foster capitalist growth and development that has become especially dominant since the 1970s. It is the view held by the dominant actors in the global economy—the most powerful nation-states and the institutions and organizations that represent their interests and impose their will on all the other states that wish to participate in the global market—the United States, G8, OECD, IMF, World Bank, Tri-Lateral Commission, and so on. (Held, 1998, p. 25). Held and many other critics of "hyperglobalism" point out that it is a political project, rather than some inevitable or natural force and, as such, it has to be supported and promoted if it is to be sustained. However, this criticism should not be taken to mean that it is a false view of the contemporary world.

It is better understood as an ideological explanation and an ideological project, one that tells only part of the story and therefore distorts the full truth of reality. Nevertheless, it is based on enough truth to persuade many people that this is the way things are and, moreover, must be. And when an ideology becomes as dominant—or hegemonic in the Gramscian sense of convincing people and winning consent—as this one is, it also becomes a material force capable of shaping our lives. Even though it has its origins in economic processes, it can acquire a quasi-independent force of its own that begins to act back on and shape the ongoing development of those processes. Globalization has thus become an important area of debate and discussion. I will try to recount the various types of interpretations and responses it has engendered from the Left, but I must begin by trying to clarify why the Left has been far from unified in their response. Please note that when I refer to "groups" in the following discussion I am categorizing people who share similar views and analyses rather than a collection of people who necessarily share a common identity.

Even before Marx, socialism was proposed as the only democratic alternative to capitalism; however, the advocates of socialism have always been divided on many issues, often very important ones. One of the most fundamental of these, and one that lies at the heart of many other disputes, is the actual meaning of socialism. A majority of the Left have always defined socialism as primarily an alternative system of distributing the results of production, which is brought about by abolishing the private ownership of the means of production. Others have understood socialism to be a process of total social, political and economic transformation—one of the results of which is the equitable distribution of the wealth produced by society. Wealth, however, is conceived not in monetary terms, but in terms of the goods and services produced by society, and just what these are to be and how they are to be produced is decided democratically by the members of the society. Private ownership of the means of production is inconceivable, of course, within such a society. This was the idea of socialism that Marx and Engels promoted. They actually referred to it as the first stage of communism rather than socialism, and they thought that it would necessarily entail the changing of many social relations and, thereby, of people as well, so that they would relate to one another in a more humane way than is possible within capitalist social relations (Marx and Engels, 1846, 1848). These different meanings of socialism lead to two quite different conceptions of the state and its role.

"Distributional socialists," or social democrats, assume that the state is a semiautonomous democratic institution that can be used by politicians of the Left, when in power, to legislate measures designed to bring about a more equitable distribution of wealth and the creation, generally, of a more just and equal society. "Transformational or revolutionary socialists" do not see the state as a neutral institution. Modern nation-states are seen as a form of social organization that developed together with capitalism and that have been both necessary for and largely beneficial to its development (Wood, 1995, 1999). Even when the governments of capitalist states are controlled by social democratic parties, the capitalist "rules of the game" apply, such that when concessions of a distributional nature are made, they are set within limits determined by the "health" of the capitalist economy. In other words, the capitalist economy—the logic of capitalism that must be adhered to—frames the "horizon" of democratic debate and limits the parameters of socialist inspired policy (Hall, 1982). With these distinctions and qualifications in mind, it becomes much easier to understand why the response of the Left to globalization has been so varied and why it often appears confusing and contradictory.

From the social-democratic, or "distributional" Left, there are basically two types of responses to globalization, both of which advocate the need for governmental intervention. They argue that intervention is needed to rectify the effect of unfettered market forces, or, alternatively, governmental capitulation or overreaction to neoliberalism's "hyperglobalist" agenda. Both camps are highly critical of purportedly social democratic governments like Bill Clinton's democratic administration and Tony Blair's "New Labour Party." One group bases its argument on the considerable empirical evidence that refutes the claims that the world market has become more open and highly integrated than previously in world history—especially the idea that global integration is greater than it was in the period leading up to 1914 (see, for example, the evidence reported by Hirst and Thompson, 1996, that refutes these claims). They stress important evidence like the tendencies for multinationals to locate their foreign direct investments primarily in developed nations rather than dispersing these investments globally. Their overall assessment of globalization is that it is a myth. They argue that governments are still quite capable of applying Keynesian measures to control and direct their national economies and create more equitable societies, but that politicians lack the will to do so.

The other group appears to accept certain aspects of this argument. They do not think, however, that the process of globalization is entirely a myth, just not as advanced or as pervasive as the hyperglobalists claim. Nevertheless, they think that a process of globalization is taking place and will continue to do so along the lines projected by the globalization thesis. Therefore, they argue that nation-states must act in concert to establish supranational and international modes of regulation and governance at both regional and international levels in order to curb the worst effects of global market forces and also to preserve, sustain and further develop democracy. In the latter group there is a further split between those who think that there is no longer any alternative economic system to capitalism and the market (e.g., Anthony Giddens, 1998) and those that think that eventually we will develop a democratic world government that will establish a worldwide socialist economic system of fair distribution and justice (e.g., Samir Amin, 1997). All those whose responses to globalization take one or another of these forms think that parties of the Left currently in power in many Western states could be taking a much greater defensive or offensive (to use Habermas's, 1999, distinction) than is currently the case. They stress the need not only for measures aimed at greater social cohesion and justice but also at much greater environmental protection and sustainability.

Revolutionary/transformational socialists—those whose thinking basically adheres to Marx's and Engels's concept of socialism (see Allman, 1999) and who therefore never considered the Soviet Union or its satellite states as representatives of that concept—agree that since World War II capitalism has increasingly become the fully internationalized system that had been predicted by Marx and Engels in the *Communist Manifesto* of 1848. Here too, however, we find differences in interpretation with reference to both globalization and other issues. One group, although fundamentally disagreeing with globalization orthodoxy, agrees that a process of globalization is taking place and that nation-states have been extremely weakened—virtually transcended as a result—At best "national governments as territorially bound juridical units . . . [have been] transformed into transmission belts and filtering devices for the imposition of the transnational agenda" (Robinson, 1996, p. 19).

In contrast to the "hyperglobalist" view or any view of globalization per se, another group stresses the international nature of capitalism. By this they mean the penetration of capitalist relations internationally and the expanding scope and depth of the global market as well as the more highly integrated relations between nations, rather than the global transcendence of the nation-state. They argue that capitalism will always need the nation-state and political leaders of the state who will act in the interest of the growth and development of capitalism within their countries (e.g., Wood, 1999). Revolutionary/transformational socialists are also divided over other issues in ways that may reflect fundamentally diverging interpretations of Marx's economic writings. Where they stand with respect to the dynamic of capitalism ostensibly lies at the heart of their differences and disagreements. However, it is entirely possible that, at least in some cases, these differences are more apparent than real—that is, they may be more a matter of emphasis and focus rather than something of a more substantive nature.

One influential "group" includes people like William Robinson, A. Sivanandan and Roger Burbach, whose writings often focus on "Third World" issues and the neoimperialism, particularly, of the United States and certain European nations. These authors have stressed the importance of the technological revolution that has displaced labor in the North, or more highly developed nations, and led to the increasing exploitation of labor in the South, or the underdeveloped and newly developing nations. In their writings they suggest that advances in technology have facilitated and accelerated the rapid movement of capital across the globe, creating "seas" of "Third World"-type poverty within even the most highly developed nations of North America and Europe and "lakes" or enclaves of the superwealthy within Latin American, Asian and even some of the poorest African nations (Robinson, 1996, p. 23). Most of the writers in this group argue that an "epochal shift" in capitalism has occurred and that a new global class of capitalist elites has been formed, which is contesting the power of the traditional nationally based bourgeoisie throughout the world (Burbach and Robinson, 1999). These authors suggest that the "hyperglobalist" view, or neoliberalism, is the ideology that specifically serves the interest of this new class.

Because various authors in this grouping emphasize the role that advances in telecommunications—the electronic, especially the digital revolution—have played in the process of globalization, others have accused them of "technological determinism" (e.g., see the debate between Sivanandan and Wood, 1997). Wood, especially, refers to Sivanandan's remark that "[i]f '. . . the steam-mill gives you the industrial capitalist,' the microchip gives you society with the global capitalist" (p. 20). In other words, the dynamic of capitalist development is technological advance. While this may not be the actual stance that Sivanandan and others are taking, the problem with an undue emphasis on technology is that authors who take this stance seem to come unstuck over what is happening with Marx's "Law of Value." I discuss this "law" in detail in chapters 2 and 3, but here it will, hopefully, suffice to say that what it basically involves is the idea that one of the historically specific features of capitalism is that *live* human labor is the source of all value and hence the basis of profit and thus all capital accumulation. Obviously this is a most important "law" in Marx's economics. For socialists who think that it is only the industrial proletariat, or workers who produce material objects, who produce value, the technological replacement of labor means that the capitalists' search for profitable investment must switch to the newly industrialized or underdeveloped nations, where cheap labor rather than advanced technology can be used to produce material objects that will be competitively priced on the world market. In this sense, therefore, technology has initiated the whole globalization process. To survive capitalism needs human labor to produce value; and since labor in the developed world, or the type of labor that produces value, can no longer do this in sufficient numbers, capitalism must spread out to the far reaches of the world. Following on from this line of thinking, some have argued that since the majority of workers in the developed world no longer serve as a source of value but are still needed by capitalism as consumers, governments will have to pay their citizens a "social wage," and thus a type of socialism—consumer socialism—will come about by default (Gorz, 1985).

Other revolutionary/transformational socialists have focused on the "laws" or inherent tendencies (e.g., laws of movement, especially the "Law of Value" mentioned earlier) that constitute capitalism as a historically specific form of socioeconomic human organization. They stress that these have always governed the movement and development of capitalism, and they use them to explain the dynamic or trajectory of what Ellen Meiksins Wood (1999) refers to as the "universalization," or full internationalization, of capitalism. Most writers in this group specifically refer to one particular tendency—*the falling rate of profit* (e.g., Brenner, 1998; or for a critique of Brenner and a more dialectical interpretation of the situation in Fine et al., 1999). Here too, however, we find further differences that pertain to the other laws—that is, tendencies or dynamics—that they see as particularly related to or interacting with the falling rate of profit at this conjuncture in history. Some writers emphasize the drive to accumulate and

concentrate capital and to dominate markets and the competition between capitalists that this fosters as each firm strives to maximize profitability as a basis for
further accumulation and growth. Others suggest that the main dynamic of
internationalization or globalization, a term used with reservations, is the struggle
between capital and labor; while still others argue that the competitive struggle
for investment and power between financial and industrial capital is the driving
force. Those who focus on the class struggle between labor and capital argue that
it was the effectiveness of working-class action against capital that ended the
long period of capitalist prosperity after World War II, setting off a fall in the rate
of profit and sending some sectors of manufacturing capital on the "move" in
search of cheap and unorganized labor.

On the other hand, writers who focus on the struggle for dominance between
financial and industrial capitalists, with each competing for the overall power to
control the flow of capital investments, stress how technology has aided financial
capital in this struggle. With the ability to transfer capital rapidly via the electronic superhighway and thus holding out the promise of increasing profitability
through speculative ventures, financial capital has managed, as mentioned previously, to lure investment away from the industrial base. Therefore, financial
capital, with the aid of technology and by unleashing the forces of the world
market and propelling the process of globalization, has gained the upper hand.
They argue that while industrial capital may once have had the power to influence the policies of national governments, it is now financial capital's power of
disinvestment that can force the hand of governments. And neoliberal policies
that governments have been forced or persuaded to adopt have primarily served
the interest of this faction of the capitalist class—note, however, not creating a
new class, but bolstering the power of a faction of the capitalist class already in
existence in many nation-states, albeit a class faction heavily involved in international finance.

In my opinion, the writers who begin from the premise that capitalism moves
and develops according to its own historically specific "laws" and tendencies
offer the most effective explanations. However, even they, to my knowledge,
have not proffered a fully comprehensive interpretation of contemporary global
capitalism; and as a consequence, there does not as yet exist a fully effective
challenge to the hyperglobalist view. Nevertheless, they do show us how best to
approach the problem. This is especially true of Fine et al. (1999) who, in
critiquing Brenner (1998), remind us that the approach must be based on Marx's
"Law of Value," which allows us to connect "the competitive struggle between
[various] capitals with the capital–labor relation and [establish] the link between
horizontal inter-capitalist relations with vertical class relations and class conflict"
(p. 81). Having said this, there are valuable insights that critical educators can
draw from all of these interpretations. It is important to recognize, however, that
none of them deal with all of the variables that need to be considered or the
relation between the variables. When it comes to that type of analysis, Marx's
economic writings remain the most comprehensive interpretation, for two rea-

sons: (1) Since we are seeking to understand capitalism—a dynamic process and not a fixed structure or "thing"—there can be no final or conclusive interpretation or answer, so to speak; this is not what we should be seeking. What we need are "tools" of analysis that we can employ in understanding capitalism as it moves and develops in a dialectic process of progress and regress. This is what Marx offers us. And (2) Marx's comprehensive exposition of capitalism remains the only one that enables us to identify the panoply of variables that must be considered if we are to grasp the true nature of capitalism in a way that will allow us to first challenge and then transform it into an entirely new form of human social-economic organization.

REFERENCES

Allman, P. (1999). *Revolutionary Social Transformation: Democratic Hopes, Political Possibilities and Critical Education.* Westport, CT: Bergin & Garvey.

Amin, S. (1997). *Capitalism in the Age of Globalization. The Management of Contemporary Society.* London: Zed.

Berger, J. (1998/99). "Against the Defeat of the World." *Race & Class,* 40 (No. 2/3 (October/March), 1–4.

Brenner, R. (1998). "The Economics of Global Turbulence." *New Left Review,* 224 (May/June), 1–264.

Burbach, R., and Robinson, W. I. (1999). "The Fin De Siècle Debate: Globalization as Epochal Shift." *Science & Society,* 63 (No. 1, Spring), 10–39.

Davis, J., and Stack, M. (1997). "The Digital Advantage." In J. Davis, T. Hirschl, and M. Stack (Eds.), *Cutting Edge: Technology, Information, Capitalism and Social Revolution* (Ch. 8). London: Verso.

Fine, B., Lapavitsas, C., and Milonakis, D. (1999). "Addressing the World Economy: Two Steps Back." *Capital & Class,* 67 (Spring), 47–90.

Freire, P. (1974). "Authority versus Authoritarianism." Audiotape, in series: *Thinking with Paulo Freire.* Sydney, Australia: Australian Council of Churches.

George, S. (1986). *How the Other Half Dies: The Real Reasons for World Hunger.* Harmondsworth, U.K.: Penguin.

Giddens, A. (1998). *The Third Way: The Renewal of Social Democracy.* Cambridge: Polity Press.

Gorz, A. (1985). *Paths to Paradise: On the Liberation from Work.* London: Pluto Press.

Habermas, J. (1999). "The European Nation-State and the Pressures of Globalisation, *New Left Review,* 235 (May/June), 46–59.

Hall, S. (1982). "Managing Conflict, Producing Consent." Unit 21, in Block 5: *Conformity, Consensus and Conflict, D102 Social Sciences: A Foundation Course.* Milton Keynes, U.K.: Open University Press.

Harman, C. (1996). "Globalization: Critique of a New Orthodoxy." *International Socialism,* 73 (Winter), 3–33.

Harris, J. (1998/99). "Globalization and the Technological Transformation of Capitalism." *Race & Class,* 40 (No. 2/3), 21–35.

Harvey, D. (1989). *The Condition of Postmodernity*. Oxford: Basil Blackwell.

Harvey, D. (1995). "Globalisation in Question." *Rethinking Marxism*, 8 (No. 4), 1–17.

Held, D. (1998). "The Timid Tendency." *Marxism Today, Special Issue* (November/December), 24–27.

Hirschl, T. (1997). "Structural Unemployment and the Qualitative Transformation of Capitalism." In J. Davis, T. Hirschl, and M. Stack (Eds.), *Cutting Edge: Technology, Information, Capitalism and Social Revolution* (Ch. 10). London: Verso.

Hirst, P., and Thompson, G. (1996). *Globalization in Question: The International Economy and Possibilities for Governance.* Cambridge: Polity.

Hobsbawm, E. (1998). "The Death of Neo-Liberalism." *Marxism Today, Special Issue* (November/December), 4–8.

Holloway, J. (1995). "Capital Moves." *Capital & Class*, 57 (Autumn), 136–144.

Hutton, W. (1998). "The State We Should Be In." *Marxism Today, Special Issue* (November/December), 34–37.

King, J. (1997). "The Biotechnology Revolution: Self-Replicating Factories and the Ownership of Life Forms." In J. Davis, T. Hirschl, and M. Stack (Eds.), *Cutting Edge: Technology, Information, Capitalism and Social Revolution* (Ch. 9). London: Verso.

Kloppenburg, J. R., Jr. (1988). *First Seed: The Political Economy of Plant Biotechnology, 1492–2000.* Cambridge: Cambridge University Press.

Kundnani, A. (1998/99). "Where Do You Want to Go Today: The Rise of Information Capitalism." *Race & Class*, 40 (No. 2/3), 49–71.

Lerner, S. (1997). "How Will North America Work in the Twenty-First Century?" in J. Davis, T. Hirschl, and M. Stack (Eds.), *Cutting Edge: Technology, Information, Capitalism and Social Revolution* (Ch. 11). London: Verso.

Lo, D. (1999). "The East Asian Phenomenon." *Capital & Class*, 67 (Spring), 1–23.

MacGregor, S. (1999). "Welfare, Neo-Liberalism and New Paternalism: Three Ways for Social Policy in Late Capitalist Societies." *Capital & Class*, 67 (Spring), 91–118.

Marx, K. (1858). *Grundrisse*, translated and with a Foreword by Martin Nicolaus. Harmondsworth, U.K.: Penguin, 1973.

Marx, K., and Engels, F. (1846). *The German Ideology.* Moscow: Progress, 1976.

Marx, K., and Engels, F. (1848). "The Communist Manifesto." In D. McLellan (Ed.), *Karl Marx: Selected Writings* (pp. 221–247). Oxford: Oxford University Press, 1977.

Pilger, J. (1998). *Hidden Agendas.* London: Vintage.

Reich, R. (1991). *The Work of Nations: A Blueprint for the Future.* New York: Vintage.

Richards, D. (1997). "The Political Economy of Neo-Liberal Reform in Latin America: A Critical Appraisal." *Capital & Class*, 61 (Spring), 19–43.

Robertson, W. I. (1996). "Globalisation: Nine Theses of Our Epoch." *Race & Class*, 38 (No. 2), 13–31.

Schiller, D. (1997). "The Information Commodity: A Preliminary View." In J. Davis, T. Hirschl, and M. Stack (Eds.), *Cutting Edge: Technology, Information, Capital and Social Revolution* (Ch. 7). London: Verso.

Sivanandan, A. (1998/99). "Globalism and the Left." *Race & Class*, 40 (No. 2/3), 3–19.

Sivanandan, A., and Wood, E. M. (1997). "Capitalism, Globalization, and Epochal Shifts: An Exchange." *Monthly Review*, 48 (No. 9), 19–32.

Tickell, A. (1999). "Unstable Futures: Controlling and Creating Risk in International Money." In L. Panitch and C. Leys (Eds.), *Socialist Register 1999, Global Capitalism versus Democracy* (pp. 248–269). Rendlesham, U.K.: Merlin.

Wilkinson, R. (1998). "Why Inequality Is Bad for You." *Marxism Today, Special Issue* (November/December), 38–39.

Wood, E. M. (1995). *Democracy Against Capitalism: Renewing Historical Materialism*. Cambridge: Cambridge University Press.

Wood, E. M. (1999). "Unhappy Families: Global Capitalism in a World of Nation-States." *Monthly Review*, 51 (No. 3) [www.monthlyreview.org].

2

Unfolding the Essence of Capitalism— From the Simple Commodity to Global Social Domination: Capitalism, Part I

"READING" MARX—"READING" THE WORLD

As I have forewarned, "reading" Marx, even through a secondary filter such as this, is not an easy task. However, the journey into understanding that we make in this chapter and the next can be made far less arduous if we first "unpack" some of the basic ingredients of Marx's approach. As I said in the introduction to this book, my interpretation or "reading" of Marx falls within a specific tradition— one that, disastrously, remains a minority tradition. The other people whom I identify as belonging to this tradition differ on certain areas of their interpretations, but the one factor that we all share is a dialectical "reading" or understanding of Marx's writings. Unfortunately, however, as I mentioned before, some people in this tradition tend to interpret Marx in terms of Hegel's dialectic rather than recognizing the distinctive nature of Marx's approach.[1] My discussion of capitalism, in this chapter and the next, is based on an understanding of Marx's distinctive dialectical conceptualization of capitalism. In the Introduction to this book, I mentioned several people whom I identify as being part of this tradition. When appropriate in the following discussion, I will mention or reference those authors who not only specifically concur with a particular aspect of my explanation but also accentuate it in their own work.

In this chapter, we embark on the first half of our journey. Here I discuss the "essence" of capitalism or, as Rosdolsky (1977) calls it, "Capital in General," and then, in chapter 3, I explain how this essence appears and is manifested in the concrete and complex reality of capitalist society. However, as I said before, our journey will be made far easier and also more rewarding if I first explain certain fundamental aspects of Marx's approach to analyzing and writing about capitalism. I begin with a discussion of the overall scheme or plan of the approach and how my presentation relates to this, as well as with a discussion of two fundamental aspects of the approach that constitute leitmotivs, or guiding threads, in Marx's writings. Next, and most importantly, I explain the conceptual orientation—viz., the dialectical conceptualization—that underpins his approach, and I also discuss the conceptual "tools" that he uses in his analysis and exposition of capitalism.

Marx's ideas about and critique of capitalism can be found in almost everything he wrote. In this chapter and chapter 3, my discussion focuses primarily on the three volumes of his *Capital* and on the *Grundrisse* (however, I also draw on Marx, 1859, 1863a, 1863b, and 1863c). As I mentioned before, the first volume of *Capital* was the only one of the three volumes that he saw through to publication himself; the others were made ready for publication by his friend and collaborator, Friedrich Engels. Marx's *Theories of Surplus Value*, Parts 1, 2 and 3 (1863a, 1863b, 1863c) is often referred to as the fourth volume of *Capital;* in these volumes, his crucial insights into the nature of capitalism are interwoven with his critique of both bourgeois and socialist political economy. Karl Kautsky published them in 1905, after Engels's death. Volume 1 of *Capital* is the best known and most widely read of all these works. It is essential, however, to recognize how the first volume relates to the second and third volumes. Unfortunately, even this is a matter of controversy among those who make up the far-from-homogeneous grouping known as Marxism. Since my interpretation of Marx is a dialectical one, it seems clear to me that the relation between the three volumes is a dialectical one. By this I mean that he presents his analysis and critique of capitalism in a way that is meant to help readers to conceptualize capitalism dialectically.

In the first volume, Marx primarily focuses on the most fundamental social relation of capitalism or of capital's essence—a relation that he locates in the sphere of production or, more precisely, within those activities within which people produce their material world. But prior to this, in part 1 of volume 1, he sets out the most general or abstract model through which we can discern the most basic contradictions and preconditions of capitalism. He shows how the "essence" of capitalism develops out of the rudimentary commodity form, tracing the development or unfolding of this form from the direct exchange of commodities between commodity producers through their circulation and exchange in commodity markets. Then, through the rest of the first volume, he takes us from the dawn of capitalism through its full development into a mature socioeconomic formation by exploring the capitalist process of production—the process through which the commodity becomes a fully developed form and through which capital is created. Here we see the most fundamental aspects of capital's essence and how this essence is formed and continually reproduced.

The dynamic of the essence, or "Capital in General," is completed in the sphere, or activities, of circulation and exchange; and the activities that take place in this sphere are the focus of *Capital*, volume 2. Therefore, with Volumes 1 (Marx, 1867) and 2 (Marx, 1878) we get the full picture of "Capital in General"—the full process or movement and development of the "essence" of capitalism. The way in which this essence is manifested in the forms, or categories, tendencies and laws of the complex and concrete totality of capitalism, where we find many capitalist firms in competition with one another, is the subject of Volume 3 (Marx, 1865). One very useful way of viewing the relationship between the volumes and their sequence is to see them as moving from *essence*, or a more general and simplified or abstract model, to the *appearance*, or the concrete, complex totality of capitalism. The essence is manifested in this concrete, complex totality but can only be grasped through analyzing the dialectical unfolding of the categories, or forms, that we experience in the day-to-day workings of the capitalist system.

Many Marxists and also non-Marxists view the three volumes as a history of the development of capitalism. It can be tempting to read particularly the first volume as a historical account, but to do so is to lose the power that Marx's analysis gives us to expose the fundamental and inherent contradictions of capitalism—contradictions that are as real today as they were in Marx's time. It is tempting to read Volume 1 in this way because it is a mixture of different types of history. As I suggested earlier, it is in this volume that Marx explains the "unfolding" of the essence, or the most basic forms or categories in which the contradictions of capitalism are manifested—the process through which the essence (its relations and forms, or categories) moves, develops and is continuously reproduced through the activity of human beings. In explaining this unfolding and also the actual process through which capital is produced, Marx furnished both historical evidence and a wealth of detail so that the logic and tendencies that emanate from the essence could be identified within the experiences and not-too-distant memories of the readers who were Marx's contemporaries. For us, of course, all of this detail comes across as a historical account of capitalism. It is important to remember that Marx wrote *Capital* for working-class readers—to enable them to understand fully just how the capitalist system oppressed and exploited them—how, in fact, they made the system possible—and how they might challenge and replace it.

The best or most accurate way to view Volume 1 is as both a general model abstracted from a concrete and complex reality—the totality of many capitals in competition—and a history of how the preconditions of capitalism developed on the margins of precapitalist societies—that is, in the activities of individuals operating on the margins of older social formations. In addition, it also depicts the historical conditions in which capitalism first appeared as a fully developed socioeconomic system—a historically specific social form.[2] As Rosdolsky (1977) says, the sequence of Marx's analysis of capitalism is both "historical and logical" (p. 39). The idea of historical specificity, which I just mentioned, is extremely important in Marx's explanation, and I will return to this idea shortly. It is one of the leitmotivs I mentioned previously that run through Marx's writings. First, however, I consider the other leitmotiv—the relationship between preconditions and results.

To understand fully or grasp the truth of capitalism, capital must be thought of as both a *process* and a *relation*. Marx often speaks of the presuppositions or preconditions of both the process and the relation. He is especially explicit about preconditions and results in the notebooks in which he worked out his rough drafts of *Capital* and his entire project for the presentation of the capitalist economy and in which we can see evidence of his own process of self-clarification [see Martin Nicolaus's (1973) "Foreword" to the *Grundrisse* (1858), the fairly recently published notebooks he kept during the winter of 1857–58]. The important idea that Marx conveys is that what begins as a precondition and in a more simplified form becomes a result or consequence—and also a more highly developed form (Wood, 1995). Moreover, the result at one moment in time can become the precondition for the reproduction of the process or even its further development at a higher level of complexity. The preconditions are identified through a logical, or reasoned, analysis of the results—an analysis of their dialectical unfolding, which provides the basis for an exhaustive explanation of how the results came into being. This notion of preconditions and results constituting moments in the dynamic process of capitalism—a process through which the essence moves and develops into new levels of maturity and complexity—is fundamental to Marx's thinking. The movement from preconditions to results is both logical—or movement from the simple, abstract essence to the complex, concrete totality—and historical. Marx unfolds the logic and the history of capital as we move in our reading of Volume 1 from the early development of commodity exchange to the early stages of capitalism and then finally to its fully developed general form or the full realization of the essence. In other words, Marx presents the categories, or forms, through which he analyzes capital according to their logical relation with one another and according to the historical development of their embryonic forms. These concepts will, hopefully, become completely clear when I refer to preconditions and results at various points in my discussion of Marx's explanation of capitalism.

Historical specificity is the other general concept or leitmotiv in Marx's thinking that is, I think, important to highlight. It is one of the most important and crucial aspects of his analysis and critique of capitalism. In his "Foreword" to the *Grundrisse*, Nicolaus (1973, pp. 39–42) points to its centrality; and the importance of the historically specific nature of capitalism is also emphasized by Sayer (1987), Wood (1995), Postone (1996) and, to some extent, by Ollman (1976). Marx's use of this concept means that his critique of capitalism—including its form of universality, its totalizing effects of domination and its teleological, recurring movement toward a predetermined end—namely, profit maximization and capital accumulation—is a critique of features that are specific to capitalism. They are no more inevitable or natural than are other features of capitalism such as its historically specific forms of poverty, injustice and exploitation and would figure equally in its abolition. This means, of course, that terms such as *essence* and *appearance* refer to that which is historically specific to capitalism—that is, the part of our total experience of life that is directly attributable to capitalism. Ironically, Marx and Marxism have been attacked, especially by postmodernist critics, for offering totalizing, "essentialist" and teleological theories of society. Were it not for the unfortunate fact that some Marxists have actually presented Marx in just that manner, these criticisms could be dismissed as gross misinterpretations or misrepresentations of Marx's thinking. I have no intention of engaging in this debate other than to use Marx himself as the best defense for his theory of capitalist society. This problem of misinterpretation would never have arisen in the first place if the historical specificity of his social theory had been recognized. That Marx's explanations pertain to capitalism rather than to other socioeconomic systems, or for that matter, to every single aspect of life in capitalist societies is an extremely important and now, I trust, explicit assumption that underpins my discussion of his ideas. The final important and often either contentious or unrecognized aspect of Marx's approach has to do with the way in which he dialectically conceptualizes capitalism and thus the way he uses concepts or categories and the precision he employs in their use.

The Basic Concepts and Conceptual Tools of Marx's Dialectical Conceptualization

Throughout this book, whether in my discussions of Marx or of critical education, I hope to convey the idea that thinking is an active process—an extremely active, rather than a passive or contemplative one. In the case of Marx, or, in fact, of any critical, dialectical thinker, this involves an uncommonly active, almost forceful, yet at the same time careful, process of grasping and also frequently penetrating the object that is being investigated. It is a type of activity that is not easy to describe, but one that you can see and feel working in Marx's texts. It will become clearer as I identify and discuss the concepts that are fundamental to understanding Marx's specific way of thinking. Not only do these concepts underpin his thought, but he also uses them almost as if they were "tools" that enable him to uncover or expose and then explain the complex development and movement of capitalism—the way in which the system functions both normally and during its periodic crises. At times he uses one or another of them like the knife of the surgeon to cut through the surface *appearances* of capitalism in order to discover some aspect of its organic, inherent *essence*. At other times he uses some of them like the tools of the builder or carpenter in order to construct his explanation of the network of forms and relations that comprise the whole structure of human activity that constitutes capitalism. It is also important to realize that all of his concepts or conceptual "tools" are interrelated—that the definition of each often overlaps with or is related to and thus necessary to the others. Therefore, even though I discuss them sequentially, they should be thought of as forming a unity within Marx's dialectical conceptualization of capitalism.

Perhaps the most unusual aspect of Marx's use of concepts is that he often employs different concepts to refer to the same thing or, alternatively, the same concept to refer to things that appear to be different (Ollman, 1976). When he uses the same concept to refer to things that seem different or seem to express separate forms of existence, he is signaling their *inner* connection. And it is because he uses concepts like precision tools to expose how relations and forms move and develop that he often needs to use different conceptual labels or categories to express both the development and the movement. With each new concept, he beckons us to look at and consider the relation or form from a different angle—that is, one aspect of it rather than another or, alternatively, the same aspect at a different moment in the dialectical process (Allman, 1999). In particular, he has been accused for not leaving a clear concept of class; however, as I discuss later in this chapter, nothing could be further from the truth. E. P. Thompson (1974) clearly recognized this in his classic study of the English working class where, drawing on Marx, he portrayed class not as a thing but a relation and also a relation in the "making." I should note that Marx's definitions of his concepts—the meaning that he attributes to them—is something that must be inferred from the way in which he uses them. However, when you understand the way he is using concepts, his precision and also consistency in the use of them makes it possible to interpret him in a straightforward and, I think, reliable manner.

One of the "building blocks" of dialectical thinking is the *dialectical contradiction*. The closest Marx ever comes to defining or explaining his concept of this type of contradiction is in an early piece he coauthored with Engels (Marx and Engels, 1844), where he talks specifically about the antithesis or dialectical contradiction between the proletariat and capital.[3] In later works he often refers to this contradiction as the "social relation of production" (e.g., Marx, 1866, p. 1060; 1867, p. 170), and he often calls a dialectical contradiction a *unity of opposites* (e.g., Marx, 1867, p. 199) and also frequently refers to polar opposites or oppositions but more importantly to "real contradictions" (e.g., Marx, 1867, p. 198) and to "antithesis" (e.g., p. 209). Our normal concept of a contradiction is drawn from formal logic, wherein contradictions are illogical assertions or arguments or even aspects of a person's behavior that don't fit together or make sense. A dialectical contradiction is a different type of contradiction. Formal, or logical, contradictions reside in people's thinking and behavior, whereas dialectical contradictions are located in our material reality or, more precisely, in the social relations of our material world. Thinking about contradictions in this way—that is, according to a dialectical conceptualization—can be traced back to ancient Greek philosophy and, in Marx's time, the philosophy of G. W. F. Hegel. The definition of a dialectical contradiction that I have drawn from Marx's writings is stated as follows. It is a single whole comprised of a unity of two opposites, which could not exist as they presently do or have done historically outside the way in which they are related. Furthermore, the internal nature of each of the opposites and its development is shaped and determined by its relation with the other.

Marx's analysis focuses on dialectical contradictions that are antagonistic. A full definition, therefore, should also point out that one of the opposites is the "positive" in the sense of trying to preserve the relation—it positively favors and benefits from the relation; the other opposite is the "negative" in the sense that the relation is detrimental or antagonistic to it. Neither opposite can change *fundamentally* while it remains in the relation—what each is and how it develops and moves depends on the other. The only way for the "negative" to end this antagonism is to abolish the relation. Marx calls this the "negation of the negation" (Marx, 1867, p. 929). Therefore, in the example of the dialectical contradiction between the proletariat and capital, the result of the "negation of the negation" would be the creation of a classless society. The proletariat would no longer exist as a separate and exploited class, and thus there would no longer be a capitalist class either, but this does not mean that the people who once comprised these classes would cease to exist. In other words it is the relation that is abolished, rather than necessarily the people that are involved in it, and since it is this relation that has determined and shaped the way that they are as human beings, this negation liberates them or frees them to create new relations within which they can exist differently, thus realizing their full potential in terms of their individuality as well as their social identity, or humanity. This means that for Marx, revolution involves not just the transformation of our social and economic conditions but also the transformation of ourselves and the way we relate to one another as social beings.

These antagonistic dialectical contradictions are also logically contradictory, because although each opposite "needs" the other to be what it is, the freedom and actual existence of both are variously hampered and constrained by their dependency on the other. In addition, progress or advance in either one undermines or works to the detriment of the other, thus in the long term undermining the relation. The relation is also conflictual and antagonistic because what one of the opposites is is not what it would choose to be if the alternatives were known. It is limited, dominated, exploited and often oppressed due to its position within the relation. Here I am discussing the opposites as if they were people or groups of people, which in many cases they are. The opposites in a dialectical contradiction can also be structures, processes or spheres that encompass some aspect of human existence, but in all these cases it is the activity of human beings within these areas of experience that is limited or restricted in some sense and thus antagonistic. To understand a dialectical contradiction comprehensively, it is necessary to consider the actual nature of the relation that forms the *inner* connection between the opposites. This is the next concept or conceptual "tool" I discuss.

Marx's dialectical thinking and conceptualization is a relational form of thinking. However, it is not just any form of relational thinking, but a very specific way of thinking in terms of relations. As far as I know, Bertell Ollman (1976, first published in 1971) was the first to emphasize the importance of the "philosophy of internal relations" in Marx's thinking. Ollman says that this is one of the important aspects of Hegel's dialectic that Marx retained and that it is essential to the understanding of dialectical thinking (p. 35). To explain this "philosophy"— conceptual "tool," or mode of conceptualizing, as I have called it—and how thinking in terms of *internal relations* differs from thinking in terms of external relations, the other form of relational thinking, I also draw on Tolman (1981) rather than relying solely on Ollman's account (see also Allman, 1999). I begin with nonrelational or categorical thinking in order to make the distinctions clear.

We form or construct categories or concepts to help us make sense of and organize the seemingly disparate and complex evidence that we encounter in the real world. When we find that certain ostensibly different entities share a collection of attributes or features that distinguishes them from all other entities, it simplifies or clarifies our thinking and also facilitates our ability to communicate this thinking if we can use a single category or concept to refer to all of them. The two most general categories of the natural world are plants and animals, if we consider them in terms of their biological attributes; alternatively, we can classify or categorize the physical world in terms of solids, liquids and gases. Some specialized fields of knowledge may pertain to a single category or to one of its subcomponents, but many of the modern sciences and other fields of study consider the relations between categories.

As I indicated before, there are two ways of thinking relationally. When we understand things as being externally related, we focus on what results when the attributes of one entity *interact* with those of another entity. The attributes, or the internal nature of the entities, do not change (or are not perceived as changing). The only change is the production of a result that is separate from and distinguishable from either entity on its own; it is a combination of some number of their separate attributes. Once it is created, it no longer depends on the existence of the entities that produced it—to reiterate, it is totally separate and distinguishable. On the other hand, when we conceptualize things in terms of internal relations, we focus on the *inner* relation between the two entities or opposites and how the nature of that relation shapes and regulates or determines the internal development of the attributes inherent to each of the opposites, sometimes creating new attributes that become inherent within one or another of the opposites. We also focus on the results that develop out of this process of shaping and determining, results that normally serve to "mediate" or bind the two opposites within the relation. In this case, however, the result remains inherently connected to the relation—its existence, or the repeated reproduction of its existence, depends on the continuing existence of the relation. These results are also what we immediately perceive rather than the internal relation of the opposites, and in this way they tend to mediate or mask the relation from which they originate and sometimes even one or both of the opposites as well.

The concept of internal relations underpins Marx's entire explanation of capitalism, and it is the most essential ingredient of his dialectical conceptualization. For example, the "building block" of dialectical thinking—the dialectical contradiction—is actually an internally related "unity of opposites." These terms can be used interchangeably; nevertheless, I frequently employ all of them simultaneously in order to stress their meaning. However—and this is a crucial point—internal relations, or dialectical contradictions, are important in Marx's explanation of capitalism because Marx found them to be inherent in the material reality of capitalism. If it had not been for his Hegelian intellectual background, Marx might have failed to recognize the internally related, dialectical nature of capitalism, just as so many before and after him have done. Nevertheless, as I have argued elsewhere (Allman, 1999), Marx's application of dialectical conceptualization, and thus also a "philosophy of internal relations," to the real world enabled him to remain more faithful to the dialectic than Hegel's idealism would ever have permitted. Most importantly he retains its openness as a system of thinking rather than condemning it to Hegelian teleological closure.

Capitalism's internal relations actually create the openness that Marx grasps with his dialectical thought. Internal relations lead to this openness because they create a tension between the opposites, or more precisely a tension between the people whose active existence constitutes each opposite. This tension gives rise to both determinacy and indeterminacy. On the one hand, people's actions and their actual nature are determined by their particular position within the relation, but on the other hand, the final outcome of the relation is indeterminate. Furthermore, when people choose to challenge their determination within the relation, they can attenuate the degree to which they are determined and shaped; however, if their challenges are uncritical, their resistance can actually accentuate the effects of the determination. Nevertheless, the determination is not set or teleological in nature and is therefore always open to contestation. Moreover, when people become critically conscious of the source of their determination, they can engage in critical/revolutionary praxis through which they can change themselves, together with their conditions of existence. In other words, the relation can be abolished through the critically purposeful activity of the negative opposite. On the other hand, unfortunately—or, rather, disastrously—when people are not critically conscious, the relation can be allowed to deteriorate and transmute into an even more antagonistic or diabolical one. The outcome is open, or, as Rosa Luxembourg is reputed to have warned, the result will be either an authentically progressive social formation—that is, socialism/communism—or a regressive form, such as barbarism. Needless to say, this more open, essentially dialectical, understanding of Marx stands in stark contrast to the type of Marxism that is associated with either or both historical and economic determinism or any form of "vulgar Marxism."

Marx often speaks of the *forms* and *mediations* that he finds in the material reality of capitalism, and the basic concepts or categories he employs to express these are of extreme importance to his thinking and, as a consequence, to his presentation of the capitalist economy. I have already used these terms, but here I can elaborate on their meanings by using other dialectical concepts. A form is the surface appearance or manifestation of a dialectical contradiction or an internally related "unity of opposites." It can be thought of as the form or phenomenon that results from the "unfolding" of the contradiction—the form that reflects and encapsulates the "mode of being," or dynamic existence, of the contradiction or internal relation. Since according to Marx's theory of consciousness/praxis our active existence is internally related to our consciousness, these are "at once forms of being and consciousness" (Postone, 1996, p. 220).

We also need to grasp the forms as part of a process, or in their movement. Forms, as I noted previously, are the results that appear to us in our immediate experience of capitalist relations—they mediate or move between, and also stand between, ourselves and their relational origin. In addition, some forms move between and explicitly bind or concretely connect the opposites within their relation with one another, and they also move between one internal relation, or dialectical contradiction, and another. When they move in any of these ways, they are said to "mediate" the opposites and the relations and, as a consequence, our perceptions of them; therefore, they are referred to as mediations. The way in which Marx uses these terms is a good example of the way he employs different concepts to beckon us to look at something from another perspective. In other words, when he wants us to consider a particular movement of a form—to conceptualize it in this movement or as part of a process—he refers to it as a mediation rather than a form. One particular form, the *value form*, which I discuss in detail later, actually moves between and binds all the social relations and habituated practices of capitalism into an interlocking network that constitutes what is often referred to as the social structure of capitalist society.

The social structure of capitalism is actually a human structure—the structured relations of human beings into which they enter routinely in order to produce their material existence. Forms of organization and physical structures, as well as the legal system that gives legitimacy to the structure, are created in order to "cement" this structuring of human relations, but the real or material substance of the structure is the daily, sensuous activity of human beings. Obviously people within a society enter into or become a part of a number of social relations, but there are certain relations that underpin and constitute the distinguishing characteristics of a particular socioeconomic formation—thus rendering it a distinct and historically specific form of human social organization. The value form arises from the most fundamental of these relations;[4] and it is, at one and the same time, the form that is an expression of that relation and the mediation that binds it together. Moreover, it also binds together all the other relations that constitute the capitalist structure—thereby mediating and creating the totality. Capital is value in motion—a fundamental point to which I return later (Postone, 1996, pp. 263–265).

The other social relations that pertain within a capitalist society may not, in theory, be necessary to capitalism and often predate this social form. Nevertheless, they help to sustain the essential relations, and they are shaped, or reconstituted into a form, that is historically specific to capitalism. For example, the social relations that lie at the basis of gender and racial oppression are not technically—that is, theoretically—necessary to capitalism and also predate capitalism, but they serve to sustain the necessary division of labor in capitalism and thus can be advantageous—in fact, indispensable—to capitalism at certain times (Wood, 1995). Moreover, they are normally, although not always, expressed in the more covert manner that is characteristic of capitalism.

Forms such as commodities and money appear on the surface of society. They appear as, and are, the mediations that move between people, linking and binding them and their activities in production, circulation and exchange in the internally related social relations of capitalism—relations that separate people, yet also hold them together within positions of opposition. Like any aspect of our concrete experience, they can be affected by the activity of human beings. They are the result of that activity—thus adding to the indeterminacy or openness of the system—its inherent potential for change through human intervention rather than the mechanical reproduction of its predetermined results. Unfortunately, so far in capitalist history the type of change that has occurred has been limited or framed within a horizon or framework determined by the internally related dialectical contradictions that are historically specific to capitalism. Total change or revolution is dependent upon the abolition of the internal relation between labor and capital, the most fundamental dialectical contradiction of capitalism, together with the value form of wealth that arises from that relation—the form of wealth that is historically specific to capitalism (Postone, 1996). This will be explained in detail later in this chapter and also in chapter 3.

Finally, Marx has a very specific concept of science and scientific thinking that he distinguishes from ideology or ideological thinking. Although he has a specific concept of science, it is not unique but, in fact, very similar to the concept held by most scientists. It may, however, differ quite radically from the way many lay people think about science, especially scientific "laws." The common-sense notion of science views scientific knowledge as immutable truth, and scientific laws are seen as straightforward statements of this truth. The modern science laboratory, replete with technology and scientific apparatuses of all shapes and forms, often creates a mystique around the scientific process. Prior to the development of modern scientific equipment, scientific thinking and experimentation were conducted on the basis of abstractions that scientists derived from observation and thinking. Most scientists continue to operate in this way, at least in the initial stages of their investigations. The abstractions are often formulated as hypotheses or null hypotheses. These are predictive explanations that often stipulate what unobservable factors might constitute the "hidden essence" or cause of some observable phenomenon. As I said before, modern scientists operate in the same way, often assisted by technology, sometimes influencing the development of new technology that can assist them in their discoveries. In all areas of science, the idea is to formulate an exhaustive explanation, or one that can account for every aspect of the phenomenon under investigation. When possible, experiments are then devised or evidence is gathered in some way in order to test the hypothesis or prediction.

Shortly after Marx discovered the "hidden essence" of capitalism, the Austrian monk, Gregor Mendel, working in the gardens of a monastery, devised his experiments with pea plants in order to test his ideas about genes and how their various combinations produced the observable hereditary characteristics that distinguish one pea plant from another. As a result, he established the basis of modern genetic theory—Mendelian genetics. Atoms and even their internal components, which, like genes, are unobservable with the naked eye, were known to be the basic substance of matter long before we had the scientific apparatus that would allow verification of this "truth." Scientific truths and laws are more than just facts. They are statements of systematic or regular tendencies in behaviors or events that lead to certain results. They often state how something works under defined conditions—or in the absence of extraneous variables.

This is the way in which Marx uses the term "law"; and he also used the scientific processes of observation and thought leading to abstractions and the formulations of hypotheses that could be verified by empirical evidence. He is known to have spent a great deal of his time in the British Museum poring over economic data that not only added to his other observations of the capitalist system but that he also used as evidence to test the dialectical conceptualization of capitalism, which he was forming from his observations. Moreover, he used this evidence to good effect in formulating his exhaustive explanation of how capitalism worked. When it comes to laws, he consistently explains the counteracting influences, or those that work against the systematic or regular operation of a particular tendency or law—often thwarting and even reversing it (e.g., Marx, 1865, pp. 339–348).

Marx's science, however, does differ from other science in a fundamental way. Scientists usually assume that whatever truth they discover—truth, that is, with all of its normal conditions and qualifications—is a transhistorical truth. It is a truth that has always existed and always will exist but that had to be discovered by the scientific processes of thought and experimentation. Sometimes, of course, these truths are not predicted beforehand but arise by chance during an experiment or from trial-and-error experimentation. Many areas of modern science, at least since Einstein formulated his "Theory of Relativity," have become much less positive or certain about the comprehensive applicability of particular truths. For example, some scientists have had to accept that certain natural phenomena such as light, might act as a particle in some cases and a wave in others or when seen from different perspectives, and thus they accept that it may take more than one truth to explain exhaustively the behavior of a particular phenomenon. Nevertheless, once they have discovered this more complex truth, it then also becomes a transhistorical truth. Marx's truths or discoveries relate to the hidden "essence" of capitalism and the laws and tendencies that regulate or govern its movement and development; they are, thus, historically specific to capitalism. In other words, they pertain only to capitalism and will be a matter of historical record once capitalism is abolished or transformed into something entirely different—for better or worse. Nevertheless, to understand capitalism, we need science—that is, Marx's dialectical science—because capitalism's conditions of possibility are not obvious or transparent. One of the main reasons for this lack of transparency is that the "unity of opposites"—the internal relations, or dialectical contradictions—that comprise the system are often separated in time and space.

This separation in time and space creates problems for our thinking. As I mentioned in the Introduction, according to Marx's theory of consciousness, our conscious thought results from our active, sensuous experience within the social relations of our existence. Thought and action, or practice, are an internally related unity of opposites—they are praxis or the unity of thought and action. However, since the activities that are fundamental to our understanding of the system are separated in time and space, it is difficult to grasp the relations in which they occur. The natural tendency is to think of things as separated or fragmented and dichotomized. Opposites are not understood as related to one another, but as binary opposites or oppositions, thus creating a characteristic form of dualistic or dichotomized/binary thinking. Ideological thinking draws on the fragments in an attempt to give them a coherence that serves to legitimize or naturalize the way things appear. In so doing, it either deliberately or naïvely masks or conceals the internal relations, or "essence," of capitalism and thereby the truth of the system. As Marx notes in Volume 3 of *Capital,* ideological thinking reflects "the notions of agents trapped within bourgeois relations of production. . . . all science would be superfluous if the form of appearance of things directly coincided with their essence" (1865, p. 956). Here, in fact, he is talking about all the ways in which the "essence" is concealed, but I will come to these other processes later, especially in chapter 3.

I must note before leaving this brief discussion of ideology that when it comes to ideology, many Marxists take their lead from Lenin rather than from Marx. They use it to refer to a system of beliefs, sometimes the knowledge that is meant to serve the interest of a particular class, sometimes a way of seeing the world conditioned by one's class position and sometimes both of these. Marxism is therefore seen as the ideology of the working class and the ideology of socialism. For Marx, ideology is a defective way of thinking; it is the opposite of science, and thus, as I said in the Introduction, it is a negative concept and often the focus of his critique (Larrain, 1983; Marx, 1863a, 1863b, 1863c; Marx and Engels, 1846).[5] To use Marxism to refer to a particular ideology would surely have both appalled and offended him. I am sure that the only positive use of this term acceptable to Marx would be one that used it to designate a mode of critique based on dialectical conceptualization or analysis—in other words, in the way that Gramsci referred to Marxism or, rather, his euphemism for it—"the philosophy of praxis"—as ideology. As I have argued elsewhere (e.g., Allman, 1999), for Gramsci ideology was a method of inquiry or the "analysis of the origin of ideas" (Gramsci, 1971, pp. 370–371), and this is how he used the word in conjunction with Marxism. Even then, Marx would probably protest, as he did on one occasion, that he himself was not a Marxist. Nevertheless, the normal usage of both terms—that is, ideology and Marxism—is Lenin's not Marx's. This is why I continually stress the negative concept of ideology and try to avoid, as far as possible, using the term Marxism.

THE INTERNAL RELATIONS: THE "ESSENCE" OF CAPITALISM OR "CAPITAL IN GENERAL"

In Volume 1 of *Capital*, Marx begins his explanation of capitalism with an analysis of the commodity—the concrete form in which the embryonic "essence" of capitalism first appears. The commodity is not a creation of nature but results from the activity of human beings within human history. At first it existed only on the margins of society as a particular type of product, but by no means the most common result, of people's productive activities. In fact, it is only within capitalism that the commodity becomes a fully developed and dominant form (Marx, 1867, p. 174 fn.). Its essence is both the germ, or precondition, of that society and its result, or consequence. In the final pages of Volume 1—that is, the appendix, known as *Resultate*—he offers this useful summary:

We regard the commodity as . . . a premiss [precondition] and we proceed from the commodity . . . in its simplest form. On the other hand, however, the *commodity* is a . . . result of capitalist production. . . . Only on the basis of capitalist production will the commodity become the general form of product. [Marx, 1866, p. 1060]

Marx explains that the commodity is different from the simple products of human labor that are used by those who produce them or alternatively traded in kind for another useful product. The commodity has a twofold or dialectical character; it is both a use-value and value (Marx, 1867, p. 152). Use-values or products of human labor are not necessarily commodities; they are material values that can exist in any type of society. For a product to become a commodity, it must be produced for someone else and transmitted to someone else through exchange. When this happens, value becomes exchange-value. Use-value and exchange-value are both social values and therefore result from historically specific social relations (p. 131). Marx explains the historical process through which the products of human labor become commodities—how, with the growth of trade, products acquire a dual nature and are thus transformed into commodities.

As I indicated earlier, the trade of commodities was originally an activity that took place on the margins of society, between different societies rather within a particular society where production for use and tribute continued for a long period of history (Marx, 1867, pp. 170–173). Eventually, however, the external trade of commodities between societies grew in volume and scope, and the products within societies—in reaction to this—also became commodities (p. 182). Before this, internal trade took place through tacit agreements between the private producers and involved the trade of products and services in kind. Although this type of trade might have existed alongside the exchange of commodities for a period of time, increasingly producers began to produce intentionally for exchange, and as a result the production of commodities and commodity exchange spread throughout the entire society (Marx, 1867, p. 182). Commodities may become distinguishable from products or use-values in exchange, but we need to consider their internal nature more closely, as Marx did, in order to see why and how they differ. Therefore, I briefly recap Marx's analysis of the development of the commodity form—the historical process through which the internal nature of this form came into existence and eventually led to the emergence of capitalism.

In order for any exchange to take place, the direct producers had to produce an excess or surplus of use-values—a surplus to their own requirements. And in order to ensure that the exchange of these was equitable and also to prevent it from breaking down into conflict or haggling, it became necessary to identify a property that all use-values shared. They all differed from one another in terms of their use; therefore use-value could not be used to establish exchange equivalency. The one property they all shared was that they were the result of human labor. The actual types of labor, the concrete forms, also varied from the making of things, to farming the land, herding livestock, extracting resources from nature, and so on; therefore, equivalency could not be based on the specific types of labor or what Marx calls "concrete labor" (1867, p. 128). Labor in general, or "abstract" labor, is the only factor all commodities share—labor is the substance of their value, but it is the magnitude of labor that makes them exchangeable, and this magnitude is measured by labor-time (pp. 128, 131, 141, 308). All concrete labor takes place within a certain period of time, and time can be divided into units of equal measure. Labor-time was the only property inherent in every commodity—internally related to its use-value—that could be used to establish equivalency and therefore serve as a basis for establishing the commodity's exchange-value.

In contrast to concrete labor, Marx, as I said before, refers to abstract labor or, more precisely, abstract social labor (p. 308). Once commodities were produced specifically for the market where they would be in competition with other commodities of the same type, one problem remained, and this is where the concept of abstract social labor becomes extremely important. If the exchange-value was based on the actual time it took to produce a particular use-value, then the products of the least skillful and/or least energetic workers would have the highest exchange-value. Instead, the exchange-value or value form of the commodity had to be based on an average, the average amount of time that it took under "normal" conditions to produce the commodity—the average amount of time in which a use-value could be produced with the average level of skill and intensity of labor prevalent in society at a particular point in history. Marx calls this the "socially necessary labor-time" (p. 129). Marx's Law of Value, to which I referred in chapter 1, states that the "magnitude of value" of any commodity is determined by the "labor-time socially necessary for its production" (p. 129). This is an extremely important concept in Marx's economics, and I will return to it often, especially in terms of how it operates at a higher level of complexity within fully developed capitalist societies and also the global market.

Eventually, in order to facilitate the growing volume of trade—especially foreign trade that was separated in space and time from the producers—a single commodity was needed that could stand in for or reflect the exchange-value of all commodities. In other words, the exchange-value of all commodities, rather than being established individually in relation to or relative to every other commodity, could be rendered commensurable with one single commodity or "universal equivalent" (Marx, 1867, p. 159). This was the money commodity or money form of value. Prior to gold and silver becoming money, other commodities that had a special significance within a community, such as cattle and grain, might have been used as universal equivalents (p. 183). But as trade developed, a more flexible and durable commodity—one whose properties allowed for it to be divided into smaller units with standard weights—became necessary. Gold and silver fulfilled both requirements. We often forget, however, that they are commodities themselves. They have a use-value, and it takes a certain amount of "socially necessary labor-time" to extract them from nature and make them available for exchange. If their "production" were not dependent upon a certain amount of "socially necessary labor-time," they would not be commensurable with other commodities—their equivalency could not be established (pp. 183–187).

Like other commodities, when money first came into existence it was used only on the margins of precapitalist societies, usually in external or foreign trade. Usurers who made profits from lending money and merchants who grew wealthy from buying cheap and selling dear or commissioning a number of people and then collecting their products to sell at a profit were not, at this point, capitalists (Marx, 1866, p. 1023). Some may have accumulated enough money to become capitalists at the dawn of capitalism, but this was not always the case. Usury and mercantile capitalism are precursors or embryonic forms of financial and commercial capitalism—forms of capitalism that develop out of industrial capitalism, or the first fully developed form of capitalist production—that is, the production of capital. These less developed financial and commercial activities formed the ground from which capitalism could grow—a ground for transition—and they continue to play that role today, often existing alongside their more developed forms in the world of global capitalism (Marx, 1866, p. 1023).

Merchants sometimes used the profits they made to buy other commodities cheaply and then sell them for further profit, thus increasing their wealth. However, this was not a systematic process, nor was it a process by which the totality of wealth increased throughout a society or the world. It was simply an exchange that involved the redistribution of wealth from the pockets of one person to the pockets of another. Sometimes the profits were hoarded and new commodities were acquired through plunder or extortion. Nevertheless, the hoarding of wealth, especially in the form of money, made possible by whatever means— trade, theft, extortion—was one of the preconditions that made capitalism possible; but by no means was it the most important. The prior development of the rudimentary form of the commodity, the money commodity, the circulation of commodities, markets and mercantile trade were also preconditions (Marx, 1867, pp. 256–269). However, even if these had been more pervasive, capitalism would not have developed where it did and when it did without one very special commodity: a commodity that only became available with the appearance of the "free" wage-laborer (pp. 272–274).

When the feudal system in Europe came to an end for various social, economic and political reasons, the serfs—the direct producers—were freed from feudal bondage. Particularly in England, they were freed not only from their bondage but were also "freed" in the double-edged sense by being separated from the land and often from their means of production—the implements and inputs they had used to produce their own necessities, along with their tithe to the feudal lord. From the end of the fifteenth century and well into the sixteenth, the peasants' or serfs' rights to land were forcibly usurped, and arable land was turned into pasture, driving even more people from the land and into either wage-labor or, alternatively, vagabondage or vagrancy. Marx says that the rapid expansion of wool manufacturing in Flanders forced prices to rise in England, and this was the immediate incentive for the eviction of people from the land—England needed wage-labor if it was to compete (Marx, 1867, pp. 878–879). By the eighteenth century the process had gone much further, with what Marx calls parliamentary robbery through the "Bills for Inclosure of Commons," driving the peasants even from the common land that then became the private property of the landowners (p. 885). Further legislation made their itinerant existence precarious and illegal, forcing them, eventually, to sell the only commodity they possessed—their labor-power (pp. 270–274).

Labor-power is the very special commodity that makes capitalism possible (Marx, 1867, p. 270). Once labor-power becomes a commodity, then all production becomes production for the market, and with this the commodity and money become fully developed and dominant forms within society (p. 274). They become the concrete forms through which value, or the value form—that is, abstract labor, or more precisely, labor-time—is expressed. To understand this, we need to follow Marx's dialectical explanation of how the special commodity— labor-power, or the worker's capacity to work for a specified duration of time— becomes the basis for capitalism and the production of capital. We need to conceptualize the commodity—labor-power—dialectically.

Like any other commodity that we find on the market, in this case the labor market, labor-power is a commodity comprised of use-value and exchange-value. The latter, the derivation or source of which I will come to in a minute, is called the wage. It is based on the "socially necessary labor-time" that it takes to sustain workers' capacities to work—in other words, the price of their necessities (Marx, 1867, p. 275). Unlike the exchange-value of other commodities, the determination of the wage contains a moral and social dimension, and this is reflected in what is considered to be the "socially necessary labor-time" that it takes for the reproduction and the sustaining of labor-power at a particular conjuncture in history (Marx, 1867, pp. 274–275). (I should mention at this point that Marx explains "Capital in General" or the "essence" of capitalism in terms of industrial production; however, it is clear from what he says elsewhere that given the ongoing development of capitalism and the spread of capitalist relations, his general analysis applies to many other types of work—even, eventually, to some of the salaried work of people in contemporary capitalism.) In the market, it *appears* that the wage is equivalent to the value it purchases—that capitalists pay for the full value of the labor-power they purchase, as would be and, in fact, is the case with any of the other inputs purchased for the production process. In a technical, or theoretical, sense this is what they do. However, Marx calls the market the "noisy sphere"—the sphere from which the laws, the common sense, the values and principles of bourgeois society emanate. He beckons us to switch our focus away from the market—to enter the "hidden abode" of production (p. 279). It is here that the "secret of profit-making" is revealed and where we can see "not only how capital produces, but how capital is itself produced" (p. 280). And this is where our journey to understanding will take us next.

As I have explained, Marx found capitalism to be comprised of various dialectical contradictions, or internally related opposites. In the following sections, I discuss the capitalist production process, which "taken as a whole, is a unity of the production and circulation processes" (Marx, 1865, p. 117). I divide the process into three general dialectical contradictions, all of which are comprised of other internal relations or dialectical contradictions. These three general contradictions can be seen as forming the framework or "essence" of capitalism—that is, the framework of "Capital in General" within which all the other contradictions, or internally related opposites, both those I have already mentioned and those yet to be discussed, operate.

The Capitalist Production Process:
The Labor–Capital Relation (Dialectical Contradiction 1)

"The use[-value] of labour-power is labour itself" (Marx, 1867, p. 283). Like the labor involved in all commodities, this labor has a twofold (dialectical) character: At one and the same time, the worker's labor is both concrete and abstract. As I mentioned earlier, concrete labor is labor that entails specific skills and procedures, and it produces the use-value of the commodity. Abstract labor, or labor in general, is measured by its duration, or the labor-time during which commodities are impregnated with value (pp. 142, 308). Value in general is, therefore, congealed labor-time (p. 325). In other words, as I also mentioned before, the substance of value is labor (abstract labor), and the measure of its magnitude is labor-time (p. 131; Rubin, 1972, p. 119). The capitalist production process—that is, the "immediate" process of production in which surplus-value and potential capital are created—involves the simultaneous twofold use of labor-power. It is at one and the same time a process by which use-values are produced—a labor process—and a process of creating value; the capitalist process of production is a unity of these two processes (Marx, 1867, p. 293). Therefore, these two processes simultaneously and reciprocally determine or shape one another. Within the value-creating process, or the process wherein new value is created, labor is used both to create the value that replaces its own value and also to "valorize" or produce an additional amount of new value (pp. 293–302). The process of valorization is simply a continuation of the process of creating value beyond a definite point or beyond a definite amount of time (p. 302). Herein lies the true significance—the real use-value—of labor-power for capital. Human labor is not only the source of value but is capable of creating more value than it possesses itself. "This is the specific service the capitalist expects from [the commodity] labour-power" (p. 301).

From this we can see that value, or congealed labor-time, also has a twofold character within the labor–capital relations of production. Some of it is necessary labor-time or the time it takes to produce the exchange-value of labor, that is, the wage—or, at least, the value around which the price of labor fluctuates. This is the derivation or source of the exchange-value of the commodity, labor-power, to which I referred previously. However, and most essentially, some of the value created is constituted by surplus labor-time. Both necessary labor and surplus labor produce value, and both are measured by the duration of labor. Marx calls surplus labor *surplus-value*; it is surplus-value that forms the basis of profit, and thus it is the life-blood of capital itself (Marx, 1867, p. 251). It is important to recognize that all of this can be traced back to the twofold, or dialectical, nature of the commodity and likewise the labor that produces it—that is, the properties of labor when it is used within the twofold nature of capitalist production, which is a unity of opposites—namely, the labor process and the process of creating value that includes, and must include, the process of valorization (p. 304). In other words, the twofold nature of the commodity's value—its use-value and its exchange-value—that results from this process has to do with the two properties of labor, one through which the value already present in the means of production and auxiliary materials is preserved and transferred and through which use-values are created (concrete labor) and one through which new value is created (abstract labor) (p. 307). The exact relationship between exchange-value and price, and surplus-value and profit, is examined in chapter 3, when I discuss how the "essence" of capitalism is masked or veiled by the appearances that are created when there are many capitals in competition with one another.

In addition, it is important to hold on to and always recognize that value and surplus-value are the basis of capital, and therefore they make capitalism possible and also constitute it as a distinct—that is, historically specific—socioeconomic formation. Moreover, it is also important to remember that surplus-value or surplus labor-time is derived from living labor-power—the utilization of labor within the labor–capital social relation of production. The labor–capital relation is the dialectical contradiction, or internally related "unity of opposites," that lies at the heart of capitalism. These conceptual distinctions—especially the distinction between concrete and abstract labor that we recognize when we grasp the twofold or dialectical nature of labor—are excellent examples of the way in which Marx's analysis enables us to examine something from different perspectives. In other words, it is an example of how he uses concepts to enable us, or beckon us, to consider something—in this case, different aspects of the immediate production process and, thus, also the labor–capital relation—from different perspectives, so that we can conceptualize dialectically and thus understand more comprehensively.

The creation of profit, the creation of capital itself, depends upon the creation of surplus-value. And the amount of surplus-value is determined by the ratio between necessary and surplus labor (Marx, 1867, pp. 325–326; 338–339). In striving to create, maintain or increase profits, capitalists will use every means at their disposal to increase the ratio between necessary and surplus labor-time—increasing the latter relative to the former. There are two general methods by which this can be accomplished, and each results in a specific form of surplus-value—specific in terms of how it is produced and in terms of how it affects the entire system. However, before explaining these, I should mention that the easiest way for capitalists to extort surplus-value is simply to pay their workers less than the value of their labor-power. Although Marx recognizes that capitalists sometimes do this, his scientific, dialectical explanation of capitalism is based on the assumption that capitalists obtain their inputs, including labor-power, by purchasing them at their value—that is, their exchange-value; therefore, when looked at in terms of market exchange, they do not, in theory, break the rule of equal exchange (p. 301).

Absolute surplus-value is produced by the first method, which involves extending the length of the working day or working period beyond the time necessary to create the value of labor-power (Marx, 1867, pp. 283–426—or Part 3, Vol. 1). At the dawn of capitalism, many workers were brought together in one place, where, instead of working for themselves, they labored for a capitalist, using the same labor process as they had done previously. However, since they sold their labor-power to the capitalists and then expended their labor within the labor–capital relation, the capitalists could use their labor for a duration that extended beyond the time necessary to create their wages. The surplus-value created—that is, extorted—within this extended period of labor-time belonged to the capitalists and became the basis of their profits and their ability to accumulate capital (pp. 340–344). Marx uses the term "capital" to designate both the main result that is derived from the capitalist production process and anything that the capitalists can then use their money—i. e., capital—for in order to create more capital or bring about the growth and accumulation of capital—in other words, to create, or extort, value and especially surplus-value and to increase or augment the latter (p. 342, pp. 317–319). Absolute surplus-value continued to be the basis of capitalist profit even when the division of labor was first employed, whereby the labor process of each individual worker became fragmented and thus more directly controllable by the capitalists or their representatives within the production process—when this fragmented labor was forced to work cooperatively under capitalist control. However, when legislation was passed that limited the length of the working day, capitalists needed to use another method of extorting surplus-value (pp. 439–491). Fortunately, for them, this other method was already available and being used to some extent.

Relative surplus-value is also produced by increasing the ratio between necessary and surplus labor. There are three ways this can happen, one of which is a derivative or off-shoot of the other two. I will deal with the derivative first, but first there are a few general points that I must make about relative surplus-value. The creation—or, more precisely, the extortion/extraction—of relative surplus-value always involves increasing the productivity of labor, which, in turn, cheapens the cost of commodities. It might seem puzzling that capitalists always strive to increase productivity when this leads to a decrease in the value of their commodities. However, we must remember that the total value of the commodity is not what capitalists are interested in; all that really counts is how much surplus-value is present and can be realized in the sale of their commodities (Marx, 1867, p. 437). I hasten also to add that since the creation of relative surplus-value leads to the production of more commodities, it also means that capitalists must expand their markets—that is, expand the demand for their commodities. It is important always to remember that even though surplus-value is created in production, this is only potential, or latent, value that must be realized through the sale of commodity.

When the process of creating—extorting—relative surplus-value takes hold in the industries that produce the workers' necessities, thus cheapening the cost of these necessities, it leads to a reduction in the value of labor-power. Therefore, all capitalists benefit—they all produce more relative surplus-value—because there is a decrease in the value of necessary labor and thus a relative increase in surplus labor. Clearly, this derivative form of relative surplus-value creation can only happen if first individual capitalists, who produce the workers' necessities, use one of the other two methods of creating relative surplus-value. In fact, once there are legal restrictions on the length of the working day, all capitalist commodity producers have an interest in pursuing one of these methods of surplus-value extraction.

Although both methods result in an increased number of commodities, Marx calls the first method increasing the "productivity of labor" (Marx, 1867, p. 655). This involves producing commodities in less time or producing more commodities in "a given time with the *same* expenditure of labor" (p. 534, emphasis added). In a working day of a fixed duration, the same value is created, since value is measured by labor-time, but it is spread over more commodities, thus reducing the value of each (p. 534). The capitalists, who do this first, can still sell their commodities at the market-value (which is determined by the "socially necessary labor-time") or even slightly less, and, in so doing they will be increasing their surplus-value by attracting, or realizing, what is, in fact, the surplus-value produced by capitalists whose workforces have a lower level of productivity (pp. 433–434). I go into greater detail about this redistribution of surplus-value in chapter 3. Of course, their competitors will not allow this situation to continue indefinitely (p. 530). They will adopt similar methods, and when they do, the "socially necessary labor-time" will be reduced. As a result, those who were first to adopt the new methods will no longer have a market advantage.

Marx says that the second method of creating, or extorting, relative surplus-value has to do with the "intensification of labor" (p. 655). More commodities are produced in a given time with a *greater,* or "increased expenditure of labor" (Marx, 1867, p. 660). Marx often stresses that "[t]he same labor . . . performed for the same length of time, always yields the same amount of value, independently of any variations in productivity" (p. 137). However, in this case, we find a temporary breach in this general rule (p. 661). For example, let us say we have a situation in which capitalists who once produced one commodity in an hour, by exacting a more "intensive magnitude" of labor from their workers, begin to produce two commodities in an hour (p. 655). It still takes an hour to produce each commodity, but at the end of the hour there are two commodities where before there was only one. As a result, the capitalists who do this first will have impregnated two commodities with an hour of labor-time and therefore will have produced a value twice as great as their competitors in the same amount of time. They, or more precisely their workers, will have created a greater amount of value in one hour than they did previously (Marx, 1867, pp. 660–662; Postone, 1996, p. 290), because an hour of labor from their workers has become a denser or less porous hour than it was before—the more condensed labor hour contains more minutes of actual labor than the more porous hour (Marx, 1867, p. 534; Postone, 1996, p. 292). Since these capitalists still pay their workers the same as before, each commodity will contain a relatively larger proportion of surplus-value (p. 435). Let us say that originally they were producing a commodity that contained a newly created value of 60, of which 30 was necessary labor and 30 surplus labor. When they produce two commodities in an hour and, thus, a total value of 120, the necessary labor is divided between the two commodities, creating a ratio of 15 necessary labor to 45 surplus labor in each commodity. Even though each commodity still contains a value of 60, the capitalist can sell them for a value of 59 each or even considerably less—say, at a ratio of 15:35 or a value of 50—and still have increased the proportion of surplus-value in each commodity. They not only will have increased their productivity and their surplus-value but also will have cheapened their commodities and thus made them more competitive in the market than those of their competitors.

Once again, other commodity producers will not tolerate this situation for long. Just as with the first method of creating relative surplus-value, the competition will be compelled to adopt similar techniques. When this happens, the new more condensed labor hour will become the basis for a reconstituted "socially necessary labor-time," and the capitalists who were first to adopt the new techniques will no longer have a market advantage. In other words, they will no longer produce a greater amount of value in an hour than their competitors (Marx, 1867, p. 661). Once again Marx's general rule—the same labor, for the same time, yields the same value—will hold true. It should be fairly clear now why capitalists will always strive to increase productivity. However, any position of advantage they gain in the market only lasts until their competitors catch up, which many invariably do; and, of course, they have many more commodities that they must sell before they can realize their surplus-value in the form of profits (p. 432–434). I will discuss all of this, especially the impact of the less porous social labor hour as well as the continuous reduction of "socially necessary labor-time," in much greater detail later in this chapter and also in chapter 3.

Marx says that absolute surplus-value is the main form of surplus-value when labor is only *formally subsumed* within the capitalist production process or when the labor process has not yet taken on its specific capitalist characteristics (Marx, 1866, pp. 1019–1023; 1867, p. 645). When the labor process itself is changed to become specifically a capitalist labor process—especially with the introduction of machinery in large-scale industry (Marx, 1867, pp. 492 ff.), then the *real subsumption* of labor by capital begins and relative surplus-value becomes the dominant type of surplus-value produced within the labor–capital relation (Marx, 1866, pp. 1023–1025; 1867, p. 645). However, since it is usually more costly for the capitalist to extract, or extort, relative surplus-value because it often involves either or both a greater division and concentration of labor and thus also a greater supervision of labor or the adoption of more advanced technology (means of production), absolute surplus-value extraction will continue to be used even after the real subsumption of labor (Marx, 1867, pp. 645–646; 1866, pp. 1023–1025). It is often the first measure used to increase profitability and will always be used whenever possible in combination with the extraction of relative surplus-value.

The period now known as the "Golden Age" of capitalism—the period of relative prosperity for both workers and capitalists that followed World War II and that lasted until the late 1960s or early 1970s—was a relatively long period during which relative surplus-value extortion was the main method applied within the industrial production of the developed countries. However, since that time there has been an increase in the extortion of absolute surplus-value. This can be witnessed in the sweatshop factories of the developing world, and also increasingly in the developed world, as labor resistance has been minimized through both the existence and the threat of unemployment and also the general malaise arising from employment insecurity, thus creating a situation in which

workers dare not complain when they are expected to work beyond their contrac-
tual hours of employment. It has also increased with the growth in part-time
employment as well as casualized labor, mixing bouts of overwork with under-
work and no work at all—all the types of contingent employment to which
I referred in chapter 1 and which Marx had the prescience to anticipate
as a common and persistent feature of capitalism (Harvey, 1989; Marx, 1867,
pp. 350–357). Since my intention in this chapter is to explain "Capital in General" or the "essence" of capitalism, I will say no more, specifically, about
contemporary capitalism at this point. However, it is important to stress that what
we see happening and what we are experiencing in our contemporary circumstances are the consequences of how the essence continually produces the concrete reality of capitalism or, more precisely, the concrete totality of global
capitalism.

In discussing surplus-value, there are several points to emphasize or reemphasize. Whether we consider absolute surplus-value or relative surplus-value or
even both being created simultaneously, it is the ratio between necessary and
surplus labor (the rate of surplus-value) that is of fundamental importance. And
of equal importance, it is abstract labor or labor-time that constitutes value in
capitalist societies; and, thus, it is living human labor that creates value. Moreover, Marx stresses that within capitalist relations, productive labor is labor that
produces surplus-value (Marx, 1867, pp. 643 ff.). We must also recall that Marx
repeatedly emphasizes that capital is a relation and not a "thing" (e.g., pp. 164–
165). In discussing the part of the production process in which value is created,
Marx points out that part of the capital is expended on "means of production, i. e.
the raw material, the auxiliary materials and the implements of labor"; however,
the value, or objectified, congealed, past labor-time contained in this capital
undergoes no quantitative change in the production process (pp. 317–318). It
adds no new value but simply passes on its value all at once or bit by bit as the
means of production wear out. He, therefore, calls this the *constant* capital. In
contrast, the capital that is expended on labor-power does undergo a quantitative
change; therefore, Marx calls this the *variable* capital. "It both reproduces the
equivalent of its own value and produces an excess, a surplus-value, which may
itself vary . . ." (Marx, 1867, p. 317).

As I noted before, the part of the value-creating process that goes beyond the
production of the variable capital, and during which the surplus-value is created,
is what Marx calls the valorization process (pp. 293–306). Yet another, and very
important, example of how Marx uses different concepts in order to beckon us to
consider something from another angle can be seen in his discussion of constant
and variable capital in the process of valorization. He says:

The same elements of capital, which from the point of view of the labor process, can
be distinguished respectively as the objective and subjective factors, as means of
production and labour-power, can be distinguished from the point of view of the
valorization process, as constant and variable capital. [p. 317]

I will return to the relation between constant and variable capital in chapter 3, when I discuss the *organic* composition of capital. Before considering Dialectical Contradiction 2, there are two subjects that require a more focused and detailed discussion—namely, wealth and class.

Capitalist Wealth

In the drive to create relative surplus-value in the valorization process, productivity is increased; therefore, capitalist societies—especially advanced ones— produce a great mass of commodities or use-values. These could be used to meet or satisfy human needs; however, under capitalism wealth is based on value— labor-time—rather than use-values (Marx, 1867, p. 236; Postone, 1996). Capitalist wealth is, therefore, a historically specific form of wealth. This is one of the greatest absurdities of capitalism. It results from a dialectical contradiction and is, in itself, a logical contradiction or the reflection of a breakdown in human reasoning, albeit one that is internally related to the dialectical contradiction in reality. In pursuing the money form of wealth, capital (here I use the term to represent the entire capitalist class) raises the productive powers of human beings to such a degree that, if production were reasonably planned, the needs of all human beings could be met. Capitalism actually creates the potential to overcome scarcity. However, because the use-values—material wealth—that are created are internally related to their exchange-value, as they must be in the commodity form, real need is denied. The only needs that are recognized are those that can be expressed through "effective" demand—the ability to "realize" the exchange-value or, as we say, pay the price. Even the workers whose labor constitutes the value of a particular commodity are denied access to its use-value if they cannot pay for its exchange-value.

Furthermore, since it is only the pursuit of value that counts rather than the suitability, or sometimes even the quality, of use-values, commodities are often produced that are not conducive to either human beings or the environment. And also since the pursuit of the value form of wealth leads to unplanned and irrational increases in productivity, the form of economic growth fostered by capitalism is also detrimental (Postone, 1996). There is every reason to believe that scientific "know-how" already exists or could be rapidly developed to enable us to adapt capitalist technology in ways that would be compatible with both maintaining high levels of productivity and sustaining the environment—possibly even enhancing it, together with the human condition. Marx frequently mentions that human beings' relations to nature will be determined—for better or worse—by their historically specific mode of production (e.g., Marx, 1867, pp. 637–638).

Another, and equally insidious, consequence of capitalism and its historically specific form of wealth, especially in terms of our duplicity in the process, has to do with the fact that the "truth" of our reality is veiled or concealed within our concrete experience of capitalism. We tend to think that the value of a commodity has to do with its inherent properties. We relate to "things" that, in truth, are merely the forms of existence in the market of a social relation between human beings—the social relation between labor and capital, the social relation of production within which value is produced and labor exploited (Marx, 1867, p. 165). As I said before, this is the dialectical contradiction—the internally related "unity of opposites"—that lies at the heart of capitalism. The reification of this social relation—that is, perceiving it as a thing and, moreover, a thing that is revered and often desired or even lusted after—is what Marx calls a fetish. To fetishize, or more generally, to reify, and thus mystify the social relations of capitalism is one of the chief characteristics of bourgeois or capitalist ideological thinking. In the case of the commodity, Marx speaks of the "commodity fetish" (pp. 165–177). When challenging bourgeois or capitalist ideological thought, as I mentioned in the Introduction, it is always important to remember and also stress that whenever we use capital as a noun we are referring to a relation between human beings, and also the process through which they produce their material world within these relations. Capital is not a thing. Just as structures—social structures—are human, so, too, is capital. It follows, therefore, that what we are like as human beings—our human nature and our subjectivity—is also shaped by the relations in which we exist. These important dimensions of ourselves do not preexist our social relations. This point is fundamental to critical educators and to any discussion of social transformation; and I consider it in much greater detail in later chapters.

Class

As I explained, Marx calls the process of creating surplus-value valorization, and he uses industrial capitalism to illustrate "Capital in General" because fully developed capitalism arose, initially, on the basis of industrial production; therefore, he discusses valorization within that context. Unfortunately, this has led many people, including many Marxists, to assume that the process of valorization—the creation of surplus-value—takes place only in industrial production. Many of those who interpret Marx in this way also assume that the *Law of Value* means that physiological—or what is often called manual—labor is the only source of value.

Some Marxists, whose interpretations are similar to mine or with whom I usually concur, suggest that Marx is not entirely clear on this point. I do not agree. I think Marx is perfectly clear. Particularly in the "Resultate" (the Appendix to the edition of *Capital* cited here), the *Grundrisse* and *Theories of Surplus Value*, he stresses that productive labor is labor that produces surplus-value within the labor–capital relation. In other words, it is not the labor that produces a particular type of use-value; thus it is not either a particular or a general category of concrete labor. In the "Resultate," he also gives examples of various types of work, usually classed as services or even professional jobs—including teaching—that can become productive labor when the work takes place within the labor–capital relation (Marx, 1866, pp. 1039–1044). Even in the main text of *Capital*, Volume 1, he states this very clearly:

The only worker who is productive is one who produces surplus-value for the capitalist . . . [who] contributes towards the self-valorization of capital. If we may take an example from outside the sphere of material production, a school-master is a productive worker when, in addition to belabouring the heads of his pupils, he works himself into the ground to enrich the owner of the school. That the latter has laid out his capital in a teaching factory, instead of a sausage factory, makes no difference to the relation. [1867, p. 644]

What is essential, therefore, is not the type of concrete labor performed but whether it takes place within the labor–capital relation and thus produces value and surplus-value measured in labor-time. Clearly, the capitalist social relation of production—the labor–capital relation—is the relation within which value and ultimately capital are produced, and therefore it is not solely the relation between labor and capital within industrial production.

This should obviously bring into question many traditional concepts of the working class or proletariat as well as contemporary epitaphs to the demise of the working class. By looking at what Marx actually meant by the working class, or the class that was the polar opposite of capital, we can understand why he predicted, and why in fact it is the case, that rather than shrinking, the working class, or proletariat, is growing—in fact, expanding dramatically as more and more branches of employment are brought under the dictates of capitalist production (Marx, 1866, pp. 1036, 1041; 1867, p. 929). With the full universalization of capitalism, not only are more and more people in the developing and underdeveloped countries being forced out of peasant production in agriculture and handicrafts and into the capitalist relations of production in agriculture, industry and services, but increasing numbers of people in the developed countries are finding their work recast or reconstituted within capitalist relations. Just as more and more products and services become commodities, so too are an increasing number of people selling their labor-power—their capacity to valorize capital, to create surplus-value—for either wages or salaries.

They may not realize that their work has been subsumed within the social relations of capitalist production, but they, especially those who experience the transition, will realize that their work has become more controlled, supervised or managed and often deskilled or what some people have referred to as de-intellectualized, thus betraying at least a subjective awareness of what is happening as well as an awareness that skill is a category of power as well as ability or agility (CCCS, 1981). Marx's full concept of the working class, or proletariat, also includes the growing numbers of people who are either temporarily or "permanently" unemployed in so far as they constitute a reserve of productive labor that can be drawn into the labor–capital relation according to the varying needs of capitalist employers.

Circulation and the Possibility of Crisis:
The "Unity of Production and Circulation" (Dialectical
Contradiction 2 of the Capitalist Production Process)

"Capital in General," the total abstract or simple model of capitalism's "essence," can only be seen when we grasp the "unity of production and circulation"—with exchange being one very essential moment within the process of circulation. Abstract labor—human labor in general as measured by labor-time—impregnates commodities with value during the value-creating process and with surplus-value during the valorization process, but this is only latent or potential value/surplus-value. If capitalists are to use the value created in production, in particular the part that is the surplus-value, as either their revenue, which they spend on their own consumption of necessities and luxuries, or as capital, then value in the form of commodities must be transformed into the money form of value through the exchange or sale of commodities. Therefore, in order to grasp the entire production process of capital—the entire circuit through which value moves—it is necessary to widen our gaze so that it includes not only the "hidden abode" of production but also how capital operates, while still in its inner organic life, on the surface of society in the sphere of circulation. It is important to grasp capital's "essence"—the totality of its internal relations—before it enters into its external relations of competition with other capitals (Marx, 1865, p. 117; 1867, pp. 433–434). This general form of capital—that is, its "essence" or the totality of its internal relations—underpins those external relations and the complexities thrown up by them; and it enables us to understand the dynamic way in which it impacts on and shapes these external relations. When the capitalist production process is seen in its entirety—as a dialectical unity of production and circulation—we can see why Marx said, in Volume 1 of *Capital*, that "the possibility of crises, though no more than a possibility . . . [is] immanent in the commodity [form] . . . [in the] . . . antithesis . . . between use-value and exchange-value . . ." (1867, p. 209). This possibility comes about as soon as commodities begin to circulate rather than being exchanged between their direct producers. "Circulation bursts through all the temporal, spatial and personal barriers" that hold together the unity of use-value and exchange-value in direct exchange; thus the possibility of crisis is immanent in the separation of purchase and sale (pp. 207–209). Whether or not this possibility becomes a reality depends on many other conditions that come into being with the full development of capitalism and thus the full development of the commodity form.

The conditions that can lead to crisis are present at several points in the capitalist production process—a process, or circuit, that begins with the purchase of the commodity, labor-power, and which only ends when the commodity that has been valorized by that labor-power is sold and consumed. (This is the process that Marx was specifically referring to when he said that crisis was immanent in the commodity form and in the separation between purchase and sale.) For example, one of these conditions is inherent in the valorization process, within the internal relation between necessary labor-time and surplus labor-time. As I have explained, capitalists extract surplus-value by making sure that the total labor-time is in excess of the value of labor-power—by increasing the ratio between necessary and surplus labor in favor of the latter. When this can only be accomplished by reducing the value of labor-power, workers, in their role as consumers, have less to spend. The necessities that determine the value of their labor-power may be cheaper, but they still have less to spend on other commodities. As a consequence, the possibility of realizing the surplus-value latent in these other commodities is reduced. When we consider the total process of production as a unity of production and circulation, we can see that the process of valorization is only completed when surplus-value is realized in the sphere of circulation. Until the commodity is sold, there is only *potential* value and surplus-value. When the total process is considered, it is also possible to see how the interests of individual capitalists can often become pitted against those of the entire capitalist class. It is in the interest of individual capitalists to keep the wages of their own labor force as low as possible; yet it is also in their interest for other workers to be well enough paid that they make good consumers (Marx, 1858, p. 420).

However, there is also another side to this. When individual capitalists keep their own workers' wages low, even though they limit their workers' ability to consume, they produce more surplus-value that not only benefits them but also benefits the entire system. By using their labor force to create as much surplus-value as possible for themselves, they increase the total mass of surplus-value in society, and this, as you will see in chapter 3, helps to sustain and maintain as well as promote the further development of the system. This type of logically contradictory situation is one of the main characteristics of capitalism. It is a characteristic that arises from the dialectical contradictions that lie at the heart of capitalism and from which the possibilities of crisis originate. Capitalism's contradictory nature makes it extremely difficult for all of us who are enmeshed in the system to understand what is happening and even more difficult to understand why it is happening.

When the capitalist system is viewed from the perspective of the individual representatives of capital, whose primary interests are to make a profit, it is extremely difficult, even for them—in fact, even more so for them—to understand the system; and the necessary relation between production and circulation adds to this confusion in many ways. One of the most central of these has to do with money being the most general form of value. Since it is within circulation that the commodity is transformed into money and the surplus-value realized, many capitalists assume that their profits come from exchange rather than from production (Marx, 1865, p. 135; 1878, p. 137). How this assumption develops into further confusions when capitalists come into competition with one another is discussed in chapter 3.

Increasing productivity is one of the main objectives of every capitalist because increases in productivity normally lead to at least temporary increases in profits. I explained before how the drive to create relative surplus-value invariably leads to greater productivity. Moreover, the accumulation of capital that brings more and more workers into cooperation, concentrating labor-power and means of production in larger units, along with the further division and fine-tuning of labor skills, also increases productivity. In fact, almost everything that capitalists can do to increase or maintain profitability also increases productivity, and, as a consequence, there are more commodities that must be sold. I consider the place of productivity within the capitalist system in greater detail in chapter 3. For now, it is important to recognize that increases in productivity, brought about by any of the factors mentioned earlier, mean that capitalists must forever be searching for new markets or trying to expand existing ones (Marx, 1865, pp. 344, 353, 359; 1878, p. 190). With the total surplus-value divided between an ever-increasing number of commodities, more and more commodities must be sold before this surplus-value can be realized. The separation of purchase and sale—purchase of labor-power and means of production and sale of commodities impregnated with surplus-value—becomes increasingly precarious as the system develops; and the possibility of crises of overproduction is always present (Marx, 1865, pp. 359–367; 1878, p. 156). Of course this is overproduction, in terms of the capitalist's need to realize surplus-value, not, in the vast majority of cases, overproduction in terms of human need (Marx, 1865 pp. 359–367; 1878, p. 156).

It is in *Capital*, Volume 2 (1878), that Marx focuses most directly on circulation and thus completes the model of the capitalist production process and his discussion of "Capital in General." Here, just as before, he depicts capital as a process as well as a relation. He analyzes the circuit of one sum of capital invested in production and follows it through the process of circulation where value changes from the commodity form of capital into the money form (pp. 110–206). In the money form some of the surplus-value that has been realized from the sale of the commodity becomes the capitalist's revenue, but the rest is returned to production, and thus the accumulation of capital takes place and so, too, of course, does the reproduction of the entire process.

Marx also examines how the total turnover of capital works within the whole system or in terms of social rather than individual capital. To do this, he divides the total productive activities of the capitalists into two "Departments." One of these Departments—Department I—produces constant capital, that is, the means of production, and the other—Department II—produces consumer items, or necessities and luxuries (Marx, 1878, p. 471). He depicts the proportions of each Department's activities of reproduction and accumulation that would enable the capitalist system to function in equilibrium—first in terms of simple reproduction (pp. 468–564) and then on an expanded scale (pp. 565–599). For example, he considers the proportion of the means of production that Department I must produce in order to meet the requirements of the capitalists in Department II who need to produce consumer goods on an expanded scale. However, since the oppositions in the inner life of capitalism—the opposites in the "unity of opposites"—seem indifferent to one another and thus attempt to develop independently of one another, their inner necessity or unity only asserts or shows itself in crisis when the opposites must be forced back into their relation with one another (this is most clearly stated in Marx, 1858, pp. 443–444). They are forced back into unity only by the devaluation and destruction of a certain amount of the existing capital. This sacrifice of some of the existing capital and capitalists, too, temporarily rectifies the imbalances, or overproduction. Therefore, what Marx actually demonstrates with his equilibrium model—his schemes of reproduction and expanded reproduction—is that equilibrium or harmony in the system is only ever achieved for limited periods and that these arise out of crisis, not the normal functioning of capital (Rosdolsky, 1977, p. 332).

In Volume 2, Marx repeatedly considers the relation between production time in the sphere of production and circulation time. He does this not just to depict the necessity of their unity, but because, as I mentioned before, many capitalists are misled into thinking that their profit is made within circulation rather than being based on the labor-time expended in production. It is the constant inter-twining of production time and circulation time, the way in which the two processes constantly run into one another, that blurs the distinctive aspects of each to those who participate in these processes. As I said before, this misleads the capitalists, but labor, too, is misled by this blurring of the two processes or, more specifically, by Dialectical Contradiction 2—that is, the unity of production and circulation, or the internal relation between production and circulation. How-ever, productive labor is in a better position to have at least a subjective knowl-edge of Dialectical Contradiction 1—that is, the internal relation between labor and capital—because it endures the experience of alienation and exploitation with daily regularity.

In his consideration of the circulation process, Marx also enables us to broaden our concept of productive labor. He distinguishes between the kind of labor that takes place within the sphere of circulation that is productive labor—adds further surplus-value to the commodity—and the type of labor that simply facilitates the movement of value or its transformation from the commodity to the money form (Marx, 1878, pp. 225–227). For example, if a commodity cannot be exchanged until it is transported from one place to another, the labor-time involved in the transportation is productive labor since it creates additional value and surplus-value and thus augments the final value of the commodity. However, the labor-time of the person who collects money for the finished commodity and places it in the till is not productive labor, even though this type of labor facilitates the realization of the surplus-value contained in the commodity (pp. 225–227). In chapter 3, I consider in greater detail the position vis-à-vis capital of people doing this type of work.

The entire turnover time of a particular sum of capital is one of the perspec-tives Marx uses to analyze the relation between circulation time and production time (Marx, 1878, pp. 233–424). In the *Grundrisse*, he points out that the ideal for the capitalist would be "circulation without circulation time" (1858, p. 659). This is because increasing the velocity of circulation time means that money capital can more quickly be converted back into productive capital—that is, capital that purchases labor-power and the other commodities necessary for the immediate production process—and capital accumulation can proceed as rapidly as possible. He demonstrates that circulation time does not add surplus-value to the commodity—that surplus-value is only created by productive labor or labor-time not circulation time (1878, p. 203). However, increasing the velocity of the turnover means that within a certain period of time—say, one year—the same capital can be valorized more times, and thus the total volume or mass of surplus-value is increased. This works in much the same way as when capitalists increase the total volume of capital they employ in a year—increasing the size of their operation, which is a norm and, in fact, an inherent tendency with the accumulation of capital (1858, p. 519; 1878, p. 375).

As capitalism develops, capitalists use an increasing number of devices to accelerate the velocity of turnover—the movement of value—through the compression of time and space (Harvey, 1989; 1999). The central concern is to shorten the time between the purchase of constant and variable capital and the sale of commodities and to prevent that separation from becoming permanent. In the first instance, the process is held in continuity and made continuous by value changing into its various forms. In other words, its continuity is made possible because value can exist simultaneously as commodity capital and money capital in circulation while it also functions as productive capital within the immediate production process. The turnover of capital is a unity of these three circuits of capital (Marx, 1878, p. 183). Even then the necessary equilibrium is never totally achieved but only approached to greater and lesser degrees; and this is why other devices or means must be used to maintain, as far as possible, the internal relation between production and circulation. Credit is the most important of all the devices, and its use as well as its forms increase with the development of capitalism. Without the transformation of value into its different forms and without credit—which is really an extension of the money form—the movement of capital would work in spasms, and the whole system would collapse (pp. 181–182, 195).

Marx discusses the role of credit in greater detail in Volume 3 of *Capital*, and there we can see that even with credit the capitalist system remains not only exploitative of labor-power but also precarious for the capitalist. I digress here from the general model in order to offer some examples of what I mean about the precariousness of the system. Production decisions for each new cycle are based on the results of previous cycles, and this, of course, increases the risk of getting these decisions wrong. Of course, capitalists use a variety of methods to minimize risk, including consumer surveys, advertising and the use of hedge funds or derivatives such as futures and options. Nevertheless, if the internal relation between production and circulation/exchange breaks down completely, a crisis will occur. Sometimes this is more like a crisis in waiting, or one that takes a while to erupt. When production or supply is less than demand, prices rise above the commodities' real values, and this encourages the capitalists to produce more or increase the supply. However, the higher prices will influence many consumers to change their pattern of demand. Therefore, the firms that have rushed to produce more often end up with commodities that are no longer wanted or at best ones that can only be sold by reducing their price below their real value or at least to a point where no surplus-value can be realized. When supply exceeds demand and prices fall or markets are glutted with unsold commodities, value is either depleted or totally destroyed. Sometimes capitalists try to circumvent this by forming "mountains" of the surplus—thus keeping the commodities off the market until the balance is corrected in their favor. In other cases the unwanted commodities are dumped cheaply onto foreign domestic markets, thereby depressing the prices of domestic equivalents and often forcing domestic producers into bankruptcy or ruin. Please note, and I will go into this later, supply and demand may influence the way that prices fluctuate around value, but they are not—as I hope I have made clear—what determines value or for that matter the range through which the prices can fluctuate (Harvey, 1999, pp. 17–18; Marx, 1865, p. 282).

It is essential to remember that the origin of capitalist crises—in fact, the precondition for capitalism's contradictions—resides in the commodity form and the value form of wealth that arises from the commodity form, whereby the use-values produced within society cannot be acquired independently from their exchange-values. Use-values are even destroyed or wasted rather than used to meet human needs when people cannot afford their exchange-values. And, as I discussed earlier, this has negative consequences not just for those whose needs are denied but for many capitalists as well. In other words, the necessary unity, or internal relation, between production and circulation/exchange that enables capitalists to accumulate their historically specific form of wealth is also a constant source of conflict and worry for them. As a consequence, they have long sought ways to adapt the system and minimize the risks involved. Marx was able to forecast these adaptations even before they had become established as part of the system. He was able to do this because his model of "Capital in General"—his dialectical conceptualization of capitalism's "essence"—allowed him to understand how the inherent contradictions of capitalism moved and developed, creating specific tendencies and the possibility of crisis. From this he was able to describe the types of measures that might be used to forestall these tendencies or rather measures that would allow capital's contradictions more room to move (Marx, 1867, p. 198). Thus capital's contradictions are never really resolved but simply displaced, often positing them at higher levels of complexity with more dire and total consequences (Harvey, 1999, p. 21; Marx, 1867, p. 198). I mention just a few of these measures here, but elaborate on them and others as appropriate in chapter 3.

There will always be individual capitalists who own their own firms, but this had ceased being the primary type of ownership by the end of the nineteenth century. Individual ownership proved too risky because of the possibility that surplus-value might not be realized or at least not by the time the capitalist needed to purchase new inputs—the gap between valorization and accumulation. As I mentioned before, credit became necessary. One of the forms of credit or ways of minimizing the risk was to share it; therefore joint stock companies and share capital were adopted as forms for controlling the risk or spreading it more evenly over a number of individuals and also eventually other corporations and institutions (Marx, 1865, pp. 567–572, 1045–1047; 1878, pp. 311, 433). Although these have been the dominant forms of capital ownership for most of the twentieth century, share ownership has increased dramatically during the last twenty-five years, and institutions such as pension funds have begun to play a commanding role in the capital share market (Blackburn, 1999).

The use of derivatives has also proliferated (Tickell, 1999), and the role of credit in consumer spending has become pervasive and problematical, forcing many people into debt and dire financial situations. Both of these are measures that protect capitalists from fluctuations in the market, especially decreases in consumer demand that might force the prices of their commodities to fall below their values. Credit is in fact as old a feature of capitalism as the "free" wage-labor that made the whole system possible. Marx notes that it has always been the custom in capitalist economies to pay for labor-power after and not before its use (Marx, 1867, p. 712). Thus wage-labor itself was capital's first creditor. However, this, in turn, forced the workers into debt. Since they were compelled to work for a fixed duration—a day, week or month—before receiving their wages, they often had to buy their necessities on credit—often at inflated prices in the company's shop. These early uses of credit within capitalism were the precursors for the worldwide credit system we see today as well as the onerous situation of the "Third World" debt crisis that is an example of capitalism displacing its crises—allowing its contradictions room to move. In chapter 3, I discuss further the role that credit plays in the concrete totality of capitalism—how it drives capital beyond its limits and becomes a vehicle for crisis and the opening up of the possibility—but only the possibility—of the "abolition of capital itself" (Marx, 1865, p. 742).

In a period of capitalist history such as our own, when the idea of the "free" market has become so dominant, it may seem surprising, at first, to realize that the long-term tendency in capitalism's development has been for capitalists to try to gain greater control of not just production, as one would expect, but also circulation and exchange. However, this becomes much easier to understand once capitalism is conceptualized dialectically—when we see that the "essence" of capitalism is comprised of internally related opposites that capitalists must strive to maintain in their inner connection. (I am by no means implying that capitalists have a dialectical understanding of the system; they simply follow what is commonly referred to as the "logic" of the system). Nevertheless, there are times and conditions when growth can only be stimulated by relaxing control, and this is when we see capitalists stressing the need for the "invisible hand" of the market to be uncuffed and given its freedom. Once again, this is something

it can lead to either the mechanistic reading of Marx known as technological determinism or alternatively a voluntarist or subjectivist reading that can be characterized as class determinism. In the first case, technological development is seen as the motor force or dynamic behind capitalist development, and in the second all movement and development within capitalism is seen to be the result of class struggle (Milonakis, 1997). A dialectical reading of Marx, and thus conceptualization of capitalism, focuses on the internal relation between the forces and relation of production and also, as I said previously, the relation between this contradiction and the other two—the labor–capital relation and the internal relation between production and circulation. Obviously the labor–capital relation constitutes one part of Contradiction 3, but in this case we need to consider how it is internally related to the productive forces—how the development of each of these opposites is determined and shaped within its relation with the other.

Once labor is totally subsumed (real rather than formal subsumption), under the domination of capital, capitalists promote the further development of the means of production—technology, the application of new forms of energy, and so on—so that they can be used to increase labor productivity—that is, in order to increase the ratio between necessary and surplus labor, always seeking to shorten the duration of the former relative to the latter (Marx, 1866, pp. 1023–1025). In other words, they seek to increase the surplus-value created within a specified amount of time. This is usually understood, from the perspective of capital, as increasing labor productivity. Thus the social forces are developed in a particular way, one that enhances their capacity to exploit labor-power, and if we remember that it is the ratio between necessary and surplus labor that is fundamental, we can understand Marx's point that the rate of surplus-value, or rate of exploitation, can even be increased when wages are rising (Marx, 1867, p. 753). Competition between capitalist firms drives each one to try constantly to increase the rate of surplus-value and the overall productivity of their workforce, and this is what drives them to adopt new technology and sometimes even to go to the expense of financing the research and development of new technology. These new means of labor, the objectification of previous labor-time, are then used to extort more surplus labor-time from the current workforce. Once again we can see how the result of a previous relation, in this case the new constant capital or technology, becomes a precondition—the precondition for further valorization.

Marx stressed that a machine was only a machine and only became capital within certain social relations—capitalist ones (Marx, 1847, p. 256). Rather than understanding this to mean that the instruments of labor only become capital when used within the historically specific social relations of capitalist production, many Marxists think that Marx was saying that technology is neutral. Therefore, they think that the technology that is developed within these relations can be used, with no problems arising, within socialist or communist production. I will consider the dangers attached to this interpretation later in the book, but, hopefully, the possibility of problems is already apparent. If technology is devel-

that can be discussed in greater detail when we consider many capitals in co[ ]tition in chapter 3.

One of the most fundamental things to remember about the "unity of proc[ ]tion and circulation"—Dialectical Contradiction 2—is that our experience[ ]capitalism takes place within this contradiction. It underpins and frames our to[ ]experience of life and therefore also the constitution of our consciousness, and, a consequence, our understanding of the system. As I mentioned before, tl[ ]constant intertwining of production time and circulation time and the way i[ ]which value—the constituting mediation of the system—is experienced in diffei[ ]ent forms blurs our consciousness, thereby distorting our understanding of th[ ]system just as much as our experiencing of the internally related opposites at[ ]different times and places does. Thus without Marx's dialectical analysis it is impossible to grasp the "truth" of capitalism.

The Social Forces and Social Relation of Production (Dialectical Contradiction 3 of the Capitalist Production Process)

The third and final contradiction that, together with the other two, constitutes the "essence" of capitalism—or "Capital in General"—is the dialectical contradiction between the social forces of production and the social relation of production. Unlike the other two, Marx does not devote a separate volume to this contradiction. His discussion of the social relation and social forces of production runs throughout all three volumes of *Capital*. I include it as part of the "essence" of capital because by analyzing it, we can grasp more adequately the dialectical movement within the "essence" and thus the movement within the entire system. This contradiction is often located within the sphere of production, but, as I have stressed with the other two contradictions, none of them can be fully understood outside their relation to one another. Moreover, in certain respects this contradiction extends beyond the capitalist process of production. It reaches out into every aspect of our social existence, sometimes impacting on and influencing these other dimensions of our lives. At other times, its effects work in the opposite direction. It pulls or incorporates factors that seem to be external to the production process into its frame—encompassing them within the "essence" of capitalism. And education is one of the most important dimensions of our lives that is affected in both these respects. However, to comprehend this, we need a more inclusive concept of the forces of production; and we need to think in a more fluid or dialectical way—to consider the movement or flow that exists both within and between the dialectical relations.

In a great deal of Marxist literature the forces of production refer only to the means of production. Marx uses the expression "productive forces" in this sense but also in a more inclusive and dialectical sense, which I discuss later in this section. When we focus on this contradiction only in terms of the means of production or when we focus on it in a way that excludes the other contradictions,

oped in order to maximize the exploitation of labor, we can hardly assume that it is conducive to either human beings or the environment. Therefore, it seems highly probable that at least some of the technology developed within capitalist relations would not be appropriate in a socialist society, and other technology might have to be transformed in order to render it amenable to human beings and nature.

When Marx refers to the forces of production, he, as I said, alludes to much more than just the means of production or the present level of development of technology. He uses this term to refer to anything that can be used to increase productivity and the further accumulation of capital within a society—to increase what Marx calls "social capital" (e.g., Marx, 1865, p. 263). Therefore, even the social relation between capital and labor is a social force of production or can be conceptualized as such, especially when labor is really subsumed under capital and the means of production use labor rather than being used by labor (Marx, 1866, p. 1025; 1867, p. 645). Moreover, when looked at from this perspective, we can see that instead of being held in a position of opposition to capital within the relation, labor is drawn into and becomes a part of capital, functioning for capital's benefit. And it is not just technology that draws labor into identity with capital, the way labor is organized in production can also be a factor in increasing productivity (Marx, 1867, p. 439ff.; Marx and Engels, 1846, p. 49). As we have seen, when labor is forced to work in cooperation under the control of capital, as it has been from the very beginning of capitalism, it can be considered to be functioning as a productive force. Other forms of organization or variations on the cooperative theme have also been used, such as the contemporary use of quality circles. When these forms of organization are used within the context of the labor–capital relation, they increase labor productivity and/or the intensity with which labor is applied—thus condensing the social labor hour or decreasing its porosity—and eventually bring about a reduction in and/or a reconstitution of "socially necessary labor-time" (Marx, 1867, pp. 431, 534–536, 661). Again we find an example of the way in which Marx uses concepts—in this case his concept of the dialectical opposition between the social relation and social forces of production and their movement into and out of identity with one another—in order to help us consider every dimension of a situation. When we consider labor in its internal relation or dialectical opposition to capital, we can understand how labor actually creates capital and how the actual character of the worker is shaped within this antagonistic relation. Alternatively or from another perspective, when we consider labor's subsumption by capital, the identity of labor and capital, we can also see how labor becomes capital—within the dialectical movement or flow that is internal to the labor–capital relation.

Ideas, or ideological forms of thinking and also scientific knowledge, can also become social forces of production. It is fairly easy to understand how scientific knowledge can be used to increase productivity in the sense of increasing use-values or material wealth. However, it also works as a productive force for the individual capitalist when it ceases to be part of the public domain and becomes a commodity. It can then be used to give its owners a temporary competitive advantage by either increasing labor productivity or by increasing the intensity of labor and thus allowing them to undercut the prices of their competitors. That ideological thinking can also serve as a productive force is less obvious; nevertheless, it can serve as an equally effective and powerful force for increasing the production of capital.

The ideas that become dominant are nothing more than an expression of the material relations that are dominant in society (Marx and Engels, 1846, p. 67). As I mentioned in the Introduction in my discussion of Marx's theory of consciousness, these material relations become integrated into our thinking through *uncritical/reproductive praxis*. Therefore, our consciousness becomes susceptible to the ideological expression of the prevailing tendencies in these relations. For example, those elements of the ideology of globalization—the "hyperglobalist" theory I referred to in chapter 1—that place working people at the mercy of global market forces serve to strengthen the productive force of social capital. They do so by persuading people to work for lower pay and to accept the increasing insecurity or uncertainty of employment and therefore convince them of the necessity of adopting flexibility in their attitudes, working practices and also their life-styles. Once the vast majority of working people have adopted these dispositions and attitudes or have been inculcated with them through the processes of education and training, it is much easier for capital to extort a greater amount of either or both absolute and relative surplus-value from them under conditions of heightened global competition. Nevertheless, the power or force of any ideological explanation, no matter how hegemonic, depends upon its inner relation with the real world; therefore its power to persuade only lasts as long as this relation or a particular tendency associated with it holds. This brings me back to the fundamental importance of capitalism's social relation of production.

When we conceptualize the social relation of production moving into and becoming a social force of production, we should understand this to be a fleeting or temporary situation, yet also a recurring one. The contradiction or opposition between labor and capital is continuously reasserted as the social relation moves out of identity with the social forces, once again becoming a "unity of opposites"—an antithesis held together by a necessary but inherently antagonistic internal relation (Marx, 1865, pp. 358–359; 1867, p. 929). According to Marx, however, this movement in and out of identity eventually ceases, and the antagonism is held in place as the type of growth and development that is historically specific to capitalism comes to a halt. One of the most frequently cited passages from Marx's writings states unequivocally that the social relations of production will become fetters on the social forces of production—thus holding back their further development as well as their capacity to increase productivity (Marx, 1859, pp. 19–23).

Unfortunately, that particular passage has been used to bolster the conclusions that are linked to two types of interpretation, which, I think, are totally erroneous and also damaging to Marx's project for human emancipation. Many Marxists who think that the social relations of production are those of private property assume that the fetter is due to the capitalists' ownership of the means of production; therefore, the problem is solved by a transfer of ownership. Some also think that when capitalism comes to a halt or is fettered, it will collapse under its own contradictions and will inevitably and automatically be replaced by socialism. In contrast, when the social relations are understood, first and fore-most, as the relation between capital and labor in the immediate production process—in the sphere of production—rather than as the relations of distribution, we can see more clearly what Marx meant when he said that they would become fetters. Every advance in capitalism that brings about a reduction in "socially necessary labor-time" or that compacts the social labor hour, allowing, for exam-ple, one worker to produce in an hour what it had taken two to do before, undermines the value form of wealth—the historically specific form of capitalist wealth—that arises from the way in which capital uses labor in the value-creating process, especially the valorization part of that process, in other words, the form of wealth that arises from the labor–capital relation. Very simply, if capitalists were successful in eventually driving down necessary labor-time to zero, then there would be no surplus labor-time either—no surplus-value. Necessary labor and surplus labor are a "unity of opposites"—a dialectical contradiction, or internal relation—in which the existence of one depends upon the existence of the other. And, of course, capitalists will have no reason to produce material wealth when they can no longer produce surplus-value.

As Postone (1996) argues and as I have argued elsewhere (Allman 1999), Marx was not primarily, or in the first instance, criticizing a property relation or a problem of distribution; he argued that the relations of distribution were a result of the social relation of production (Marx, 1875, pp. 569–570). In other words, the only way for the problems of distribution to be truly eradicated is to abolish the social relation between labor and capital—yet another "unity of opposites." The focus of his critique was the social relation of production within which labor was alienated and dehumanized through a process of exploitation and within which a type of social wealth was created that actually denied human need regardless of the level of social productivity. Although the relations of distribu-tion also place limits on people consuming the material wealth that can poten-tially be created by further advances in the forces of production and thus in that way might act as fetters on these advances, Marx was trying to show us that the problems of capitalism could not be rectified by alterations in these relations alone. In fact, if we were to simply have a social form of ownership, without any fundamental changes in the social relation of production or the value form of wealth, the same problems of distribution would reemerge (Marx, 1875, pp. 569–570). Therefore, when capitalism is abolished, the labor–capital relation will be abolished and the actual relation of production and also the specific capitalist mode of production—not just property relations—will need to be transformed.

And, of course, as far as the inevitability of socialism is concerned, hopefully it is clear that whatever type of society results when capitalism ceases to function will be a matter of the presence or absence of *critical/revolutionary praxis*.

THE PROCESS: VALUE MOVES AND MEDIATES

In my discussion of capitalism's "essence," I have tried to convey a sense of the movement that can be grasped by a dialectical conceptualization of capitalism. It is a movement that arises out of the internal relations—dialectical contradictions—that form the "essence" of capitalism. It arises both from the antagonistic tension inherent in these relations and also from the value form that is produced and realized within them. As John Holloway (1995) has stressed, "capital moves," but it is only through a dialectical conceptualization of capitalist reality that we can see why it moves and develops according to the specific inherent necessities I have described. In this section I want to stress that capital and the entire capitalist system moves because value moves and to recap that movement by focusing on value from its moment of creation through its various transformations. I also stress the role that value plays as a mediation within the system. I begin with a brief summary of the origin of value and the value form.

As I have explained, the substance of value is abstract labor and its measure is labor-time (Marx, 1867, p. 131; Rubin, 1972). Value is created by the way in which capital uses labor in the process of production—a process that is a unity of the actual concrete labor process and a process of creating value. During the process of creating value, some of the labor-time involved is necessary labor-time, or the amount of time it takes to reproduce the value of labor-power—the very special commodity that makes capitalism possible. Marx calls the part of the value-creating process that extends beyond the point of creating the value of labor-power the process of valorization: it "is nothing but the continuation of the former beyond a definite point" (Marx, 1867, p. 302). During the process of valorization, labor creates or is used to create surplus-value—the basis of the capitalist's profits and thus capital itself. Value, therefore, is the result of the labor–capital relation, and the value form is the expression of that relation or its mode of existence from the very moment that valorization takes place. Value is also a precondition of capitalism and the substance of capitalism's historically specific form of wealth. An economy that ceased being based on the creation of value would no longer be a capitalist economy.

Value's first movement arises from the actual sensuous expression of the laborer's vital activity, functioning not as a particular type of labor but in its abstract social form. This abstract labor is transformed into abstract units of temporal duration—time. Labor-time therefore constitutes value; it impregnates, or becomes incorporated within, the commodity, whether it is a tangible object or a service or even an event, and thus value undergoes its first metamorphosis into the commodity form. Often the commodity is fully completed in the process of production and is then ready to be moved through the process of circulation to the point where it is exchanged and the latent value within it is realized. In this process, value, embodied in its commodity form, passes from the social relations between people engaged in the sphere of production to those engaged in circulation, wherein they facilitate the movement of value and its transformation from its commodity form to its money form at the point of exchange. Value mediates or binds the activities of the individuals engaged in these activities, and thus it brings them into social relations with one another. In other words, just as it mediates labor and capital within the process of production, it also mediates the activities of those engaged in that relation with the activities of people engaged in the process of circulation and exchange. It constitutes and binds the internal relation between labor and capital and also the internal relation, or unity, of production and circulation.

In other cases, the commodity is not completed in the first labor process and must move from the original site of production to a second one and sometimes to others in succession before it is constituted in the manner in which it will be exchanged. In some of these cases new value may be added within capitalist social relations, and thus more surplus-value may be incorporated in the commodity. Some of these subsequent sites may be located in the sphere of production while others will be in the sphere of circulation. With every movement of the commodity, value moves, and thus latent, or potential, capital also moves. With every one of these movements, value also mediates the relations of the people involved because they engage in social relations with one another for the sole purpose of either creating value or facilitating its movement from production through circulation to the point of exchange. At the point of exchange, the use-value of the commodity is separated from its exchange-value and enters into the sphere of consumption, and exchange-value is transformed into the money form, the most general form of value. Even upon separation, the use-value retains traces of its relation with value. It will have been shaped or to some extent determined within this relation. Furthermore, it would not even exist as a use-value unless it could form a unity with exchange-value, and the way it is constituted—its quality—will have been largely determined, if necessary, restricted, according to the dictates of surplus-value creation. This is the case with any dialectical/internal relation. For example, people engaged in the labor–capital relation that is mediated by value retain the subjective and objective effects of their position within the relation even when they are not actively engaged within it.

When the commodity is sold, value is liberated from the commodity form, and once divorced from its use-value and thus commodity form, value in its money form is then free to move in a variety of ways and, accordingly, to perform a number of functions. The newly created value that is realized from the sale of the commodity and transformed into money is comprised of necessary labor-time and surplus labor-time. Any other value realized from the sale of the commodity is not newly created value but simply replaces the value, or past labor-time, that is objectified in the raw materials and means of production, and in the case of the latter, some of it is only transferred to the commodity's price bit by bit in each production cycle. The newly created value that is comprised of necessary labor-time is used as variable capital by the capitalists to pay for labor-power, thereby mediating the exchange relation between capital and the worker who is the purveyor of the commodity, labor-power.[6] The other part of the newly created value is surplus-value. Some of the surplus-value realized from the sale of the commodity is used by capitalists as their revenue for the purchase of necessities and luxuries; therefore it functions as a means of payment. Some of it is used to facilitate the movement of other commodities, in other words, as a means of circulation. The remaining surplus-value is used to accumulate capital, often in the form of constant capital used in the process of production. At every moment in the process, it is value that moves and propels the process, and it is also value, in its various objective forms, that mediates the social relations of all the people involved in the process. In other words, it is value that brings them together or binds them together in social relations with one another and that mediates or links one cluster of activities with every other cluster.

The social relations that people enter into in the turnover of capital, whether in one turnover cycle or in expanded and continuous reproduction cycles, are their most fundamental social relations. Of course, people enter into other social relations too, but those they enter into in order to produce their material reality and thus the basis of their consciousness as well as their actual mode of existence are fundamental or basic to all the others (Marx and Engels, 1846). Value's dynamic and mediating movements hold the entire framework, or capital's "essence," together. These movements work within that framework, binding all the internally related opposites, and the necessary human social relations of the opposites, into a network or web-like pattern that constitutes the socioeconomic structure of capitalist society in its national as well as global forms. As Postone (1996) says, value is the historically specific intrinsic or immanent dynamic of capitalism and also its quasi-objective form of social mediation. I return to the importance of this shortly when I consider the nature of capitalism's historically specific form of social domination.

When surplus-value becomes separated from the use-value of the commodity and enters the money form, it is often returned to the sphere of production; however, it can also continue to function in the sphere of circulation, as I mentioned earlier, by facilitating the movement of commodities. In addition, surplus-value that is not returned to the production process can also be transformed into other forms of capital that may also operate outside the sphere of production. The surplus-value that originates in production, once it assumes the money form, can be transformed into commercial capital and interest-bearing capital and used to develop financial capital—a host of financial commodities such as derivatives, stocks and bonds or share capital. It also constitutes the rent that becomes the basis of the landlord's/landowner's capital. As value assumes these various forms and moves further and further away from its point of origin, it becomes more difficult to trace it back to its source—its constitution by labor within the labor–capital social relation of production. However, if the link is actually broken, then the real value content of these other forms of capital can be called into question. At some point, the link must be reestablished and value must move back into capital accumulation where it can be used to set in motion the creation of new value—new valorization. If not, devaluation, even crisis, will occur. I discuss this in more detail in chapter 3. As value spins off into these other forms, it continues to propel the economic process and to mediate the social relations of people in an ever-expanding arena of employment and vital social, political and economic activities. In sum, the flow or movement and mediation of value is of ultimate importance to capitalism. In this sense it *is* capitalism—its dynamic and its raison d'être. And so long as we must live and function in capitalist societies, it is our raison d'être too, whether we like it or not.

VALUE, TIME AND SOCIAL DOMINATION: CAPITALISM'S HISTORICALLY SPECIFIC FORM OF SOCIAL DOMINATION

In this final section, I focus on the historical specificity of capitalism's form of social domination. My interpretation has been influenced by Moishe Postone's "reinterpretation" of Marx's theory that was first published in 1993. Postone not only offers, in my opinion, an accurate interpretation of some important aspects of Marx's explanation of capitalism but also usefully emphasizes certain areas of Marx's critique that were either implicit or at least not stressed in an emphatic way by Marx himself. By bringing these to light, Postone has posed an important challenge to undialectical interpretations of Marx and thus furnished support for the type of dialectical interpretation presented here. His "reinterpretation" also highlights certain crucial elements implicit in Marx's theory that I, for one, had not previously recognized—primarily those having to do with capital's historically specific form of social domination. Just as Marx, himself, so often does, Postone enables us to look at the internal nature of capitalism—the nature that Marx exposed—from yet another perspective. It is not possible in this brief discussion to do full justice to Postone's exegesis or to summarize his arguments, and this is not my intention. In fact, drawing on Marx, I slightly expand on his notion of the compulsion that is inherent in "socially necessary labor-time." Moreover, my discussion of the role of the state in capitalist societies differs from his in certain respects not because I disagree with him but because I want to emphasize different aspects of this role; and with reference to these and also the democratic form of governance, my interpretation primarily draws on the writings of Ellen Meiksins Wood (in particular, Wood, 1995, 1999).

We normally think of social domination as something that emanates from the state, politics or even our interpersonal social relationships as opposed to the more public and organized social relations we enter into in civil society—relations such as those involved in the economic sphere of human activity.[7] For example, we think of the state's exercise of legitimate force through the police and military and its legal juridical functions, or the political exercise of power by the national and the local state. Alternatively, to the extent that we do locate power or domination within civil society, we might think of the forms of manipulation and control that arise within interpersonal relations or social relationships generally. Or we locate power and control in either macro or micro discourses, the latter arising from specific sites of human practice and the former as aspects of the dominant ideology or ideological discourses perpetuated by social institutions and the media. According to Marx, all of these sources of power are secondary forms of social domination, and many forms of power that arise within civil society are not necessarily related to capitalism. Nevertheless, they are shaped in specific ways by capital's historically specific intrinsic dynamic—the dynamic that constitutes capital's actual form of social domination. Postone (1996) argues that this is an abstract form of social domination and that this is one of the factors that make capitalism entirely different from any other social formation that has ever existed. It is easier to understand this if we consider these other forms of social domination before going into further detail about capitalism's historically specific form.

In the societies that predate capitalism, it was a particular class or social group—sometimes even an extended family—that overtly dominated the most fundamental aspects of a subordinate group's social existence. Moreover, they overtly exploited this other social group by exerting their command and control over the surplus production of the latter group. This was not necessarily surplus to the requirements of the exploited group or an excess beyond what they needed in order to sustain their capacity to work but a surplus in terms of what they were allowed to keep for themselves. Therefore overt and personal forms of power and control were needed to enforce such an arrangement. As I mentioned earlier in this chapter, capitalism first emerged in Britain for various reasons; therefore the advent of capitalism was not simply a matter of economic evolution or development. The type of society from which it emerged was a feudal system of socioeconomic organization. Some of the features of feudalism were similar to those that pertained in the Roman Empire as well as in many other ancient forms of governance elsewhere in the world of antiquity—some of which endured throughout the centuries until fairly recent times, such as China's dynasties and Japan's shogunates. All these forms of social organization have in common an overt, concrete and personal form of social domination. For example, the Roman legions, or those who commanded them and represented the will of the Roman Emperor, were able to demand tribute or taxes from even the most remote reaches of the Empire by force or threat of force, which was, of course, how these places became part of the Empire in the first place. Although they were not nearly as powerful as Rome, the feudal lords operated in much the same way.

The legitimacy or naturalness of such overt forms of domination and exploitation had to be established and sustained by a particular type of ideology. Usually divine intervention was necessary. God—sometimes a multiplicity of gods—was called on to explain and justify the system, as in the "Divine Right of Kings" or, in the case of the feudal lord, nobility bequeathed by birth or favor. It is doubtful, however, that this alone could have maintained the system. The feudal lords, or any other type of exploiter, had to justify their positions of domination and their right to demand a tax or a tithe of surplus product or surplus labor by promising to protect those they dominated from external or foreign invasion. They also had to demonstrate their ability to do this by the possession of weapons, a defensive structure such as a fort or castle and often a permanent military force. Feudal jousting matches were no doubt a form of entertainment, but more importantly a demonstration and reminder of the force commanded by the feudal hierarchy—a demonstration of their power to maintain social order and to ward off any internal or external challenges to their authority. European feudalism, like the other forms of this type of society mentioned before, was first and foremost a political social structure in which the social relations of production or economic relations were embedded, in contrast to capitalism, wherein the social structure is constituted by the economic relations (Wood, 1995). Therefore in the societies that predate capitalism, the main form of social domination is external to or comes from outside the relations of production. Moreover, because the source of domination is concrete and personal, and thus obvious, it must be, but also can be, rendered natural and legitimate by a type of ideology that is equally obvious and straight-forward. In other words, there is no second-guessing about one's place or status in the social order. These are determined by birth and remain fixed for life. People were not equal, and everyone knew this to be the fact and ostensibly accepted it as a natural state of affairs.

The oppressed and exploited in such situations have one advantage over people who live under capitalism's historically specific form of social domina-tion. Since the real source of their domination is obvious, when and if they decide to challenge their situation, they know who it is they must challenge. Of course normally they do not have the physical force—offensive or defensive weap-onry—to either attain or sustain victory over their oppressors. Nor do they have any established and generally accepted values or rights with which they might undertake a political or moral/ethical challenge to the system. Their only strength is in numbers and in some cases in their ability to withhold their surplus produc-tion. Nevertheless, if they could secure some of the force they need from outside the system, then they have the clear advantage of knowing with whom and where the source of domination and their oppression lies.

Capitalism's form of social domination is entirely different, even in postliberal capitalism, where the state plays a more interventionist role in the economy. The real source of domination and compulsion under capitalism is abstract. It is value constituted by abstract labor and measured by labor-time or abstract temporal units. Yet since value is also dynamic and thus transmutes into objective forms—that is, commodity, money and capital—Postone (1996) says that while it is abstract, it is also a quasi-objective form of social mediation and domination. It is quasi-objective because it is concrete and thus observable—and, in that sense objective—at one and the same time that it is also abstract and also subjective. In other words, value is an abstract form of domination and social mediation, but we experience it in concrete or objective forms, and these objective forms are constituted subjectively—by the activity of human beings, that is, productive labor. Moreover, we also experience value's social domination subjectively, or within our feelings and emotions. Therefore, even though we experience the constraints and compulsion of this abstract form of domination through objective and impersonal forms, we need to remember its subjective and social origin, its constitution by abstract labor within the capitalist social relation of production, and also its effects on our subjectivity. By designating value as an abstract quasi-objective form of social domination, we can more readily hold on to these distinctions.

In tracing the movement of value or following its dynamic, I indicated how it serves as a social mediation that binds the most fundamental social relations of society into a total human structure, or the "essence" of capitalism, interweaving its internal social relations into a framework or structure with set boundaries. Following Marx and also Postone's reinterpretation of Marx's critical theory, I explained that the most fundamental social relations were those in which people produce their material world and those in which they circulate, exchange and consume the results of that production (Marx, 1867, pp. 165–166, 176; Marx and Engels, 1846, pp. 41, 47; Postone, 1996, p. 153). We may not immediately think of these as our most fundamental social relations, but without them there would be no society; and since we are social beings who are interdependent upon one another, soon there would be no individuals either. Of course, as I have stressed before, there are many other social relations within capitalist societies, and importantly for this aspect of my discussion, other forms of power and domination. Some of these emanate from the national and local state, others from relations of discrimination and micro and macro discourses of power and control. However, it is value that weaves together the framework or total structure of oppression and domination. It creates a web that not only sets the outer limits, boundaries, or the horizon, of the system but also reaches in all directions within the interior of this web. It is intrinsic to the fundamental relations therein, arising from and binding individuals in the fundamental relations that shape the total network of social relations that comprise the society.

The other relations and forms of domination operate in the pockets of the web and are not historically specific to capitalism. Therefore, they are not technically necessary to the system, but they are molded or shaped in a specific way by capitalism's quasi-objective form of abstract social domination. In theory, they could be eliminated, and capitalism would remain; however, in the real world they serve capitalism well (Wood, 1995). For example, they help to keep individuals divided in a variety of ways that reinforces the division of labor and deflects attention away from the fundamental structuring of the opposition between labor and capital. Moreover, they focus our attention on more overt and personal forms of domination rather than capitalism's abstract quasi-objective form. Clearly, this abstract form of domination is a more difficult form of domination to understand and also challenge, and even when value appears in objective forms, such as commodities and money, its source within a social relation between human beings remains veiled. This is why we need Marx's dialectical conceptualization—his science—to understand or fully grasp how it works.

One of the main characteristics of this quasi-objective form of social domination is compulsion—the way our lives are driven, dominated and controlled by the compulsion to create value, especially surplus-value. Marx stresses that it is living labor that creates value rather than previous labor or, as he calls it, "dead labor" embodied in machines (Marx, 1866, p. 1017), and thus it is living labor that creates the value form of wealth that is historically specific to capitalism. It is the incessant drive to create and augment value that drives the system and those engaged within it and that creates the necessity for continuous, unplanned and often irrational growth. With the emergence of fully developed industrial capitalism, the labor process, in which material wealth, or use-value, is created, becomes shaped and determined by the value-creating process, especially that part of it that entails the process of valorization (Postone, 1996, p. 346). Machinery incorporates labor as an appendage—subsumes it—within the immediate production process and increases the productivity of labor. More and more material wealth (which does not really count under capitalism) is produced in the same labor-time, and when that same labor-time is simply spread over more commodities, no more value can be created than was created before because value is measured by labor-time. Nevertheless, in order to increase the portion of that labor-time that produces surplus-value, the capitalist is constantly compelled to increase the productivity of the workforce and thus reduce "socially necessary labor-time."

Alternatively, or sometimes even in addition, capitalists are also compelled, and in turn they compel their workers, continuously to transform "socially necessary labor-time," or the nature of the social labor hour inherent in it, by intensifying the expenditure of labor-power within each hour. (I return to these points later.) These measures—that is, increasing both the productivity and the intensity of labor—together with the continuous accumulation of capital that they tend to necessitate, result in an irrational form of growth or growth that does not benefit the vast majority of human beings and is detrimental to the environment, but it is the form of growth that capitalists are compelled to engage in—the only "rational" choice they can make within the confines of an irrational system. I explain the nature of this growth more fully in chapter 3.

It is not only value that is measured in abstract units of time: Our daily activities also adhere to this regimen. We frequently assess others and are, in turn, assessed or held accountable on the basis of time or the efficient use of time. Postone points out that the dominance of abstract time was necessitated by capitalism (1996, pp. 200–216). He explains that in precapitalist societies concrete time prevailed. He means by this that time depended on another concrete variable rather than being an independent variable composed of equal and standard numerical units, as is the case with abstract time. For example, in agrarian societies the length of the working day was determined by seasonal variations that depended on the rising and setting of the sun that was, of course, determined by the earth's rotation on its axis and also its simultaneous movement around the sun. While these factors may continue to determine the various time zones around the globe, it is abstract time that governs our daily lives in accord with the dictates or logic of capitalism. Devices capable of measuring abstract time predate capitalism by centuries; however, their use only became a necessity under capitalism, and thus they became the common method of measuring time (Postone, 1996, pp. 200–216).

If we think about it, we all know how time creates pressure in our lives and that it compels us to pattern our daily existence in ways that are often stressful and less than satisfying. In many ways we are constantly being compelled to work more efficiently or organize our lives more efficiently—as the saying goes, to be more economical with our use of time—just as the capitalists do who manage to reduce the time it takes to produce their commodities. In other words, the method used to create relative surplus-value, which leads to a reduction in "socially necessary labor-time," becomes the model of efficiency that we are compelled to emulate. Postone draws our attention to yet another aspect of compulsion, one that is also inherent in "socially necessary labor-time." Marx also discusses this, but I did not recognize its importance in terms of social domination until I read Postone's account.

As I explained previously, "socially necessary labor-time" is the average time it takes for labor of average skill and intensity in specific social and historical condition to produce a particular type of commodity. Moreover, the actual value of each commodity is not based on the amount of labor-time objectified in it but is determined by the "socially necessary labor-time" for the production of that commodity. Labor-time is always measured in units of an hour; and "socially necessary labor-time" is measured according to what Postone calls the "social labor hour" (p. 288). This hour, like any other hour, is composed of minutes and seconds; therefore, one hour can contain more or fewer minutes and seconds of labor than another hour. As I noted earlier, according to Marx it can have either greater porosity or greater density (1867, p. 534). And I also explained that when capitalists work their labor forces more intensively, thus increasing the number of commodities produced in an hour, and as a consequence temporarily increase the total amount of value yielded in that unit of time, they gain surplus profits for a while but also compel their competitors to adopt the same or similar techniques. Eventually the more condensed labor hour becomes the standard reflected in the "socially necessary labor-time," and the capitalists, who were first to intensify the labor of their workers, will no longer produce a greater amount of value in an hour than do their competitors. In other words, the more compacted labor hour will become the new norm—the "social labor hour" that forms the basis of the reconstituted "socially necessary labor-time" (Marx, 1867, pp. 533–535, 661; Postone, 1996, p. 289).

When "socially necessary labor-time" is reconstituted due to an intensification of the labor it contains, there are more minutes and/or seconds of labor in every hour; however, this does not mean that the "socially necessary labor-time" is reduced as would be the case with an increase in what Marx calls the "productivity" of labor (Marx, 1867, p. 655). Focusing primarily on the more condensed social labor hour, Postone depicts the immanent dynamic of capitalism as one of transformation and reconstitution or a treadmill type of movement that is constantly propelling the system forward but then pulling it back—never superseding necessity (the need for human labor that can be exploited) but constantly reconstituting it (Postone, 1996, pp. 289, 346–347). In terms of the productivity of material wealth (which also increases with an intensification of labor) and the density of the social labor hour, it's a forward movement, but in terms of value it is a treadmill effect or a reconstitution at the previous level (p. 293). This helps us to understand better what Marx meant when he said that the same labor performed for the same amount of time "always yields the same amount of value," regardless of changes in productivity (Marx, 1867, p. 137). As I said before, this is the general rule that is temporarily breached with the intensification of labor but then reinstated as competition forces the reconstitution of the "socially necessary labor-time." Postone argues that the time unit itself changes as it becomes more compact. It is still an hour, but "the *standard* of what constitutes that amount of time" varies (Postone, 1996, p. 289). Tomaney (1990), in his study of workplace flexibility, describes how workers actually experience this compacted social labor hour. He found that they described it—or, rather, their experience of new flexible working practices—in terms of being forced into 60 minutes of work in every hour. Not only does this constant compulsion associated with "socially necessary labor-time" dominate workers in the workplace, it also forms part of an overarching form of compulsion or domination that determines the overall goals of a capitalist society and the objectives it must achieve if it is to remain viable and thus survive in the global market. However, I think that the overall effect of this domination as well as the nature of value's dynamic is more complex than the treadmill movement that Postone describes.

It seems to me that Postone conflates the two methods that individual capitalists use to extort relative surplus-value, and he then focuses primarily on the effects of the compacted social labor hour that result from the intensification of labor. As I see it, there are two main types of compulsion, usually occurring simultaneously in the world of global capitalism. Coupled with the treadmill movement brought about by the reconstitution of the social labor hour, capitalists are also reducing "socially necessary labor-time" when they increase what Marx calls the "productivity" of labor, and thus unwittingly they are reducing their need for labor. Although it is not a perfect metaphor, I see the total or combined movement as more like a ratchet effect or a movement forward, with a slight but never full movement back to the point of departure. First, there is a movement forward as the labor hour becomes denser, then a move backward as the "social labor hour" is reconstituted and with it "socially necessary labor-time," but with increasing labor productivity there is also a recurring reduction in "socially necessary labor-time" and thus another but normally not as great a movement forward. The total movement or effect is brought about by a dual or combined movement of value, or the magnitude of value produced in an hour of labor-time (a movement first forward and then back), and the movement of the time that is socially necessary for the production of a particular commodity (a recurring movement forward). In terms of the overall feeling of compulsion this creates in our lives, it is a constant feeling of being both pressed, or compressed, downward and pushed, or shoved, forward at the same time—feeling heavy and claustro-phobic and simultaneously rushed off our feet and "strung out." In fact it is a bit like running the same distance over and over, but each time being expected to run it faster, with more and heavier weights attached to our legs and arms.

The way in which value functions as a quasi-objective form of abstract social domination is often masked by other aspects of our lives—aspects that, however, are themselves constituted and determined in a specific way by value's domina-tion. Ellen Meiksins Wood (1999) argues that the modern nation-state developed in concert with capitalism—each promoting and to some extent shaping the development of the other. Although capitalism exists under different forms of governance, Marx (1843, 1875) points out that the most conducive form of governance is liberal democracy. One reason for this is that under liberal democ-racy the state is seen as a separate and autonomous sphere of activity, and this disguises the way in which the state actually functions to sustain and promote the capitalist system—the way in which the domination of value is embedded in the institutions and practices of government.

Liberal democracies also profess certain values and rights, such as equality and freedom, that only operate abstractly or formally and thus help to conceal not just the obvious but also the obtuse forms of inequality and unfreedom that affect the lives of many—the so-called losers when it comes to the zero-sum game of capitalism. Furthermore, liberal democracies demarcate and interlink the citi-zen's rights and responsibilities. However, since the rights are formal and often devalued as well (Taylor, 1991) and the responsibilities are frequently used to focus blame on the individual—to individuate or locate blame with individuals rather than their conditions of existence—this serves as a convenient scapegoat for capitalism's culpability in constituting those conditions. The overall effect of liberal democratic ideals is to camouflage their contradictory nature—their inter-nally related antithetical nature (Allman, 1999). For example, citizens are guaran-teed the right to own private property, but this has little meaning if you have no means by which you can purchase it or, alternatively, any possibility of inheriting it; nevertheless, everyone is responsible for respecting the property of those who do possess it. Freedom of speech and assembly are normally guaranteed, and it would be difficult to challenge capitalism if this were not the case; however, it is clearly the words of the dominant—the words that justify and support rather than undermine capitalism—that we encounter habitually and repeatedly in education, work and through the media. Moreover, since they seem to speak to or express what is rational within the "logic" of the system and also natural and inevitable, no plan or conspiracy is necessarily needed to sustain their dominance. This is done, first and foremost, by the value form as it moves through our social relations, structuring our existence and determining what action is necessary and equally what is not permitted or is unreasonable. Value determines our objective and subjective responses—our actions as well as our feelings and desires—as it constitutes and frames the "essence" of our material world. And it even determines the patterns and exact forms of democratic governance that are feasible within the time constraints of capitalist societies and that are also required to establish and maintain the ideological components of capitalist hegemony.

It should come as no surprise when social-democratic parties or parties of the Left manage to come into government but not to live up to our expectations or even their election pledges. They can only make concessions to social justice when the economy is booming or, alternatively, when it is so close to collapse that the legitimacy of the nation-state comes into question. Nevertheless, in either case there are definite limits to these concessions, and these are set by capitalism's necessary quest for the value form of social wealth. *Value is the social form of capitalism's "essence"—its mode of being—and without value as constituted by abstract labor within the labor–capital relation of capitalist production, capitalism would cease to exist.*

We can see that the abstract form of social domination that is historically specific to capitalism can be traced back to the twofold (dialectical) nature of the commodity form and the twofold nature of the labor that produces commodities. This should indicate what would have to be abolished if we are to create a world of peace and social and economic justice. Clearly, transferring the ownership of the means of production to either the "associated producers" or the state is not the solution. It may be a step in a much more complex process of revolutionary transformation, but when it is seen as the main criterion of socialism, the results, as history has testified, are disastrous. This becomes painfully obvious when capitalism becomes a global system, and socialist nations are forced to or attempt to compete in the world market. The compulsion of "socially necessary labor-time" and the whole force of value's social domination comes crashing down on them, just as the walls did that were supposed to keep the full thrust of capitalism contained.

With the full universalization of capitalism, the value form of social domination becomes even more pervasive and forceful. Marx and Engels depicted capitalism as a universal system more than 150 years ago (Marx and Engels, 1848). It was clear to them that the dynamic set in motion by the capitalist system would lead to the creation of a world market and the subsumption of increasing numbers of people and nations within a universal capitalist system. What we are witnessing at present is the simultaneous spread of capitalist social relations outwards into geographical space—into the furthest reaches and depths of the globe—and the spread of these relations inward as well. In long-established areas of capital's domination, more and more areas of work are being reconstituted so that an ever-increasing number of people can become the source of surplus-value. Postone identifies the origin of capital's trajectory in the dialectic of labor and time and the transformation and reconstitution of the social labor hour. That same trajectory—or, rather, that trajectory with my slight amendments—is responsible for this specific pattern of capitalist globalization. To fully grasp why capitalism's "essence" and its immanent dynamic necessitate a universal system and also this specific pattern of globalization, our focus must shift from the "essence," or "Capital in General," to the concrete totality of capitalism where we find many capitalist firms in competition. This will also facilitate a more comprehensive understanding of capitalism's totalizing and universalizing tendencies and thus its historically specific form of global social domination.

NOTES

1. The German philosopher G. W. F. Hegel's dialectical philosophy had a great influence on Marx, and Marx acknowledged his debt to Hegel. However, he also moved away from Hegel's dialectical idealism when he developed his distinctive form of materialism, which is referred to as either dialectical or historical materialism. I shall attempt to show that Marx's approach was both dialectical (a type of logic) and historical.

2. I have culled this interpretation from Rosdolsky (1977); Ollman (1976); Sekine (1998); Smith (1998) and Arthur (1998).

3. It is clear from the Table of Contents that Marx wrote this section.

4. Marx (1863b) says that the relation between capital and wage labor determines the entire character of the mode of production. This relation "reveals [capitalism's] *differentia specifica*" (p. 153).

5. Marx doesn't use the term ideology very often in his later economic writings; however, Marx's *Theories of Surplus Value* (1863a, 1863b, 1863c) is, in fact, a sustained and brilliant ideology critique.

6. At this point the relation between the capitalist and the worker is, technically, just the same as the relation between any buyer and seller in commodity exchange—that is, the market, except for the fact that in the actual transaction capitalist breach the rule of "equal exchange," or can be seen to do so if we recognize that they pay less than the potential value they acquire.

7. I use the term civil society in the same way that Marx used it, and also in the way that it is normally used within Marxism, to designate that part of the social world that lies outside the state or the sphere of political governance. It includes, for example, the economy, the family, organized religion, voluntary organizations, etc.

REFERENCES

Allman, P. (1999). *Revolutionary Social Transformation: Democratic Hopes, Political Possibilities and Critical Education.* Westport, CT: Bergin & Garvey.

Arthur, C. (1998). "Systematic Dialectics." *Science & Society,* 62 (No. 3, Autumn), 447–459.

Blackburn, R. (1999). "The New Collectivism: Pension Reform, Grey Capitalism and Complex Socialism." *New Left Review,* 233 (January/February), 3–65.

CCCS (1981). *Unpopular Education.* Education Group, Centre for Contemporary Cultural Studies. London: Hutchinson.

Gramsci, A. (1971). *Selections from the Prison Notebooks of Antonio Gramsci*, edited and translated by Quinton Hoare and Geoffrey Nowell Smith. London: Lawrence and Wishart.

Harvey, D. (1989). *The Condition of Postmodernity.* Oxford: Basil Blackwell.

Harvey, D. (1999). *The Limits to Capital* (new edition). London: Verso.

Holloway, J. (1995). "Capital Moves." *Capital & Class,* 54 (Autumn), 136–144.

Larrain J. (1979). *The Concept of Ideology.* London: Hutchinson.

Larrain, J. (1983). *Marxism and Ideology.* London: Macmillan.

Marx, K. (1843). "On the Jewish Question." In D. McLellan (Ed.), *Karl Marx: Selected Writings* (pp. 39–62). Oxford: Oxford University Press, 1977.

Marx, K. (1847). "Wage-Labour and Capital." In D. McLellan (Ed.), *Karl Marx: Selected Writings* (pp. 248–268). Oxford: Oxford University Press, 1977.

Marx, K. (1858). *Grundrisse*, translated and with a Foreword by Martin Nicolaus. Harmondsworth, U.K.: Penguin, 1973.

Marx, K. (1859). *A Contribution to the Critique of Political Economy*, translated by S. W. Ryazanskaya and edited by Maurice Dobb. London: Lawrence & Wishart, 1981.

Marx, K. (1863a). *Theories of Surplus Value,* Part 1. London: Lawrence & Wishart, 1969.

Marx, K. (1863b). *Theories of Surplus Value,* Part 2. London: Lawrence & Wishart, 1969.

Marx, K. (1863c). *Theories of Surplus Value,* Part 3. London: Lawrence & Wishart, 1972.

Marx, K. (1865) *Capital,* Vol. 3, translated by David Fernbach, Introduction by Ernest Mandel. Harmondsworth, U.K.: Penguin, 1981.

Marx, K. (1866). "Resultate" in *Capital*, Vol. 1 (Appendix, pp. 943–1084). Harmondsworth, U.K.: Penguin, 1976.

Marx, K. (1867). *Capital*, Vol. 1, translated by Ben Fowkes, Introduction by Ernest Mandel. Harmondsworth, U.K.: Penguin, 1976.

Marx, K. (1875). "Critique of the Gotha Programme." In D. McLellan (Ed.), *Karl Marx: Selected Writings* (pp. 564–570). Oxford: Oxford University Press, 1977.

Marx, K. (1878). *Capital*, Vol. 2, translated by David Fernbach, Introduction by Ernest Mandel. Harmondsworth, U.K.: Penguin, 1978.

Marx, K., and Engels, F. (1844). *The Holy Family.* In K. Marx and F. Engels, *Collected Works*, Vol. 4 (pp. 5–211). London: Lawrence & Wishart, 1975.

Marx, K., and Engels, F. (1846). *The German Ideology.* Moscow: Progress, 1976.

Marx, K., and Engels, F. (1848). "The Communist Manifesto." In D. McLellan (Ed.), *Karl Marx: Selected Writings* (pp. 221–247). Oxford: Oxford University Press, 1977.

Milonakis, D. (1997). "The Dynamics of History: Structure and Agency in Historical Evolution." *Science & Society*, 61 (No. 2, Autumn), 302–329.

Nicolaus, M. (1973). "Foreword." In K. Marx, *Grundrisse* (pp. 7–63), 1858. Harmondsworth, U.K.: Penguin.

Ollman, B. (1976). *Alienation: Marx's Conception of Man in Capitalist Society* (second edition). Cambridge: Cambridge University Press.

Postone, M. (1996). *Time, Labor, and Social Domination: A Reinterpretation of Marx's Critical Theory.* Cambridge: Cambridge University Press.

Rosdolsky, R. (1977). *The Making of Marx's Capital.* London: Pluto Press.

Rubin, I. I. (1972). *Essays on Marx's Theory of Value*, translated from the third edition, 1928, by M. Samardija and F. Perlman. Detroit, MI: Black & Red.

Sayer, D. (1983). *Marx's Method: Ideology, Science and Critique in "Capital"* (second edition). Brighton: Harvester Press.

Sayer, D. (1987). *The Violence of Abstraction: The Analytical Foundations of Historical Materialism.* Oxford: Basil Blackwell.

Sekine, T. (1998). "The Dialectic of Capital: A Unoist Interpretation." *Science & Society,* 62 (No. 3), 434–445.

Smith, T. (1998). "Value Theory and Dialectics." *Science & Society,* 62 (No. 3), 460–470.

Taylor, C. (1991). *The Ethics of Authenticity.* Cambridge, MA: Harvard University Press.

Thompson, E., P. (1974). *The Making of the English Working Class.* Harmondsworth, U.K.: Penguin.

Tickell, A. (1999). "Unstable Futures: Controlling and Creating Risks in International Money." In L. Panitch and C. Leys (Eds.), *Socialist Register 1999, Global Capitalism Versus Democracy* (pp. 248–268). Rendlesham, U.K.: Merlin.

Tolman, C. (1981). "The Metaphysics of Relations in Klaus Reigel's Dialectics of Human Development." *Human Development,* 24, 33–51.

Tomaney, J. (1990). "The Reality of Workplace Flexibility." *Capital & Class*, 40 (Spring), 29–60.

Wood, E. M. (1995). *Democracy Against Capitalism; Renewing Historical Materialism.* Cambridge: Cambridge University Press.

Wood, E. M. (1999). "Unhappy Families: Global Capitalism in a World of Nation-States." *Monthly Review,* 51 (No. 3) [http://www.monthlyreview.org].

3

From Essence to Appearance: Capitalism, Part II

In chapter 2, I discussed the "essence" of capitalism. This chapter is about the concrete totality of capitalism or the way in which the essence operates under the competitive conditions that pertain when many capitalist firms are in competition with one another. These competitive conditions are absolutely necessary for the full realization or functioning of capital's essence (Marx, 1865, p. 1020). For the most part, I will still be discussing capitalism in terms of generalizations that would apply to any fully developed capitalist society rather than referring to specific aspects of a particular capitalist society at a particular point in time. When speaking of the essence, I also employed Rosdolsky's (1977) expression, "Capital in General," and in a sense I am still talking about "capital in general" but, in this case, at a higher level of complexity—the complexity that we need to grasp when considering fully developed capitalist societies and the world market. To develop a comprehensive understanding of global capitalism, we must follow Marx by moving from the abstract and simple to the more concrete and complex reality of many capitals in competition. Marx explains the concrete reality of capitalism by dividing it into two sections; I will follow the same procedure because it adds clarity to the explanation. By proceeding in this way, I will be adhering to my previous discussion of the total process of capitalist production—that is, the internal relation, or dialectical contradiction, between production and circulation/exchange.

To recap: I first discussed the contradiction between capital and labor in the "immediate" production process wherein surplus-value is created, and then I brought in the contradiction between production and circulation to complete the picture of the entire capitalist production process—in other words, my explanation followed first the creation and then the realization of surplus-value (Marx, 1865, p. 117). In the same vein, here I first discuss the total capital of society—social capital—in terms of the competition between industrial, or productive, capitalists, and then I expand the discussion to include commercial capital—the capitalists who deal with circulation—in order to provide a full explanation of the concrete totality of capitalism. My explanation is drawn primarily from Volume 3 of *Capital*; however, it is not my intent, nor would it be possible in a book of this length, to go into all the detail that Marx offers. Instead, I provide only the detail that is necessary to explain how capitalism actually works and to offer an understanding of how the inherent tendencies of capitalism lead to the necessary development of the particular type or pattern of globalization we are experiencing. I begin by considering briefly how the capitalists themselves normally operate and how they perceive what is going on.

Every industrial capitalist—or, for that matter, any commodity-producing capitalist or productive capitalist—invests a certain amount of capital in each production cycle.[1] Some of this capital—that is, value in its money form that is being used as capital—is used to purchase raw materials, auxiliary materials (such as energy supplies) and means of production; and some purchases labor-power. The latter sum is, of course, the most fundamental investment, because it provides the basis for the creation of the capitalists' profits. However, capitalists simply consider the capital they lay out in wages—or what Marx calls variable capital—as part of their total investment, or outlay, of capital. I explain, in this chapter, why Marx's distinction between variable capital that is used to purchase labor-power and constant capital that is used to purchase raw materials, means of production, and so on is so important to his scientific exposition of capitalism. The sum of the variable and constant capital is called the cost price of the commodity (Marx, 1865, p. 127). Capitalists think that this sum of money represents the actual value of their commodities (p. 127).

When a commodity enters the sphere of circulation and comes into competition with other commodities, capitalists try to sell the commodity for at least the market price, or the average price, commanded by that particular type of commodity. If competition is intense, those who can afford to do so will sell their commodities below the market price; however, they can only do this if they can recoup what they consider to be the actual value of their commodity—its cost price—plus at least some profit. However, if selling at the market price allows no margin for profit, then there is a problem, and if this problem continues over a period of time, it means ruin for the capitalist. Whatever the situation, capitalists are focused on the market price and the prices their commodities can command or must command in order, at a minimum, to repay their costs. When they make a profit, they consider this to have happened as a result of keeping their costs down—by obtaining their inputs more cheaply than the competition. If they make an exceptionally high profit, they attribute this to their ability to sell the commodity at a price above its cost price. However, most importantly, they assume that their profits derive from the total capital they have employed; and they estimate their profit rate by dividing the increment, or surplus, over the cost price of the commodity by the total capital employed—as reflected in the formula: s/C, where s is the surplus and C is the total capital (p. 133).

If a firm manages to make a good rate of profit compared to the average rate of profit on a particular commodity, this attracts investment in this firm—either convincing the same capitalist to reinvest or possibly also encouraging the inward flow of investment from other capitalists. And this leads to capital accumulation and expanded reproduction as far as this firm is concerned or even capitalism as a whole if no other firms are adversely affected. This further accumulation might result in the capitalist investing more in both variable and constant capital or increasing expenditure on only the constant capital—investing, for example, in new technology in order to increase the productivity of the existing or even a reduced labor force. Either decision is a reasonable one for capitalists, given their perception of the situation. However, when we consider what is actually happening, it is a far from reasonable decision for capitalism as a whole—the entire capitalist system and its continuing survival.

THE ORGANIC COMPOSITION OF CAPITAL
AND THE REDISTRIBUTION OF SURPLUS-VALUE
AMONG CAPITALISTS

So much for how capitalists perceive the situation! From Marx's dialectical analysis, we know that the value contained in the commodity is equal to the sum of the constant capital *plus* the variable capital *plus* the surplus-value, or $c + v + s$. All the newly created value is expressed in the sum of $v + s$. The amount or mass of surplus-value created depends on the rate of surplus-value. The mass of surplus-value can be calculated by multiplying the variable capital by the rate of surplus-value—this rate is the ratio of the surplus-value to the total variable capital—or s/v (Marx, 1865, pp. 141, 249). For convenience, Marx often assumes that the rate of surplus-value is 100%—which means that there is the same amount of necessary labor as there is surplus labor, or workers work the same amount of time for themselves as they do for the capitalists. In this case, the surplus-value is expressed in the same quantity as the variable capital; for example, a capital of 100 units composed of $c80 + v20$ would produce a surplus-value of 20 and can be represented by the formula: $C100 = c80 + v20 + s20$ (Marx uses C to stand for the total capital; therefore, this formula actually includes both what the capitalists see and what they do not). For this discussion, we can retain the assumption that s/v is 100%, so long as it is understood that the rate depends on the ratio of the surplus-value to the variable capital and therefore can alter with a lowering or a heightening of the ratio between necessary and surplus labor—s/v is an index of the degree to which labor is exploited (pp. 132–133). Therefore, the mass of surplus-value, or total amount of surplus-value, in the commodity depends upon the rate of surplus-value. In the example, with a variable capital of 20, if the rate of surplus-value were 75% not 100%, the total amount of surplus-value would be 15 rather than 20 (20 × .75, not 20 × 1.00).

In addition, we also know from Marx's analysis that the "socially necessary labor-time" actually determines the value of the commodity once it is produced for market exchange. Therefore, the actual value of the commodity is based not on the real value it contains but on the amount of labor-time that is socially necessary for its production. As I explained in chapter 2, if the value of a commodity were determined by the actual time expended in its production, then it would be possible for the least skillful or even the laziest worker to create the commodity with the greatest value, and this is why the value of commodities produced for the market must be based on an average, or more precisely, the "socially necessary labor-time" it takes for their production. This value—that is, "socially necessary labor-time"—is usually expressed as the market value (pp. 279, 281–284).[2] The market price, which is what captures the attention of the capitalists engaged in competitive struggle, fluctuates around this market value according to supply and demand. Therefore, market value is the central point around which deviations in price move in one direction or another according to supply and demand (Marx, 1865, pp. 279, 281–284).

When demand is greater than supply, then the market price will be higher than the market value; when it is less than the supply, then the market price will be less. When supply and demand are equal (which happens only by chance or accident), they cancel each other out and have no effect on the price; and the market price is then equal to the market value or is determined directly by the market value, or "socially necessary labor-time" (p. 291). Assuming that market value and market price coincide, the capitalist whose commodity's value coincides with the market value—which might be, for example, $c80 + v20 + s20$— can even sell the commodity for less than its value of 120, in fact for any price between 100.01 and 120, and still realize a profit or an excess above the cost price of the commodity. Therefore, any price above 100 will return not only the cost price, or what the capitalist thinks is the value of the commodity, but also an increment, or profit, that is in excess of this, and this will be true even when the commodity is sold for less than its value as determined by the "socially necessary labor-time" (pp. 127, 180).

So far, I have discussed what happens in very simple terms, or in terms of the competition that exists between capitalists selling the same commodity, produced with the same inputs. In this case, we can see that the problem with capitalists' perceptions of the situation involves a simple misunderstanding. The surplus-value that is latent in the commodity only becomes visible to the capitalist when it changes into the money form. And as this only happens when the commodity is sold, it appears as if the profit or money form of the surplus has just been created in exchange. Remember, they think that the value of their commodities is composed of just their cost price (or k), or the sum of their constant and variable capital; in other words, $k = c + v$, which in the example I have given is the same as C, or the total capital employed, and this would only be the case when the capitalist uses up the total constant capital in producing the commodity. They don't realize that the value of their commodity actually equals $c + v + s$. There has been a simple change in form as value moves and is transformed from its commodity form to its money form, but the latter is the form in which capitalists actually see their profits for the first time (pp. 128, 267). In other words, it is only when the commodity is sold that they become aware of s, or what we know is the unpaid labor—or the surplus-value—and therefore they think it has come from the act of selling. However, if the situation were as simple as this, it might be fairly easy to challenge the misconception. To understand the full complexity (or nearly the full complexity) of what is happening, we need to take into considera-tion the different composition of the capitals involved in this competition—to consider what Marx calls their organic composition, the different quantities of constant capital in relation to variable capital.

Let us take two capitalists, each investing 100 units of total capital (units of whatever denomination or currency the capitalists are employing). Looking where capitalists fail to look, we can see that in the case of one of these capitalists, the 100 is composed of 95 in constant capital and only 5 in variable capital; while the other capital of 100 is composed of only 5 constant capital but 95 variable capital (labor-power). Both have a 100% rate of surplus-value or exploit their labor force to the same extent; therefore the amount of surplus-value they create is the same quantity as their variable capital. The value contained in the first commodity is $c95 + v5 + s5 = 105$; and the value contained in the second is $c5 + v95 + s95 = 195$. Since the capitalists in this example represent exactly opposite positions, one is more than likely to be producing in less than "socially necessary labor-time" and one in more than that time, and therefore the market value for their commodities will lie somewhere between these two extremes. If the market value and price are the same—say, 150—and both capitalists sell at this price, then the first capitalist—the one with more constant capital—receives 45 over the value of the commodity and an increment of 50 over the cost price. The second, who spends more on variable capital, also receives an increment of 50 over the cost price; but in this case the capitalists receives 45 less than the value contained in the commodity—in other words, much less surplus-value than has been produced. These two capitalists have produced very different amounts of surplus-value, but this has worked in favor of the one who produces less surplus-value rather than the one who produces more, which is obviously very contradictory and seems absurd. This has happened because the competition between all the capitalists involved has the effect of redistributing the total surplus-value created. Before explaining exactly how this happens, I want to stress that it is important to remember that the "socially necessary labor-time" around which market prices fluctuate is established when commodities come to the market or are produced for the purpose of market exchange, and it is this that determines whether a commodity is sold for more than or less than the newly created value—labor-time—it contains. Let us consider precisely how the extremely contradictory redistribution of surplus-value occurs.

The Formation of a General Rate of Profit and the Transformation of Value into Prices of Production

Capitalist competition involves more than the competition between commodity producers, or owners, trying to sell the same commodities on the market. Apart from the competition between two capitalists trying to sell televisions there is, for example, competition between those capitalists and others trying to sell consumers a computer rather than a television. However, there is also another type of competition as well—one that has the most important effect on the entire economy. Capitalist firms compete for the investment of capital, and this results in the constant inflow and outflow of capital, into firms with higher profit rates and out of those with lower ones (Marx, 1865, p. 297). It is this continuous migration and redistribution of capital investments that leads to the redistribution of surplus-value (pp. 297–301; Rubin, 1972, p. 227). This happens because capitalists invest where they can receive the highest return on their investment, or at least they try to do so if they are operating in the spirit of true capitalists. Therefore, it is perfectly reasonable for capitalists to invest some of their profits in firms other than their own. We will see how this becomes a much more common occurrence as the division of "labor" between capitalists themselves develops. However, the point to keep in mind is that capital will flow out of firms with low rates of profit and into firms with high or higher rates of profit. Within this competitive process of capital flows, the organic composition of the different capitals plays a significant and crucial role—a role to which capitalists are oblivious.

As I indicated in a previous example, capitalist firms have varying proportions of constant and variable capital that form what Marx calls their organic composition. Let us begin by considering three different spheres of production with different organic compositions. I will focus on the capital in each of these spheres that has the mean, or average, organic composition for that sphere and also assume that these capitals are of equal size and that they all have a 100% rate of surplus-value, and, therefore, the amount of surplus-value or profit will be the same as the variable capital. (Please note that when I begin to discuss the total social capital—that is, the total capital in society—as I am beginning to do here, the term "profit" can be substituted for surplus-value because the total amount of profit produced in society is the same as the total amount of surplus-value (Marx, 1865, p. 273). In the case of the first capital, which I will designate as **A**, the total capital of 100 invested is made up of 80 constant capital and 20 variable capital, and the profit produced is 20. In the second capital or **B**, there is 60 constant and 40 variable, and thus it produces a profit of 40; and in **C**, the third capital, there is

95 constant, 5 variable and 5 profit. The rate of profit in each case is the surplus, profit, increment or whatever we call it, divided by the total capital, which in each case is 100—the total capital invested and the cost price in this case are the same and are therefore the quantity that represents to the capitalist the actual value of the commodity. In the case of **A**, the profit rate would be 20%; in **B**, it would be 40% and in **C**, it would be 5%. If such profit rates on capitals of equal size actually existed, it would be a disaster for capitalism. Capital would flow into the least advanced, or more labor-intensive, firms or the spheres of production in which these firm were predominant—firms with a lower organic composition, which is a characteristic of less developed forms of capitalism. Firms with a lower organic composition signify that the overall social productivity of society is less developed. In this example, capital would flow into firm **B** or the sphere of production for which **B** reflects the average rate of profit, because **B** has the highest rate of profit—40%. These different averages do not exist, because competition leads to an equalization of the profit rates between the different spheres (pp. 267–268, 281–299).

It is important to remember that in every sphere of production there will be some firms with higher organic compositions actually producing below the average rate of profit and some with lower organic compositions producing above the average. As in the previous example, those who produce below the average but can still sell at the market value, will receive the same increment over their cost price—the same increment on a capital of equal size—and thus the same profit as those with average and below-average organic compositions for a capital of 100. Moreover, they can afford to sell for less than the average price and thus should sell more commodities, and even when this is at a slightly lower profit on each item, they still stand to make either the same or even a larger profit on the total capital of 100 than other firms. For example, the capitalist who sells three commodities at 10% makes more total profit on an investment of 100 than does the capitalist who sells one commodity for 20%. All of these processes of production, selling, buying, investing and competing, both within and between spheres, take place simultaneously on a daily basis, and the competition for the investment of capital that results tends to equalize the different profit rates, creating a general or average rate of profit across all the spheres (pp. 257–258, 297). The averages for each sphere do not exist once capitalism is fully developed because they are always tending toward the general rate of profit that results from the overall competition—competition among all the spheres—for capital investment (p. 297).

There is, therefore, a continuous equalization of the "ever-renewed inequalities" that exist between different spheres and firms (p. 298). Furthermore, this equalization is accomplished more readily when capital is more mobile and can thus be transferred between spheres more easily and also when labor-power can be moved more rapidly from one sphere to another (p. 298). The general rate of profit adjusts the various profits to the rate of those that have the mean or average organic composition—that is, those that reflect the average for the total social capital and in which profit coincides with surplus-value (p. 273).

When we are therefore dealing with a fully developed capitalist economy, this general rate of profit affects the value of every commodity in much the same way as the "socially necessary labor-time" for the production of a particular commodity affects the value of the commodity once it is produced for the market. Remember: in that case it was the "socially necessary labor-time" that determined the actual value of the commodity rather than the real or exact value—that is, labor-time—that the commodity contained. When we look at the situation on a more concrete and complex level, instead of the value of the commodity being based on either the sum of $c + v + s$ or the "socially necessary labor-time" for the production of that commodity, the value of the commodity is transformed into what Marx calls the price of production (Marx, 1865, pp. 257, 263, 274). The price of production of a commodity is the sum of the constant capital, or c, plus the variable capital, or v, plus the general rate of profit, p. I hasten to add that this is no more the actual price of the commodity than $c + v + s$, or the value was (pp. 263–274, 281). Just as before, we are looking at the value of the commodity—that is, the transformed form of value—rather than price, a form of value that still reflects "socially necessary labor-time" and that is, therefore, the central point around which prices oscillate (p. 281). Value—especially surplus-value—still governs this price of production. However, the price of production no longer reflects either the precise value, or labor-time, contained in each commodity or that which is determined by the "socially necessary labor-time" for the production of a particular commodity (p. 277). Instead, when we bring competition into the picture and thus consider capitalism in its full concrete complexity, we find that the value of each commodity is determined by the ratio between the total mass of surplus-value produced in the economy and the total capital—the entire social capital employed (pp. 267–268, 273, 299).

Therefore, when capitalists sell their commodities, they do not receive back either the surplus-value they produce or even the surplus-value or profit produced in their own sphere of production. Instead, they receive back a share of the total surplus-value produced during "a given [period of] time" according to the size of their capital investment, regardless of its organic composition (p. 258). To reiterate, this takes place because competition leads to the formation of a general rate of profit, which transforms the value of commodities, or $c + v + s$, into prices of production, or $c + v + p$, where p is the general rate of profit on each 100 units of capital advanced (pp. 257–259, 273–279, 297). I should also note, here, another point that I do not explain in great detail because it is not necessary to the level of understanding I am trying to convey. In the price of production of a commodity, the c and v, or the cost price of the commodity, remain specific to their sphere of production and therefore reflect the "socially necessary labor-time" for that sphere (p. 259; for a more complete explanation, see Marx, 1865, pp. 258–266). It is the surplus-value that is transformed in the price of production and which relates to the total social capital and the total mass of surplus-value produced.

Marx offers numerous examples to support his scientific analysis of what is actually happening. Obviously, space does not permit me to reproduce that degree of detail. My examples are, therefore, not proof of the explanation but simply representative examples of the proof Marx offers. There is another aspect that enters into the formation of the general rate of profit, to which I turn after the following brief summary of the explanation just given.

In a fully developed capitalist economy, a general rate of profit is formed as competition drives capital through the various spheres of production, always seeking to invest where the rate of return is the highest. The Law of Value underpins the whole process (Marx, 1865, pp. 267–269, 280–281). However, when capitalism is considered in its full complexity, which involves the fundamental factor of competition, we find that the values of commodities are transformed into prices of production. Now, rather than being sold at a price that, as a minimum requirement, reflects the market value or "socially necessary labor-time," they must be sold at prices that "deliver the average profit [per 100 units of social capital, or the general rate of profit], i.e. at prices of production" (p. 297). Since the general rate of profit is equal to the total mass of surplus-value divided by the total social capital—that is, the total capital in society—the total mass of profit produced in society is equal to the total mass of surplus-value (pp. 273–274). Furthermore, if all the prices of production were added together, we would get the same sum as we would if we were to add together the value of all the commodities produced (p. 273). As I noted before, the general rate of profit is also affected by another factor that is extremely important when we consider the globalization of capitalism—that is, when we consider it in light of the further explanations that follow throughout this chapter.

The level of the general rate of profit also is affected by how much of the total social capital is invested in different spheres of production (p. 262). If a large proportion is invested in spheres with a high organic composition—that is, those with a greater value of constant capital in relation to the variable capital, which usually indicates more advanced technology—then this will weight the average in the direction of the rate of profit of those spheres. Conversely, if a greater proportion of the total capital is invested in labor-intensive industries, then the average will be weighted in that direction (Marx, 1865, p. 262). For example, if we take a very simple example of how the amount of capital advanced affects the outcome, we can begin by considering a total social capital of 200 units of capital made up of only 2 capitalist firms, each with 100 units of capital. If one of these has a variable capital of 60 and at a 100% rate of surplus-value it produces a profit of 60 and the other has a variable capital of 5 (with the same rate of surplus-value) and produces a profit of 5, then the total profit on the social capital is 65. This is divided by 200, or simply 2 (that is, 2 capitals of 100 units each) to arrive at a general rate of profit of 32.5%. However, if the firm with the variable capital of 5 advanced 500 instead of 100 units, then the total profit would be 85—that is, 60 + 25 (or $5v \times 5$ units of 100). The sum of 85 is divided by 600, or simply 6—that is, 1 capital of 100 units and another of 500 and therefore 100 + 500 = 600, or simply 1 + 5 = 6—and this gives a general rate of profit of approximately 14%. Conversely, if the firm with more variable capital were to advance 500 while the other firm continued with 100 units, then the total profit would be 305 (60 × 5 + 5 = 305) and the general rate of profit approximately 50% (305/6). (For a slightly more complicated example of this, see Marx, 1865, p. 262.) Thus the general rate of profit is not only an average of the profits in the different spheres, but also a matter of "the relative weight which these different rates of profit assume in the formation of this average" (p. 262). However, if the investment is evenly distributed, it is an average, as I said before, that reflects the mean organic composition (p. 273).

If we look again at how the situation is perceived by the capitalists, we can see that they have an even greater reason to misread the situation than they did when things were much simpler. The actual appearance is even more misleading once the general rate of profit enters the picture. The main problem is that capitalists are not aware that the organic composition of their total investment plays a very significant role. They think that profit relates to their total capital and have no idea of the crucial role played by variable capital. And, once the general rate of profit has been established, the crucial role that variable capital plays relates to the total social capital rather than directly to the capitalist who has employed it. Thus the idea that the rate of profit has nothing to do with their own variable capital or, for that matter, the variable capital and thus surplus-value produced in their own sphere of production is reinforced (Marx, 1865, pp. 267–268). Obviously, they also have no idea of the role their variable capital plays when it comes to the total social capital and thus the health and survival of the capitalist system as well as their own profits. Moreover, when we consider the concrete complexity of a fully developed capitalist society and all the daily activities that take place on the surface of society, the essence of capitalism, that governs the whole process and the movements involved, becomes further and further removed from view—further submerged below the surface of capitalist society (p. 269). This is why it takes a dialectical, scientific process of thought and analysis to penetrate this surface complexity or the forms in which the essence is expressed. And it is also why the analysis must be carefully presented as a dialectical unfolding of the results in the way that Marx demonstrates. However, his painstaking presentation of the results can only be fully understood if grasped dialectically.

Marx offers an example in which he uses five capitals of 100 units each but with varying organic compositions, and he treats them as the averages for five different spheres comprising a total economy (Marx, 1865, p. 255). The average rate of profit works out at 22% (we can ignore the weight they assume in forming the average as they all represent capitals of equal size). I will use just the three capitals in one of my previous examples in order to be as brief as possible and also so that there are only three capitals to think about at one time. In fact, the rate of profit for just those three works out at a figure very close to 22%; so I will retain 22% as the average rate of profit rather than complicating the arithmetic with fractions. (Once again the rate of surplus-value is 100%.) The price of production for capital **A** is $c80 + v20 + p22 = 122$, and this is 2 above its value. Capitals **B** ($c60 + v40$) and **C** ($c95 + v5$) also have production prices of 122, but this is 18 below the value of **B** and 17 above the value of **C**. In other words, **B**'s value is 140, and 140 minus the production price of 122 comes to a loss of 18; and **C**'s value is 105, or 17 less than the production price and therefore a gain of 17. If I had used all the capitals in Marx's example, there would have been exactly the same number or sum of values below as there are above the production price (pp. 256–257). In terms of understanding capital's tendencies, the way it moves and develops for better or worse, it is important to focus on capital **C**—the one with the highest organic composition.

Capital **C** produces commodities containing less newly created value than the other capitals, but because its total size is equal to all the others, it can command the same rate of profit as the others, since the rate of profit is calculated on the total capital and the price of production is the same for capitals of equal size (Marx, 1865, p. 257). [Remember again, however, that prices of production are not the same thing as prices paid for the commodities—just as values were not the same as prices. However, in conditions of equilibrium between supply and demand (which only happens by chance or accident and thus rarely), production prices coincide with the market price—just as market values, which were based on the "socially necessary labor-time" for a particular species of commodity, did—but when the equilibrium is disturbed, then they serve as a central point around which market prices fluctuate (pp. 277–281).] Capital **C**'s commodities have less newly created value because capital **C** has a high organic composition and thus a greater proporton of value tied up in constant than variable capital, a great deal more relative to the average (pp. 244–255). This normally reflects that capital **C** uses more advanced machinery—automated machinery or advanced technology in general—and thus has the capacity for higher productivity—the production of more use-values in a given amount of time with the same expenditure of labor. [In other words, each use-value is produced in less time; here my examples are based on the productivity of labor rather than its intensity in order to keep my explanation as straightforward as possible.] This higher productivity results in the situation to which I referred previously. If the other capitals only produce one commodity during a specific period of time (e.g., a day or week) but capital **C** produces two, then capital **C**'s cost price is spread over two commodities rather than being absorbed totally within the one, as it is for the others. Each commodity has a cost price of 50 rather than 100; they could therefore be sold even at a lower rate of profit—as low as 11%, for 61 or half the price of production (122)—yet this capital of 100 would still command a rate of profit of 22% on the total capital invested, just like its competitors. And if capital **C** produces three or more commodities to everyone else's one, then it will receive a higher rate of profit on the total investment of 100. Alternatively, when demand for the commodity is good, capital **C**'s two commodities can be sold at their price of production or the same production price as all the others. And then capital **C** will make what Marx calls a "surplus profit" (p. 279).

Obviously increasing productivity becomes very important to capitalists when they see this kind of effect; and also, obviously, their perception of what actually lies behind the surplus profit will be more blurred than ever. They cannot see how the total mass of surplus-value produced in society effects the general rate of profit and, as a consequence, the possibility of some capitalists, precisely those who have contributed the least surplus-value, obtaining surplus profits—the type of profits that are, of course, extremely attractive to investors. Because the investments flowing into these firms lead to the equalization of the rate of profit and thus the redistribution of surplus-value, Marx referred to this facetiously in a letter to Engels as capitalist communism—"from each capitalist according to his total workforce and to each capitalist according to his total investment" (cited in Harvey, 1999, p. 63). Here I need to consider in closer detail the effect that capital **C**'s success will have on the other capitalists with whom capital **C** competes in the commodity market and, as a consequence, the effect it will have on the entire economy.

The Law of the Falling Rate of Profit

Each of the two commodities produced by capital **C**, which has an organic composition of $c95:v5$, contains even less paid labor than one commodity would have done but also less unpaid or surplus labor as well—half as much. Even if capitalist **C** were aware of this, it would not be cause for concern in his or her individual case because the surplus-value realized when these commodities are sold is not the surplus-value they contain (Marx, 1865, p. 270). To reiterate, it is not even the average surplus-value produced in their sphere of production. Instead, it is a share of the total social surplus-value—produced in a given time— that falls to each 100 units of capital advanced (p. 258). However, the fact that capital **C** receives back this general rate of profit even though it is composed of more constant than variable capital can, and invariably does, lead to a problem for capitalism as a whole.

If capitalist **C** manages to sell both commodities, then just as much surplus-value will have been contributed to the total surplus-value of society as capital **C** contributed with a lower level of productivity. In either case, however, capital **C** contributes much less surplus-value to the total than do capitals with more living labor. Furthermore, if capital **C** fails to sell either one or both commodities, and this is true when any commodity remains unsold, then the latent surplus-value in the commodity diminishes—that is, the process of devaluation begins. If a commodity is never sold, then value is totally destroyed. Even if capital **C** manages to sell both commodities at a reduced price and still command the average rate of profit or more, this often means that other commodity producers/owners will not be able to sell their commodities, and thus the overall effect is a reduction of the total surplus-value in the economy. It is important to recognize that value must keep moving in order to remain value. If it remains too long in the commodity form—that is, unsold, or unrealized—it eventually disappears. And not only must value in the commodity form be transformed into the money form, it must be used again, in the production of commodities, if the original value is to increase and thus continue to function as capital.

Let us look at what happens in the situation where capital **C** receives surplus profit or when supply has not yet caught up with demand and, as a result, capital **C** can sell the commodities either at the price of production or at a price just below that value. In fact, if capital **C** takes that latter option, the existence of the cheaper commodities will probably increase the number of people who can express effective demand—who can afford to pay the price of the commodity. Therefore, demand will remain buoyant initially. However, capitalists **B** and **A** and any others involved in competition with **C** will not settle for this state of affairs indefinitely, and those who fail to make the necessary adjustments as quickly as the others, perhaps beguiled by the increased demand, will not survive for long. The capitalists who recognize what must be done in order to remain competitive and viable in the market will make every attempt to increase their own productivity. For example, they might try to increase the exploitation of their workforce directly—a tactic normally preferred rather than incurring greater costs. However, since there are social limits on the degree to which they can exploit their labor force, or raise the rate of surplus-value, in relation to their competitors, they will eventually end up having to increase the organic composition of their own capital. When competition forces these capitalists to adopt the same or similar techniques, it brings an end to the first capitalist's—capital **C**'s— advantageous position. As a consequence, it will not be long before the market value (the newly established "socially necessary labor-time") will be altered. [Of course, as I indicated before, prices of production take the place of market values once the general rate of profit is established, but the movement of these is still governed by "socially necessary labor-time" and therefore the Law of Value (Marx, 1865, pp. 280–281).] The gap that existed between capital **C**'s price and the average market price closes, and with this comes the end of surplus profits— at least until the whole process is repeated again in other circumstances. In addition, this situation usually foments other problems.

If all the conditions remain the same—that is, the rate of surplus-value remains the same as does the size of the capitals—but all the capitalists in competition with capital **C** start producing their commodities with capital of a higher organic composition, then the total amount of surplus-value produced will decline. When this is a general tendency or one affecting several spheres of production, then it will impact on the general rate of profit because the latter is determined by the ratio between the total surplus-value and the total social capital—S/C. Using simple figures, it is easy to see what happens to the general rate of profit when the total mass of surplus-value decreases, with the total social capital remaining the same. If there is a total social capital of 2000 and a total mass of surplus-value of

500, then the general rate of profit is 500/2,000 or 25%. However, if the total mass of surplus-value is reduced to 400, then the general rate of profit is 400/2,000 or 20%—the general rate falls from 25 to 20%. Marx calls this "The Law of the Tendential Fall in the Rate of Profit" (p. 318). He also explains that it operates as a tendency because there are many counteracting or countervailing factors that slow down the fall and that can even, under certain conditions, temporarily reverse it. Nevertheless, he also explains that it is a necessary or inherent tendency that will constantly reassert itself (p. 339). Therefore, for the sake of brevity it is simpler to refer to it as the Law of the Falling Rate of Profit.

The Law of the Falling Rate of Profit results from the way in which the Law of Value asserts itself in a fully developed capitalist society wherein capitalists engage in competition with one another both in selling their commodities and in attempting to attract the investment of capital. The falling rate of profit encapsulates the contradictory nature of capitalism. As a mode of production in the history of humanity, capitalism can be seen to have a purpose or a task to be achieved. It is a mode of production that increases the productive capacity of human beings, accelerating the productivity of society and thus the production of an ever-increasing mass of use-values or material wealth. As I explained in chapter 2, the irony is that despite the fact that material wealth or abundance, and with it the elimination of scarcity, is what most people actually want and need, capitalist wealth is based on value, not use-value, or material wealth. Therefore, despite the fantastic productivity that capitalism breeds, scarcity remains and, as a consequence, poverty, hunger, homelessness, and so on remain long after they could have been eliminated. In fact, they will never be, nor can they be, eliminated under capitalism because—if for no other reason—they serve the purpose of constantly reminding people of what might happen to them if they do not accept capital's conditions. But the irony does not stop here.

For example, the competition that drives capitalists to increase their productivity leads them to do this by increasing the organic composition of their capital—to acquire the most advanced and productive technology and to reduce labor costs in any way possible and thus to reduce their variable capital relative to their constant capital. Since capitalism must always be understood in terms of relationships and ratios, it is important to note that this decrease in variable relative to constant capital even happens while increasing numbers of people are being drawn into the labor–capital relation—when the actual number of working people is increasing. Therefore, no matter how much the total surplus-value grows, it always decreases relative to the total capital employed. The falling rate of profit has to do with this relationship between constant and variable capital—the organic composition rather than absolute magnitudes (Marx, 1865, p. 323). Furthermore, at the same time as the higher organic composition increases productivity and thus the mass of commodities produced, it increases the necessity of selling all the commodities produced. Each commodity, on its own, returns less profit, and with no plan or limits to the increases in productivity of all the capitalists in competition with one another, supply often outstrips demand—even when the commodities become cheaper. This results in the recurring crises of overproduction that are characteristic of capitalism and which, when they extend throughout the system, threaten everyone's well-being.

Competition, therefore, forces capitalists, or a number of them, to adopt the new more productive technology and/or organizational forms (which can also increase productivity with or without technological change), leading to a situation in which the total output of commodities will be massively increased. As a consequence, supply soon exceeds demand. This is precisely what Marx meant when he stressed that the social forces of production would come into opposition or contradiction with the social relation of production. The social forces of production that capitalism brings forth—forces capable of producing in abundance—are in contradiction with the social relation of production because this relation results in the value form of wealth that has a tendency to decrease in relative terms as the social forces are developed, and it also determines the relations of distribution and thus consumption (Marx, 1865, p. 367; 1858, p. 832; 1875, pp. 569–570). Within these relations, the needs of the vast majority of humanity are denied because they do not have the purchasing power to realize the value of the commodities, no matter how much they need them. Moreover, often even the collective purchasing inclination of those who do have the means to acquire what they want is not sufficient to realize the value of all of the commodities produced; and therefore a great deal of productive effort as well as the natural resources used are simply wasted. In other words, since there is no plan to production other than the making of profit, the commodities that are produced in abundance may not even be what people need or want. And, of course, as we all know, a great deal of effort then needs to be expended on convincing us that we do need these commodities.

Furthermore, although capitalism fosters the development of advanced technology, which is capable of replacing human labor, because it is based upon a form of wealth—the value form—that can only be created by live human labor, it must limit the extent to which labor-saving technology is used. And once capitalism becomes a global or fully universalized system, these limits can be placed in a discriminatory fashion (yet another case of dumping) on some areas of the world and/or some spheres of production rather than others. This will be the case for as long as labor is the substance of value and labor-time the measure of its magnitude; in other words, as long as capitalism is the mode of production. However, all of this is something that capitalists do not seem to understand, since they constantly strive to lower their labor costs by using labor-saving devices or techniques.

Marx remarks that given a dialectical, scientific understanding of the internal laws and tendencies of capitalism and thus the ability to grasp the movement and development of capitalism, what remains surprising is that the rate of profit does not fall more rapidly and to a further extent than it actually does (Marx, 1865, p. 339). Therefore, it is essential to understand why this is so—to understand the counteracting tendencies that slow and sometimes even reverse the falling rate of profit. When we consider the counteracting tendencies, it will become clear why globalization is necessary to capitalism and why it produces a particular form of universalization, a historically and capitalist specific form of universalization. However, before considering these tendencies, it is important to remember that capitalism is "essentially . . . a process of accumulation" (p. 324) and to focus briefly on the implications of this—on the process and consequences of capitalist accumulation. Among other things, this suggests that environmental destruction—or, at the very least, abuse—is a necessary feature of capitalism.

As I have explained, progress in capitalist terms implies a greater and greater accumulation of constant capital or the means of increasing labor's productivity. Marx points out that with greater accumulation, "the mass of surplus labour that can be and is appropriated *must* grow, and with it too the absolute mass of profit appropriated by the social capital" (p. 325). However, the same laws that govern this bring about an increase in the value of constant capital along with its mass, and this grows more quickly than does the variable capital spent on labor-power; therefore, as a result there is a progressive fall in the rate of profit (Marx, 1865, p. 325). This process seems very contradictory and this is why it is so important to think dialectically when we are trying to understand it—to grasp simultaneously two seemingly opposite tendencies or the possibility, if we put this in logical terms, of A being both A and not-A. Marx describes how the changes in organic composition that bring about a decrease in the surplus-value or profit produced by one firm give rise to an increase in the surplus-value or mass of profits appropriated by social capital or all the capitalists combined. The only way that the total mass of surplus-value or profit can grow when the general rate of profit is falling is for the total social capital to grow—and, further, to grow by an extraordinary amount. And this same rule also applies for individual capitalists. Since the same rule applies for the individual as for the total capitalist economy, we can consider the implications for the whole of society—and, for that matter, the global economy—by looking at precisely what this would entail for an individual capitalist; but in so doing, once again for purposes of clarity, I will assume a lower level of complexity or one prior to the formation of a general rate of profit, as this makes it easier to see the relations involved.

Let us focus this time on the organic composition of capital **B** in the previous example. The organic composition of capital **B** was 60 constant, 40 variable, and at a 100% rate of surplus-value; the surplus-value, or profit, was also 40, and the rate of profit (i.e., the rate of profit that would exist in the absence of a general rate of profit) was, therefore, 40% (40/100 = 40%) (Marx, 1865, p. 328). If we consider the same proportional relations—the same organic composition—for a capital of 1 million, we can see the dramatic growth that must take place in order to maintain capital **B**'s position when the organic composition of the capital is increased. With a total capital of 1 million and the original composition of 60–40, the total surplus-value and profit would amount to 400,000 (40% × 1,000,000). If competition forces capital **B** to change the organic composition to 80 constant and 20 variable, assuming the rate of surplus-value remains unchanged, the profit, now at a rate of 20%, would decrease to 200,000. (If we were looking at this at the higher level of complexity and thus where there is a general rate of profit, then, providing that $c80 : v20$ was the mean composition for the total social capital, there would be the same effect even if capital **B** did not alter its organic composition.) However, capital **B** can avoid this decrease if it doubles the total amount of capital invested so that instead of 1 million, there is now a capital of 2 million; then the total profit would remain at 400,000 (20% × 2,000,000). Even though the rate of profit has fallen to 20% (400,000/2,000,000), doubling the capital invested compensates for what would have been a fall by half in the total profits brought about by the change in the organic composition. Therefore, it takes double the investment of capital to produce the same result in terms of the mass of profit produced when the rate of profit falls by half. If capital **B** had wanted to increase its profits from 400,000 to 440,000 with the original composition of $c60:v40$, it would only have been necessary to invest 100,000 more (40% × 1,100,000 = 440,000). Of course, this would be potential profit and would probably not be realized if capital **B** is competing with more productive firms, for example, firms with compositions of $c80:v20$—firms that, if they need to, can sell their commodities more cheaply. Nevertheless, if capital **B** wanted to increase its profits to 440,000 with the new organic composition of 80:20, a total investment of 2,220,000 would be required—in other words, a 220% rise on the original value (p. 328).

Marx offers a general rule or formula to express this relation: " if the mass of profit is to remain the same with a declining rate of profit, the multiplier that indicates the growth in the total capital must be the same as the divisor that indicates the fall in the profit rate" (Marx, 1865, p. 329). However, as is demonstrated in the example, if the mass of profit is to grow, the total capital must increase by a greater amount or in a higher ratio—a larger multiplier—than the ratio in which the rate of profit falls (Marx, 1865, p. 329). In other words, even though the variable capital is declining as a percentage of the total, the total capital will increase, so that the same amount of labor-power than before, or even more, is absorbed. "[T]he total capital must grow in a higher ratio than that at which the percentage of variable capital falls" (p. 229), so that it requires more not less labor-power if it is going to sustain or increase the total mass of surplus-value. If you can hold on to these two opposite tendencies for a minute longer, I will summarize what happens using Marx's exact words. "[T]he relative decline in the variable capital and profit goes together with an absolute increase in both. This twofold effect . . . can be expressed only in a growth in the total capital that takes place more rapidly than the fall in the rate of profit" (pp. 329–330). This may appear contradictory and certainly, as Marx remarks, confuses the capitalists, who end up with an *upside-down consciousness*; yet, it only expresses the "inner and necessary connection between two apparently contradictory phenomena" (p. 331). In Marx's time, capitalists and bourgeois economists were, of course, aware of the fall in the average or general rate of profit; however, they thought that the increase in the mass of profit compensated for it. But since they did not understand the inner mechanism, they were baffled when at times the total capital would grow without the mass of profit rising or even on occasion falling (p. 330).

Before leaving these points about accumulation and its importance and going on to the counteracting factors, it is important to note that a large capital will always amass more profit in absolute terms than a smaller capital with a higher rate of profit. And often, in times of heightened competition, this enables the larger capital to lower its profit rate, thus driving the smaller capital out and making more room for itself in the market (Marx, 1865, p. 331). It is important to recognize that this unplanned and unpredictable growth on a large scale is a necessity for capitalism's survival, no matter how detrimental it might be for humanity and the natural environment.

Counteracting Factors, or Factors That Attenuate the Falling Rate of Profit. When the rate of surplus-value is increased and there is no increase in the constant capital relative to the variable capital, then the rate and the mass of profit increase. And when this happens in a relatively large number of capitalist firms that contribute to the total social capital, then the tendency toward a falling rate of profit is slowed. Marx always stresses that the law or tendency is "not annulled" but, rather, slowed or weakened (Marx, 1865, p. 341). There also is a limit on this counteracting factor because there is a limit to the intensive exploitation of labor. The porosity of the labor hour is not infinite either in real terms or in terms of what workers can endure. In addition, the ratio between paid, or necessary labor, and unpaid, or surplus labor, can only be reduced in favor of the latter to the extent that workers are still paid sufficiently to maintain and reproduce their labor-power—their capacity for work—which also involves sustaining their capacity to consume at least a considerable amount of the commodities that capitalists must sell. Moreover, the same factors that tend to increase the rate of surplus-value usually lead to a decrease in the number of people employed and thus in the ratio between variable and constant capital. And this causes the general law to be reasserted.

The extensive exploitation of labor—that is, an increase in the length of the working day—also slows down the falling rate of profit for the individual capitalist; if this happens on a large-enough scale, it is attenuated for the total social capital as well. Marx also mentions that a reduction in wages below their value or the necessary level for the sustaining of labor-power would also weaken the tendency for the rate of profit to fall. However, he suggests that this is not an inherent feature of capitalism in that, as I mentioned before, it breaks the law of equal exchange of values. Nevertheless, the use of sweatshop labor, illegal workers—adults and children—and even the semislavery conditions entailed in prison labor can be important factors in stemming the falling rate of profit (p. 342).

The increased productivity of labor that is brought about by the higher organic composition of capital also, as I noted, brings about the cheapening of the commodities produced. This includes not only the cheapening of consumer items, but also the cheapening of constant capital, in particular raw materials and means of production. Therefore, it is possible that at certain times the mass of constant capital will grow faster than its value, such that the value of constant capital does not actually grow relative to the variable capital. Marx says that it is even possible for the mass of constant capital to grow with there being no change or even a fall in its value (p. 343). Once again, however, this will only attenuate the fall in the rate of profit and not annul the tendency. The tendency would eventually be reasserted because the same level of social productivity that causes a cheapening in constant capital would also bring about a cheapening of the value of labor-power—in other words, a cheapening of the necessities required for the sustenance of labor-power.

The counteracting factor that impacts most negatively on working people is capital's inner necessity to create a surplus population—the unemployed (Marx, 1865, p. 343). The increasing labor productivity that is brought about by the higher organic composition of capital means that firms shed labor, thus casting people into unemployment. Once again, we are faced with a contradictory tendency. The unceasing accumulation of capital, as I explained, is constantly incorporating more and more people into the labor–capital relation, at the same time as the increasing organic composition of capital throws still other people into unemployment, creating a surplus population. These dual processes take place unevenly across and within different sectors of employment. Sometimes unemployment is fairly evenly dispersed across the entire society, resulting in what is now called structural unemployment. At other times it takes place in a particular geographical region or sector of industry, resulting in what is called frictional unemployment. Whichever situation prevails at a particular juncture, it simply reflects the inner necessity in capitalism to create a surplus population. This surplus population affects the capitalist system in different ways.

Since unemployed people quite often are willing to work for lower wages, this gives capitalists the option of remaining competitive not through investment in constant capital, but through more intensive exploitation of their existing or even an expanding labor force. When this happens, what Marx calls the incomplete, or only formal, subsumption of labor by capital may persist in certain branches of industry because of the continuing existence of often quite large numbers of low-wage workers being available in the labor market (p. 343). This will then slow down the overall increase in the organic composition of the total social capital and thus also the fall in the rate of profit. The availability of large numbers of low-wage workers also encourages the growth of labor-intensive branches of industry that specialize in the production of luxuries. These firms tend to employ large numbers of low-paid workers and only pass through the stages of capitalist development very slowly. And since these firms also participate in the equalization of the general rate of profit, they tend to put a brake on the falling rate of profit by boosting the total mass of surplus-value produced relative to the total social capital (p. 344).

Foreign trade is another counteracting factor and is one that has a twofold effect (Marx, 1865, p. 344). The importation of foreign goods often cheapens the cost of constant capital, and thus produces the effect mentioned earlier, where the mass of constant capital grows faster than its value relative to the variable capital. Of course, this importation can also cheapen the cost of workers' necessities and thus reduce the value of wages. It might seem that this would compensate for the fall in the value of constant capital, leaving the law to operate normally. However, providing the workforce remains the same numerically or does not decrease too drastically, what actually happens is that this decrease in the value of the wage has a greater effect on raising the rate of surplus-value, thus increasing the overall mass of surplus-value—that is, relative surplus-value—produced (pp. 344, 347). As a consequence, the falling rate of profit is attenuated. In this way the importation of foreign goods has a twofold or dual effect, both of which slow the decline in the rate of profit.

Foreign trade also opens up the possibility of capitalist production processes being moved abroad. Capitalists searching for lower cost prices, for both raw materials and labor, can transfer their production to foreign locales. When this results in a readjustment of the overall organic composition of a corporation, or on a large scale an entire capitalist economy, thus reducing the overall organic composition, there will be an attenuation in the falling rate of profit. Alternatively, capital can often simply be invested abroad at a higher rate of profit, and as long as its base is national and thus the investment and profits enter into the equalization of the general rate of profit, this, too, will act as a brake on the fall in the general rate of profit (pp. 345–346).

Marx points to foreign trade and colonialism (the latter of which persists in our own time as solely an economic rather than a political relation of domination often referred to as neocolonialism or neoimperialism) as good examples of how capitalist nation-states deal with their inherent contradictions. This method of dealing with or temporarily resolving contradictions had already begun in Marx's life time and went on to become a common and pervasive feature of twentieth-century capitalism. Marx sums it up as follows: "The internal contradiction seeks resolution by extending the external field of production" (Marx, 1865, p. 353). It is clear that Marx is referring to a continuous process of temporarily resolving contradictions. He also points out that the growth of foreign trade has contradictory consequences. It allows the scale of production to expand, thereby encouraging the greater accumulation of capital (thus attenuating the fall), while also bringing about a decrease in variable relative to constant capital, which, in turn, promotes the fall in the rate of profit (p. 344). Finally, foreign trade is yet another example of a precondition that becomes a result. As I mentioned in chapter 2, the development of commodity exchange and the use of money began first as a peripheral activity on the margins of society in foreign trade or trade external to the community. But in a fully developed capitalist society the importance of foreign trade grows. It accelerates, becoming an "inner necessity," because it is one of the main devices for the temporary displacement of capitalism's internal contradiction (i.e., internal to a particular capitalist economy), or their movement onto a wider and more complex level of operation (p. 344).

Turnover time is not discussed in the section where Marx lists the factors that attenuate the falling rate of profit; nor is it discussed in great detail elsewhere in Volume 3. In fact, many of the comments related to turnover time in the third volume are additions made by Engels (e.g., Marx, 1865, pp. 163–169). However, Marx does clearly indicate that a faster turnover time—that is, a capital that turns over more than once per annum—produces a greater mass of surplus-value (p. 243–244); thus he reinforces the points about turnover time that he makes in Volume 2—points that I discussed in chapter 2. And even though he does not include turnover time among the other counteracting factors, he does suggest, in at least a few other places, that an increase in the speed of turnover, if it were to affect the total social capital, could also serve to attenuate the falling rate of profit (pp. 261, 334, 424–425). Since one of the main features of globalization—one that is both a precondition and a result—is the acceleration of life brought about by advances in telecommunications and transport, there is a strong probability that this has increased the speed of turnover on a global scale. The impact on the total mass of surplus-value produced globally may have been considerable. However, this would only be the case to the extent that the acceleration has affected the turnover of commodity-producing capital—that is, capital that produces surplus-value (p. 426). And we know, for example, that a great deal of what is being turned over daily through high-tech global trade is fictitious capital rather the real commodities, or commodities produced by productive labor. Nevertheless, my point is that it seems reasonable to expect that the outcome of a global increase in the mass of surplus-value would be an attenuation of the falling rate of profit.

Throughout his discussion of the counteracting factors, Marx stresses that they do not annul the Law of the Falling Rate of Profit. They simply weaken its effect, so that it works more like a tendency that "is decisive only under certain particular circumstances and over long periods" (Marx, 1865, p. 346). Therefore, returning to the point I made in chapter 2, even for readers who are not aware that this is normally the case for scientific laws, Marx tries to make his use of the terms "science" and "law" very clear. This should have countered vulgar or dogmatic interpretations of his explanations but, unfortunately, it has not. The Law of the Falling Rate of Profit would be very difficult to understand in the absence of Mark's explanation. It is important to recognize that both the falling rate of profit and the rising rate of surplus-value are indications of the increasing productivity of labor (p. 347). In order to grasp fully how capitalism works, we need to hold fast to the dual effects created by capitalism's dialectical nature—to the dialectical or internal relations involved.

[T]he same mode of production that reduces the total mass of additional living labour in a commodity is accompanied by a rise in the absolute and relative surplus-value. The tendential fall in the rate of profit is linked with the tendential rise in the rate of surplus-value, i.e. in the level of exploitation of labour. [p. 347]

In other words, the same factor, the rising organic composition of capital, that makes the rate of profit fall, enables capital to raise the rate of surplus-value. This happens for two interacting reasons. Advanced machinery or technology allows for labor to be worked more intensively—at a higher level of exploitation—thus increasing relative surplus-value and productivity. When this increased productivity decreases the cost of the workers' necessities and thus lowers the value of labor, this also decreases necessary labor relative to surplus labor, further increasing the rate of surplus-value and thus the mass of surplus-value produced; but, at the same time, the rising organic composition means that the constant capital increases relative to the variable more quickly than the mass of surplus-value increases. Thus the overall tendency is a fall in the general rate of profit.

Furthermore, the increasing organic composition that brings about a reduction in the amount of living labor also leads to the increasing accumulation of capital or an increase in the total mass of social capital. As a consequence, as labor is shed in one firm or one sphere of production, more and more labor is simultaneously being incorporated into the labor–capital relation elsewhere. And if and when the original firm, or the entire sphere, decides to expand and thus engage in further accumulation, some labor will then be reincorporated there as well. The effect this has on the overall organic composition of social capital and thus the falling rate of profit will depend on the organic composition of the firms where labor is being incorporated. In some cases, it might involve a huge industrial plant where more labor needs to be employed to tend the increasing mass of constant capital. In others, it might involve the imposition of the labor–capital relations on new areas of work that often, at least initially, tend to be labor-intensive and thus lower in organic composition—such as when services are turned into commodities or there is an increase in the production of luxuries. In either of these cases, there could be an increase in the mass of surplus-value or profit produced in society; however, in the long term the increase in variable capital that brings this about is never as great proportionally as the increase in constant capital, even if at certain stages there may be a compensatory effect that attenuates the fall in the rate of profit. As I said before, although the absolute amount, or mass, of surplus-value increases, it decreases relative to, or in comparison with, constant capital (Marx, 1865, pp. 323–325). Capitalists often blame the falling rate of profit on workers' demands for higher wages in the absence of increased productivity. To the contrary, once the real relationships are grasped, the absurdity of this idea is apparent. Marx's explanation clearly demonstrates that the rate of profit falls because labor has become more not less productive (p. 347).[3]

THE DIVISION OF "LABOR" AMONG CAPITALISTS
AND THE DIVISION OF SURPLUS-VALUE

To this point, I have explained that the competition between industrial capitalists brings about the equalization of the profit rate, an equalization that is brought about by the continuous flow of capital from firms with low rates of profit into firms with higher rates of profit, and the resulting redistribution of the total surplus-value that has been created. It is time to consider how this redistributed surplus-value is divided among various capitalists according to their function within a fully developed capitalist economy. When Marx refers to the division of labor among capitalists, he is facetiously referring to the way in which different functions are divided among capitalists, constituting a necessary internal relation between them, which often divides them into class factions or subdivisions of their class. This division is made not only possible but also necessary by the movement of value (capital)—its continuous transformation into and out of its money and commodity forms. In chapter 2, I discussed how this movement mediates the internal dialectical relation between production and circulation (including the latter's crucial moment of exchange) and stressed that this relation constitutes the whole or complete capitalist production process (Marx, 1865, p. 117). I also pointed out that both mercantile capitalism and usury existed prior to capitalism and thus served as preconditions for capitalism, preconditions that would arise in a more developed form as results of the full development of industrial capitalism. It is important to bring all these factors together in order to complete my explanation of the concrete totality of a fully developed capitalist society. This entails considering how the equalization of the rate of profit and the transformation of the value of commodities into prices of production, which that equalization brings about, together with the redistribution of surplus-value among capitalists, operates when the division of functions among capitalists is brought into view.

At one point, earlier, I hinted that I was not yet explaining the full complexity, but I did not hint very emphatically for fear that you might grow weary if you knew then that there was more to come. However, once these final aspects of the totality of capitalism have been considered, I promise that you will have a comprehensive picture or operational model of how in general a fully developed national or global capitalist economy moves and develops according to its own internal logic or, more precisely, its inherent dialectical contradictions—contradictions from which general laws or tendencies emerge. Everything I have explained up to this point holds true because it is based on the assumption of a fully developed capitalist system where the division of functions among capitalists is in place. However, because this division of functions adds yet another layer of complexity, it was best to discuss the general laws and tendencies first, just as I explained the Law of Value and all the other aspects of capital's essence prior to bringing in the concrete complexity that emerges when we consider the competition among capitalists first within one sphere of production and then across the different spheres. By unfolding the explanation of capitalism in this way, I am following Marx's approach—his dialectical method of presenting and explaining capital, a method that always involves moving from the most abstract and simple forms and processes to the more concrete and complex. It is only by adhering to this approach that we can come to grasp capitalism dialectically, or in the way that Marx did, and thus understand fully its dialectical complexity and, equally, its absurdity. I reemphasize that I do not go into the detailed proof, examples and depth of explanation that Marx offers.[4] Instead, as I said before, I have tried to cull in a coherent form the elements of his explanation that enable one to comprehensively grasp the basic character of capitalism as well as the way in which it must of necessity move and develop.

In the early stages of capitalist development, and also often the early stages of the development of a particular capitalist firm, industrial capitalists often oversee the entire production process and thus are just as concerned with the circulation and exchange of their commodities as they are with their actual production. However, as capitalism develops, the circulation and exchange functions are increasingly turned over to commercial capitalists. In contemporary multi-national and transnational corporations, these functions are once again often subsumed within one corporate body. Nevertheless, even in these giant con-glomerates, there will be a division of "labor" or functions—that is, a division of what the representatives of capital think of as their labor. As I noted in chapter 2 and also previously in this chapter, the velocity of turnover affects the mass of surplus-value that is produced annually (Marx, 1865, pp. 163, 243, 424; 1878, pp. 369 ff.). A capital with a given amount of variable capital that turns over the constant capital several times during the year will produce more surplus-value than a capital of the same organic composition that has only one turnover per annum (Marx, 1865, pp. 424–425). This is one of the reasons why it makes a great deal of sense to divide the functions of production and circulation.

When each capitalist can devote his or her entire energies and resources to a single function, it should accelerate the production cycle. In other words, by allowing the industrial capitalists to realize some of their surplus-value immedi-ately on completion of the production process and thus reinvest this capital in further production, it helps to increase the velocity of the annual, immediate production process. Whether or not this results in a greater mass of surplus-value being realized is contingent, of course, on whether those dealing with circulation can just as quickly circulate and sell the increased volume of commodities produced. However, once the functions are divided and the industrialists have sold their commodities, this is no longer an obvious or pressing concern for them. The value of their commodities will have been transformed into money and can therefore be reinvested in production and made to function as capital. Therefore, this division of "labor" between industrial and commercial capitalists means that industrial capital can be reinvested more quickly, and this, as I said, is one of the main reasons why the division of "labor" becomes a normal practice. It also leads to other consequences, such as, laying the foundations for the full development of the credit system, which I discuss in greater detail later. At this point, it is important to consider the complexity that this division of "labor" adds to the processes taking place, especially the effect it has on prices of production. Marx's explanation of what is actually going on within the entire process of capitalist production offers a deeper or more complete understanding of the price of production of the commodity—that is, the transformation of value that takes place through the equalization of rates of profit into a general rate of profit.

To begin with, we must assume that the total social capital includes not only industrial, or productive, capital but also commercial capital. If all the industrial capitalists in a society, during the course of one year, invest 720 in constant capital plus 180 in variable capital (e.g., in millions of either dollars or pounds or whatever), the total industrial capital is 900. The cost price of the total industrial capital would then be $k = 900$, with k being the symbol for cost price. If we assume a rate of surplus-value of 100%, then the price of production of this total industrial capital is $c720 + v180 + p180 = 1,080$ (note that the rate of profit on this total capital of 900 would be 20%; therefore, this is the general rate of profit calculated on the total industrial capital in society—Marx, 1865, p. 398). However, let us take into consideration that in addition to the industrial, or productive, capital, commercial capital is also included in the total social capital, and, thus, it also figures in the equalization of the rate of profit. If we assume that this commercial capital is 100 (again in millions), then the total social capital is 1,000 and not 900 (i.e., the total of the industrial capital). In which case the rate of profit, or general rate of profit since I am talking about the total social capital, is 18% rather than 20%—that is, 180/1,000 and not 180/900.

Let us consider this new rate of profit first for the commercial capitalists and then for the industrialists. The commercial capital is one tenth, or 10%, of the total capital of 1,000 and can claim a share of the total profit according to its size. Therefore, commercial capitalists can claim 10% of the 180, or 18; and this means that their profit rate is 18%: 18/100 = 18%. Industrial, or productive, capitalists can only claim nine-tenths of the profit of 180 as they comprise only 90% of the total social capital, and therefore, rather than a profit, or surplus-value, of 180, their profit is only 162, or 180 − 18 = 162. As a consequence, they also end up with a profit rate of 18%: 162/900 = 18%, or the same rate of profit as the commercial capital. And this is, in fact, the actual general rate of profit rather than 20%, which it would have been if only industrial capital had made up the total social capital. This means that the industrial, or productive, capitalists sell their commodities to the commercial capitalists for $c720 + v180 + p162 = 1,062$, instead of $c720 + v180 + p180 = 1,080$. The 1,062 is the commercial capitalists' cost price to which they add a profit of 18% and sell the commodity for what, in the first instance, appeared to be the industrialists' price of production—that is, 1,080. Now it becomes clear that this is actually made up of $c + v + p + m$, where m is the commercial capitalists' profit (p. 399). In summary, rather than the price of production of the commodity being $c720 + v180 + p180 = 1,080$ (with a general rate of profit of 20%), the price of production is, instead, $c720 + v180 + p162 + m18 = 1,080$, and the general rate of profit is 18%. The latter formula signifies the value of the total social capital. As I mentioned previously, the sum of all the prices of production is equal to the sum of all of the value of commodities produced by the total social capital (Marx, 1865, pp. 259, 273). [As I also mentioned before, the cost price of commodities is specific to their sphere of production and is related to the "socially necessary labor-time," or value, of the constant and variable capital in that sphere, but the profit on top of the cost price is independent of any particular sphere—it is the general rate of profit derived from the total social capital, or the total productive and commercial capital in a society (p. 259).]

All the industrial, or all the productive, capitalists, therefore, sell their commodities to the commercial capitalists for less than their value because commercial capital is part of the total social capital and enters into the equalization of the rates of profit and the creation of the general rate of profit. This means that the industrial capitalists' prices of production are based on a lower rate of profit than they would be if commercial capital were not included in the total, and consequently they sell their commodities to the commercial capitalists for less than their value (p. 398). Even though commercial capital does not produce the surplus-value in the commodity, it does enter into the average profits in each sphere of production. As a consequence, the general rate of profit that results from the equalization of these rates of profit will take into account the deduction from the industrialists' rates of profit that have already gone to commercial capital (p. 400). Clearly, the larger the commercial capital as a proportion of the total social capital, the smaller will be the industrialists' profits (p. 400).

Marx frequently notes that the rate of profit, which is calculated on the total capital, is always smaller than the rate of surplus-value, or the index of the exploitation of labor, because the latter rate is calculated only on the variable capital. Of course, once the general rate of profit is formed, which is calculated on the total social capital, it is further removed from the specific rate of surplus-value in a firm, and when commercial capital is calculated into the total capital, the rate of profit is removed further still from this specific rate of surplus-value. As a consequence, it is even more difficult to form an accurate idea of the level of exploitation (Marx, 1865, p. 400). Moreover, the larger commercial capital becomes relative to the total capital, the more blurred the picture will be.

As I noted in chapter 2, with the exception of belated or additional production processes within circulation—processes that make the commodity saleable, such as dispatch, transport and storage—no further surplus-value is added to the commodity during the circulation process; however, commercial capitalists will often have additional costs having to do solely with circulation or the transformation of commodities into money and money into commodities (pp. 402–403). These costs do not have to do with the production of surplus-value but, rather, with its realization; however, they do entail the expenditure of variable capital, or the purchase of labor-power. From the standpoint of the commercial employee, he or she is a wage-laborer, just like any other wage-laborer. However, in relation to the workers employed by industrial capitalists, they stand in the same position as the commercial capitalist does to the industrial capitalist (p. 406). As I have explained, merchants do not pay industrialists for the full amount of unpaid labor their commodities contain. The amount they can claim—that is, the profit they can claim—depends entirely on the size of capital they employ. And they can employ more and more capital in the buying and selling of commodities, the greater the unpaid labor of their workers—the more they exploit their workforce. Therefore, even though the unpaid labor of the commercial employees does not create surplus-value—stands in no relation to the surplus-value realized in the commodities—it enables the commercial capitalists to appropriate surplus-value from the industrial capitalists (p. 414). As far as the commercial capitalists are concerned, then, this unpaid labor is also a source of profit—it gives them a share of the surplus-value or profit created by the industrialists (pp. 407–408). It also helps commercial capitalists to reduce the costs of realizing surplus-value (p. 414). While holding onto Marx's explanation of what actually takes place, it is also important to consider how this appears to commercial capitalists as opposed to industrial capitalists, and vice versa. And in order to understand their perspectives, it helps to see how they were developed historically.

As mentioned before, prior to the advent of industrial capitalism, there was mercantile "capitalism," based on commercial trade. The general rate of profit was first formed in circulation wherein commercial capital "fixes the price of commodities more or less according to their values . . ." (Marx, 1865, p. 400). Therefore, when industrial capitalism first emerged, industrial profit was determined by commercial profit (p. 401). However, once capitalism has fully developed through its industrial basis and industrial capitalists, at least initially, become their own merchants, commercial profit assumes a subordinate role. And even when the industrial and commercial functions are eventually divided, commercial profit continues in its subordinate role. Commercial capitalists can lay claim to only a portion of the surplus-value produced by the industrial, or productive, capitalists. In other words, the profit rate no longer originates from a commercial base (p. 401).

The upshot of all this is that the commercial function is perceived very differently by industrial and commercial capitalists. When the commercial function is performed by the industrialists, it appears to them as something that adds to their costs and thus reduces their profits. However, when commercial capitalists take over this function, they perceive the process as one in which they pay money for the industrialists' prices of production; therefore, they invest money capital in a commodity that they sell for a profit—a process that they perceive as $M–M'$, or money, becoming money with an augmented value (Marx, 1865, p. 401). In other words, to the industrialists, money spent in this way seems to be, and is, an addition to their costs, but to the commercial capitalists it appears to be, and is, an investment—an investment that is the source of their profits. Therefore, to the commercial capitalists this also appears to be a productive investment and, from their perspective, commercial laborers can be considered to be "directly productive" (p. 416). Nevertheless, according to Marx, even though they help to produce a profit for their employers, this profit is only a claim on the surplus-value already produced. Commercial employees' wages stand in no relation to the surplus-value in the commodity or, in other words, the amount of profit they help the commercial capitalists to realize (p. 414).

On the other hand, as far as class interests are concerned, commercial workers are in the labor–capital relation and are subjected to the same forces of exploitation as their industrial counterparts. As capitalism develops, there is also a tendency to divide commercial labor into smaller and less skilled tasks; therefore, commercial labor, which once demanded a higher level of intellectual skill than did industrial labor, tends to become deskilled and thus paid at an increasingly lower wage than it was originally. The general spread of education and thus literacy skills also hastens this process of deskilling. Therefore, as Marx remarks, workers who are accustomed to a lower standard of living increasingly take on this work for lower pay (Marx, 1865, pp. 414–415). It is important to remember, in connection with this consideration of commercial employees' position with respect to the creation of surplus-value, that this does not mean that it is only industrial workers who create surplus-value. For example, in contemporary capitalism, many services have become commodified, and usually this means that the respective service workers are involved in creating these intangible service commodities within the labor–capital relation. The difference in the case of the commercial workers is that their unpaid labor, although it is a use-value, creates no value—their unpaid labor forms no part of the surplus-value of any commodity.

I have offered a comprehensive summary of Marx's explanation of the transformation of the value of commodities into prices of production. This transformation that is brought about through the equalization of different profit rates of the total social capital—including commercial as well as industrial capital—into a general rate of profit is impossible to comprehend in the absence of Marx's scientific analysis of what is actually happening (p. 956). In other words, it cannot be understood from merely observing what takes place on the surface of society in the day-to-day activities, or concrete reality, of a capitalist society. This aspect of Marx's analysis of capitalism is often referred to as "the transformation problem." Many people, including some Marxist economists, think that Marx is trying to explain how value is transformed into prices—the actual prices paid for commodities—in a fully developed capitalist economy. This is not the problem that Marx was addressing. Marx's analysis of the transformation of value into prices of production, as I explained, pertains to the distribution of social labor and redistribution of surplus-value among capitalists in conditions of competition (Harvey, 1999; Marx, 1865, pp. 298, 1020; Rubin, 1972). A theory of prices could be formulated from Marx's analysis, but Marx did not do so, as that was not the problem he set out to solve.

Summary: I will offer a brief summary of the conceptual journey—that is, the journey of dialectical conceptualization—on which Marx takes us as we follow value from the beginning of Volume 1 through Volume 3. In the beginning of Volume 1, Marx first discusses the early days of commodity exchange between the direct producers of the commodities and explains that the value of a commodity is determined by the labor-time it contains and that it is this that establishes the equivalency and thus exchangeability of commodities between their producers. However, when these commodities are produced in order to be traded in the market, their value is no longer determined by the actual amount of labor-time they contain, but instead by the "socially necessary labor-time" that it takes for the production or a particular type of commodity during a particular period of time. In Volume 3, he explains how value is once again transformed when we consider the complex and concrete totality of the capitalist system, where we find many different productive capitalists competing with one another both in terms of the selling of commodities and in terms of attracting the investment of capital. This competition tends to equalize all the different rates of profit, thus creating a general rate of profit. Therefore, instead of the simple and more abstract formula for the value of the commodity, or $c + v + s$, that pertained when the commodity's value was determined directly by the "socially necessary labor-time" for the production of that particular commodity, we now have a more concrete formula that reflects the more complex situation that arises due to competition, viz. $c + v + p$, where p reflects the general rate of profit, or the rate of profit for all the commodities produced by the total social capital, and the value of the commodity is now expressed in what Marx calls the price of production. Finally, due to the division of labor between industrial, or productive, capital and commercial capital, the total social capital comes to include both of them, and the formula for the value of the commodity changes once again. The price of production is now expressed as $c + v + p + m$, where m stands for the commercial profit and p the industrial, or productive, profit. In every case labor-time is the constitutive element of the commodity's value, and in every case Marx is talking about the value of the commodity, or the point around which prices fluctuate. This value, therefore, determines the space or parameters through which prices move. And the Law of Value, which states that the value of a commodity is based on the labor-time socially necessary for its production, pertains throughout all of these transformations.

Having discussed how different functions and also the different portions of the surplus-value are divided among industrial, or productive, and commercial capitalists, I consider still further divisions that also take place within a fully developed capitalist society. Once again, it is necessary to focus on the movement of value and its continuous transformation into and out of the money and commodity forms.

With the development of commercial capital, the money form of value appears to become completely autonomous from the commodity form. At least, it can operate as though it were autonomous, and the distinction between money capital and commodity capital comes into full force. Money capital and commodity capital become, therefore, two separate and distinct forms of capital; but, of course, they are derived from the same source (Marx, 1865, p. 431). Money capital, whether invested in the production of commodities or commercially in the sphere of circulation, yields the same rate of profit as commodity capital because both form part of the total capital involved in the production of capital and thus participate in the creation of the general rate of profit (pp. 402, 459, 463). However, once money capital becomes autonomous, it can also separate from, or "spin off" from, the continuous reproduction cycle and perform different functions for different factions of capital. These functions and the processes involved in them are aided and facilitated by the development of credit money. Credit money is any token that functions in the place of real money—that is, the money commodity that contains value—tokens like the bills of exchange, which industrial and commercial capitalists often use in their transactions in place of cash. In fact, these bills of exchange lay the foundation for the credit system (p. 525). The use of credit allows for a greater period of time to exist between the acts of buying and selling, and thus the transfer of actual money. This encourages speculation or speculative investment because the real money can be used for these activities while credit stands in its place.

Another consequence of money capital becoming autonomous is that money can be used as capital by people other than the industrial, or productive, and the commercial capitalists, and often the other people lend it as capital to the capitalists who are functioning in industry and commerce. This money capital is transferred to them by the money capitalists as a use-value with no immediate exchange-value or exchange of money involved in the transfer. It is then used by, for example, the industrial capitalists in their function of producing surplus-value. At the end of the production process, a portion of the profit created is returned to the money capitalists in the form of interest; and in this way the money capitalists' capital, or what Marx calls interest-bearing capital, is repeatedly augmented (Marx, 1865, pp. 459–479). However, when money capital is lent by money capitalists to productive or commercial capitalists, it does not earn the general rate of profit for the money capitalists. Instead, it earns the rate of interest, and this is why, when it is used in this way, Marx calls it interest-bearing capital rather than money capital. Another consequence, of course, is that money capital can be invested such that it does not flow directly into the immediate reproduction cycle. For example, it can be invested in derivatives related to future, rather than current, production or large-scale fixed capital investments, such as railways, superhighways, and so on.

The rate of interest, which determines how much is returned to the money capitalists, depends on the amount of money capital available and the demand for it. Once the banks and other financial institutions socialize the greater part of interest-bearing capital (bring it into an alienated form of common rather than individual, private ownership), the supply, which is comprised of the savings of all classes, greatly increases (pp. 512, 742). With this mass of money available for productive investment, the reproduction of capital is accelerated, and the accumulation of capital is greatly increased. Although the rate of interest depends on supply and demand, the level of the rate of interest has a limit, which is determined by the general rate of profit. "The rate of interest is related to the profit rate [general rate of profit] in a similar way as the market price of a commodity is [related] to its value [or the "socially necessary labor-time as expressed in market-value]" (Marx, 1865, p. 487). When the general rate of profit is relatively higher (relative to its tendency to fall), the interest rate will be low, which is a general indication of prosperity. However, as prosperity wanes, interest rates begin to rise (p. 482). Rates of interest reach their highest peak at times of crisis—overproduction, stagnation and inactivity (p. 483). However, interest rates can also fall independently of movements in the general rate of profit. For example, they can fall when there is a large concentration of savings in banks and thus more money capital available for lending. This increased supply pushes down the interest rate (p. 484).

Some capitalists operate with their own rather than borrowed capital. The only difference is that they are able to keep their total share of the profit, whereas those who borrow only keep $p - I$ (or industrial profit minus the interest). Of course, the closer the rate of interest is to zero, the less difference there is between those who employ their own capital and those who borrow from the money capitalists. This difference is only a quantitative one, but it comes to be seen as a qualitative one (Marx, 1865, p. 495). Capitalists always think in terms of the total capital employed, and gross profit is seen as deriving from this total capital. Gross profit is divided into net profit and interest, and the former, often referred to as profit of enterprise, comes to be seen as the part that is the result of performing a function, whereas interest is seen as deriving solely from ownership. Profit of enterprise appears to have come entirely from the functions that capitalists perform in the reproduction process, especially those "functions that he[or she] performs as an entrepreneur in industry or trade" (p. 497). In contrast, interest appears as the mere result of the ownership of capital—of property—"abstracted from the reproductive process of capital . . ." (Marx, 1865, p. 497). Industrial capitalists think that it is their own activity—in contrast to the total inactivity of the owners of interest-bearing capital—that produces profit (p. 497). Once functions are divided in this way, it is no longer a matter of a simple or straightforward illusion but rests on the objective fact that interest does accrue to the money capitalists simply because of the ownership of capital—property in capital that exists prior to the production process concerned and external to it (pp. 497–498).

This situation, and conception related to it, is even more strongly reinforced by the fact that interest-bearing capital has its historical roots in usury and therefore existed prior to the advent of capitalist production. Once again, this is a case of a precondition of capitalism emerging in a more developed form as a result of capitalist production, but a result that continues to be perceived as a precondition by those involved in the daily reproduction of capitalist relations. "In the popular mind, therefore, money capital or interest-bearing capital is still seen as capital as such, capital *par excellence*" (Marx, 1865, p. 499). Moreover, since loan capital returns interest even when it is not actually used as capital but rather borrowed for consumption, the impression of it as something that exists totally independently of production—and thus the constitution of value by labor-time—is doubly reinforced. The only situation that might reveal that interest derives from surplus-value would be one in which the vast majority of capitalists converted their capital into money capital. If this were to happen, it would bring about a dramatic fall in the rate of interest, as there would be an oversupply of interest-bearing capital. At which point, these capitalists would quickly learn that they cannot live from interest alone—or, rather, the capitalist system as a whole would soon learn this lesson (p. 501)

With interest-bearing capital, we arrive at the full fetishization of the capital relation (Marx, 1865, p. 515). At least with commercial capital, even though the profit-making process takes place within circulation and can seem totally remote from production, there is at least a process that can be represented as "$M–C–M'$," (money invested in buying commodities that are sold for more money). There is actually a process wherein money is mediated by the commodity, even though commercial capitalists often think in terms of $M–M'$ because their employees rather than themselves are normally the ones involved with the mediation—the actual commodities. In contrast, money capitalists are not involved in any intermediary processes. In other words, commercial capitalists are still involved in *social relations*, whereas for the money capitalists the social relation is totally obliterated. Money capitalists relate only to a thing—interest-bearing capital (p. 515). They are totally involved in a fetishized relation, one that totally veils the real processes that are taking place.

As I noted before, the use of credit and credit money is fundamental to fully developed capitalism. Real money, or value in its money form, comes to act less and less as a means of circulation and functions primarily as a means of payment (Marx, 1865, p. 525). Circulation is propelled by credit money (p. 567). Bills of exchange, or promises to pay, between producers and merchants form the foundation of the credit system that both expands as capitalism develops and accelerates its growth (p. 525). The other side of the credit system also develops, with the management of interest-bearing, or money, capital becoming the specialized business of money-dealers (p. 528). They act as go-betweens or middle-persons between those who actually loan money capital and the commercial and industrial capitalists who borrow it. The banking system develops as it concentrates in a central location large masses of money capital that can be made available for loans. Banks, and later other financial institutions, thereby act as representatives for the individual lenders and become, in general, the managers of money capital (p. 528). Banknotes are actually forms of credit, circulating tokens of credit, which serve as legal tender, backed by government credit (p. 529). As I mentioned before, credit allows for a tremendous acceleration in the reproduction of capital, but it also means that the acts of buying and selling can be further separated in time. This separation then leads to the speculative use of money that is not being used immediately as a means of payment (p. 567). Credit, or a form of credit in stocks and shares, moreover, facilitates the separation of the owner-ship of capital from the actual function of capitalist production, which is left in the hands of managers (p. 567). As such the credit system is the primary stimulus to overproduction as well as the excessive speculation in commerce (p. 572). Since the reproduction of capital is elastic in nature, the credit system stretches it to its limits as the social capital tends more and more to be applied or invested by those who are not actually functioning as capitalists. When the functioning capitalists are the owners, they tend to be more cautious and consider the limits to their private capital more carefully (p. 572).

Thus the credit system has a dual character (Marx, 1865, p. 572). On the one hand, it accelerates the development of the productive forces and creates a world market, but on the other hand it accelerates the development of capital's contra-dictions and as a consequence the outbreak of crises (p. 572). As I mentioned before but reemphasize here, the credit system is immanent in capitalism and drives it to develop into a fully universal or global form, but it also sows the seeds of its destruction (p. 572). I have explained that the average profit of the indi-vidual capitalists, or any jointly owned capital, does not come from the surplus-value it produces, but, instead, it derives from the total surplus-value produced in society. Each capital draws its proportional share of this total according to its size. Capital, thus, has a social character, and this is realized in full with the development of the credit system, especially specific parts of that system such as banking and the stock exchange. The problem is that those who are neither the owners nor the producers of capital put all the available or potential capital that is not already committed at one point in time at the disposal of commercial and industrial capitalists who also are not the owners or producers of the capital (p. 742). This to a large extent abolishes the private character of capital (estab-lishing in an antithetical form its social character) and also abolishes the respon-sibility and caution that accompanied the private character (p. 572). The credit system, thus, drives capitalist production beyond its barriers and also becomes a powerful impetus for swindling and ultimately crisis (p. 742). When the system becomes overladen with credit money and fictitious capital, or the title claims to value or capital that circulate in place of real money, financial crises can arise (pp. 597–602, 614–615, 625). This happens when there is a rush to liquidate or claim the real value rather than its mere representation. In the case of fictitious capital or shares that repay dividends on earnings and derivatives—all of which are claims on the future production of value—the situation is at its worst and, in fact, can be disastrous for those who own these when there is a rush to liquidate (pp. 598–599).

Just as Marx shows how interest-bearing capital, whether it is loaned as money or fixed capital (e.g., machinery), makes a claim in the form of interest on the surplus-value produced by industrial capital, he also shows how rent also is a claim on surplus-value that accrues to landowners (Marx, 1865, pp. 751–787, 859, 870, 882–911, 917–950). In addition, he once again explains why this is not the way that people living within capitalism perceive the situation. Marx's analysis of capitalism is simultaneously an analysis of the type of distorted consciousness that capitalist relations foster, and this sort of analysis is crucial for critical educators. To people living within these relations, it appears that all the money or revenue in a capitalist society derives from three separate and unrelated sources—capital, land and labor (pp. 953–954). Marx breaks through the appearances, or forms, in which the social relations present themselves in a capitalist society by means of a penetrating analysis that unveils the relations and the laws, or tendencies, that these relations, or dialectical contradictions, create, which then act back on them, governing their movement and development. (Of course, when we talk about social relations, or internal relations and dialectical contradictions, we must remember that these are comprised of human beings, behaving in ways that are determined by their positions within the relations, and who are thus actively involved in producing the laws, or tendencies.) Moreover, Marx enables us to understand why our own and others', especially the capitalists', perceptions are distorted by our actual engagement in the material reality of capitalism.

The questions Marx posed that led him to challenge the prevailing ideas of how the system worked were not difficult questions. For example, if supply and demand were responsible for determining the price of commodities, as many lay people and economists thought then and still do now, what happens when supply and demand are balanced? (pp. 291, 478). What then determines prices? When confronted with this type of question, the capitalist or bourgeois economists will dig a bit deeper and contend that the value of a commodity is a sum of wages, profits and rent—the fruits of labor, capital and land (presuming the value of all the other inputs for a given commodity are the same across all commodities of that type). Marx explains that it appears like this because the capitalist, like a person involved in any other mode of production, "constantly reproduces not only the material product but also the socio-economic relations," or the determining factors (p. 1011). Within these relations, the results—the profits, wages and rent—appear as preconditions. The results are assumed in the contracts that are made prior to production. Wages are agreed as is rent, and the average profit is known as well as the rate of interest; therefore, capitalists consider that their costs and margins are predetermined. The elements of this configuration of the commodity's value, no matter how much their relative proportions may vary, are "presupposed because [they are] constantly reproduced, and . . . constantly reproduced because [they are] constantly presupposed" (p. 1012). Furthermore, as I explained before, the capitalists have no real concern over whether their commodities are sold at their actual value, since it is not their values but their prices of production that govern the averages prices in each sphere of production. Therefore, capitalists have no awareness, nor do they have any reason to have an awareness of what goes on behind their backs—namely, the processes that result from their social relations and that are constantly reproduced by their and others' activities within these relations but which, once set in motion, then also work independently of their own activities.

Although the explanation I have given is obviously in no way as extensive or detailed as Marx's, it is sufficient to form a fairly comprehensive understanding of how capitalism works, an understanding that should enable an adequate grasp of global capitalism and the actual process of globalization. To understand why globalization has been essential for the survival of capitalism and why capitalism produces a very specific pattern of globalization with specific results or consequences, this type of understanding is indispensable. At this point, I want to reemphasize and expand on some of the points and relate them more directly to our contemporary experience of capitalism.

SEEING MORE CLEARLY NOW: CAPITALISM RIGHT-SIDE UP

I explained that capitalism has an immanent dynamic that raises social productivity to an unfathomable level—a level that could, but does not, eliminate scarcity. The relations of distribution, which, as Marx's analyses show, are simply expressions, or results, of the relations of production, place a limit on consumption by limiting the "effective" demand of the vast majority of the world's population (Marx, 1865, pp. 367, 615, 1017–1024). Material use-values are only available in the commodity form, and therefore the use-value is internally related to and thus bound to or inseparable from the exchange-value of the commodity, which is determined by labor-time. It is value, rather than the massive array of material use-values internally linked with value (as well as an increasing number of immaterial use-values, such as services) that constitutes wealth in capitalist societies and that creates its immanent dynamic and also its raison d'être (Postone, 1996). The quest to realize value—especially surplus-value—and to find the best conditions for its production has driven capital all over the world and established capitalism as a global socioeconomic form of organization—one with an ever-expanding world market in goods, services, and also capital itself, in its real commodity and money forms and also its various fictitious forms, which are no more than claims to future production (Marx, 1965, pp. 599, 608–609). This same quest necessitated the development of a credit system that could accelerate the reproduction of capital and lubricate the flow of commodities and money. Eventually this credit system resulted in a giant world-wide network of credit and debt; and all of these developments were inherent within capitalism even at its inception (p. 525).

Once we begin to understand how capitalism works, and must work, it becomes a great deal easier to understand what is actually happening and why it is happening. For example, it is easy to see why the use of consumer credit has become so important and also why the "Third World" debt crisis has occurred. To begin with consumer credit: Not only does it allow the consumer to buy without needing to use real money and the capitalists to realize their surplus-value more rapidly and so also proceed more rapidly with accumulation, but it also helps to keep the rate of interest on loan capital at a reasonable (i.e., lucrative) level by increasing the demand for loans while also increasing the supply when interest is repaid. Consider for a minute what would happen to the interest rate on interest-bearing capital that is loaned out to industry, once all the money not currently committed to reproduction becomes amassed in large financial institutions and available for loan. The supply might increase much faster than it is needed by the functioning capitalists—especially in times of stagnation due to overaccumulation, that is, excess capacity and overproduction—thus driving the interest rate close to zero, in which case it would no longer be possible to survive as a money-dealing capitalist. Capitalism needs borrowers or users of credit other than the capitalists themselves in order to try to achieve some sort of reasonable balance between supply and demand for interest-bearing capital. If we turn to "Third World" debt, it is also fairly easy to understand one of the major reasons why this came about and why it was also necessary for capitalism's survival—that is, how it provided a temporary solution at a particular point in time.

During periods of stagnation and the buildup to crisis, when there is not only a high level of unemployment, or a surplus population, but also surplus, or unemployed, capital, the system is flooded with excess or surplus funds. By the early 1970s, there were signs that this type of situation had begun to develop throughout much of the capitalist world. But it was then exacerbated in 1974, when the cartel of oil-producing countries forced up the price of oil. Industrial production had already begun to stagnate due to overproduction, and there was, therefore, a decreased demand on loan capital for productive purposes. Not only did the rising price of oil frustrate this situation, it also greatly increased the profits on oil, which flooded into banks, thus further increasing the supply of loan capital. As a result during the 1970s loans were increasingly sold as commodities and peddled at low—in fact, irresistibly low—rates of interest to developing and underdeveloped countries (George, 1988; George and Sabelli, 1994). Although there were other factors involved, this low-interest honeymoon period was sent into reverse in the 1980s primarily because the U.S. government, having launched the Star Wars project and thereby massively increased its defense spending, suddenly became the world's largest debtor (Bonefeld, 1999; George, 1988). Demand for loan capital suddenly outstripped supply, and interest rates soared, plunging the "Third World" into the now familiar debt crisis. Claims on this debt are now sold as commodities—just one of many examples of a world financial system that has been flooded with fictitious capital (Bonefeld, 1999). And the trade in this and other forms of fictitious capital has been accelerated by the massive improvements in telecommunications, which allow value, or its fictitious representatives to move around the globe, changing hands between buyers and sellers with the speed of light. Harvey (1989) calls the overall effect of this accelerated movement of capital time–space compression. The last thirty years of the twentieth century have been characterized by capital's accelerating search to find new outlets for the resolution of its inherent contradictions (Bonefeld, 1999).

The same recurring cycle of boom–stagnation–bust that necessarily bedevils capitalism almost brought the system down in the late 1920s to early 1930s—precipitated by the famous crash of 1929. When capitalism overproduces, value begins to deteriorate; and the only way to restore the value of money and commodities is to destroy a great deal of what has been already produced (Harvey, 1999). Massive devaluation has to take place in order to restore value. A single nation can dump its excess production cheaply on other countries, often wrecking their domestic economies as a result; it can stockpile or create mountains of the surplus by removing commodities from the market or it can even pay or reward, by the taxation system, producers for not producing. However, such strategies only serve to exacerbate a global financial crisis. The only strategy, if we can call it that, which was able to save capitalism in the 1930s and lay the basis for its eventual full recovery and the regeneration of growth, or capital accumulation, was the most effective and comprehensive form of devaluation possible—total war (Bonefeld, 1999; Harvey, 1999). World War II effectively cleansed the system, clearing capitalism of its excess production and creating a clean slate on which unprecedented production and growth would be able to proceed for an unprecedented number of years, often referred to now as capitalism's postwar "Golden Age." But just as there was not a divorce between politics and the economy in bringing about the war, so, too, was there no divorce in economic recovery.

During the twenty-year period that followed the war, wages, productivity and profits grew in concert, and so there appeared to be a period of relative harmony between capital and labor. Of course, the harmony was largely an appearance, with wages rising only through hard negotiation. Nevertheless, labor did operate from a position of greater strength than it had done prior to the war, a position won through political compromise, albeit compromise that was often instigated by either the threat or the real existence of labor militancy. Nevertheless, trade union strength and the legitimacy of trade union action grew, relative to the past. Productivity also grew, and growth in capitalist terms was extremely progressive—almost becoming routine. Had the destruction wrought by World War II been less complete, however, then this period, even with the aid of Keynesian demand management as a form of government intervention, would not have lasted so long. Nor would it have been so prosperous, first for the United States, and then, with recovery, for Western Europe as well. The contradictions were bound to reappear. The massive destruction and thus devaluation that resulted from the war simply meant that they reappeared later than they might have done otherwise. However, this time their resolution would demand that each nation—particularly the most advanced, or developed, capitalists countries and especially the United States, which emerged from the war as the world's strongest economy—would need to try to displace the contradictions beyond its own borders. Industrial or productive capitalists needed time to try to find new organizational patterns or patterns of accumulation that might restore their profitability.

The multinational and transnational corporate forms were one result. These corporations operate in much the same way as a national economy, equalizing the rate of profit internally (Harvey, 1999) and thus redistributing surplus-value from one sector or department of the corporation to another and maintaining the overall profit rate of the firm—that is, on the massive amount of total capital invested. It is worth noting that multi- and transnational corporations require a global financial structure and thus have fostered and accelerated the growth and consolidation of the world financial system and also the global telecommunications structure that supports it, eventually leading to financial capital's current dominance over industrial or productive capital in the global market (McNally, 1999). Equally important as these new forms of organization, industrial capitalists needed time for the full effect of unemployment to be felt and to thus exert the heavy hammer of discipline on their nations' workforces—forcing working people into accepting lower wages as well as new patterns of working and new, less favorable conditions of employment. In the meantime, capital in search of profitable investment flowed into financial institutions, encouraging profitmaking through speculation rather than production (Fine, Lapavitsas, and Milonakis, 1999; McNally, 1999). This bolstered the strength of money or financial capital in comparison to industrial, or productive, capital, but it also created new dilemmas for capitalism that have yet to be resolved. The first and foremost response to these problems has been the reassertion of liberal capitalism or neoliberalism, as it has come to be called, and with it the full unleashing or unfettering of market forces, along with various other forms of deregulation.

Since the end of the nineteenth century, individual capitalists, faced with the riskiness of capitalism, have sought to minimize these risks by adopting new forms of organization—from the joint stock companies of Marx's time to the multinational corporations of today—and also by attempting to control unfettered competition. In other words, they have sought ways of controlling the market or bettering their position within it. Yet, as Marx explains with great care and detail, the Law of Value, with all its consequences for capitalists—both positive and negative—only comes into force and functions so as to create and increase capitalist wealth under competitive conditions (Marx, 1865, p. 1020). Neoliberalism expresses a recognition (albeit no doubt not a full understanding) of this basic fact of life under capitalism—a fact of life with harsh consequences for the vast majority of humanity, including many capitalists. However, the proponents of neoliberal policies fail to realize that it is the competition between capitalist commodity producers that is crucial to capitalism, not the current type of competition, which focuses primarily on currency speculation rather than competitive production strategies (McNally, 1999). Recently there has been an outcry against neoliberalism and the assertion of a need to put brakes on it and against the process of complete and unrelenting globalization that it has unleashed, as well as the financial speculation that is both one of its preconditions and one of its results. However, when we remember that capital's contradiction must find resolution, even if only temporarily, somewhere, it seems unlikely that we will experience much more than the apparent softening of neoliberal policies—a softening that is more a matter of discourse than action or veritable policy changes. Nevertheless, there is one change we might expect.

In countries such as the United States, and to a lesser extent Western Europe—to say nothing of the former socialist states, where unemployment or its continuing threat has quite effectively disciplined the working population—we may find that the resolution of the contradictions is increasingly brought home again to the nation-state or region where the movements and developments—the immanent buildup of tension—within the contradictions will begin their cycle once more. Brenner's (1998) report on globalization gives a fair indication that this is what lies behind the recent economic recovery in the United States. It is also one of the reasons why the centralizing forces of globalization are simultaneously accompanied by decentralizing forces and even fragmentation, both nationally and/or regionally. In other words, the displacement of the contradictions and their resolution works in both directions geographically or spatially (Harvey, 1999). Thus it works in much the same way as it often does in general with capital accumulation—from the massive centralization and concentration of capital to its devaluation, disintegration and dispersal into new small ventures, where the cycle of accumulation and growth can begin once more. However, since the next time around will take place in a fully globalized, and thus more complex, system, the consequences of the contradictions may well be even more insidious—a gloomy prognosis, I admit, especially when, as yet, there is no guarantee that the capitalist system has actually begun to recover from its present crisis.

For the capitalists, as well as everyone else at the mercy of the system, the only way to deal—that is, cope—with capital's laws and tendencies, which operate as blind and ultimately uncontrollable forces, is to try to readjust and maneuver the ossified forms that result from value's movement, development and then separation into these ossified forms (Marx, 1865, pp. 967–969). Since that which actually governs these forms—be they money capital in its various manifestations, both real and fictitious, commodity capital or productive capital—is the social relation from which they are derived and of whose role the players in the game have little or no critical awareness, it is little wonder that crises occur and that seemingly unexplainable and absurd consequences continue to bedevil us in an ever-increasing manner.

Even if capitalists actually understood how the system works, they could not rectify it. Capitalism is based on contradictory, dialectically, or internally, related opposites—opposites the movements and developments of which mutually determine one another. As I explained, when we move toward favoring one opposite—for example, capital rather than labor—or placing emphasis on it, this worsens the situation of the other, and yet the existence of each opposite depends upon and determines the mode of existence of the other. Obviously this applies to the contradictory relation between labor and capital, but it is also true of the relations between the various capitalists with each other—both those who perform the same function and those who perform different functions. There is no possibility of a lasting equilibrium between the various opposites in capitalism—equilibrium is only ever achieved accidentally and fleetingly. The only way that human beings can gain control over the socioeconomic conditions of their lives—that is, the most basic and determining aspect of their lives—is to abolish the relations that unleash the uncontrollable consequences that are produced by capitalism's immanent dynamic. Anything less—especially attempts to make the relations of distribution or social relations in general more equitable—is no more than a palliative that loses its strength with repeated doses. Moreover, palliatives that have worked in the past may become unfeasible as capital's contradictions are played out globally or even locally and regionally within a global framework, becoming increasingly complex and all-encompassing.

One of the most crucial problems that capitalism faces in the new millennium is the increasingly questionable substance—that is, underpinning basis—of currency. Money has become a bit like Peter Pan's shadow, the further it has become separated from its real substance. Only, in this case, it is a matter of the shadow searching for Peter. This problem was set in motion with the dissolution of the Bretton Woods Agreement in 1971. Rather than the U.S. dollar acting as world money (in place of gold), exchange rates were floated; and, as I mentioned before, the value of national currencies became one of the main focuses for financial speculation. This situation has been exacerbated, especially since 1985, when the Paris Accord resulted in the devaluation of the U.S. dollar. The devaluation of the dollar made U.S. commodities highly competitive with their European and Japanese counterparts. And, as also mentioned previously, this focused competition on currencies and subsequently led to other strategic as well as IMF-imposed devaluations that have created turbulence in the world market (McNally, 1999). More recently, the devaluation of Japan's and China's currencies have led to crisis in the Southeast Asian economies (McNally, 1999).

The value of national currencies has become, more than ever before, influenced by factors other than economic performance or factors only indirectly related to a nation's economic strength—for example, factors such as political stability and power on the world stage (Marazzi, 1996). There are currently at least three other national currencies that vie with the U.S. dollar for dominance in the world's money markets and in the worldwide trade of other commodities—the pound sterling, the yen and the Euro/Deutschmark. The attempt of the United States to establish itself as the world's only superpower after the fall of the Berlin Wall has more to do with economics than sheer political bravado—or at least the latter is fostered by the former. Moreover, it should be clear to anyone who understands capitalism that the U.S. display of high-tech military superiority, whether in the Gulf War or more recently in Bosnia or wherever, figures centrally in its overall economic strategy. In the first instance, superpower status impacts on the value of the dollar—a shadow currency like all the others, seeking to find a new substance that can constitute its value, thus attempting to replace abstract human labor. In the second instance, it is about prestige and the association of this prestige with U.S. commodities. In other words, it is about giving U.S. business a competitive advantage in the newly created market for commodities that will be needed for the reconstruction of the war-torn and devastated communities and their economies. It is also about the struggle over which country's troops supervise the peace in a particular area, thus establishing influence over economic decisions through the giving of aid and establishing relations of indebtedness for the protection offered by the occupying forces against internal and external aggressors. I am by no means implying a conspiracy, for none is needed. What I am suggesting is simply good business sense within established capitalist relations, especially since in the aftermath of World War II this type of approach proved so successful to the U.S. economy with the institution of the Marshall Plan.

The success for the U.S. economy of the Marshall Plan is a brilliant example of how capital's dialectic works. U.S. firms prospered by promoting European recovery (George, 1986). Among other things, this meant that they made massive investments in fixed capital—plant and machinery—the cost of which takes approximately ten years to recoup while its value constantly deteriorates. However, once Europe recovered, it became, once again, a formidable competitor with the United States in both domestic and foreign trade. Virtually the same thing happened with Japan, whose recovery was supervised and thus influenced by the United States. While this may be healthy for the capitalist system as a whole, it was less than healthy for U.S. corporations that had accumulated rapidly and grown to enormous size when privileged with the near-monopoly conditions that prevailed in the immediate aftermath of World War II. Having grown used to noncompetitive conditions, these giant corporations often proved to be too inflexible when they were once again faced with competition. To make things worse, the competition came equipped with more advanced technology—fixed capital—and, as a result, higher levels of productivity (McNally, 1999). It is little wonder that the multinational organizational form developed first in the United States and grew as a necessity in order to disperse these large centralized concentrations of capital, placing them globally in positions of better access to the world market and also decentralizing certain levels of decision-making in order to increase flexibility, while simultaneously retaining the necessary advantages of large-scale investment—in fact, offering many advantages, including those mentioned previously.

The postwar period may have been a prosperous one for capitalism and one during which many ordinary working people felt the benefits of capitalist growth.

However, it may prove to be a dangerous period for humanity when it is looked back on in future years. This period of prosperity lulled people into a false sense of security and a belief that capitalism could deliver progress to all people, or at least it would do so eventually. In fact, it added considerable reinforcement to the "ideology of progress" that is part of capitalist ideology more generally—an untrammeled faith in science (that is, a misconceived notion of science), progress and the type of modernism that is synonymous with capitalism. With a dialectical understanding of capitalism, it is possible to position capital's postwar boom more accurately. It was a more or less protracted "blip" between a period when capitalism had finally reached a stage of permanent rather than cyclical crisis—a stage interrupted and then temporarily forestalled by the "cleansing" mechanisms of World War II—and the present, when capitalism seems once again to have entered a stage of permanent crisis (Bonefeld, 1999).

The only way to bring about a more just and humane existence for all human beings is to abolish the relations of capitalism. Critical educators can help people to understand these relations and how they lead to specific unalterable negative consequences. Moreover, they can help people to understand the dialectical nature of capital's contradictions and thus to grasp the positive potential that has also been created within these relations but that lies dormant and thwarted so long as the relations prevail—the possibilities of a very different and much better future for humanity. It is a propitious time for critical education, but also a time when the need for critical education is urgent.

As capitalism has become a fully global, universal system with an abstract form of social domination that increasingly penetrates every aspect of our existence, its contradictions and necessary consequences have become more pervasive and apparent. People in increasing numbers and for various reasons are expressing their desire for change, but thus far their focus has been on the results, or problems, rather than the causes. Thus there is a gap between wanting change and knowing what needs to be changed, or at least knowing what needs to be changed in order to really make a difference—what must be abolished and what can be salvaged if transformed within alternative relations. For example, global campaigns have sprung up to challenge neoliberalism, but neoliberalism is only the most recent and drastic response—that is, the most drastic response thus far devised—to managing capital's contradictions. It may be the immediate enemy, but its elimination would by no means eliminate the contradictions. In other words, we need to understand and *name* the real enemy. If we do not do so, then the specter of capitalism will simply come to hover over humanity in an even more menacing form. Critical educators can play an important role in helping people to develop a more accurate comprehension of the real causes of the problems they are experiencing—the relations that are actually devastating the lives of millions of people. And, as I suggested before, it is increasingly necessary and urgent for critical educators to seize the initiative. The rest of this book addresses this important and urgent project by exploring the relation between critical education and global capitalism from a variety of perspectives.

NOTES

1. As I mentioned in chapter 2, Marx discusses capitalist commodity production in terms of industrial production. This was the first fully developed form of commodity production. However, in contemporary capitalism many services are also produced as commodities, just as Marx suggested they would be, in his discussions of productive labor. Since, in this chapter, I follow Marx's explanation in Volume 3 of *Capital*, I also discuss commodity production only in terms of industrial production. However, it should be understood that the explanation pertains, in general, to capitalist commodity production, or all production based on productive capital—that is, capital that is invested in order to produce surplus-value.

2. When production of a commodity is evenly distributed throughout a sphere of production, "socially necessary labor-time," and therefore market value, is determined by average conditions; however, if the great mass of commodities is produced under either the best or the worst conditions, then these determine the market value—that is, the market, or social, value deviates, accordingly, from the "socially necessary labor-time" (Marx, 1865, pp. 284–285). This type of deviation would also occur when, for example, demand is so much stronger than supply that people are not deterred from buying commodities produced under the worst conditions; or when, conversely, supply exceeds demand, and commodities can only be sold below their value as determined by "socially necessary labor-time" (pp. 279–280). In order to simplify the discussion in the main text, I treat market value as being synonymous with "socially necessary labor-time." Although they usually converge, hopefully it is clear that there is a distinction that might need to be taken into consideration in more specialized analyses of contemporary capitalism.

3. Marx also suggests that the rate of profit would be even lower if capital invested in large-scale fixed capital projects like railways—that is, capital that pays out dividends or interest on these investments—entered into the equalization process. It would be lower because it is these that have the very highest ratio of constant to variable capital (Marx, 1865, pp. 347–348).

4. In arguing his explanation of capitalism against bourgeois economists and political economy in general, Marx goes through innumerable possible combinations of factors and considers almost every conceivable result in addition to stating the general tendencies of capitalism. I offer, instead, just the tendencies and what I consider to be the most appropriate examples to explain them. I add, here, one necessary but I think relatively unimportant caveat—that is, unimportant in terms of developing a comprehensive, albeit nonspecialist, understanding of capitalism. Some authors, for example Harvey (1999), bring up a few factors that Marx fails to consider; but in the case of Harvey and many others, this does not deter them from basically agreeing with Marx's explanation—most importantly, his explication of the Law of Value.

REFERENCES

Bonefeld, W. (1999). "The Politics of Change." *Common Sense*, 24, 76–90.

Brenner, R. (1998). "The Economics of Global Turbulence." *New Left Review*, 229, 1–264.

Fine, B., Lapavitsas, C., and Milonakis, D. (1999). "Addressing the World Economy: Two Steps Back." *Capital & Class*, 67 (Spring), 47–90.

George, S. (1986). *How the Other Half Dies: The Real Reasons for World Hunger*. Harmondsworth, U.K.: Penguin, 1986.

George, S. (1988). *A Fate Worse Than Debt*. Harmondsworth, U.K.: Penguin.

George, S., and Sabelli, F. (1994). *Faith and Credit: The World Bank's Secular Empire*. Harmondsworth, U.K.: Penguin.

Harvey, D. (1989). *The Condition of Postmodernity*. Oxford: Basil Blackwell.

Harvey, D. (1999). *The Limits to Capital* (new edition). London: Verso.

Marazzi, C. (1996). "Money in the World Crisis: The New Basis of Capitalist Power." In W. Bonefeld and J. Holloway (Eds.), *Global Capital, National State and the Politics of Money* (pp. 69–91). London: Macmillan.

Marx, K. (1858). *Grundrisse*, translated and with a Foreword by Martin Nicolaus. Harmondsworth, U.K.: Penguin, 1973.

Marx, K. (1865). *Capital*, Vol. 3, translated by David Fernbach, Introduction by Ernest Mandel. Harmondsworth, U.K.: Penguin, 1981.

Marx, K. (1875). "Critique of the Gotha Programme." In D. McLellan (Ed.), *Karl Marx: Selected Writings* (pp. 564–570). Oxford: Oxford University Press, 1977.

Marx, K. (1878). *Capital*, Vol. 2, translated by David Fernbach, Introduction by Ernest Mandel. Harmondsworth, U.K.: Penguin, 1978.

McNally, D. (1999). "Turbulence in the World Economy." *Monthly Review*, 51 (No. 2, June) [www.monthlyreview.org].

Rosdolsky, R. (1977). *The Making of Marx's Capital*. London: Pluto Press.

Rubin, I. I. (1972). *Essays on Marx's Theory of Value*, translated from the third edition, 1928, by M. Samardija and F. Perlman. Detroit, MI: Black & Red.

4

Ya Basta [Enough]!
Challenging Capitalism
in the New Millennium

Irony and uncertainty abound as we enter the third millennium. The fall of communism/socialism left capitalism and liberal democracy the undisputed victors of the twentieth century. Ostensibly the contest between competing economic systems and worldviews or "ideologies"—a contest that cost millions in lives and dollars, pounds, yens, marks, and so on—had come to an end. Yet, despite the triumphalism of the victors, there is little to celebrate. Capitalism—global capital—continues to be in crisis, regardless of claims to the contrary, and liberal democracy is increasingly seen as a sham as many citizens, in the established democracies, have lost faith in politicians and government bureaucracies. Free elections have become little more than media sideshows, with soundbites and hard cash the main determinants of election outcomes (to say nothing of the recent fiasco with the U.S. presidential election). For these as well as other reasons ranging from environmental destruction to the harsh consequences of neoliberal policies, discontent is growing and being expressed in a multitude of forms.

In this chapter, I consider the nature of this discontent, together with the challenge it may or may not pose to capitalism and the liberal democratic state—the problems and the possibilities. I also consider various misconceptions that need to be rectified in order to mount an effective challenge to capitalism and to create an authentic socialist/communist alternative to it. I endeavor to make it clear that it is one thing—and an extremely important one at that—to say "NO" to the forces unleashed by capitalism, as, for example, the Zapatistas in Mexico have been doing since 1994 and as the tens of thousands who demonstrated in

Seattle in November 1999, Washington, D.C., in April 2000 and in London and elsewhere on the first May Day weekend of the new millennium have done, but it is another to understand what creating a better future for humanity entails. The first step to that understanding, as I have explained in the preceding chapters, is a dialectical comprehension of capitalism; in other words, we need to uncover the source of the problems because it is this source that must be the focus of change and transformation. In concluding his book, the *Age of Extremes: The Short Twentieth Century 1914–1991*, Eric Hobsbawm makes another thing very clear:

> If humanity is to have a recognizable future, it cannot be by prolonging the past or present. If we try to build the third millennium on that basis, we shall fail. And the price of failure, that is to say, the alternative to a changed society, is darkness. [1995, p. 585]

The urgent need for change, in the current situation where the possibility of finding an alternative to capitalism seems so remote, has left many socialists both puzzled and perplexed. Some have more or less dug their heels in and become increasingly defensive about the necessary leading role of the working class (i.e., the industrial workers) in revolutionary change. Others, who share an equally limited concept of the working class—and, by implication, an equally limited concept of the extent of capitalist exploitation—have all too hastily dismissed the potential and importance of class struggle and have launched into a somewhat frenetic search for new subjects who might become the agents of historical change. The search has been far from difficult, as an increasing number of groups have become vocal in expressing their discontent. However, this discontent is rarely directed at capitalism itself.

One of the largest and best-publicized public displays of discontent took place in Seattle, Washington, during the final days of the twentieth century. Individuals and various groups representative of many of the world's discontented gathered in Seattle in late November 1999 to take part in what was to become the last mass demonstration of the century. They were protesting against the newly formed World Trade Organization, the WTO, which was set up by the 1995 Uruguay round of GATT (the General Agreement on Tariffs and Trade). The WTO is an organization of 137 member states that is supposed to be a forum for negotiating international trade agreements and a monitoring and regulatory authority for enforcing these agreements. In general, the people demonstrating in Seattle were protesting because the WTO is seen to reflect the interests of business rather than workers and consumers. This mass demonstration, as well as some of the others that have taken place since then, brought together people reflecting an amalgam of different interests. For example, the Seattle demonstration included those who were protesting against working conditions and various grass-root organizations with interests ranging from the rights of indigenous peoples, human rights more generally, environmental issues, feminism, the antihomophobic and gay rights struggle, the plight of small farmers, animal liberation, as well as individuals and groups promoting greater democratization and in some instances even socialist values and aspirations.

According to Elaine Bernard (1999), the Executive Director of the Harvard Trade Union Program, the two factors that united this disparate group of protesters were their resistance to the free-trade agenda of corporations and also to the corporations' continual drive to undermine processes of social decision-making and thus democracy. As far as these protesters are concerned, the WTO is the international organization that was created in order to promote this global corporate agenda. Therefore, the challenge mounted in Seattle, and also to varying degrees in demonstrations that have followed it, was directed at corporations and those who run them or the organizations that support their interests rather than capitalism as a form of national and global socioeconomic organization. Bernard notes that the protesters were divided between those who wanted to abolish the WTO and those who thought that the only possibility was to call for its reform. The latter group want to transform the WTO by making it accept certain core labor rights, or what Europeans call a "social clause," and objectives aimed at environmental protection.

Burbach, Núñez and Kagarlitsky (1997) in their book, *Globalization and Its Discontents*, say:

Humanity is in a tumultuous stage of its development. There are enormous possibilities for increasing the general well-being, and yet the globe is mired in an unprecedented era of misery, alienation and turbulence . . . [we need] new actors and social forces that c[an] enable humanity to break through this impasse. [p. 1]

These authors go on to complain that there is no longer any world view or vision capable of forging a mass movement and that those who once offered reformist programs are unable to come up with viable solutions for dealing with the increasing polarization between the rich and poor and the developed and underdeveloped nations. Yet they also claim that globalization has created "a global army of discontents" who are capable of acting as an "antisystemic force" (p. 5). Those whom they consider to be the new antagonists include radical environmental groups, militant feminists, indigenous societies, human rights organizations, fundamentalist religious movements and the urban underclasses, who, they note, periodically revolt and demonstrate their anger by pillaging the property of those who are materially comfortable. They see all of these groups as offering a challenge to the authority of those in positions of power, and as a consequence they conclude: "All of these challenges to the system of domination are 'antisystemic' . . . [t]hey shake capitalism at its roots rather than engaging in a frontal attack as the Bolsheviks and Third World liberation movements did" (p. 21). I return to these authors' discussion of the discontents later, but here I will simply note that what these authors see as the roots of capitalism are not roots at all but the consequences that derive from capital's essence—the "essence" that I discussed in chapter 2. Furthermore, if we look at what the discontents they identify are seeking to accomplish, worthy though many of these causes and campaigns are, they clearly are not challenging capitalism. In fact, their last group, the urban underclasses in their periodic rioting and looting, as these authors also seem to acknowledge or at least imply, are quite simply succumbing to capitalism's commodity fetishism through desperate acts of violence.

The problem of mistaking the symptoms or consequences for the causes or "roots" of capitalism lies at the heart of Marx's critique. To reiterate, his critique of capitalism is equally and simultaneously both a critique of the way people think about or understand the system and an explanation of how capitalism leads to this type of thinking or understanding—that is, how it fosters a characteristic type of misconception that provides the raw material for what Marx refers to as ideological thought. Moreover, his critique was pitched not just at bourgeois thinking but also some socialist thinking that also focused on symptoms and consequences rather than the real contradictions from which they arise. In fact, Marx's entire project was aimed at enabling people to understand a system that was not decipherable from even the most rigorous empirical observations and investigations of the surface, or concrete, manifestations of capitalism's essence. Although he scathingly criticized those who willfully misinterpreted reality, he understood how easy it was for even the most serious and committed adversaries of capitalism to be misled by its dialectical nature. Yet, despite his efforts—the copious detail with which he presents his arguments and explanations—it is not only his detractors but also many from among those who are his supporters who fail to grasp some of the most essential aspects of his thinking. To move beyond the present impasse that has been created by these misconceptions, it is necessary to highlight these essential aspects of Marx's thought. But before going into them, I want to make some other general points about the nature of contemporary discontent.

Whether you read progressive and left-wing literature, listen to the news or surf the Internet to listen to the voices of the discontented, you will find their protests directed at one or the other foe or some combination of four "enemies": (1) globalization; (2) neoliberalism; (3) corporations, especially the multi- and transnational varieties, and the international institutions that are seen as promoting their agendas and (4) any nation, group, corporation or institution that is infringing human rights or interfering with democratic processes and thus undermining liberal democracy. The most sophisticated challenges attack all of these, assuming that they are all linked together in various unclearly defined ways. However, whatever the challenge or its level of sophistication, most of the solutions being proposed are basically the same. For example, environmentalists and defenders of the poor and starving call for greater regulation of the forces unleashed by neoliberalism, or what, in fact, as I explained, is simply the neoliberal response to the most recent crises in capitalism—crises that began to emerge in the early 1970s. You may remember me mentioning in chapter 1 that even some of the capitalists who grew wealthy from the tidal wave of neoliberal policies that swept the globe from the late 1970s through the 1980s, especially the financial deregulation that fostered the rapid and unrelenting globalization of capitalist relations, are now calling for a halt to the process and stressing the need for greater regulatory mechanisms. In clamoring for regulation, these individuals, as well as various groups, increasingly call for greater transparency and account-ability regarding the actions of both public and private institutions.

Some of the discontented have argued for far-reaching regulatory mechanisms to be enshrined in legislation. Experience has taught them how easy it is for capital to circumvent the highly compromised regulations imposed by regulatory agencies, such as, the Environmental Protection Agency (EPA) in the United States. For example, they have seen how piecemeal restrictions, such as limiting the amount of a particular poisonous substance that can be emitted by a particular industry, can be easily diluted and are far from what is really needed to effec-tively promote and sustain the environment. As a result, they now demand more all-encompassing legislation, which would effectively prevent every industry from emitting any type of pollutant (Grossman, 1998). Yet even these challenges fall short of actually challenging capitalism, and it is often far from clear whether those who promote this type of reform see any direct connection between these environmental problems and capitalist social relations.

This is hardly surprising when some of the most incisive critics of the devasta-tion wreaked by capitalism—people like Noam Chomsky (e.g., 1998) and Susan George (e.g., 1999), who have assiduously compiled a considerable amount of damning evidence against capitalism's consequences and who also wage untiring and courageous campaigns against capitalist absurdities—repeatedly call for institutional change, together with greater legal controls and firmer regulations, rather than for structural change or the abolition of capitalism, and when, from the center-Left to the far Left, scholars such as David Held (e.g., 1995) and Samir Amin (e.g., 1997) place their faith in the emergence of a cosmopolitan or global form of democratic governance that could ensure a fairer distribution of the world's wealth and also implement regulations capable of protecting the environ-ment and promoting sustainable development. In other words, it should not be surprising that current expressions of discontent fail to name the real enemy or to question the limited form of democracy that serves this enemy so well when some of our finest minds and most ardent critics seem to frame their criticisms entirely within the horizon, or the parameters, of capitalism and liberal democ-racy.

Almost every critic of the current world order agrees on the need to re-invigorate and democratize civil society and thus the necessity of making it possible for people to engage in shaping their communities and their destinies. They also agree that existing political structures—that is, organizations and governing bodies as well as the practices within them—must be made much more transparent, accountable and responsive to the expressed needs and aspirations of citizens. Yet there appears to be a general acceptance of the concept of liberal democracy or a resigned acceptance of the commonsense notion that this is as democratic as it is possible to be in complex social orders. And this acceptance persists even though there is also considerable unease or concern that liberal democracies are not operating as effectively as they should. People seem to think that measures designed to increase transparency and accountability and make liberal democracy work more effectively will make it possible to hold capital to account and force it to become a fairer and more responsible system. Somehow people must be encouraged to give up such ill-founded utopian thinking, and this is where critical education—or more precisely what I call revolutionary critical education—has an important and crucial role to play, a role I focus on directly in chapters 5–7.

Behind most of these voices of discontent, therefore, there is a tacit acceptance of capitalism and its handmaiden, liberal democracy, although for some it is quite obviously a reluctant acceptance. There is little doubt that the failure and dissolution of many of the professed socialist nations—the failure and dissolution of what for so long many believed to be the alternative to capitalism—have fostered this acceptance. Nonetheless, as far as economic problems are concerned, in my opinion something much more fundamental underlies a great deal of this often tacit acceptance of capitalism as well as the pervasive misrecognition and misidentification of the "enemy." Those who assume that greater legal control and regulation of capitalism can correct or ameliorate the problems they identify do not understand fully—that is, dialectically—how the capitalist system works. Not only do they think that it is possible to cure the problems through reform, but they locate the problems and therefore the solutions either with individual capitalists or with particular corporations and/or institutions. Having to function within capitalist social relations and to compete in order to be successful or simply to survive is bound to cultivate the development of certain personal characteristics or organizational styles like self-centeredness and greed, but to blame individual capitalists or corporations or even the institutions set up to facilitate and orchestrate the system and the cut-throat competition that abounds, particularly when capital is in crisis, gets us nowhere in terms of creating a more just society.

Furthermore, claims that the only way to save the ecosystem and biosphere is to curtail growth, when growth is always assumed on a capitalist basis and when the vast majority of the world's population has thus far not benefited one jot from capitalist-induced growth, may not only be misguided but also border on being unethical. Whether or not growth and productivity must be limited in any future society is something we cannot properly decide until adequate scientific research and other resources are redirected away from wasteful uses, such as defense and military programs and the pursuit of profits. In other words, we cannot come to these conclusions—or, for that matter, any others—until we have considered growth in terms of transformed social relations in which all of the necessary intellectual and material resources could be concentrated on finding ways of both sustaining and enhancing the environment while also providing for the general well-being of humanity. At present even most of the well-informed prognoses pertaining to the health of the planet are made within a framework of assumptions delimited by capitalist social relations as they have operated within both liberal democracies and also so-called socialist societies or command economies, such as the Soviet Union and its satellite states in Eastern Europe.

Having said this, it does not follow and I want to be clear that I am not saying that reform is unimportant or unnecessary. The millions who are dying of starvation and malnutrition and the precarious health of the earth cannot wait for a new society to emerge. Reform, and struggling for it, is crucial both because we must attempt to make life more palatable for those suffering the harshest consequences of capitalism and because we must try to forestall environmental collapse. But it is also important as well as essential because it is through and within the struggles for reform—whether these pertain to issues emanating from the shop floor, the community, the environment or any other site where the ramifications of capitalism are experienced—that critical/revolutionary praxis develops. These struggles are some of the most important sites in which critical education can and must take place. Moreover, if this critical education takes place within changed relations (as I discuss in later chapters), people will be transforming not only their consciousness but their subjectivity and sensibility as well. This type of preparatory struggle is seen as a necessity and is thus advocated by Marx and also by Gramsci and Freire, all of whom argue that this is the main reason why struggling for reform is essential for authentic socialist transformation (see Allman, 1999; Allman and Wallis, 1995).

Even though the various types of challenges to which I have referred misrecognize the "enemy" and thus cannot rectify the problems that are their chief concern, they have produced some interesting ideas and real possibilities that could be extremely beneficial once capitalism is abolished. Of more immediate importance, however, is the emergence, within some of these struggles, of certain creative and fundamental insights that are important not only for a socialist/communist future, but also for the way in which we go about challenging capitalism and creating a just and equitable alternative to it. I return to these later in this chapter. First, however, as I indicated earlier, I want to identify some of the problems or misconceptions pertaining to Marx's thinking that are barriers to formulating an effective challenge to capitalism. Throughout this book, I have discussed various misconceptions of Marx's ideas, but here I want to highlight those that I consider to be the most formidable barriers to mounting an effective challenge to capitalism. Some of them, if they persist, will also thwart any attempts we might make to create a better society.

BARRIERS TO A BETTER FUTURE:
MISCONCEPTIONS OF MARX

When Marx speaks of the social relations of capitalism determining the way in which it moves and develops and of how these give rise to its contradictory nature, many socialists, and others too, as I said before, think that he is referring to property relations and therefore the private ownership of the means of production as well as the private relations of exchange that buyers and seller enter into in market transactions—relations mediated by money. Accordingly, they think that the inequitable distribution that characterizes capitalist societies results from property relations—in particular, the private ownership of the means of production. Clearly Marx was critical of all of these relations. Free-wage laborers only came into existence because their means of production, the land and implements they needed to produce their subsistence, had been expropriated through private ownership. The only way they could survive was to sell their labor-power as a commodity in the market. But the social relation that lies at the heart of capitalism, that turns all the preconditions for capitalism's emergence on the historical scene into ever-recurring results, is the internal, or dialectical, relation that exists between labor and capital in the capitalist production process—that is, the immediate process of production.

This is the relation in which already existing value is preserved and new value—necessary and surplus-value—is created by "live" human labor. It is also the relation that leads to the inequitable and unjust distribution of use-values, the accumulation of capital and the enrichment of the capitalist class through the exploitation of labor. It is the relation that designates production for the market, thus sustaining and fostering market relations and competition, in particular the competitive struggle between capitalists that then acts back on the relations of production, setting into motion the dialectical movements and developments that produce the historically specific laws and tendencies of capitalism. And it is also this relation between labor and capital that perpetuates and thus makes possible the continuing determination of wealth in terms of value rather than use-values, thus creating and expediting the growing polarization of humanity as well as capital's dynamic that propels its abstract form of social domination across the face of the globe.

Therefore, while private property, along with other features that we associate with capitalism such as commodities and markets, all predate the specific labor–capital relation of production and serve as preconditions for it, once capitalism has developed, they are the results of that relation. They cease being the actual cause of any of its dire consequences. Clearly, then, it is the social relation between labor and capital that must be abolished if we are to bring an end to any of these results as well as the even more dire consequences of capitalism. Marx's discussion of cooperatives in Volume 1 of *Capital* indicates that the same relations can prevail even in the absence of private ownership. The type of market exchange and social relations of distribution that have arisen and spread pervasively as well as invasively within capitalism—the exchange and distribution of labor, products and services as commodities—must always be based on exploitative relations of production. They are locked into internal symbiotic relations, which would exist even under a system of social ownership.

These distinctions between the various social relations of capitalism and their respective locations within the recurring sequence of preconditions, or causes, and results, or effects and consequences, are important because they help to determine what constitutes reform, or temporary ameliorative measures, as opposed to authentic transformation—in other words, revolutionary social transformation. In fact, it is through making these distinctions that we can understand that certain reforms, such as those aimed at redistribution, can never be anything but temporary and that, in the long term, they can also have counterproductive consequences. These would occur if the reforms lulled people into a false sense of victory and nurtured a unidirectional conception of progress, thus deflecting attention away from the real causes—or dialectical contradictions—that, in the meantime, continue to develop, reaching new levels of complexity capable of creating even more dire and devastating consequences and doing so on a larger scale. On the other hand, reforms and the struggles that take place to bring them about are necessary and important, and they need not be counterproductive. They can be the exact opposite when those involved are fully aware of the limits of reform, and when equally they are aware of the organizational and educational potential of these struggles. This is a point to which I return later in this book.

Capitalism's postwar "Golden Age" created the illusion that reforms could permanently change the system and that the accumulation of reforms would eventually turn capitalism into a much fairer and more equitable system. This illusion simply feeds into and is bolstered by the more encompassing and pervasive "ideology of progress" that arose with the Enlightenment philosophy of the eighteenth century and modernism in the nineteenth century. It is an illusion that is still prevalent, despite the fairly recent dismantling and dilution of many of the progressive social democratic reforms made during the postwar period of relative harmony and economic growth. And it is the illusion that underpins many of the confused and misguided responses to our current problems. For example, people who advocate global governance and regulatory mechanisms—the creation of something like what David Held (1993, 1995) calls cosmopolitan democracy—seem to assume that the social democratic compromise, or Keynesian mode of economic regulation, failed, or, rather, its effectiveness was exhausted, at the level of the nation-state because of globalization. As a consequence, they assume that this mode of managing capitalism can still work if applied supranationally. Other people, like Samir Amin, have a more radical concept of the potential of social democracy. Amin (1997) advocates global governance as a means of making the voices of the excluded majority of humanity count, thus creating a global democratic process whereby socialism or some global form of socioeconomic organization capable of delivering justice and equality for all human beings will evolve and eventually replace capitalism.

Those who advocate global governance from either of these perspectives or motivations seem unaware of capitalism's essence, and especially of how its dialectical contradictions move and develop in conditions of intense global competition. They fail to see, as do those who think that consumer pressure can persuade businesses to act fairly and with a sense of social responsibility, that capitalist nation-states and transnational corporations—or, for that matter, all firms that depend on export markets—are locked into a fierce competitive struggle (moreover, a competitive struggle that is absolutely necessary to the appropriate functioning of capitalism). It is these competitive social relations that force firms to search the globe for conditions that allow them to cut their cost prices—conditions that usually mean cheaper labor costs and lower standards of working conditions, deregulated markets, and so on. They also force governments to create an atmosphere (such as adopting certain types of educational policies and practices) that is highly attractive to capital—both the retention of nationally based firms and the attraction of foreign investment.

The race is to the bottom, not the top; in other words, it is a race to see who can get by with the minimum or lowest standards of social and economic justice as well as environmental protection and sustainability. This is not because governments, people and corporations are necessarily greedy, unscrupulous, mean or uncaring, though they may be all of these. It is due to the fact that they are locked into historically specific social relations, a form of wealth and an abstract form of social domination that now engulfs the entire globe. They cannot escape from or circumvent these relations, and if they are to survive within them, they cannot choose to do other than what is necessary to compete in the global market or, for that matter, regional and national markets. The same situation would exist even if markets were primarily domestic or only national or regional in scope. The global factor simply increases the competitive pressure and increases the complexity and risks involved in either winning or just surviving. As Wood (1999) argues, markets are constraining, not enabling, mechanisms that dictate certain types of behaviors that preclude the possibility of people or individual corporations acting responsibly and fairly. No matter how much corporations' mission statements and projections of their corporate image incorporate the discourses of fairness, partnership and human rights, attempting to persuade us that this is their intent, it is the social relations of capitalism that determine what they can and must do. And this is also true for governments that wish to support them. A global form of governance might give a greater voice to the majority of human beings who are now excluded, but if their voices call only for a fairer distribution of the world's wealth rather than the abolition of capitalism, then the best that can be hoped for is the highly compromised limits of reform.

Another extremely problematical misconception has to do with Marx's concept of class (which I discussed previously) and, by way of extension, the notion of the revolutionary subject. According to Marxist–Leninist theory (as opposed to the concept conveyed in the main corpus of Marx's writings),[1] the industrial proletariat is the revolutionary subject, the class that is destined to challenge and ultimately overthrow capitalism. However, and this is where Lenin's interpretation of Marx figures centrally, this class can only recognize and rise to its historical mission under the guidance of the revolutionary vanguard—the communists party members who must bring Marx's scientific understanding of capitalism to the revolutionary subjects, thereby turning them into a class aware of its historical role (McLellan, 1983).[2] There are two problems that arise from these ideas. One has to do with the notion of a revolutionary vanguard. This, however, is a problem that I will deal with in subsequent chapters, when I focus directly on critical education. The other problem is related to the concept of class.

Over the past thirty years, in the developed countries, industrial production has declined dramatically, and with it the number of people who could be considered the industrial proletariat. Some industrial production has been transferred to less developed countries, where it can be carried out under conditions more favorable to capital. Although there are some indications that industrial production is picking up once again in the developed world, it is only doing so in altered conditions that require much less labor-power. This sequence of events has led to two different conclusions, both of which I have mentioned before and briefly summarize here. Some people think that when and if world revolution ever becomes feasible, it will begin in the so-called "Third World" countries, where there are still considerable concentrations of labor-intensive industries. Others seem to have given up on the industrial proletariat or at least no longer consider it to be the primary agent in revolutionary change; and they have begun therefore to look to other groups of discontented and exploited people in the hope of finding a possible successor. I have attempted to encapsulate an extremely complex situation in a few sentences only because I want to focus my discussion on the misconception that, I think, lies behind these varying responses to the contemporary reality of global capital—the misconception of Marx's concept of class. However, I return to the point about the search for an alternative revolutionary subject after a brief recap of Marx's dialectical concept of class.

When I presented Marx's explanation of capitalism, I frequently noted that he used the industrial proletariat throughout his discussions of the labor–capital relation because industrial production was the form of commodity production from which fully developed capitalism first arose. It was still the prevalent type of commodity production when Marx undertook his critique of capitalism and political economy; and by focusing on it, he was able not only to lay bare the laws and motions of the fully developed capitalist social formation, but also to elaborate these with a plethora of evidence and rich contemporary as well as historical detail that was highly relevant to his intended working-class readers. Nevertheless, as I explained previously, he frequently stressed that productive labor—the type of labor internally related to capital—is labor that produces surplus-value rather than a particular form of labor that produces a particular type of commodity. And when he makes this point, on more than one occasion, as I previously cited, he gives examples that include various service occupations, such as teaching, painting and decorating and even acting or performing on stage in the theater. This means that for Marx class was and is a relation, not a thing, fixed status or category pertaining to a specific category of concrete labor. Marx's concept of class was a dialectical and open concept. And once this is understood, it is possible to see not only why he predicted that capitalism would eventually develop into a society divided basically into two classes—that is, labor, or the proletariat, and capital—but also that his prediction was correct. At least, this seems to be the direction in which we are increasingly headed.

So where does this take us in terms of considering the revolutionary subject? The industrial proletariat may be shrinking, but nationally and globally the proletariat—that is, productive labor—is growing as more and more people and their areas of work or occupations are incorporated within the labor–capital relation. In other words, more and more products and services are being commodified, and the labor-power of those who produce and provide them is increasingly commodified as well—that is, recast within the labor–capital relation and thus drawn into and exploited within the valorization process. Sometimes this commodification of labor takes place rapidly and at other times it transpires only over a relatively long period of time. In the latter case, the result of a labor process might be commodified for quite some time before the labor that produces it is actually sold as the commodity labor-power and used to create surplus-value. Therefore, the transition period between a particular job or labor process simply providing revenue and the same job or labor process providing surplus-value can vary in length. Whether the transition is rapid or slow, once the product or service is commodified, then those whose labor produces it will be subjected to tighter control, supervision and monitoring or accountability. Often the actual job or labor process will be subdivided among various people in order to increase efficiency and facilitate monitoring and control. This means that areas of work that once required a certain level of skill, either or both mental and manual, are subdivided so that each new subdivision of the job demands little or no skill at all, thus operating in the same way that Marx describes it happening with commercial labor—a process I mentioned in chapter 3. Currently, even some professional people are experiencing this type of transition in some if not all aspects of their work, and some have described it as a process of deskilling or deintellectualization.

The point to all of this is that there is no longer, if there ever was, one revolutionary subject—that is, one particular, dominated or exploited group of working people who sell their capacity to work and whose objective interest in the abolition of capitalism is greater than that of any other group. With a dialectical and, thus, relational concept of class, we can understand that the proletariat (thereby revolutionary subject) is fast becoming the class to which the vast majority of humanity belongs. Potentially and essentially this is a positive development so far as challenging and abolishing capitalism is concerned. Nevertheless, there remains the problem of critical awareness or class-consciousness. For Marx, the proletariat was the revolutionary subject because the interests, concerns and problems of the working class (whatever its composition at a particular point in time) coincided with the interests of humanity—both the survival and the full and enriched development of human beings. And their interests coincided because, as Marx foresaw, in the long term the vast majority of humanity would be incorporated into and exploited within the labor–capital relation. They would have become the dialectical, internally related, antagonistic opposite of capital— the potential critically conscious negatives in that "unity of opposites."

Furthermore, Marx's critique of capitalism indicates that the interests of humanity coincide with the interests or well-being of the natural world because human beings, from the moment they intervene in nature, become internally related with nature. The existence, development and thus well-being of each depend upon the existence, development and well-being of the other. Marx, like most people of his time with an interest in the sciences, thought that human beings should be in control of nature. But unlike many who advocated this, he thought that they should use their scientific knowledge not to exploit nature but to make sure that natural resources were managed and used in a rational and sensible manner. He assumed that advances in science and human reason could be used to foster the harmonious coexistence and mutual dependence of life forms that share the natural world. Or at least they would be used in this way in a socialist/communist society. He never said all of this in so many words, but the logic of his thought concerning the full development of human beings and his critique of capitalism and its potential for producing devastating consequences, such as those that arise from its destructive and exploitative approach to nature and natural resources, can only lead to this type of conclusion. In particular, his critique of capital's drive to create its historically specific form of wealth based on value, with little regard to the nature of the use-values to which it must be related, or attached, or to how they are produced, indicates that Marx was well aware of and concerned about capitalism's potential devastation of the environment (Burkett, 1999).

There are many misconceptions of Marx's thinking; however, there are two remaining ones that are important to this discussion. One is fairly straightforward, but the other leads to several other mistaken ideas. I will start with the latter after reiterating that I am considering the misconceptions that, I think, present the greatest barriers to the formation of a social movement capable of effectively challenging capitalism. In other words, a social movement with a realistic alternative vision—a movement capable of initiating the struggle to create a social formation based on the first principle of communism: "from each according to his[her] ability, to each according to his[her] needs" (Marx, 1875, p. 569); and also one, in keeping with Marx's ideas, that would be based on a material base, which would enable people to be rich in needs (Heller, 1976). The first of the remaining misconceptions—that is, the one that leads to further problems—has to do with Marx's explanation of the Law of Value.

Even among Marxists who base their thinking primarily on the writings of Marx, rather than on the various schools or renditions of Marxism that arose after his death, there are fundamental differences in the interpretation of Marx's "Labor Theory of Value" or what Marx normally refers to as the "Law of Value." Before Marx, both Adam Smith and David Ricardo had formulated "Labor" theories of value. However, it was Marx who was able to explain and formulate the theory in a comprehensive manner that explicated the entire basis of the movement and development of a fully developed capitalist system. Some Marxists and many non-Marxists, who do not fully grasp Marx's explanation, tend to think that the "Labor Theory of Value," or "Law of Value," pertained only to commodity production prior to the advent of fully developed capitalism. But this is not the problem that is my central concern in this discussion. Marxists who do accept the centrality of the "Labor Theory of Value," or "Law of Value" to Marx's entire explanation and critique of capitalism are divided over their inter-pretations of what Marx meant by labor. It is this difference that feeds back into the misconception of his concept of class, or more specifically productive labor. But this is not the only problem that results.

For some Marxists, the labor that constitutes value is physiological labor. In other words, they may realize that labor other than industrial labor can create value, but they still hold on to the idea that it must be a type of labor that involves physical manipulation or the expenditure of physical energy. One of the main problems that arises from this is that not only do they tend to elevate, or idolize, physical labor, they also tend to ignore the problems associated with the value, as opposed to use-value, form of wealth. For others, like myself, value is constituted by abstract labor, or social labor in general. Abstract labor is the substance of value, but the magnitude of value is measured in labor-time; and the labor that Marx is referring to in the "Law of Value" is the labor that constitutes "socially necessary labor-time," part of which is the surplus labor that creates surplus-value. Furthermore, the value form of wealth that is created by abstract labor is one of the most obscene problems of the capitalist form of socioeconomic organization.

One of the reasons for the confusion over what Marx actually meant may have to do with the way in which he presented his explanation of "socially necessary labor-time" in the first chapter of Volume 1 of Capital (Marx, 1867, pp. 125–177). This explanation is presented, as are most of Marx's explanations, with the painstaking detailed unfolding of an exhaustive scientific (dialectical) explana-tion of empirical or observable, concrete processes and phenomena. As I noted in chapter 2, it is a logical/historical explanation of how something comes into being and is then sustained in a specific form of existence. In this particular explanation, Marx has to move from an exhaustive exposition or proof that abstract labor, measured in abstract temporal units, is the only factor that all commodities share in common and thus the only factor that can establish their equivalency in the simple, or direct, exchange between two commodity produc-ers to an equally exhaustive explanation of why and how this changes when production takes place solely for market exchange. As I explained in chapters 2 and 3, when the latter occurs, the value of commodities is then based on the time socially necessary for their production. Of course, as you have seen, he then goes on, in the third volume of *Capital*, to explain how even this is modified—that is, the "socially necessary labor-time" pertaining to particular commodities is modi-fied—when we consider the competition between capitalists in the different spheres of production and how it leads to the equalization of different rates of profit and the creation of a general rate of profit and how, as a result of this, prices of production come to be a transformed expression of the commodity's value when it enters into market relations. Nevertheless, it is the first chapter of Volume 1 that leads, I think, to the basic confusion. It is here that he discusses the difference between concrete and abstract labor, and it is also in this section that his use of abstraction or logical deductive analysis is employed with great rigor, but in a manner that somehow leads to not only the confusion over his distinction between abstract and concrete labor but also the problem of many people thinking that he is referring to a strictly historical sequence of events. The later problem leads some people to think that the "Law of Value" does not pertain in contemporary capitalism, or even the fully developed capitalism of the nineteenth century. However, as I said before, the confusion over abstract and concrete labor leads to important disagreements even among those who are aware of the central and absolutely fundamental role that the "Law of Value" continues to play in our own experience of the fully universalized system of global capitalism.

Moishe Postone (1996) and, before him, I. I. Rubin (1972), have both focused particularly on the confusion over abstract and concrete labor that plagues Marxist thought. Somewhere (unfortunately I can't trace where) I read that it was Rubin's insistence on a correct reading of Marx's theory that led to his banishment by Stalin and his eventual execution in one of Stalin's death camps. Although many, perhaps even the majority, of Marxists still seem to think that Marx meant that it was only physical labor that could create value, I am quite certain that Rubin's fate does not await those like Postone and myself who continue to insist on a more accurate reading of Marx—that is, the only reading that is consistent with his use of the "Labor Theory of Value," or "Law of Value," to explain the laws and motions of capitalism and also to critique the historically specific form of wealth in capitalist societies. However, the continued existence of this confusion over Marx's thinking does not bode well for the future of humanity if that future, as I argue, depends on a credible and effective challenge to capitalism.

Postone (1996) argues, and I fully concur, as would anyone who has a concept of internal relations, that Marx was actually criticizing the capitalist production process and that he deplored the alienation and dehumanization that workers suffered once they were locked into an internal relation with capital (e.g., see Ollman, 1976). In other words, he was not elevating the image of the industrial worker or the capitalist industrial production process in a way that suggested that these should become the basis of a future socialist society; however, this is what those who adhere to the physiological concept—that is, the notion that only physical labor creates value—tend to do. Worse still, as I have just suggested, some of these people do not recognize—at least, they make no mention of the fact—that the value form of wealth must be abolished if we are to create a socially and economically just alternative to capitalism.

Marx's dialectical conceptualization suggests that everything—people, processes, social forms and objects such as technology or machinery—that is created within antagonistic capitalist social relations must be critically scrutinized in the process of creating an alternative, socialist society. This is because people, things and social forms that develop within or from capitalists relations will have been shaped and to some degree or another determined within these relations, and this may have produced consequences that are not conducive or salutary and may, in fact, even be antagonistic to a transformed society. Until we take on board what Marx was actually trying to explain to us, any attempts we make to transform our existence will be tainted by the residue, or, in Marx's words, the "muck" of capitalism. According to Marx, socialism was to be a movement, or process, leading to a communist social formation—a movement that would involve the creation of new social relations and the transformation of people, processes and objects within these newly created relations. In other words, socialism was to be a collective, collaborative and critical movement to create new harmonious relations in which we and the products of our labor are transformed for the betterment of humanity and the natural world (Allman, 1999). Moreover, these transformed relations would also foster the full development of our individual potentials—in other words, the full unfolding and enrichment of our individuality.

Of course, it is not simply the one chapter in Volume 1 that has led to these fundamental differences in interpretation. The way that people read that chapter or any other will be influenced by a number of factors, not the least of which is what Marx said in his other writings. Clearly, Marx could not qualify or fully elaborate on everything he said in every context in which he wrote and spoke. Unfortunately, this has led to problems. One very famous phrase from one of his more accessible sources has indirectly bolstered the notion to which I referred as well as other misconceptions I discussed previously—namely, that socialism would entail only the transfer of the already existing means of production from private to social ownership. In stressing that capital is a relation not a thing, Marx said: "A cotton-spinning jenny is a machine for spinning cotton, it becomes capital only in certain relations" (Marx, 1847, p. 256). This has led many people to the conclusion that capitalist means of production, without any alteration, can be transferred to the "associated producers" for their collective use within a socialist society—a conclusion that is erroneous from a dialectical point of view and therefore Marx's own perspective. This perspective, based on the concept of internal, or dialectical, relations, indicates, as I said earlier, that everything produced within capitalist social relations as well as every aspect of the capitalist production process will need to be critically scrutinized in order to determine whether it is beneficial or potentially destructive, or detrimental in any way, to our human nature or physical and mental well-being or to the health and sustainability of the natural world. It is important to emphasize that, according to Marx, even human nature does not preexist the relations within which it is formed and is therefore amenable to improvement within transformed social relations. This idea underpins one of the key principles of critical education that I will be discussing more fully in later chapters. As for the products of human labor that have been created within capitalist social relation—the massive wealth of use-values that results from capitalist production and the processes and technology by which they are created—sometimes only minor adaptation to a particular machine, product or labor process would be necessary in order to render them conducive to a socialist society; however, there will undoubtedly be others that require considerable adjustments as well as some that must be totally scrapped or destroyed. In the passage cited, Marx is saying that a machine would no longer be capital once it is used outside the labor–capital relation; but this does not mean that the machine will have escaped the relations unscathed, any more than the workers or anyone else who has been involved in or touched by these relations will have done. Both human beings and the products of human labor will have been contaminated to some degree by capitalist relations; and in the case of machinery this may mean that its continued use, in an unaltered form, could be potentially detrimental to humanity and the environment.

The idea of historical inevitability is the final misconception I want to discuss. It is possibly the greatest barrier of all to initiating an effective challenge to capitalism. This is the notion that socialism or some more progressive alternative to capitalism will develop automatically and inevitably out of the contradictions of capitalism—the idea that history unfolds according to either its own inherent teleology or in accord with some external teleological force. Marx was well aware that barbarism was just as likely to be the successor to capitalism as socialism. In fact, in the absence of a critical understanding of capitalism, Marx's analysis suggests that barbarism, although in a more sophisticated form than it existed previously, is the most likely successor. No doubt this is what motivated his entire intellectual project and the effort that it entailed. Nevertheless, the idea of historical inevitability, and, indeed, the inevitability of progress, persists in the thinking of many who call themselves Marxists or who at least lay claim to a Marxist analysis of the contemporary scene. In particular, the idea that some social form more progressive than capitalism will actually develop within the so-called "womb of capitalism"—just as capitalism is said to have developed within the "womb of feudalism"—is so persistent that it seems to be leading to considerable ambiguity in the thinking of some socialists. The authors of the book *Globalization and its Discontents*, to which I referred earlier, convey this type of ambiguity (Burbach, Núñez and Kagarlitsky, 1997).

I suggested previously that their idea of what constitutes an antisystemic challenge is highly questionable, but the problems or ambiguities do not stop there. They claim that a new socioeconomic system—one that is more progressive in human and ecological terms—is already developing within the "womb of capitalism." However, they also send out warning signals about the advent of a new barbarism. After identifying various groups of the discontented and suggesting that the present crisis of capitalism, together with the antisystemic challenges they identify, is causing global capital to "ulcerate" and bleed from within (p. 33), they concede that barbarism is a much more likely outcome than socialism (p. 143). Yet despite this recognition, their persistent adherence to historical and progressive inevitability leads them to simultaneously claim early in their exposition and then to suggest repeatedly throughout the book that a new "postmodern" socioeconomic system is developing within capitalism, albeit thus far at the margins of the capitalist world. The following passage expresses the gist of how they see this new system developing.

In the parts of the world that capitalism discards, a new mode of production is taking hold, which comprises what we call post-modern economies. . . . [They don't compete with transnational capital but] [r]ather they lurk on the sidelines, seizing the activities the transnational world decides to dispose of. This historic process resembles the transition from feudalism to capitalism. Then capitalism first took hold in the nooks and crannies, slowly gathering momentum until it replaced feudalism as the dominant mode of production. [Burbach, Núñez and Kagarlitsky, 1997, p. 5]

There seem to be two reasons why these authors predict the eventual ascendancy of these discarded activities—that is, activities that include everything from redundant professors in the former socialist societies taking up small-scale farming to those engaged in the illegitimate economies of the *favelas* and *barrios* of the "Third World" or the urban ghettos of the developed world. The first reason has to do with the numerical force of those involved in these activities—that is, the fact that there are so many people involved in these activities already—and the authors' prognosis that their numbers are bound to grow. The second reason is that they do not think that the world can sustain the 3.5% growth rate that many experts say is necessary for capitalism's survival (p. 7). How do they bring these two predictions together to come up with the conclusion that a new mode of production is forming within the old one? Although their attempt at synthesis is not entirely clear, they seem to suggest that barbarism is the most likely outcome in the first instance, but after a time people will begin to trade harmoniously the goods and services they produce with their own labor, thereby producing a system in which, according to the authors, the ideas of Adam Smith (market exchange) and Karl Marx (justice and more equitable distribution) will be married (p. 159). I may be mistaken, but this idea of mixing liberal economics with social justice sounds very much like a recipe for that political genre commonly known as the "Third Way"—a genre that most socialists, or at least Marxists, normally berate.

I am not questioning the sincerity of these authors' attempt to identify possible new antagonists to capitalism and to outline the possibility of a better future for humanity. Nevertheless, I have devoted a fair amount of space to exposing the ambiguity and confusion that issues from their discussion because I think it exemplifies the type of misconceptions I have been describing. In fact, their book congeals or concentrates many of these misconceptions, especially the belief in the inevitability of progress, into one rather supercolossal misconceived notion of how we might go about culling something hopeful out of the present crisis of global capitalism and the related misery of the human condition. Any notion that humanity can expect a brighter future without the critically conscious effort—the revolutionary praxis—of human beings is not only a whimsical pipe-dream but also a dangerous barrier to the work that will be essential for the development of critical consciousness on the massive scale—a development that is necessary in order to initiate a fully democratized process of global social transformation.

POSITIVE TENDENCIES AND REAL POSSIBILITIES FOR A BETTER FUTURE

In considering current challenges to the consequences rather than causes or premises of capitalism together with the misconceptions that continue to plague Marxism and thus serve as one of the biggest barriers to the effectiveness of these challenges, I have been focusing on the problems or negative side of our contemporary situation. After briefly recapping the central points, I identify the positive side of this situation—the real possibilities for a better future. I have noted that one of the primary problems is that most of the current groups of discontented people are not, for the most part, challenging capitalism per se but, rather, its results or consequences, especially the harsh and drastic measures that have been instituted under global capital's neoliberal regime. Furthermore, most critics of liberal democracy are not challenging this form of democracy but instead only call for its full implementation. Often this is referred to as further democratization, which, in practice, usually means greater government transparency and accountability rather than any sort of movement toward a more radical or direct form of democratic governance. Related to this seemingly unquestioned acceptance of liberal democracy, it is also disconcerting that many socialists and social democrats have ceased looking for an alternative to capitalism and are searching, instead, for more and better ways of controlling or managing the vagaries and uncertainties of the capitalist economy. They seem resigned to this being the only hope for creating a system with some degree of fairness or a greater degree of social justice. I suggested that these latter developments are largely due to not being able to envision a future beyond the ideologically reinforced horizon of capitalism and its political handmaiden, liberal democracy, and that they are also due to misconceptions of Marx's thought and the mistaken equation of our experience of extant socialism with Marx's idea of socialism. I also suggested that the first problem had to do with a misidentification of the real enemy. In fact, all of these problems are intimately related, and the remedy to each of them lies in critical education or, as I stress in later chapters, critical/revolutionary praxis on a wide scale.

Despite all the problems I have discussed, there are, as I said, many tendencies or positive elements in our contemporary situation that could be real possibilities or potentials for creating some of the elements of an effective challenge to capitalism. Before turning to these, I want to stress that in any dialectical situation, identifying the possibilities and potential demands just as much rigor and care as engaging in critique. Grasping at any straw—as I fear the authors of *Globalization and Its Discontents* (Burbach, Núñez, and Kagarlitsky, 1997) do—is not at all satisfactory. Since I am engaging in this activity in comparative isolation, I proceed with somewhat guarded caution, and therefore I must emphasize that the possibilities and potential I identify are by no means an exhaustive list.

Firstly, both the rhetoric and the policies of neoliberalism have brought to the surface, or revealed, many of the harsh realities of capitalism—more or less exposing the "emperor without his clothes." The devastation to public services and personal lives that neoliberalism has brought not only to the "Third World" but also to the very heart of capitalism in North America and Western Europe, and also, of course, to the former socialist countries, has awakened many people to the contradictory nature of capitalism, if not, as yet, the actual contradictions that constitute capital's essence. Although the current responses may only be a call for the restitution of what has been lost or alternatively signify a resigned acceptance, this brand of capitalism has unleashed a general feeling of unease even among many who do not see themselves as being directly or adversely affected by it. This unease, together with the contemporary material reality of capitalism that has produced it, provides fertile ground for critical education—in other words, an atmosphere in which people are more receptive to questioning much of what is normally taken for granted or assumed to be natural and inevitable. Therefore, critical educators should be able to work more effectively with people than they might have done when conditions seemed to be more favorable and capitalism's problems were not so visible and widely experienced. I return to this in later chapters when I focus directly on critical education.

Secondly, the increasing awareness and concern about environmental destruction and the emergence of an international movement to protect the environment and promote sustainable development has led to a vehement critique of irresponsible industrial production as well as other pernicious consequences of unfettered market forces. Unfortunately, this critique is all too rarely linked with capitalism itself. In other words, as yet there seems to be little recognition that industrial production within capitalist social relations is a historically specific form of industrial production. Nevertheless, the environmental movement has aroused the awareness of many Marxists; and, as a consequence, many are now assuming a position much closer to that of Moishe Postone (1996), who suggests that industrial production within transformed, authentic socialist relations will have to take place according to processes that can guarantee a sustainable environment. And an increasing number of Marxists also realize that this will have to take place alongside other measures—that is, human interventions in the natural world that are designed to repair as much as possible of the damage already done.

Another positive factor that is developing or has the potential to develop in an extremely significant way has to do with organized labor. Although the most immediate effect of globalization on organized labor has been a general weakening of trade unionism and a deterioration in the wages and working conditions of many workers throughout the world, there are certain factors that could lead to more effective global working-class struggle in the future. During capitalism's "Golden Age," although organized labor may have become relatively stronger than it had been vis-à-vis capital in the past, many trade unions had become extremely bureaucratic. In addition, the leadership, in general, had lured many workers into accepting a corporatist model, or compromised way, of working more harmoniously together with capital in order to achieve capitalist objectives. This tended to undermine the avowed internationalism of the trade union movement and sometimes even served as a barrier to working-class solidarity at the national level, both of which are fundamental—or, at least, should be fundamental—to the union movement. However, there are signs that this is changing. In fact, there were indications even during the heyday of union corporatism that many unions were becoming more outward-looking in approach. Increasingly during the 1970s and 1980s unions formed alliances with various social movements that were campaigning on a range of issues, including, for example, various often local campaigns against environmental destruction, struggles against apartheid and other infringements of human rights, the abolition of "Third World" debt and the campaign for nuclear disarmament. And there is every reason to believe that these types of alliances will increase in the future.

Moreover, perhaps as a response to the growing tendency for capitalist nation-states to form regional trading blocks, unions or agreements of mutual cooperation—a tendency no doubt stimulated by globalization—many workers and their unions are becoming increasingly aware that they, too, must engage in regional alliances of cooperation and support as well as reengage in union campaigns for greater international working-class solidarity (Richards, 1995). This renewed and enhanced solidarity among unions and their greater recognition of the need to form alliances with various social movements provides another arena in which critical educators can be working with others to form the necessary critical comprehension of capitalism and thus the potential for much more effective challenges to it in the not too distant future.

Finally, although there are no doubt many other positive elements emerging from the present conditions of capitalism, one of the most important for humanity's future, in my opinion, is that some human beings have begun to develop new approaches to working together and relating to one another, which embody some of the most important aspects of Marx's vision of socialism/communism. It is important to revisit and revive Marx's vision in that it is so antithetical to much that has passed as socialism/communism and also because it is truly a vision of a better future for humanity. I have written about Marx's vision of socialism/communism in detail elsewhere (Allman, 1999); therefore, here I refer only to those aspects that are directly related to or necessary for this discussion. I think that you will see, even from this brief discussion, that Marx's vision was one that embraced a concept of radical democratic governance.

For Marx, equality is a concept he associated with its opposite—inequality. In other words, it is a concept pertinent only to capitalism or societies in which inequality was an inherent part of the system, or social relations. In capitalist societies, or more precisely those that are supported by the liberal democratic form of governance—that is, the form of democracy that helps to sustain and promote capitalist objectives—the only possible application of this principle is its formal, or juridical, use, wherein the same standards are suppose to be applied to everyone regardless of their real circumstances—to rich and poor alike. In the same source where he states the first principle of communism—that is, "from each according to his[her] ability, to each according to his[her] needs" (Marx, 1875), he says that we are not equal individuals. We have different abilities and different needs. However, from his early days onward, Marx believed that it is possible to create a society based on social relations that would foster our desire to meet one another's needs—to find our own individual fulfillment and the realization of our creative potential in and through meeting the needs of others (Marx, 1844). Therefore, the greater our diversity, the "richer" (in quality) our society will be. His idea of socialism is of a society in which individuality rather than individualism would flourish and in which we would authentically appreciate and depend upon our differences, embracing them because of their potential to enrich the quality of our lives. The key to establishing such a society is the creation of new or alternative social relations, ones in which we would begin to perceive and appreciate one another in more human terms and thus begin to act accordingly (see also Allman, 1999).

Another facet that is central to Marx's vision of socialism/communism is the disappearance of the political state. Marx thought that bourgeois democracy, or liberal democracy, is the most appropriate form of government for capitalist societies because according to this model of democracy the political state, and thus the vast majority of political activity, is separated from the activities of civil society. Civil society is a term normally used to designate those aspects of personal and communal existence where people are most involved—such as family life, work, shopping and consuming (the market), community activities, religion, what we now call the voluntary sector and to a certain extent education (modern compulsory education more or less straddles the two domains of state and civil society). He thought that this separation was wrong and that people could and should "reabsorb" their political powers rather than alienating them in the state or giving them over to political representatives (Marx, 1843). He felt that the entire community should be responsible for directing the course of society; and that when it is necessary to delegate powers or the execution of powers, then those who take on these duties and obligations would be doing work just like any other member of the community, and they also should be subject to immediate recall if they do not obey the wishes or commands of those who really hold the power—the ordinary citizens. When people take on such duties, they would do so in order to serve rather than govern the society. These ideas are expressed by Marx to some extent in his early writings (for example, Marx, 1843) but were elaborated more fully in his writings that discussed and were influenced by the accomplishments of the short-lived, but, in his mind, exemplary, Paris Commune (Marx, 1871, 1872).[3]

There are at least two recent developments that embody, or seem to embody, some important aspects of Marx's vision of socialism in particular the idea of reabsorbing our political powers. First, there is the recent history of the revolutionary struggle and the outcomes of that struggle in Eritrea. From the scarce literature that reveals some of the details of the Eritreans' struggle it appears that there are at least a few parallels with the recent struggle of the Zapatistas in Mexico. Since the latter is better documented in terms of its principles and ways of working and organizing, I will focus my discussion on the principles promulgated by the Zapatistas and practices that have arisen in the context of their struggles.

I focus, here, on the principles, values and ideas that have been put forward by the Zapatistas rather than recounting the full story of where they came from and the history or details of their struggle and what they have accomplished, because space does not permit me to do justice to the latter. Moreover, that type of account is readily available elsewhere (see, for example, Cunninghame and Corona, 1998; De Angelis, 1998, 2000; Esteva, 1999; Holloway and Peláez, 1998; and also http://www.eco.utexas.edu/faculty/Cleaver/zapincyber/html, as well as several other Internet sites; for a more qualified and critical account, see Hellman, 2000). However, I must make one important point, albeit a rather extensive one, about the context within which the Zapatistas' struggle emerged. The home of the Zapatistas, the Chiapas region of south-eastern Mexico, is an area of the world where many of the concerns raised in connection with globalization are bought together in one location. This is one of the reasons why this movement, although originating in the Lacandon Jungle area of Chiapas and remaining most firmly rooted there, has attracted the interest of people who are struggling for social justice elsewhere in Mexico and throughout the world. I will identify a number of factors that are related to these concerns.

The Lacandon Jungle is a tropical rainforest that is rich in biodiversity, and the Chiapas region has huge reserves of oil and natural gas as well as large forested areas, all of which global capital is anxious to exploit. The people are indigenous people—in fact, various groups of indigenous people with different cultural traditions that all value the earth and nature in general in ways that are directly counter to capitalist objectives and practices. During the 1980s, Mexico became one of the biggest success stories of neoliberal free-market policies—so successful that in 1993 Mexico was able to join the OECD, the organization of the world's most prosperous nations. An enormous amount of financial capital flowed into Mexico at that time (Holloway and Peláez, 1998). In 1994, this success was supposed to be ensured for the future when the United States, Canada and Mexico concluded the North American Free Trade Agreement (NAFTA), thus forming a North American trading bloc that, its signatories hope, will function along similar lines to the former European Common Market (now politically unified as the European Union). The new treaty facilitated the movement of increasing amounts of U.S. capital into Mexico—a movement originally driven by the search for cheaper labor and lower standards of working conditions that had been going on for some time. However, a great deal of this new influx of capital went into speculative rather than productive investment—a fact dramatically exposed in 1995, when the devaluation of the Mexican peso

Ya Basta

created a reverse flow of capital out of Mexico at lightning speed. This situation happened so quickly that it threatened to plunge the entire world into a financial crisis of considerable magnitude (Holloway and Peláez, 1998).

It is in this context that the Zapatistas' struggle is located. It began on a small and clandestine scale in the early 1980s and erupted with full strength on 1 January 1994, the day that NAFTA came into force (Lorenzano, 1998). The strength that the Zapatistas exhibited in their uprising on that day was a strength of unity and conviction as the men and women engaged in this struggle emphatically said "No" or, in their words, "*Ya Basta* [Enough]" to the forces of neoliberalism that were devastating their lives and robbing them of their human dignity. The Zapatistas' struggle is a struggle *against* rather than *for* power, and for this and many other reasons it has captured the imagination and won the support of tens of thousands of people around the globe (Esteva, 1999). It is a struggle that continues with no real resolution in sight. The Zapatistas by no means provide all the answers or even a clear way forward to challenging capitalism or its neoliberal variant, but their approach to struggle, their particular style of revolutionary struggle, or praxis, has led many people to question long-cherished notions of what must constitute this type of struggle. As a result, there are at least some signs that some people are beginning to think more critically and creatively about how to challenge capitalism effectively and about how we might develop an alternative way of struggling for a better future for humanity as we enter the twenty-first century. In concluding this chapter, I consider the lessons that might be drawn form the Zapatistas' praxis.

According to Esteva (1999), the Zapatistas practice a type of radical democracy that is far more radical than even the literal meaning of democracy or people's power. For them, the word democracy "does not allude to a kind of government, but to a government end. It is not a collection of institutions, but an historical project" (p. 154). Therefore, when the Zapatistas refer to democracy, they are not referring to existing democracies. Instead, they are referring to their own exercise of and belief in people's power, a concept of democracy that differs even from concepts of direct democracy (p. 154). People's power, for them, is actually a form of social existence or way of living that is expressed in the daily exercise of power and, therefore, "not only in its origin and constitution" (p. 155). Esteva says that the Zapatistas reject the formal or abstract notion of equality or homogeneity, which they see as an illusion that serves to legitimate privilege and the existence of material inequality. Instead, they recognize and appreciate individual and collective differences and heterogeneity. The diversity of individuals within the movement and their different cultural practices are embraced, and their interactions take place on equal terms, with no implicit or explicit assumptions of superiority, thus establishing the "harmonious coexistence of all the 'different'" (p. 157). From this it follows that if there are some functions that cannot be undertaken by the bodies into which the people organize themselves, then these are entrusted to newly created institutions or appointed individuals. However, either of these operates according to the principle of "command by obeying" rather than according to the ideas of representation and the delegation of power that pertain in traditional democracies (p. 157).

From Esteva's and others' accounts, it appears that the Zapatistas' idea of democracy is similar to if not synonymous with Marx's idea of people's autonomous organizations in civil society reabsorbing the powers of the state, which, in liberal or representative democracies, people have alienated or delegated to the state. Neoliberals also advocate a greater role for civil society and a diminished role for the state, but by this they mean devolution of power to private businesses or corporations. This, of course, would be anathema to the Zapatistas, who trust corporations and the market even less than they do the central state. The organizations through which they mobilize their power are meant to embrace the totality of civil society, and it is thus through civil society that they express their opposition to the state or anything that is associated with or controlled by the state. They have no desire to seize control of the government or to replace the current leaders and managers of the state with their own people. Instead, the various formal and informal organizations that act together for a variety of purposes stand together against the state in order to resist being absorbed by either it or the forces of globalization. It is in the process of saying "No" or "Enough" to the state and globalization that Zapatista civil society becomes a united and antagonistic force, which is a threat to the state (Esteva, 1999, p. 157). However, according to Esteva, it is not just their "politics of no" that are a threat to the state. The bigger threat comes from their actual concept of autonomy, which is taken from the Indian peoples, not the European tradition of decentralization. The Zapatistas' concept of autonomy would make the state superfluous because it is an idea of autonomy that "affirms people's freedom and capacity to freely determine themselves, in their own spaces, and at the same time to determine with other people and cultures forms of communion based on intercultural dialogues . . ." (p. 165).

When the Zapatistas convened the "First International Encounter of Humanity" in La Realidad in 1996, many people from all over Mexico as well as from the rest of the world attended (Cunninghame and Corona, 1998). For some there was an expectation that a positive program for a way forward would be proposed and equally that an organizational apparatus for promoting and coordinating a worldwide movement with universal ideals would be formed or at least suggested. Instead, the "International of Hope" was created. The Zapatistas refuse to impose their ideas and programs on others (Esteva, 1999, p. 162). This has nothing to do with the postmodernists' celebration of relativism. It comes from a different disposition altogether—one in which difference is embraced because it adds a strength and a richness to the whole of which it is a part. Their movement is about creating the conditions in which people can freely and collectively construct a new type of society according to their own aspirations and through their own collective participation and efforts. They are trying to create a space in which new social and political relations can develop, relations wherein there is no place for conventional concepts of power and instead only a concept of power that resides equally in the hands of everyone. And it is important to note that by everyone, the Zapatistas mean all men and women and even the children over a certain age—that is, nearly every person in their communities who is a part of the Zapatista movement.

Whether or not the Zapatistas' approach to a revolutionary politics of peaceful transition will take hold and eventually be successful is open to question. However, their approach exemplifies some of the principles that are important to effective critical education. Moreover, they have awakened interest in many ideas that seem to parallel Marx's ideas on democracy and socialism/communism—ideas that, unfortunately, have been buried under the twentieth-century experience of a type of socialism/communism that bore little resemblance to his concepts and vision. As I argue here and have done elsewhere, it is essential for us to reconsider his ideas on these subjects and to take them seriously. I think they should be enshrined in the principles and praxis of the type of critical education that is needed so urgently, especially if we take seriously, as I think we should, the warning conveyed in the following words of Lula, the Brazilian labor leader:

The Third World War has already started—it is a silent war, not for that reason any less sinister. This war is tearing down practically all the Third World. Instead of soldiers dying, there are children dying; instead of millions wounded, there are millions unemployed; instead of the destruction of bridges, there is a tearing down of factories, hospitals, schools and entire economies. [cited in Burbach, Núñez & Kagarlitsky, 1997, p. 75]

Many may think that Lula's warning is alarmist and has little relevance to the world they know and experience, but for increasing numbers of human beings global capital has already made, or is in the process of making, these words a reality. Of course, critical education on its own is clearly not the solution, but without critical education, there will never be authentic revolutionary social transformation.

NOTES

1. Here I am referring to the main corpus of Marx's theoretical as opposed to polemical writings. In the latter type of writing, as one would expect, he constantly tried to encourage working people to take on the historical role of struggling to abolish capital. Since he was usually addressing industrial workers, these writings give the impression that they are the only revolutionary subjects. In his more theoretical texts, such as *Capital*, which was also written for working people, Marx's concept of the dialectical contradiction, or relation, between labor and capital indicates that labor—that is, the proletariat as revolutionary subject—is a constantly expanding group of people. Therefore, it is a concept of the working class that is much more inclusive than just the industrial working class.

2. The idea of an exclusive revolutionary party of the working class—a communist party that would enable the proletariat to overcome their spontaneous bourgeois consciousness, or

trade-unionism—was first proposed by Lenin in his famous *What Is to Be Done?*, written in 1902. By 1921, he had become even more committed to this idea and went on to propose to the Tenth Party Congress that the Party train a vanguard of the proletariat that would have the revolutionary consciousness capable of withstanding the vacillations of the masses who had supported the 1917 Revolution (McLellan, 1983, pp. 162–164). Lenin's idea may, or may not, have been appropriate for his specific historical circumstances, but I doubt whether he or any other dialectical thinker would suggest that it be adopted unquestioningly in other circumstances.

3. In the Preface to the second German edition of the *Communist Manifesto* (1872), Marx altered one of the ideas he and Engels had promulgated in the original text (1848). Influenced by the Paris Commune, he no longer thought that the working class should take hold of the existing government machinery, thereby using it to wield power in their own interest, in the way he and Engels had advocated in 1848.

REFERENCES

Allman, P. (1999). *Revolutionary Social Transformation: Democratic Hopes, Political Possibilities and Critical Education.* Westport, CT: Bergin & Garvey.

Allman, P., and Wallis, J. (1995). "Gramsci's Challenge to the Politics of the Left in 'Our Times.'" *International Journal of Lifelong Education*, 14 (No. 2, March/April), 120–143.

Amin, S. (1997). *Capitalism in the Age of Globalization. The Management of Contemporary Society.* London: Zed.

Bernard, E. (1999). "A Short Guide to WTO, The Millennium Round and the Rumble In Seattle." Znet Free Update, 24 September [www.zmag.org/CrisesCur Evts/Globalism/GlobalEcon.htm].

Burbach, R., Núñez, O., and Kagarlitsky, B. (1997). *Globalization and Its Discontents.* London: Pluto Press.

Burkett, P. (1999). "Nature's 'Free Gifts' and the Ecological Significance of Value." *Capital & Class*, 68 (Summer), 89–110.

Chomsky, N. (1998). "Whose World Order: Conflicting Visions." Speech delivered at the University of Calgary, 22 September [www.zmag.org/CrisesCurEvts/ Globalism/GlobalEcon.htm].

Cleaver, H. (1995). "Chiapas95." [www.eco.utexas.edu/faculty/Cleaver/zapincyber/ html].

Cunninghame, P., and Corona, C. B. (1998). "A Rainbow at Midnight: Zapatistas and Autonomy." *Capital & Class*, 66 (Autumn), 12–22.

De Angelis, M. (1998). "2nd Encounter for Humanity and Against Neoliberalism. Introduction." *Capital & Class,* 65 (Summer), 135–142.

De Angelis, M. (2000). "Globalization, New Internationalism and the Zapatistas." *Capital & Class,* 70 (Spring), 9–35.

Esteva, G. (1999). "The Zapatistas and People's Power." *Capital & Class*, 68 (Summer), 153–182.

George, S. (1999). "A Short History of Neo-Liberalism: Twenty Years of Elite Economics and Emerging Opportunities for Structural Change." Speech given at the Conference on Economic Sovereignty in a Globalizing World, Bangkok, 24–26 March [www.zmag.org/CrisesCurEvts/Globalism/ GlobalEcon.htm or www.millennium.round.org].

Grossman, R. (1998). "Challenging Corporate Power." Interview by David Baramian, Provincetown, Mass., 23 August. ZNet Interviews [www.zmag.org/CrisesCurEvts/Globalism/GlobalEcon.htm].

Held, D. (Ed.) (1993). *Prospects for Democracy: North, South, East, West.* Cambridge: Polity.

Held, D. (1995). *Democracy and the Global Order: From the Modern State to Cosmopolitan Governance.* Cambridge: Polity.

Heller, A. (1976). *The Theory of Need in Marx.* London: Allison and Busby.

Hellman, J. A. (2000). "Real and Virtual Chiapas: Magic Realism and the Left." In L. Panitch and C. Leys (Eds.), *Socialist Register 2000, Necessary and Unnecessary Utopias* (pp. 161–186). Rendlesham, U.K.: Merlin.

Hobsbawm, E. (1995). *Age of Extremes: The Short Twentieth Century 1914–1991.* London: Abacus.

Holloway, J., and Peláez, E. (Eds.) (1998). *Zapatista! Reinventing Revolution in Mexico.* London: Pluto Press.

Lorenzano, L. (1998). "Zapatismo: Recomposition of Labour, Radical Democracy and Revolutionary Project." In J. Holloway and E. Peláez (Eds.), *Zapatista! Reinventing Revolution in Mexico* (pp. 126–158). London: Pluto Press.

Marx, K. (1843). "On the Jewish Question." In D. McLellan (Ed.), *Karl Marx: Selected Writings* (pp. 39–62). Oxford: Oxford University Press, 1977.

Marx, K. (1844). "On James Mill." In D. McLellan (Ed.), *Karl Marx: Selected Writings* (pp. 114–123). Oxford: Oxford University Press, 1977.

Marx, K. (1847). "Wage-Labour and Capital." In D. McLellan (Ed.), *Karl Marx: Selected Writings* (pp. 248–268). Oxford: Oxford University Press, 1977.

Marx, K. (1867). *Capital,* Vol. 1, translated by Ben Fowkes, Introduction by Ernest Mandel. Harmondsworth, U.K.: Penguin, 1976.

Marx, K. (1871). "The Civil War in France." In D. McLellan (Ed.), *Karl Marx: Selected Writings* (drafts by Marx, pp. 539–558). Oxford: Oxford University press, 1977.

Marx, K. (1872). "Preface to the Second German Edition of the *Communist Manifesto.*" In D. McLellan (Ed.), *Karl Marx: Selected Writings* (pp. 559–560). Oxford: Oxford University Press, 1977.

Marx, K. (1875). "Critique of the Gotha Programme." In D. McLellan (Ed.), *Karl Marx: Selected Writings* (pp. 564–570). Oxford: Oxford University Press, 1977.

McLellan, D. (Ed.) (1983). *Marx: The First Hundred Years.* Oxford: Fontana.

Ollman, B. (1976). *Alienation: Marx's Conception of Man in Capitalist Society* (second edition). Cambridge: Cambridge University Press.

Postone, M. (1996). *Time, Labor, and Social Domination: A Reinterpretation of Marx's Critical Theory.* Cambridge: Cambridge University Press.

Richards, D. G. (1995). "Regional Integration and Class Conflict: The Mercosur and the Argentine Labour Movement." *Capital & Class,* 57 (Autumn), 55–82.

Rubin, I. I. (1972). *Essays on Marx's Theory of Value,* translated from the third edition, 1928, by M. Samardija and F. Perlman. Detroit, MI: Black & Red.

Wood, E. M. (1999). "The Politics of Capitalism." *Monthly Review,* 51 (No. 4) [www.monthlyreview.org].

5

Critical Education
for Revolutionary Social Transformation

Peter McLaren poses the question that I address in this chapter.

Can a renewed and revivified critical pedagogy . . . serve as a point of departure for a politics of resistance and counterhegemonic struggle in the twenty-first century? [1998, p. 448]

As I have indicated from the very beginning of this book, my response is affirmative, emphatic and hopeful. Not only *can* a "renewed" and "revivified" critical pedagogy do this—it *must*. Moreover, it can do more; however, whether it *will* do anything that impacts directly on improving the human condition and thus revolutionary social transformation depends on what is meant by critical pedagogy, or (my preferred term) critical education, and what we intend it to do. McLaren (1998, pp. 441–442) positions the emergence of critical education in the United States somewhere around 1978 and suggests that it arose from a variety of influences, including the writings of the Brazilian educator, Paulo Freire.[1] He also notes that its use in the United States has become increasingly domesticated through its cooptation by a range of progressive and liberal discourses (p. 448). Cooptation and domestication are only possible when we are uncertain about the meaning and aims of critical education. Unfortunately, ambiguity has become endemic and relativism fashionable, and thus uncertainty abounds. In one sense this is not an entirely new or a postmodern phenomenon. There has never been widespread agreement over the meaning or use of this term. Its meaning varies between individuals and also varies in different historical and cultural contexts.

In the United Kingdom, as well as in other countries, the term "critical education" is often used synonymously with radical education and education for socialism or social transformation. It also is used more widely, for example, within the British tradition of Liberal Adult Education to refer to education designed to foster critical and reflective thought. In this chapter, rather than exploring all the historical, cultural and theoretical reasons for these differences in meaning—interesting though such an exploration might be—I use the term "critical education" in a very precise and unequivocal way. I offer, for your consideration, a discussion of what I think this type of education entails and what it is intended to accomplish. It will come as no surprise to those who have read the preceding chapters that my definition has to do with the eventual abolition of capitalism. Therefore, I advocate a form of critical education—one that I often refer to as *revolutionary critical education*—that is capable of preparing people to take part in the creation of what I call authentic socialism: a society engaged in revolutionary social transformation and the development of the type of communist social formation advocated by Karl Marx (see Allman, 1999, for a discussion of Marx's vision of socialism/communism—a vision that differs considerably from anything we witnessed in the twentieth century).

The need for this type of critical education has never been greater. Marx's dialectical explanation of capitalism indicates that capitalism cannot be reformed in a manner that will bring about a better future for humanity. And the contemporary experience of global capitalism clearly corroborates his theoretical analysis of the way in which the inherent laws and tendencies of capitalism lead to recurring crises—crises that have begun to take place more regularly or at closer intervals and that are played out in a highly integrated global system within which their effects are more widespread and devastating than ever before in the history of capitalism. There is no longer room in critical education for hesitancy and prevarication. We either "renew" and "revivify" critical education, as McLaren urges, and reengage in the struggle for social and economic justice—the "project for humanity," as some have called it—or we capitulate to capitalism and the continuing dehumanization of millions of human beings. In the latter case, therefore, we resign ourselves either to training people to cope as best they can with the dire consequences of capitalism or, at best, to educating them to employ their critical faculties on those areas of extant knowledge that are unrelated to social transformation or the type of social, economic and political critique capable of challenging the system.

McLaren (1998) argues, and I fully agree, that if we choose to reengage in the struggle, we need much more than good intentions. We "require a revolutionary movement of educators informed by a principled ethics of compassion and social justice, a social ethos based on solidarity and social interdependence . . ." (p. 451). I would add that this movement needs to be international in scope and composition and that it needs to be informed by a philosophy or theory of critical education for revolutionary social transformation. And in spirit and intent it would also be a movement of educators committed to "justice educated [through a critique of] injustice" (Hill, 2000). Of course, as I suggested at the end of chapter 4, critical education on its own is not capable of bringing about the transformation of society; on the other hand, it is impossible to see how a society that is capable of guaranteeing a better future for humanity will ever come into being without critical education. The approach to critical education that I advocate is not only intended to prepare people to engage in social transformation, but it is also meant to serve as a prefigurative experience of the type of social relations that would lie at the heart of a transformed society—relations, moreover, that would also be integral to the process—the struggle—that will be necessary to create that society. It is through the process of struggle that women and men, and children, too, will recreate their social relations and thus themselves as a necessary and fundamental requirement for building a new social order. This approach to critical education is based on Marx's theory of consciousness. In the introduction to this book, I made some general points about his theory and its importance to critical education. It is now the time to explain Marx's revolutionary theory of consciousness in greater detail and to reveal its important implications for critical educators.

MARX'S DIALECTICAL THEORY OF CONSCIOUSNESS: A THEORY OF CRITICAL/REVOLUTIONARY PRAXIS

I mentioned before that Marx's critique of capitalism was equally a critique of the way that people thought about it. And I also mentioned that his explanation of its essence—the dialectical contradictions that lie at the heart of capitalism—and how it moves and develops in a way that produces definite laws and tendencies is also an explanation of how a particular type of consciousness or way of thinking develops from our experience of these contradictions and processes (Marx, 1858, 1867). Consciousness, therefore, is one of Marx's central concerns (see especially Marx, 1858, 1863a, 1863b, 1863c, 1865, 1867; Marx and Engels, 1846). In fact, even before, he had worked out the precise details about how capitalism operates, his dialectical mode of conceptualizing had enabled him to develop a revolutionary theory of consciousness (Marx, 1843; Marx and Engels, 1846).

Marx's academic background was in philosophy. Long before the advent of modern disciplines, such as psychology and psychoanalysis, philosophers had focused their intellectual energies on a range of questions pertaining to the human mind. The origin of consciousness was one of these and, in fact, one of the most important topics of philosophical inquiry and debate. Although psychology and psychoanalysis are usually considered to be more scientific and thus more accurate than mere philosophical contemplation, all schools of psychology and psychoanalysis have philosophical roots. Often those working in these disciplines are unaware of these roots; nevertheless, when the history of the development of these disciplines is considered, the links with various philosophical traditions are very clear. Educational theory, of course, is premised very heavily on psychology, particularly those areas of psychology that deal with the develop-

ment of cognition, affect and identity. When I explain Marx's theory of consciousness, I think you will be able to discern certain parallels between his theory
and a great deal of the thinking that informs educational psychology and educational theory more generally. However, in my opinion and experience, Marx's
theory provides a much more effective theoretical basis for fostering the development of critical thinking and especially, as one might expect, the development of
critical dialectical conceptualization.

New theories are usually posited in opposition either to common sense or to
some extant theory. Marx's theory of consciousness—that is, his theory of the
formation of ideas—developed from his recognition that there were problems
with the other theories that were prevalent in the 1840s—the period just after
Marx completed his university studies and doctoral dissertation. At that time,
there were two categories or paradigms of philosophical thought that stood in
direct opposition to one another. According to one paradigm, called idealism,
ideas are considered to be temporally prior to reality. In other words, they are the
cause or origin of the real world. In opposition to this, the other paradigm, which
is a type of materialism, saw ideas or thoughts as merely projections of material
phenomena. As simplistic as these notions may sound, they continue to be
accepted paradigms even now. Marx, as I have explained, conceptualized dialectically, or in terms of internal relations; therefore, he rejected the dichotomization
and separation of ideas or thought from the real world. For him, consciousness—
and all the ideas and thoughts of which it is composed—is internally, or dialectically, related to reality. According to idealism, consciousness and reality are two
separate and distinct entities. Ideas have to be seen as having a separate and
temporally prior existence if they are the cause or origin of the phenomena that
exist in the material world. Separation or dichotomization is also necessary with
the type of materialism that Marx opposed—a materialism that is mechanical and
also ahistorical or devoid of the historical specificity Marx considered to be
absolutely necessary for understanding the world. With this type of materialism,
first there is a distinct and fixed material world, and then there are ideas, which
are the direct efflux of their material point of origin. In neither idealism nor
mechanical, ahistorical materialism is there a reciprocity between cause and
effect; in other words, all movement is unidirectional.

In opposition to these paradigms, Marx formulated a distinct and revolutionary
form of materialism that allowed for no dualism, separation or dichotomy between consciousness and reality. As far as Marx was concerned, both idealism
and ahistorical, mechanical materialism led to a reified—or, in their worst form,
fetishized—way of thinking (Marx, 1845, 1867; Marx and Engels, 1844; 1846).
These forms of thinking ignore or are blind to the internal relation between
consciousness and reality and more generally tend to assign a thing-like status to
that which is actually human in nature or the result of human beings' social
relations. This is the type of thinking that results in what Marx calls the "commodity fetish," or the idea that the value of commodities derives from some
quality inherent within them rather than from the social relation within which

they are produced (Marx, 1867, pp. 163–177). Furthermore, since according to Marx the real world was constantly moving and developing due to the tension between the dialectically related opposites and the movement of value, he was also critical of the reified thinking produced by both paradigms because it lacked historical specificity. This type of thinking involved using concepts uncritically to understand the present, past and future as if reality at all these points in time were static and unchanging (Marx, 1858).

Despite appearing to be diametric opposites, idealism and mechanical, ahistorical materialism are based, therefore, on the same process of dichotomizing or separating thought and reality; and as a consequence, they lead to similar theories of knowledge, or epistemologies. Knowledge can either be grasped as an eternal verity by correct philosophical thinking or, alternatively, discovered, once and for all time, by the scientific, empirical observation of reality. In either case, knowledge is seen as something that exists distinctly and separately from the real world.

Another problem, perhaps the most crucial, with both idealism and ahistorical, mechanical materialism is that they both ignore the fundamental importance of the sensuous, active experience of human beings. For Marx, our action in and on the material world is the mediation or link between our consciousness and objective reality. Our consciousness develops from our active engagement with other people, nature and the objects or processes we produce. In other words, it develops from the sensuous experiencing of reality from within the social relations in which we exist (Marx and Engels, 1846). Although Marx does not mention this, it seems to me that this aspect of his theory suggests that consciousness is not just our thoughts and ideas as they exist on an objective level; it also involves our subjective, or emotional, responses. Since both thoughts and feelings are present whenever we engage sensuously with something or somebody else, the consciousness that is produced in unison with this activity must contain both of these dimensions. They arise simultaneously and therefore must be internally related. Thus there can be no dichotomy or separate existence of cognitive and affective domains—they are intimately related, whether in our immediate awareness, or conscious thought, or submerged somewhere in our unconsciousness. Marx's theory of consciousness, therefore, involves the dialectic of internally related opposites—thought and practice as well as, by implication, objectivity and subjectivity; and it also has a temporal element.

At any moment in time our consciousness will be comprised of thoughts that have resulted from our own sensuous activity. However, it will also be comprised of thoughts that have arisen outside our own experience. Nevertheless, these thoughts will have arisen from the sensuous activity of other people at other times and in other places. Therefore, they have the same type of origin, or source, but they arise from people other than ourselves and at a different time and place. Moreover, they only become a part of our consciousness when we actively receive them from an external source. We are constantly bombarded with ideas and a plethora of information; however, under normal conditions we do not automatically or passively incorporate these into our consciousness. Reception depends upon our active engagement with them—an active engagement that is, simultaneously, physical and mental.

Certain aspects of Jean Piaget's cognitive developmental psychology—or what he calls his theory of "genetic epistemology" (Piaget, 1970)—come close to being a psychological translation of Marx's theory of consciousness. It will come as no surprise to those who are familiar with Piaget's ideas that action is fundamental to concept formation and other aspects of cognitive development. However, it is in Piaget's depiction of the child's development prior to the acquisition of language where I find the closest parallels with Marx's theory. The best way I can explain this is to ask you to visualize an infant or small child playing with a "shape box"—one of those toys that engages the child in attempting to fit various geometrically shaped objects into holes of a similar shape, usually placed at intervals around the outside of a cube-shaped box. The child picks up, for example, a round wooden or plastic dowel and tries to put it into the various holes, until finally it fits exactly and drops through the circular hole, or space, into the interior of the box. It takes some time and a great deal of rather frustrating play before the child will learn to put each shape directly into the appropriate hole. The child is actively producing a concept of the various geometrical shapes; however, this is an "action concept" rather than a mental concept. Action concepts exist externally to the child in his/her actions rather than in the mind. It is only later in the child's development that these action concepts become fully internalized mental images that can be linked to words or symbols and then communicated or reexternalized through language. When this level of development is reached, the child's concept formation no longer depends on physical activity. The same sorts of actions begin to be executed abstractly, or by mental processes; therefore, concept formation is no longer externalized in physical action, but physical action can, of course, continue to serve as an aid or reinforcement to these internalized processes.

I would add to the normal accounts of this process that the formation of the child's action concepts involves seeking out and establishing a relationship between the concrete object and the appropriately shaped hole, or empty space. Furthermore, the entire process in which the seeking is situated is a tactile process and also one that involves emotions such as frustration, satisfaction and, ultimately, pleasure. According to Marx's theory, ideas and concepts are not the mere reflection of "things." They arise from people's active and sensuous experience of relations—relations between people as well as relations between people and objects and between objects and objects. Developmental psychologists, of course, consider the acquisition of language to be a sign of progress or development, which it clearly is. However, it also has negative consequences. When concepts come to be designated by words, their active, sensuous and relational origins are extinguished or masked (Allman, 1999).

Marx's theory of consciousness indicates that this same active production—whether physical, mental, or both—of concepts and consciousness in general continues throughout life; however, once language is acquired, the processes of action, internalization and reexternalization can occur simultaneously. As I indicated earlier, this conflation of the processes and their externalization through language have the unfortunate effect of masking the actual relational origin of consciousness, and as a consequence we tend to produce static and reified concepts. This also places constraints on our ability to think dialectically, or in terms of internal relations. Clearly, the acquisition of language is an advance in the child's development, and without language human beings are severely hampered. Yet, as with many things, language has a negative side as well; however, if we are aware of the limitations it can place on our thinking, there is no reason for it to actually inhibit our ability to think dialectically. Marx's theory enables us to understand these processes and thus overcome any limitations they might place on our thinking. Unfortunately, for the most part, Marx's theory has been ignored. Perhaps the constraints I've just discussed make his theory initially difficult to understand. "Common sense" develops on the basis of these constraints, and Marx's theory obviously runs against the grain of "common sense."

I have argued elsewhere (Allman, 1999), and reemphasize here, that Marx's revolutionary theory of consciousness is actually a theory of praxis—that is, a theory of the unity of thought and action. In saying this, I am suggesting a very particular concept of praxis that may be at variance with the concept held by others. As I said in the Introduction, the term "praxis" is often used to refer to the idea that action and thought, or reflection and sometimes theory, should be united in a sequence. In other words, we act and then reflect and maybe even formulate a theory of what has happened or a theory that can be applied in future action. Alternatively, the sequence can take place in reverse, beginning with thought, reflection or theory, which are used as a basis for initiating action that is then refined, or "fine-tuned," through further thought. Marx's theory of consciousness—or, more precisely, praxis—is a theory of the dialectical unity—the internal relation—between thought and action. In other words, we do not stop thinking when we act, and thinking itself is a form of action; therefore, even when we engage in the type of sequence referred to before, thought and action should not be dichotomized or thought of as being separate and distinct—to reiterate, they are internally related. However, since not all thinking is critical thinking, Marx's theory, as I indicated before, implies two very different types of praxis.

If we simply partake in the relations and conditions that we find already existing in the world and assume that these are natural and inevitable—that this is the way things are, always, or at least for a considerable time, have been, and always will be—then our praxis is uncritical and simply reproduces the existing relations. In fact, even those who move with or engage in the most recent developments in these relations and conditions—who operate at the "cutting-edge" or forward flow of events, yet always within the horizon of capitalist reality—are still engaged in a praxis that uncritically accepts, facilitates and thus supports and eventually helps to reproduce these movements and developments. In contrast, we can choose to question critically the existing relations and conditions and actively seek to transform or abolish them and to create relations and conditions that will lead to a better future for all human beings, in which case our praxis becomes critical or revolutionary praxis as opposed to uncritical/reproductive praxis.[2] Critical/revolutionary praxis is the type of praxis we should aim to develop within critical education; it should constitute the actual process of critical education as well as being one of its main outcomes. Thus there should be no dichotomy between means and ends because it is only through the means—the process—that the ends can be achieved. Critical/revolutionary praxis would also, therefore, be the appropriate praxis for any aspect of social transformation. It is through this form of praxis that we turn social transformation into authentic, or revolutionary, social transformation—that is, the struggle to transform simultaneously not just the socioeconomic and political conditions of our existence but also ourselves.

I mentioned earlier that idealism and mechanical, ahistorical materialism produce similar theories of knowledge, or epistemologies, in which knowledge is dichotomized from reality—seen as an entity that is separate and distinct from the real world. Marx's theory of consciousness—praxis—based as it is on an entirely different and revolutionary form of materialism, produces a relational, historically specific and therefore contingent and conditional theory of knowledge. This means that the knowledge that is produced at a particular historical conjuncture will be influenced by the material conditions that prevail at its time of production. The arrival of postmodernism in the "academy" and its pervasive influence in various disciplines as well as in art, culture, architecture and even contemporary politics and life-styles is, therefore, no accident. It is a form of thinking that is related to what David Harvey (1989) has called the "condition of postmodernity": the material condition of global capitalism that he links to capital's continuing struggle to temporally overcome—that is, displace at a higher level of complexity—its inherent contradictions. Postmodernism locks into and seems to explain or make sense of what is happening in the world because it is the consciousness that is internally, dialectically related to our contemporary material conditions, or, more precisely, people's experience of the way in which these conditions are moving and developing. However, in all of its forms, both what some people have called its "ludic" forms (Ebert, 1996) and also even its most critical and insightful forms, it is indicative of an uncritical/reproductive consciousness—or more precisely, uncritical/reproductive praxis.[3] In other words, postmodern thought is internally related to a postmodern way of "being," or existing. As a consequence, it produces, as would any form of reproductive praxis, a particular theory of being, or ontology.

Postmodern dispositions that favor and celebrate incoherent, fragmented, "go with the flow" modes of living or "life-styles" and also transient or serial relationships have become pervasive. They are dismissive of any notion that human beings should be in control of their lives and also the creative and critically conscious architects of their collective destinies. Any reproductive praxis, and postmodernism is no exception, will produce theories of being, or ontologies, that mistakenly depict the present dominant mode of existence as the transhistorical human condition (Marx, 1858). Moreover, reproductive praxis, in any historical conjuncture, results in an uncritical consciousness that is highly susceptible to the dominant ideological discourses or explanations of reality.

As I also stressed in the Introduction, Marx's theory of consciousness/praxis contains a negative concept of ideology (Larrain, 1983; Marx and Engels, 1846). Ideology or ideological thinking tends to separate, dichotomize or fragment things that can only be understood in terms of their dialectical, or internally related, nature. Ideological discourses utilize these fragments, including some and leaving out others, and in so doing they produce explanations that conceal the true nature of reality. Therefore, ideological thought is not false in the normal sense of that word (Marx and Engels, 1846). Instead, it distorts one's understanding by separating the dialectically related opposites and then referring to only one or the other of them or some mediation that results from their unity rather than offering a complete or full explanation. In our daily experience of capitalism, we tend to experience the internally related opposites of the contradictions that lie at the heart of capitalism—the contradictions that comprise its essence—at different times and in different places (Marx, 1858, p. 148). Therefore, if thought tends to separate or dichotomize the opposites, it is because this is how we actually experience them; and as a consequence, uncritical consciousness—or, more precisely, uncritical/reproductive praxis—will quite understandably give way to the type of dualistic explanations that are promoted in ideological discourses. One of the main objectives of critical education based on critical/revolutionary praxis is to critique and overcome ideological thinking by developing the ability to dialectically conceptualize the world.

A very different and opposed theory of being, or ontology, arises from Marx's revolutionary theory of consciousness and, as a consequence, also critical/revolutionary praxis—a theory based on the philosophy of internal relations. According to this ontology, what we are like as human beings—our human nature as well as our potential as sentient beings—does not preexist our relations but is, instead, shaped and developed within our social relations (Marx, 1844a, 1858). Therefore, if we want to become people who not only believe in social justice and various other ethical or moral values related to the welfare and betterment of humanity but also people who embody these values in the very fiber of our being—to establish coherence not just in our thinking but also between our thinking, feeling and the way we behave toward and relate to one another—then we must transform our social relations so that existing within them enables us to live in this manner. This critical ontology, or theory of being, is predicated on the idea that people working together through critical praxis can actually shape their human nature and their destinies according to revolutionary values and beliefs and thus create a new "ethics of harmonious existence" in unity with what Charles Taylor (1991) has called an "ethics of authenticity." This critical ontology challenges the idea that destiny is a matter of chance or fate. Destiny is something we can choose and actively pursue through our own critical and creative powers.

Marx's dialectical theory of consciousness/praxis, a theory that enables us to distinguish between uncritical/reproductive and critical/revolutionary praxis, offers the necessary foundation for "renewing" and "revivifying" critical education. It is the foundation and also the most essential ingredient of the approach to critical education that I advocate. In the remainder of this chapter, I discuss the nature, principles and aims of this approach to critical education; and, in chapter 6, I describe my experience of developing and attempting to apply the approach in a particular educational context. However, first I want to point out one, perhaps obvious, implication that arises from Marx's theory of consciousness/praxis—an implication of crucial importance to critical educators.

I often argue that revolutionary critical education must offer an "abbreviated experience" or "glimpse" of the type of social relations that we are working toward establishing through revolutionary social transformation (Allman, 1999, p. 104). This idea is based on the recognition that authentic and lasting transformations in consciousness can occur only when alternative understandings and values are actually experienced "in depth"—that is, when they are experienced sensuously and subjectively as well as cognitively, or intellectually. In other words, the revolutionary transformations in self that I will discuss in greater detail can only come about through a unitary and coherent *deep transformation*, or a transformation through which, as Gramsci (1971, p. 349) suggests, knowledge becomes so well "integrated" and "assimilated" that it becomes located within our subjectivities, and thus, in addition to being known, it is felt, or subjectively experienced, as a type of "lived" compassion and commitment. Clearly this type of transformation is complicated and not just because of its depth but also because it takes place by working against the already established modes of being and thinking that have been ingrained in the fabric of the "self" through uncritical/reproductive praxis. Therefore, for each person who engages in transformation, it is a bit like taking the already woven fabric, or tapestry, of one's identity, or one's self, and reweaving it critically and creatively into something quite different. As far as certain areas of transformation are concerned, this is not as difficult as it may sound. For example, it is traditional education that creates an artificial divide between teaching and learning, first dichotomizing these processes and then assigning them to different groups of people. These processes are, or should be, internally related within each member of a learning group; therefore, the grain against which this transformation is working is an artificial one that creates barriers to the development of critical understanding, and for that reason, it should be easier to overcome. Nevertheless, critical educators need to be aware of the already existing fabric, the "deep consciousness," of members of the learning group and to take it into account when "new knowledge" is being considered or created within the learning group.

In other words, the transformation in consciousness that this "new knowledge" might bring about is a much deeper and more complicated transformation than it may appear. We must always remember that even when a person's already existing fabric works against his or her own best interests, there is still a great deal of emotional investment involved. Therefore, transformation must always be supported sympathetically and empathetically and with a full recognition of the personal space and time that may be required by some individuals.

THE EDUCATIONAL DIALECTIC OF SELF AND SOCIETY: CRITICAL EDUCATION FOR REVOLUTIONARY SOCIAL TRANSFORMATION

My experience of critical education has been in the context of British adult and community education, or, more specifically, within courses I have organized for people working within these as well as other aspects of postcompulsory education and also the social and health services and the voluntary sector. We frequently use the term "critical education," and often this is done to acknowledge our allegiance with North American critical pedagogy; however, as I mentioned before, "radical education" is the term we normally use to refer to education for social transformation or education for socialism. I tend to use the terms "critical" and "radical" interchangeably to refer to education for revolutionary social transformation. The radical tradition of education in Britain dates back at least to the second decade of the nineteenth century, and even from its earliest days there have been tensions within the tradition. Many people involved in this tradition have aimed to increase working-class and other disadvantaged and oppressed groups' access to positions of power or at least to a position offering equality of opportunity; while others have steadfastly aligned themselves with the objective of revolutionary socioeconomic and political change. I emigrated to the United Kingdom from the United States in the early 1970s, and, as unbelievable as it may sound today, I can remember thinking at that time that almost everything I was experiencing in British education seemed radical in comparison to my previous experiences of education. However, it was not until 1981 that I began to experience at least the beginnings of what I would now call radical or critical education.

During the 1980/81 academic year, "my" students initiated me into the ideas of Paulo Freire.[4] I had been introduced to Freire's ideas when I read his book, *Pedagogy of the Oppressed* (1972), in the early 1970s. Unfortunately, like so many other people, although deeply moved by this book, I thought Freire's critique could not possibly apply to my own teaching. I assured myself that I was certainly not a "banking educator," thinking that he was only referring to some rather archaic style of didactic teaching far removed from the "progressive" philosophies of education that I assumed had become, at least since the mid 1960s, widespread in both the United States and the United Kingdom. In 1981, I was forced, due to the initiation I mentioned before, to reconsider these assumptions. At the time, I was working in the department of adult education of an English university, and I was teaching the psychology component of a diploma—or postexperience professional qualification—course for adult and community educators. The student group was extremely interesting and varied that year, but as I look back on the events that have unfolded since then, I think that there was one student in particular who acted as a catalyst for my initiation. He was a Chilean political refugee who had actually worked with Freire for a short time in Chile. He managed to get the whole group talking about Freire; and eventually we became interested in undertaking a collective study of Freire's thinking on education. At some point in our study of Freire we decided to try to apply his philosophy of education to our own situation, and with this decision my initiation truly began. In chapter 6, I will continue the story of what transpired as a result of that decision. Here, I want to discuss the nature, principles and aims of the approach to critical education that was developed together with many learning colleagues, including several members of the original group, during the three-year period that followed the first attempt to apply Freire.

This approach to critical education is based primarily on Freire's philosophy of education, or at least my own and my learning colleagues' interpretation of his approach. Over the three years during which the approach was initially developed and refined, it became necessary to consider and reconsider Freire in light of further theoretical insights. Freire tends to use certain terms or expressions—ones that are fundamental to unlocking what he actually means—in a way that assumes of his readers a shared understanding or intellectual background. Therefore, to uncover his meanings and critically assess his ideas, it is important to situate his meanings in terms of contemporary theoretical debates and also to delve into his theoretical sources. These requirements led me into many interesting contemporary theoretical debates, but, most importantly and essentially, they led me to undertake an in-depth study of Marx and also Gramsci. As a result, the ideas that I discuss in the following pages reflect a synthesis of the ideas of Freire, Marx and Gramsci—a synthesis that I used to develop an approach to critical education for revolutionary social transformation. I have already explained how important Marx's theory of consciousness/praxis is for developing an approach to critical education; however, I also found that without Marx it was just about impossible to understand what Freire and Gramsci were actually saying. And, of course, I have tried in the preceding chapters to indicate how indispensable Marx is for developing a dialectical understanding of capitalist reality, or for what Freire calls critically "reading the world." I assume here, and have argued elsewhere (especially Allman, 1999) that there are many parallels between Freire's and Gramsci's ideas about education and that these parallels arise primarily from their understanding and application of Marx's theory of consciousness. I begin by trying to describe the "nature" of this approach to critical education—both the general ethos that it embodies or that must be inherent within it and its essence.

The Ethos and Essence of Revolutionary Critical Education:
An Educational Form of Critical/Revolutionary Praxis

Adopting the approach to critical education that I advocate involves a personal and professional decision to engage in a process of self-transformation. Unfortunately, teachers cannot bring about this transformation on their own—either for themselves or for the learners with whom they are working. The transformations can only be realized jointly with others in the process of learning. However, teachers must undergo a certain degree of transformation in their thinking about, or their philosophy of, education—of teaching and learning—in order to be able to initiate the approach with others. I am talking about a philosophical approach to education, not an educational method; and it is a philosophy that must not only be believed in but also lived. Freire (1974a) says that teachers must undergo an "Easter Experience." In his words, they must be "born again" as teacher–learners who learn and teach together *with* others who are learner–teachers. His analogy expresses the transformations as well as any words I could substitute. Before initiating this approach and in order to engage in it authentically, teachers must be willing to undergo the process of "rebirth" and to understand why it is necessary; however, they can only complete the process within their internal relations with the students, as they too undergo the "rebirth" of becoming learner–teachers.

It is tempting to read Freire's ideas and intentions as stemming entirely from some sort of progressive, humanistic psychology aimed at creating equitable and harmonious relationships between teachers and students. Although these types of relationships are normal and necessary within the learning process, they are not the only reason for the transformed relations between teachers and students—a transformation that involves more comprehensive ontological shifts. The transformation of the teacher–student relation—that is, the ontological transformation—is actually part of, and also the result of, a more complex and fundamental transformation—namely, a transformed theory of knowledge that requires a transformed relation to knowledge. These epistemological transformations facilitate a dialectical conceptualization and thus critical "reading" of the world (see Allman, 1999; Freire, 1985). They enable the learning group to treat knowledge as an object that can be subjected to collective, critical scrutiny and, when necessary, rejected or transformed rather than relating to it as something extant, fixed and finite that we lack and therefore need to acquire and also desire to possess. Within the transformed epistemological relations, knowledge is placed before the learning group for their consideration. However, if this is to lead to what Freire calls a "critical reading of the world" (Freire and Macedo, 1987, p. 36), then each person in the group must engage in dialectically reuniting the processes of teaching and learning within his or herself so that the group can undertake a critical co-investigation of the "knowledge object." In other words, the ontological and epistemological transformations are codependent on one another.

Each person brings to this experience different types of knowledge—some practical and experiential and some theoretical—and any of these may enhance, at one time or another, the group's ability to think critically about the "knowledge object" the group is investigating. This means that teachers who initiate this approach must have a sincere humility about what they know and also the genuine desire to place their knowledge before the group so that it can be tested and then, as appropriate, refined, rejected, or changed and developed into a deeper and richer or more complex version (see also Mayo, 1999). The teacher's knowledge, therefore, is the beginning point of the learning process—the object of reflection and scrutiny rather than *necessarily* the end point or subject matter to be acquired or the objective to be achieved. And the same holds true for the knowledge of any other member of the group whose knowledge might be the object of co-investigation at some particular point in the ongoing process of "reading" the world critically. We must always be aware that any knowledge or form of knowledge that is being considered as a starting point or an enhancement to learning may be ideologically contaminated.

On an audiotape that Freire made in 1974 during a speaking tour of Australia, he explains his approach to education with greater clarity than he does in his writings. He says that the teacher he is criticizing is the one who thinks that his or her complete, or finished, knowledge is reflected, or contained, in the lesson that this teacher prepares for the class. All that is left to do is to deliver this "finished" knowledge to the class (Freire, 1974a). He is talking about the teacher's relation to knowledge; therefore, it does not matter whether the delivery takes place through conventional or progressive methodologies. Referring to the teacher's epistemology, he says that he believes just the opposite of this, and then, as if addressing a student, or the person he calls the "educatee–educator"—that is, the person I have referred to as the learner–teacher—he says: "I need you so that I can know more. For me to know more, I need another subject of knowing" (Freire, 1974a). Freire argues that this is a very different form of education. It begins with teachers having a very different theory or concept of knowledge, which arises from and then exists in unity with a transformed relation to knowledge. And I can testify to the fact that when you take what he is saying seriously and try to apply it, you will experience the difference. It is a revolutionary—transformational—difference that acts as a catalyst for even more profound transformations. These, as I indicated earlier, involve every participant in the learning group struggling to transform simultaneously the relation between teacher and students and each person's relation to knowledge. And, in so doing, they dialectically reunite the processes of teaching and learning within themselves. The teacher's transformed relation to knowledge can only be realized in full within this total process of critical transformation—that is, within collaborative, or collective, critical/revolutionary praxis. To reiterate, teachers cannot do this "to" or "for" the learning group. They can only initiate the process by explaining it and inviting the students to join them in the struggle for transformation and also by inviting the students to join them in vigilantly monitoring the process according to certain principles and criteria, which I will discuss soon. First, however, I turn to another element that is an essential factor in the process of transformation.

Dialogue as Critical/Revolutionary Praxis. Freire (1974b) says that dialogue is "the seal" of the transformed relations (p. 21). It is also the vehicle through which the transformations take place. The best way to describe this particular form of dialogue is to say both what it is and what it is not. I will begin with the latter. It is not at all the same as a discussion, no matter how harmonious or amicable the discussion may be. Discussions require a leader or someone who is in charge of the process, and in educational contexts this is normally the teacher. In dialogue the process should be collectively led or controlled. In other words, the aim of dialogue is for the responsibilities of the leader to be shared by all members of the group, so that at all times they are mutually responsible both for their own and for everyone else's learning. However, this does not happen automatically; it becomes a reality only as a part of the struggle for transformation. This is one of the main reasons why Freire distinguishes between teacher–learners and learner–teachers or, to use his exact and even more cumbersome terms, "educators–educatees" and "educatees–educators" (1974a). Both are required to reunite within themselves the internally related processes of teaching and learning—an internal relation forcibly ripped apart in conventional educational contexts. Nevertheless, the teacher–learner has always, at the point of initiation and any other point when necessary, the responsibility for making sure that the dialogue does not lapse into a distortion of the principles and aims the group is striving to achieve.

Discussions, although often harmonious, actually involve a sharing of monologues that often bear no relation to one another except that they address the same topic or question. Ideally, each person is supposed to be given the opportunity to state his or her ideas, answers, opinions or knowledge and questions as they pertain to the topic being discussed. When discussions are used as a teaching method, teachers try to ascertain the students' current level of understanding or accumulated knowledge and also use this format to offer their knowledge and understanding to the students. They are responsible for the "ordered and managed communication of monologues" (Allman, 1999, p. 100).

In dialogue, the members of the group share their thinking about the theme or issue that they are investigating or, alternatively, some "knowledge object" that has been selected in order to help the group members think critically about the theme or issue they are investigating. The "knowledge object" might come from a source external to the group, or it might be the result of a sub-group project or simply the knowledge that an individual is sharing with the group. However, this input is only the beginning of the learning, as is any "knowledge object" or "object focus" (these are interchangeable terms) that the group might consider. The dialogical exchange that takes place between at least two and usually many more members of the group is about investigating or exploring this knowledge—

not simply a one-way, monological offering of someone's knowledge to the group, as would be the case in discussion. In other words, it is not a matter of each person or several people simply stating what they think, but it involves taking the thinking of group members and also the thinking that is expressed in the "knowledge object," as an object of collective focus, or reflection and concern and exploring why each person thinks as he or she does and where this thinking has come from (e.g., the historical and cultural context) and analyzing whether it can enable the group to understand the world more critically. As a consequence, thinking or knowledge is offered to the group so that it can be considered and critically scrutinized or problematized by the other members of the group. It is examined in terms of whether it deepens everyone's understanding of what they are seeking to know—that is, some aspect related to the development of their critical understanding of reality. Knowledge, therefore, is offered for consideration so that the person who offers it can reconsider it with the help of others. To reiterate: already existing knowledge is always the beginning of the process of knowing—the development of deeper and more critical knowledge and sometimes even the creation of new knowledge. At times the original understanding may also be the end point of the process, but only after it has been subjected to the processes of problematization and co-investigation.

In this dialogical form of communication, the objective is to *use* the knowledge or thinking of each member of the group, together with the knowledge of people who are external to the group—that is, those who can offer expertise of a theoretical or practical nature—in order to investigate critically the theme or issue that the group is considering or seeking to understand more critically. In discussion, on the other hand, the objective is for students to acquire knowledge or offer it for teachers to assess. In dialogue, knowledge, of course, is acquired, but this happens when its use has revealed deeper insights regarding the theme or issue that is the real focus of the group's attention. And in accord with Marx's theory of consciousness, because it has been acted upon and explicitly related to each person's previous understandings as well as the theme being considered, it tends to be acquired at a deeper level and is thus more readily accessible for future use.

This form of dialogue is not the type of dialogue used in political negotiations. Therefore, it is not about reaching some form of highly compromised and often reluctant consensus. When decisions have to be made concerning, for example, the direction the group should take next, then dialogue is used to enable the group to reach a consensus that everyone is committed to and thus supports in all its dimensions. This often takes time, but it is time well spent because the process of reaching consensus is itself highly educational.

Dialogue, as I am describing it, is not easy to achieve. It is a process that must be struggled for on each occasion the group meets because the transformed relations that the group is trying to achieve will exist only in the learning group. Until society itself is transformed, dialogic communication and learning will remain counterhegemonic. Therefore, each time the members of the group depart from these relations, they reenter the social relations of capitalism—the all-pervasive, hegemonic relations of their normal conditions of existence. As a consequence, the transformed relations of dialogue—the relations integral to this approach to critical education—must be recreated each time the group meets, and this involves the commitment and effort of each member of the group. In light of these difficulties, it is important to follow each learning dialogue with an evaluation dialogue or a period of reflection during which the "knowledge object" or "object focus" is the struggle to learn dialogically—that is, through the dialogue that has just taken place. Of course, this, too, is time consuming, but equally a valuable learning experience.

Every time I write about dialogue, I try to explain it in a slightly different way (e.g., Allman, 1999) in the hope that I might find the words that can add further insights into a process that is difficult to describe and that can only be fully understood by actually experiencing it or attempting to experience it. The key to every explanation of dialogue is the idea of a form of communication that involves the continuous struggle—a critically conscious effort—to transform epistemological and ontological relations. These transformations or shifts in epistemology and ontology are the most essential requirements of Freire's educational approach (Allman, 1999, p. 100). And, as I have argued elsewhere, they follow directly from Marx's revolutionary theory of consciousness/praxis, which, to reiterate, includes a negative concept of ideology, wherein ideology is not just a matter of ideas but is also ingrained in habituated practices, social relations and the symbolic domains of our existence (p. 100). Dialogue, therefore, is a process of "knowing" and "being" differently. As a form of critical/revolutionary praxis, it is meant to offer a "glimpse" of some important aspects of revolutionary social transformation—an "abbreviated experience" of self and social transformation (p. 104), the dialectic of self and social transformation within the specific context of the social relations of education. Both transformations are necessary and inseparable in the process of preparing ourselves to take part in revolutionary social transformation (p. 100).

Principles and Aims of Critical Education for Revolutionary Social Transformation: The Dialectic of Means and Ends

I am convinced that this approach to education—or at least many of its principles—can be applied in almost any context within which learning is meant to take place. However, since teachers cannot do it "to" or "for" students but only *with* them, the teacher must explain, in some detail, the reasons for engaging in the approach, and this involves sharing at least an introductory level explanation of the theory and philosophy that underpins the approach. In chapter 6, I explain how this was done in my context. When I say that this approach or many aspects of it can be accomplished in almost any context, I mean with almost every age group and in both formal and informal learning situations.[5] However, to engage in the full approach and thus all the transformations entailed so that the approach becomes a coherent experience of critical/revolutionary praxis, the teacher must have the agreement of all those who are going to participate in the process. If it is not possible to secure this agreement from the group, teachers can still try to express their commitment to the principles in the way they relate to students and also in their attitudes to their own and other people's thinking.

In this final section, I list and briefly discuss the principles and aims, the inextricably linked means and ends, of this approach to critical education—an approach I call, alternatively "Freirean education," "critical education for revolutionary social transformation" or, most simply and to the point, "revolutionary critical education." I have already referred to many of these in my previous discussion. Here I explicitly propose them as the principles and aims that must inherently inform and guide every aspect of this approach to critical education. Although I first state the principles and then go on to the aims or objectives, I reiterate that they must be understood as part of a total process through which they ultimately become internally related means and ends.

Mutual respect, humility, openness, trust and cooperation are indispensable to this approach. However, the genuine development and expression of these dispositions or virtues does not preexist engaging in the struggle for transformation. Some people, primarily as a result of their previous experiences, will be more predisposed toward expressing them than will others. Nevertheless, the support that people must necessarily offer one another in order to effect the transformations and the excitement that ensues as each new critical insight arises within dialogue facilitate the realization of these principles and the development of people's ability to express them, at least within the transformed relations of the learning group.

Commitment to learning to "read the world" critically and to transforming the conventional, hegemonic or dominant and pervasive educational relations, based on at least an initial level of understanding of why the transformations are necessary, should be elicited from all participants prior to their engagement in this approach to critical education. Any form of imposition, either from the teacher or from other members of the group, is counterproductive and antithetical to the principles and general ethos of this approach and must, therefore, be challenged and abolished if ever it occurs. This is essential because the approach can lead to the desired outcomes only when those involved are committed to expending the effort necessary to bring about the transformations and if they genuinely want to understand what is happening in the world and why it is happening and are also committed to helping every other member of the group to do likewise. Moreover, dialogue simply does not take place in the absence of such commitment. As I said before, teachers cannot impose this approach on students or do it "to" or "for" them. It only works effectively when each person involved works with everyone else to bring about the transformed student–teacher relation simultaneously with the group's—and this means each person's—transformed relation to knowledge. Needless, to say, initially not every member of the group shares the same level of commitment; but when the approach works effectively, the general level of commitment increases and continues to do so. Therefore, any initial differences tend to be erased over time, or at least they do not inhibit the energy and motivation of the learning group.

Vigilance with regard to one's own process of self-transformation and adherence to the principles and aims the group is attempting to fulfill is required from every member of the group. It is so indispensable to the process that it needs to be perceived as an integral part of the process and purposively incorporated in it. In my discussion of dialogue I mentioned that it was important to follow every dialogical learning session with an evaluation dialogue during which the group can reflect upon the preceding session. During this time the group should focus, in particular, on the whether the principles have been embodied in and expressed during the learning dialogue and should also consider whether progress is being made in relation to the aims the group is seeking to achieve. Teachers and students need to be vigilant regarding not only their own personal efforts to transform and learn within the counterhegemonic relations of learning but also with regard to the degree to which everyone is sharing responsibility for the transformations and also monitoring the processes involved. And they need to monitor vigilantly their own and the group's progress in developing a deeper and more critical understanding of whatever aspect of reality they are co-investigating at each moment in the process. In chapter 6, I discuss how this principle and all the others were translated into action in the context of my own practice and also how we dealt with any problems that arose.

Honesty, truth—or more precisely, *an "ethics of authenticity"* (Taylor, 1991) is the guiding principle to this approach—a principle that must be expressed by the teacher or person initiating the process from the very first moment of contact with any member of the learning group. The reasons for engaging in the process, the effort required, the need for individual and collective responsibility, the possibilities or potentials as well as the problems and pitfalls and, very importantly, feelings about failure as well as success should be made explicit from the outset. The same level of honesty or authenticity is required from every member of the group once the process of learning has begun, and this, along with the fact that this often involves the sharing of feelings, should be clearly stated before people's commitment to participating in the process is elicited. Honesty, truth and an ethics of authenticity work together with and underpin openness and trust and help to engender the development of mutual respect as well as each person's commitment to learning to "read" the world critically and to the transformation of self and society.

Passion may seem, at first glance, a peculiar principle to specify. It is similar to but also something more than commitment. I take it from one of my favorite passages in Antonio Gramsci's prison notebooks (1971). In this passage he is talking about revolutionary social transformation and the type of prefigurative, counterhegemonic process that is essential for its realization. Of course, any critical education process is only a small component of the preparatory phase. Nevertheless, Gramsci's words, which I paraphrased before and now cite, capture what I mean by passion—that is, its inner connection with critically "reading" the world. Moreover, they express why I think passion is a fundamental principle— not only a principle that motivates the use of this approach to critical education but also a principle to be achieved within it. In Gramsci's words:

An historic act can only be performed [collectively], and this presupposes the attainment of a "cultural–social" unity through which a multiplicity of dispersed wills, with heterogeneous aims, are welded together with a specific aim, on the basis of an equal and common conception of the world, both general and particular, . . . where the intellectual base is so well rooted, assimilated and experienced that it becomes *passion*. [1971, p. 349; emphasis added]

Passion, like mutual respect, humility, openness, trust and cooperation, nor- mally does not exist—at least, not to the degree I am suggesting—prior to our engagement in the process of transformation. Neither, however, is it only a final outcome or result, although it is that as well. All of these principles, which dialectically unite our thoughts or beliefs and feelings and which, as I indicated before, are, it is to be hoped, expressed in the very fiber of our being, develop within our struggle to transform the existing social relations. Therefore, the struggle to transform these relations—critical/revolutionary praxis *par excel- lence*—is a struggle to establish coherence in our thinking and also between our thinking, feeling and the way we express our lives—in the way we act toward and relate to others. It is through critical/revolutionary praxis that justice be- comes educated (Hill, 2000) and internalized as passion.

The aims or objectives of this approach to education are, perhaps, obvious. Nevertheless, I will try to state them as comprehensively as I can and also mention some of the unexpected outcomes that I, together with learning col- leagues, have experienced. In a certain respect it is somewhat antithetical to this approach to specify aims and objectives, because these usually suggest a point of finality or completion. And one of the most important and exciting outcomes of this approach to education is that there is no final point to the learning process that is set in motion. Once knowledge is no longer considered to be an object that can be possessed, it becomes a process of continuous unfolding and deepening. It is as open and dialectical as the movement and the development of the reality we must constantly and endlessly seek to comprehend.

Critical, Creative and Hopeful Thinking. This approach to education is aimed at the development of both critical and creative thought, which in combi- nation lead to realistic hope. "Reading the world" critically serves little purpose if this "reading" does not also develop the ability to recognize the possibilities or potential that are already present in the world, if only in some suppressed or muted form, often existing in dialectical unity with their opposites that tend to negate them or deny and inhibit their existence. Commitment to continuing self and social transformation—another aim that I discuss later—requires us to prob- lematize our current conditions of existence. But in order to problematize effectively, the learning group needs to ask persistently not only "why" and "how" questions but also "why not," "what if" and "what about" questions; and these latter types of questions require creative and hopeful thinking—thinking that can lead to a vision of a humanized future or a realistic utopia.

Transformation of Self and the Social Relations of Learning and Teaching. When we dialectically conceptualize human development, we understand that the self, or our individuality and identity, in both its subjective and its objective dimensions, is internally related to other people and also the objects that exist in nature or that have been created by human beings. In other words, the self—or our individuality and identity—does not preexist these relations but is constantly developing and being shaped within them. Therefore, in striving to transform the conventional social relations of learning—that is, our relations to one another as teachers and learners and our relations to knowledge—we are also striving to transform ourselves for the better, just as we do when we strive to transform any social relation. Every dimension of our "being"—our thoughts, feelings and habituated ways of acting—will have been shaped and determined by the existing social relations. As we transform these relations, then we are also, in a critically and creatively conscious way, reshaping and redefining the type of people we are. When we undertake these transformations in a critically conscious manner—through critical/revolutionary praxis rather than reproductive/uncritical and habituated praxis—we can overcome our fragmentation and become coherent "beings." Thus this approach to critical education aims to prepare people to be able to shape and determine their own personal and social destinies collectively, critically and creatively—to be collectively and critically in control of their future conditions of existence rather than being determined by them.

Democratization. If democracy is to become a way of living—as it must be within the type of socialism envisioned by Marx and advocated by myself and many others—rather than just an abstract or formal designation for a form of government, then it must become a process that we incorporate in every aspect of our social existence and also internalize within ourselves so that it becomes an integral part of our identity or ethical and moral makeup (Hill, 2000). This aim is inseparable from the type of self-transformation and development of our identity that I described earlier; however, it also involves learning to live and act in cooperation with others—to embrace our *inner* dependence with and need for one another as integral to our own self-fulfillment. As Freire (1974a) says: "I cannot be unless you are. I cannot grow up [develop fully] without you." Democratization involves a recognition of each individual's strengths and differences and an affirmation of how all of these contribute to and enrich whatever we are seeking to do, to learn or to understand more deeply and critically. In one of Marx's early writings he describes this manner of social existence. As I mentioned in chapter 4, he believed that it was possible to create a society based on social relations that would foster our care, concern, regard and love for one another—our desire to meet one another's needs. This is the passage where he most clearly and passionately describes this form of existence and the social relations entailed in it. He begins by contrasting it to the mode of existence that prevails within capitalist societies.

Our mutual value is for us the value of our mutual products. Thus, [human beings themselves are] for us mutually worthless.

Supposing we had produced in a human manner, each of us would in [our] production have doubly affirmed [ourselves] and [our] fellow [human beings]. I would have: (1) objectified in my production my individuality and its peculiarity and thus both in my activity enjoyed the individual expression of my life and also in looking at the object have had the individual pleasure of realizing that my personality was objective, visible to the senses, and thus a power raised beyond doubt. (2) In your enjoyment or use of my product I would have had the direct enjoyment of realizing that I had both satisfied a human need by my work and also objectified the human essence and therefore fashioned for another human being the object that met his [her] need. (3) I would have been for you the mediator between you and the species and thus been acknowledged and felt by you a completion of your own essence and as a necessary part of yourself and have thus realized that I am confirmed both in your thought and in your love. (4) In my expression of my life I would have fashioned the expression of your life, and thus in my own activity have realized my own essence, my human, my communal essence.

In that case our products would be like so many mirrors out of which our essence shone.

Thus, in this relation what occurred on my side would also occur on yours. [Marx, 1844b, pp. 121–122]

Embracing and Internalizing the Principles.   As I noted before, the principles that guide this approach are also its aims. Prior to engaging in the approach, the principles may be advocated or believed in, but the aim is not only to embrace and profess them but also to internalize them so that they become integral to, or a normal part of, our mode of "being." This internalization is only possible within the transformed relations and is brought about in the process of transformation and sustained by striving to maintain the transformations. I noted previously that the relations within the learning group are counterhegemonic; therefore, prior to the social transformation of the entire society, members of the learning group will continue to spend most of their time within capitalist, and also other, relations of domination and oppression that are a part of capitalist hegemony. Therefore, the transformations within the learning group have to be struggled for each time the group meets. This is the only way the relations can be maintained, and it is also why vigilance is so important. However, as members internalize the principles, sustaining the transformations becomes much easier, and the transformations are much more likely to endure.

I have found that this experience of critical education tends to have a lasting effect on participants. Once the principles are internalized, participants try to encourage other people to join them in bringing about these transformations in other aspects of their lives. One unanticipated outcome was the extent to which former members of the learning groups set up informal Freirean learning circles either at work or in their communities. Linked to this, and also unanticipated, was their request for us to reconvene the group at regular intervals for post-course one-day sessions focused on an issue or problem that was being widely experienced by themselves and others.

Unquenchable Thirst for Understanding, or Genuine Critical Curiosity. This approach is aimed at developing a disposition to learning or education that is open and engaged in a never-ending quest not only to understand the "as yet unknown" but to understand ever more deeply the "already known." The aim is to orient learners, and teachers too, toward what I call *genuine continuing education*—an orientation toward lifelong learning so deeply ingrained that it becomes integral to one's existence. The need to understand, therefore, becomes an internally felt need and one that, at most, can only ever be temporarily satisfied. In the contemporary world, continuing education and lifelong education are being promoted in order to convince people that they will have to continue learning in order to stay employable, and thus there is an element of fear and compulsion involved in this promotion. This is an abomination and a barrier to developing a genuine disposition and authentic desire—that is, real need—to continuously learn and deepen the level of one's understanding. In my opinion, critical educators should be taking every opportunity to problematize the current rationale for and approach to lifelong education—that is, the implicit compulsion and control that are integral to its promotion.

Solidarity and Commitment to Self and Social Transformation and the Project of Humanization. The project of humanization—or what some people call the "project for humanity"—is about the creation of a world in which people can reach their full potential as human beings and thus also as social beings and then constantly strive to expand the horizons of that potential. In other words, it is about creating a world in which humanity can become the critically and creatively conscious species that it has the potential to be (Marx, 1844a). Freire (1972) argues that the dehumanizing conditions of our current reality are dialectically related to their opposite—the possibility of humanizing the world—creating, as he says, "a world in which it will be easier to love" our fellow human beings (p. 19). It is about creating a world in which human dignity is safeguarded and nurtured and in which human beings collectively, critically and creatively shape their destiny and therefore the future destiny, or history, of humanity. The transformation of ourselves and our social relations of learning is only a small part of the project of humanization. Nevertheless, it is a place where we can choose to start this process, and it is also a necessary and essential part of this project, as are many of the other aims of this approach to critical education.

The aims I have specified may seem unrealistic and utopian, but I do not think they are. They are simply counterfactual. After all, it is only human beings who have created our current conditions of existence—conditions that are historically specific to capitalism. Capitalism is not some separate entity—reified system or structure—that is external to human beings. It is created and sustained by human beings actively engaged in capitalist social relations—in uncritical/reproductive praxis. And as Rikowski (1999), following Marx, argues, capitalism is even internalized within our subjectivities. Therefore, it stands to reason that it is only human beings who can choose critically, collectively and co-intentionally to change and, when necessary, abolish these relations and thus transform the conditions of their existence. It is only human beings who can choose to abolish dehumanization and to humanize the world. However, to know that they can do this, to know what needs to be abolished and transformed and to discover how to create social relations within which humanization can be fostered, they—that is, all of us—need to engage in critical education. And it is only an approach to critical education that embodies these aims and principles and thus offers an abbreviated experience of the future reality we are striving for that will be able to prepare people who are capable of and committed to revolutionary social transformation.

NOTES

1. North American critical pedagogy has also been influenced by many factors other than Freire; Critical Theory, that is, The Frankfurt School, Feminist Theory, the writings of Foucault and Bloch and the field of Cultural Studies, for example, are some of the most important influences. For an interesting personal account from some of Critical Pedagogy's best-known figures, see Torres, *Education, Power, and Personal Biography: Dialogues with Critical Educators* (1998).

2. I arrived at this conclusion independently but later found that it was also proposed by Kosík in his *Dialectic of the Concrete: A Study of Problems of Man and World* (1976).

3. This has serious implications. Many theories and definitions of intelligence are based on the notion that intelligent beings are those that can adapt most successfully to their environment or their circumstances. In the case of animals, other than human beings (and these definitions and theories of intelligence are drawn from the study of such animals), this is probably an accurate concept of intelligence, because animals would find it difficult to survive if they did not adapt. However, in terms of Marx's theory of consciousness, if we apply this idea to human beings, it could mean that those whom we consider to be the most intelligent are actually those most directly engaged in reproductive praxis. In other words, they are "tuned into" their material reality in a way that enables them to adapt to and embrace its general pattern of movement—to "go with the flow" and, moreover, to often be at the "cutting-edge" of that flow. This is especially problematic in capitalist conditions wherein the surface appearances conceal the real essence of the system. However, human intelligence can be conceived differently—for example, in terms of one's ability not to adapt one's self but instead to adapt or transform one's material reality or circumstances in accord with a vision or a plan of something better—that is, conditions that would be more conducive to the realization of the full potential of the human species.

4. I have placed quotation marks around "my" because Freire (1974a) drew my attention to the fact that "my" is a very possessive word. He says it is a symptom of capitalist ideology and stresses that we do not "have" people; we are "with" people—"with" students.

5. I think that many of these principles can be applied even in the education of young children. The closest I have come to doing something like this with very young children was in a British infant school. I was teaching 5- to 7-year-olds and was very frustrated by their tattle telling, which, according to Kohlberg's theory of moral development, is symptomatic of the

moral development of children in this age group. According to my understanding of some of the literature that reported applications of this theory, especially in prison education, if people at a lower stage of moral development were placed together with people at a higher stage, there was a tendency for this to foster development in those whose moral reasoning was less developed. Since my infant class had some children who were more advanced, I decided to have dialogues with the children in which the "object focus" was a moral dilemma—a make-believe problem of a moral nature related to their own circumstances—in order to see whether the more advanced children's reasoning would help to foster development in those who were tattling. There was one rule, and that was that they could not ask me what to do; my role was to explain the situation and pose further questions if they became stuck. This worked wonders, and the tattle-telling was soon eradicated. Moreover, all the children began to take greater responsibility for their actions and their thinking.

REFERENCES

Allman, P. (1999). *Revolutionary Social Transformation: Democratic Hopes, Political Possibilities and Critical Education.* Westport CT: Bergin & Garvey.

Ebert, T. (1996). *Ludic Feminism and After: Postmodernism, Desire, and Labor in Late Capitalism.* Ann Arbor, MI: The University of Michigan Press.

Freire, P. (1972). *Pedagogy of the Oppressed.* Harmondsworth, U.K.: Penguin.

Freire, P. (1974a). "Authority versus Authoritarianism." Audiotape, in series: *Thinking with Paulo Freire.* Sydney, Australia: Australian Council of Churches.

Freire, P. (1974b). "Education: Domestication or Liberation." In I. Lister (Ed.), *De-Schooling.* Cambridge: Cambridge University Press.

Freire, P. (1985). *The Politics of Education.* London: Macmillan.

Freire, P., and Macedo, D. (1987). *Literacy: Reading the Word and the World.* London: Routledge & Kegan Paul.

Gramsci, A. (1971). *Selections from the Prison Notebooks of Antonio Gramsci,* edited and translated by Quinton Hoare and Geoffrey Nowell Smith. London: Lawrence & Wishart.

Harvey, D. (1989). *The Condition of Postmodernity.* Oxford: Basil Blackwell.

Hill, D. (2000). "Review of Peter Mayo's (1999) *Gramsci, Freire and Adult Education: Possibilities for Transformative Action* (London: Zed Books, 1999)." *International Gramsci Society Newsletter,* No. 10 [www.italnet.nd.edu/gramsci].

Kosík, K. (1976). *Dialectic of the Concrete: A Study of Problems of Man and World.* Dordrecht, Holland: Reidel.

Larrain, J. (1983). *Marxism and Ideology.* London: Macmillan.

Marx, K. (1843). "Critique of Hegel's 'Philosophy of Right.'" In D. McLellan (Ed.), *Karl Marx Selected Writings* (pp. 26–35). Oxford: Oxford University Press, 1977.

Marx, K. (1844a). "Economic and Philosophical Manuscripts." In D. McLellan (Ed.), *Karl Marx: Selected Writings* (pp. 75–111). Oxford: Oxford University Press, 1977.

Marx, K. (1844b). "On James Mill." In D. McLellan (Ed.), *Karl Marx: Selected Writings* (pp. 114–123). Oxford: Oxford University Press, 1977.

Marx, K. (1845). "Theses on Feuerbach." In D. McLellan (Ed.), *Karl Marx: Selected Writings* (pp. 156–158). Oxford: Oxford University Press, 1977.

Marx, K. (1858). *Grundrisse,* translated and with a Foreword by Martin Nicolaus. Harmondsworth, U.K.: Penguin, 1973.

Marx, K. (1863a). *Theories of Surplus Value,* Part 1. London: Lawrence & Wishart, 1969.

Marx, K. (1863b). *Theories of Surplus Value,* Part 2. London: Lawrence & Wishart, 1969.

Marx, K. (1863c). *Theories of Surplus Value,* Part 3. London: Lawrence & Wishart, 1972.

Marx, K. (1865). *Capital,* Vol. 3, translated by David Fernbach, Introduction by Ernest Mandel. Harmondsworth, U.K.: Penguin, 1981.

Marx, K. (1867). *Capital,* Vol. 1, translated by Ben Fowkes, Introduction by Ernest Mandel. Harmondsworth, U.K.: Penguin, 1976.

Marx, K., and Engels, F. (1844). *The Holy Family.* In K. Marx and F. Engels, *Collected Works,* Vol. 4 (pp. 5–211). London: Lawrence & Wishart, 1975.

Marx, K., and Engels, F. (1846). *The German Ideology.* Moscow: Progress, 1976.

Mayo, P. (1999). *Gramsci, Freire and Adult Education: Possibilities for Transformative Action.* London: Zed.

McLaren, P. (1998). "Revolutionary Pedagogy in Post-Revolutionary Times: Rethinking the Political Economy of Critical Education." *Education Theory,* 48 (No. 4), 431–462.

Piaget, J. (1970). *Genetic Epistemology.* New York: Columbia University Press.

Rikowski, G. (1999). "Education, Capital and the Transhuman." In D. Hill, P. McLaren and G. Rikowski (Eds.), *Postmodernism in Educational Theory: Education and the Politics of Human Resistance* (pp. 50–84). London: The Tufnell Press.

Taylor, C. (1991). *The Ethics of Authenticity.* Cambridge, MA: Harvard University Press.

Torres, C. A. (1998). *Education, Power, and Personal Biography: Dialogues with Critical Educators.* London: Routledge.

6

Freirean Critical Education in an Unlikely Context

The theoretical understandings I have discussed in the preceding chapters arose in concert with my educational praxis. This chapter is about that praxis—a praxis in which I attempted to apply or translate Paulo Freire's philosophical approach to critical education within a specific context that was entirely different from that of Freire—one that many would deem an inappropriate context for his approach to critical education. The diaries I kept over the twelve years of this praxis no longer exist. Several years ago I made the decision never to use the diaries in my writing. I did not feel that they were mine to share, other than with the learning colleagues (learner–teachers) to whose learning experience they referred. When external events forced me to bring this trial or informal experiment in Freirean critical education to a close, I discarded the diaries, partly because I was feeling depressed, but primarily, and more rationally, to make sure that I would not be tempted to go back on my previous decision not to use them for a writing project such as this one. This chapter is, therefore, based entirely on my personal memories and critical reflection. However, to give you some idea of why I kept the diaries and how they aided what I was doing, I will give you an idea of some of the types of entries I made in them.

Each week, immediately after the teaching day, I would fill approximately two A–4 pages with comments such as these:

Week 5—I know X was on the verge of making a major shift in his thinking today, but I couldn't think of the right question to put to him that would have problematized his present position. Still can't figure out just exactly what is blocking him. Also had a bit of trouble, again, with the "gridlock" between the oppressed . . . the clash between Y and Z over which of their oppressions is the worse . . . racism or sexism. Since this is going on during our coffee breaks rather than in the group, I think I'll wait a bit before problematizing this conflict.[1]

Week 6—Finally figured out what was blocking X, but so did M, who posed just the right question to get X thinking . . . maybe by next week some real development will start. The battle of the oppressed that I was picking up on between Y and Z flared up during our dialogue session. I was hoping they might realize how futile their line of argument was once they heard themselves expressing their opinions in front of the whole group . . . so I didn't say anything this time. Maybe they need a week to reflect on what they are saying . . . the reaction—silence—from the rest of us should be cause for reflection. . . .

The diaries helped me to refocus and reflect on what had happened during the day, and this helped me to keep in mind the way that members of the group were thinking and to think of ways in which I might foster the further development of their criticality. They also helped me to monitor my own thinking and development as a critical educator—in other words, the development of my own criticality. For me, they were one expression of the type of vigilance this approach to education requires.

The account that I share in this chapter follows the chronology of the development of the Freirean course (later courses), but it is not an exact chronology in which I depict a week-by-week or term-by-term sequence of events. Instead, I talk in terms of phases—phases that have become clear to me only with hindsight. I do not mention the names of any individual, other than John Wallis, the member of staff who joined me at the beginning of Year 3 and who then shared the development of the course with me and various groups of learning colleagues (students) until the penultimate year of the Freirean courses. Since I am very aware that this project was at all times a collective activity, which involved not just John and me but also our learning colleagues, and that, therefore, the development of the course was a shared effort, I refer to "we" rather than "I" in most instances. In this chapter, I tend to refer to "Freirean education" rather than "revolutionary critical education." This is because my original intention was to apply Freire's ideas, and although the approach developed into something more complex, we always referred to it within the course and also the institution as Freirean education.

Of course, there are many individuals to whom I shall always be indebted, mainly because they supportively and often brilliantly fostered my own personal, professional and intellectual development or because they had the same effect through their challenges and sometimes even resistance and hidden agendas. In either case, however, since these reflections are my reflections, and reflections made at a considerable distance in time, with reference to these contributions, it would serve no purpose, nor would it be just, to single out (i.e., name) particular individuals from a context that was always a collective endeavor. I begin my account from where I left it in chapter 5. There, I mentioned the group who had initiated me into the ideas of Paulo Freire and how our joint reading of *Pedagogy of the Oppressed* (Freire, 1972) and initial attempts to apply Freire's ideas led to what was to become a fourteen-year trial/experience of Freirean education (i.e., two years with the group who initiated me and then twelve years of the Freirean course). First, however, I describe various aspects of the context within which this took place, including the course structure and the background of the students who participate or tend to participate in the type of courses offered by the department within which my work was located.

I mentioned in chapter 5 that I was working in a department of adult education in an English university. This department, the Department of Adult Education at the University of Nottingham, is the oldest department of its kind in the United Kingdom. Like most departments of adult education in Britain, ours ran a large extramural program of courses both for the general public and for trade unionists. Originally, this had been the main function of such departments; however, in the present climate colleagues are struggling to keep what we call the "Liberal Tradition" of adult education—learning for its own sake—alive. I should note that even though my own work is associated with the "radical tradition," which often stands in opposition to and is critical of the liberal tradition, I fully support the "liberal tradition," as, I think, all critical/radical educators should. It is a valuable service that will, it is to be hoped, thrive in a transformed society. In fact, my main argument with liberal educators is that this type of education is better suited to a socialist than to a capitalist society. Our department also runs award-bearing postexperience courses for people involved in the education and training of adults and those working in community education and development. These courses are meant to develop educators' academic, or intellectual, understanding of their work and to enable them to reflect upon and theorize their practice and also the context in which their practice takes place from either a specific or a range of disciplinary perspectives. They are also intended to develop educators' skills, including their research skills, and their ability to apply these skills in their educational practice. The awards now range from certificates to Ph.D.s, but during the period I am describing our main awards were the Diploma in Adult Education (a highly valued professional award based on academic work); the M.Ed., the title of which has since changed to M.A. (a taught master's degree); the M.Phil. (a master's degree by research and thesis) and the Ph.D. (a doctorate by research and dissertation). We began the Freirean trial first with the diploma course and five years later with the M.Ed.; however, in a few cases M.Phil. and Ph.D. students working in the area of radical/critical education committed themselves to regularly attending and fully participating in the Freirean courses. Since the M.Ed. was run on lines similar to the diploma, unless I state otherwise, this discussion will refer mainly to the diploma course.

Students pursuing any of these awards come from various backgrounds, many of which I mentioned in chapter 5. Once the Freirean course was running, we tended to recruit more people than previously from community education and development and also the social services and voluntary sector, although in principle our courses were always meant to attract applicants from these areas of informal or nonformal educational work with adults. Normally we also have students from abroad. During the twelve years of the Freirean course we were joined by students from Brazil, Mexico, Chile, Namibia, South Africa (one an ANC member in exile who was being groomed for a diplomatic post in the hoped-for ANC government of the future), Malawi, Cyprus, Pakistan, India, China, Hong Kong, Japan and Australia. These students were full-time students, as were some participants from the United Kingdom, but the majority, every year, was made up of part-time students. Due to the mixture of full and part-time students, we ran the course over two consecutive days. Part-timers attended on a day-release (from work) basis on Tuesdays in the first year and Wednesdays in the second year. Full-time students attended on both days and thus worked with two different groups of learning colleagues—the Tuesday group, as new to the situation as they were, and the Wednesday group, an experienced Freirean learning group.

The course-day usually ran from 10:30 a.m. until 5 or sometimes 5:30 p.m. There were a few years when we varied this slightly to accommodate one or more individuals who had difficulty obtaining a full-day-release from their employers. However, even in those cases, we never sacrificed any of the time allocated for dialogue. Although the pattern or structure of the day also varied slightly in order to accommodate a particular year-group's needs, normally we started the day with library and tutorial time for the first hour; then we held a one-hour dialogue session prior to an hour break for lunch—during which tutorial time could also be arranged and study circles, which I explain later, were convened. From 1:30 to 4:00, with a fifteen-minute break about halfway through, we engaged in a sustained dialogue session, leaving the last hour of the day for our evaluation dialogue and the collective "forward planning" of the next session. This pattern was flexible and could be altered whenever the group decided that an alternative pattern would better suit our learning plans for the following week; however, the evaluation period was never sacrificed unless we went on an external visit, or "field trip." In those instances, the evaluation of the day was held during the morning dialogue session of the following week. I realize this may sound very tightly structured, but it had to be if we were going to achieve the development and transformations necessary. Adhering to the timetable was the one facet of the course that I constantly had to struggle to get learning colleagues to share jointly with me. In fact, I usually prodded them less and less after a while because I understood their reluctance to take on this responsibility—this was their day away from work and the normal burden of keeping to a schedule. Nevertheless, in principle it should have been a shared responsibility, even if the best I could do was to remind people constantly of this point. This is not to say that all responsibilities in a Freirean approach to education are shared ones, and I will mention those that teachers—that is, teacher–learners—must assume or retain, but keeping to the timetable should ideally be everyone's task.

In the first year of the course, the Freirean sessions were held only in the afternoon. This was a matter of compromise with my academic colleagues and was meant to accommodate elements of the previous course structure and content. Other members of staff offered one-hour sessions on their areas of expertise during the time that later became the morning dialogue session. For a variety of reasons—including, importantly, student evaluations of the course—this hybrid arrangement was replaced after the first year by an entire day devoted to Freirean critical education, which was run according to the pattern I just described. For a while, there was a certain amount of tension between myself and some other members of the department. I was the most recent full-time appointment, having been a member of staff for only two years when the changes began to occur. I was also the only full-time woman academic. Not only were the other members of staff my seniors in terms of years of service to the department, but, for the most part, they were also well-established and well-known figures in the field of adult education, both nationally and, in some cases, internationally. Therefore, I risked treading on some very important toes. Nevertheless, the students were firmly and enthusiastically behind the trial Freirean program. In fact, to a large extent it was their idea, and because they were "fellow" professionals in the field of adult education, our academic staff listened to what they were saying and agreed to cooperate. Over the years, the tension subsided, primarily due to the extremely favorable evaluations and also support the course received from our external examiners. However, I suspect that in a few cases the apprehensions behind this tension never abated.

Certain features of the course pertained throughout the twelve years. I think it is important to discuss these before looking back over the phases through which the course developed.

In chapter 5, I stressed the importance of coherence, authenticity and honesty. For me this meant that the principles and aims of the course had to be reflected in every aspect of it, beginning with all the elements involved in recruitment, such as publicity and initial telephone contact with people making inquiries about the course. The only constraint on this was my own understanding of what Freirean education actually entailed—an understanding that deepened considerably over the first two to three years of trying to apply Freire's philosophical approach to critical education. As an expression of the principles of this approach, I was always open and honest about these limitations in my understanding—at least as soon as I became aware of them. I return to some of these limitations and the problems they caused in my discussion of the phases through which the course developed. The principles and aims of the course were also expressed as clearly as possible in the course brochure that we used to publicize the course and, as far as our limited budget would allow, in the one-off advertisement that the department allowed us to place in the *Guardian* newspaper each year. In the brochure we were also able to stress the commitment that was required from those who wished to participate and to extend an invitation, to those who were interested, to attend a mutual interview session that was meant to be as much about applicants interviewing us as it was about us interviewing them.

These interview sessions were extremely important. The actual pattern I describe emerged over the first phase of the course, but in most respects the interviews were very similar from the very beginning. To encourage the two-way or mutual process, we tried always to hold group interviews, with 3–6 applicants per session. We assumed—and this was confirmed by the participants—that people would be more relaxed and open if they were interviewed in a small group rather than individually, although anyone who chose to meet with us on an individual basis was welcome to do so. The interviews began in our teaching room (a seminar room, with a capacity to seat 20 people comfortably or a few more when necessary, where we regularly held the course sessions but that was also used by the university for other purposes). We tried to make this room as comfortable as the institution would allow—for example, we had our own resource cupboards and coffee- and tea-making facilities; photographs of past and present course members, engaged in various course-related activities, were displayed on the walls. After making coffee or tea for everyone attending the interview, we would explain the course in a fair amount of detail to the whole group, which was seated with us around the seminar table. Then we would reassemble the applicants in small groups. John would take half of those attending to his office down the corridor, and I would take the other half to mine, which was also near the teaching room (during the course, our offices were also used as small group meeting rooms, and the two professors in the department, who had quite large offices, also allowed their offices to be used as small group meeting rooms when they were not using them). In this part of the interview, we encouraged those attending the session to interview us. From this mutual process, we learned more about people's appropriateness for our particular course, especially their potential commitment, than we would have through a more conventional interview procedure. After about 40 minutes, we would have a short coffee break and then exchange the groups, repeating the process. Finally, we reconvened the whole group to see whether they had any further question that they wanted to put to the two of us.

When we were as certain as we could be that applicants who had attended the interview were committed to participating in the course, we sent them a letter of acceptance and asked them to reply with a provisional acceptance of their place on the course (we tried to limit the group to 20 members, but on one or two occasions we slightly exceeded that number). We asked only for a provisional acceptance, because we held a precourse orientation day during which they could meet the others who were likely to be participating and also sample a bit of what the course would be like before making their final commitment to join the course. Because the university administration always wanted and expected full courses, this was fairly risky on our part, even during the first seven or so years of the course, when the external climate, though changing, was such that participants could quite easily gain day-release and at least nominal support from their employers—a situation that changed drastically as the full force of the Thatcher/ Major regime began to hit the postcompulsory sector of education. Our Head of Department was, understandably, not keen on us risking drop-out prior to formal registration for the course. However, we had a waiting list during the years of abundant student numbers and were, as a result, able to defend the risk we were taking. By the time the "lean years" hit, the procedure had become so routine that no mention was made of it; and though the risk for us then grew greater, we continued to hold the orientation day. The entire process was important because, as I said in chapter 5, Freirean education cannot possibly work by imposition, and by this careful procedure from interview through precourse orientation we were doing as much as we possibly could to assure ourselves and the entire learning group that we were all committed, at least in principle, to trying to learn together in an alternative, unconventional and what we hoped would become a revolutionary way.

Another feature of the course that was always present was, of course, dialogue. During the first ten-week term we tried to initiate or orientate people into the total process of Freirean education through explanation and also by putting the principles into practice. Our main focus, of course, was dialogue, and we used a number of ways to introduce the group to the experience of this revolutionary form of communication. For the first 5 weeks, our sessions focused on the "Course Essentials" booklet. This was a spiral-bound booklet that we prepared especially for this orientation period. In addition to containing all the details about the course (term dates, specifications for the assessed written work, etc.), the booklet had sections that provided a short history of the origins of the course and an introduction to social science. We felt that it was important for the participants to have a sense of the historical development of the course—that is, an idea of the context from which it emerged and also some idea of the theoretical ground we were moving away from. In addition, since members of the course either came from a range of disciplinary backgrounds or had no formal academic background at all and thus no prior disciplinary orientation, we felt that it was necessary to introduce them to a social science approach to education. We used these sections of the *Essentials* booklet as our "object focus" during the afternoon sessions of the orientation period, and since they were written in a clear and straightforward way, this allowed us to focus on dialogue with an object that was unencumbered by a great degree of theoretical difficulty.

In the morning session of the orientation period, however, we used an even more straightforward approach to introducing the group to dialogue. Each week we asked the group to choose a "key word" from a list we had culled from listening carefully to what people were saying about their working lives during the interview sessions (this list was also part of the Essentials booklet). Many of these words were common to all the participants and fairly predictable—for example, community, education, disadvantage, and so on. Using one term each week as the object focus of our morning dialogue session, we would explore our own as well as others' understandings of the term and also the experiences or situations that had led to these understandings. These sessions were so fruitful that we often continued dialoguing about a certain term over subsequent weeks and in some cases brought in readings that enabled us to deepen our thinking about the meaning of a particular word. For example, we used Raymond Williams's *Keywords* to discover the derivation of the word and its historical development and thus its historical specificity. Of course, as I said before, we also engaged in dialogue during the longer afternoon session, but the focus of the morning sessions was kept simple, or unencumbered, in order to ease the group into using dialogue to co-investigate the generative themes that constituted our curriculum. I discuss these later. The entire five-week orientation period was intended to be a "gentle" introduction to the course—that is, a slightly slower-paced and less rigorous interlude during which learning colleagues could really focus on dialogue and begin to experience the principles of the course while engaging with some important concepts and ideas and also getting to know one another.

Each student was also the member of a study circle, wherein they could practice dialoguing with a smaller number of people. Study circles were set up during the orientation period and then continued throughout the duration of the course. They were another regular feature of the course. These groups engaged in various activities. For example, sometimes they continued to dialogue about a particular term—that is, key word—after the whole group had moved on to another. John and I decided on the membership of these groups rather than risking anyone being left out of the selection process. The study circles also functioned as tutorial groups supported by myself or John (we were the personal tutors to the people in these groups; however, depending on the particular subject a person was pursuing for a piece of assessed work, either one of us or other members of staff would also supervise the student's work). The study circles were a highly successful part of the course and were very important to our learning colleagues. They met at lunchtime and also, whenever they felt that it was necessary, prior to or after the course sessions. Study circles decided their own activities. Sometimes, as I said before, they chose to continue dialoguing on one of the key words, and at other times they arranged visits to each other's workplaces, or they collectively read a recommended text. But their most important function was to support each other's learning, including offering help to one another with the written work that had to be submitted in order to fulfill the course requirements that were specified by the University. This support was extremely important. Not only did it help those who came to the course with little or no academic experience, it also gave members of the study circle a collective sense of responsibility and interest in each others' work, thus breaking down the individuated and isolated way in which such work is usually produced.

The curriculum for the course was always based on "generative themes," that is, Freire's idea of a theme that expresses the dialectical nature of people's concrete reality—a theme or issue that is central to and manifested in the lives of the participants (in this case particularly their working lives), but which also unfolds into other themes. Generative themes are inherently and integrally related to other generative themes, and they are expressed in and embrace other contexts with national or even global dimensions (pp. 68–95). Through the co-investigation of generative themes, people learn to "read" their world critically (Freire, 1972, pp. 68–95). We often debated whether it would be more time-efficient for John and me to determine the themes prior to the course. This would have made our work a great deal easier, or at least more reasonably distributed, because we could have "resourced" the course before it began. Every time a group decided on the theme they wanted to co-investigate, John and I would do the initial research and provide each member of the group with a folder of readings (articles and extracts from books and journals) that could enable us to think more deeply and critically about the theme. This meant that during the seven to ten days after a theme was decided on, we had to work nonstop almost every waking hour in order to do a preliminary review of the available literature, reading as much of it as possible, making a selection of readings from this review and then getting individual copies prepared for everyone in the group.[2]

It would have been infinitely simpler to predetermine the themes and have all the resources selected and ready to hand out prior to the commencement of the course. However, for a number of reasons, we felt it important to draw the themes from what was currently of central concern to learning colleagues in a particular group, especially if we were to gain everyone's full commitment to co-investigating the theme. We needed to be able to listen to how they were perceiving the themes and thus expressing them. Moreover, since we understood our reality to be in constant dialectical movement and because our learning colleagues came from such a wide range of working contexts, in which the generative themes might be developing and thus being expressed in different ways, we thought it vitally important to select the themes in concert with the group. Another reason why we thought this was important was that our learning colleagues were also learning how to engage in Freirean education—learning how to become Freirean educators, if this was what they chose to do after completing the course. It was important for them, therefore, to be involved in the process of selecting the themes. Fortunately, I read fairly quickly, and this was very useful when it came to researching and then resourcing the themes, but this is far from being an essential requirement for those who wish to engage in this approach to critical education. Freirean educators tend to, and need to, engage in a continuous critical "reading of the world" and thus are likely to become tuned in to the generative themes that are figuring centrally in people's lives at a particular point in time. As a consequence, reading extensively becomes a preoccupation, and thus the researching/resourcing of a theme rarely begins from scratch.

Themes were chosen through dialogue. We tried various approaches to generating a list of themes from which the final one would be chosen. The best approach was first to break into small groups that would each produce a list of themes and then to bring these back to the whole group, wherein a comprehensive list would be compiled. Sometimes it took two to three weeks to decide on the first theme, but the dialogue and learning that was involved in this process was useful in helping the group to build an understanding of each others' working contexts and also educative on several other levels as well. Learning colleagues had to share why they thought a particular theme was important, both when they introduced it and when they were trying to convince others that it would be valuable to co-investigate it; and through this process we learned a great deal about each other and also about different aspects of the contexts within which the education of adults and also community development were taking place. When group members came from abroad, we also learned a great deal about their countries and cultures. Subsequent themes were always easier to choose because the in-depth investigation of one generative theme tends to lead almost automatically to wanting to investigate another theme to which it is integrally and inherently related.

John and I were, of course, coparticipants in all dialogues, including the process of selecting a generative theme. However, as teacher–learners, when selecting the themes, we had the added responsibility of advising the group on what was and was not a generative theme and why—a responsibility that we became better at fulfilling the more our own comprehension of the concept of a generative theme developed. We had to listen carefully so that we could "hear" what was truly of concern to members of the group. This was the only way we could translate Freire's idea of investigating the "thematic universe" of our learning colleagues (Freire, 1972, pp. 68–95). Time and circumstances would not have allowed us to spend sufficient time in the working or local environment of each member of the group. This aspect of Freire's literacy teaching was actually part of his method, his way of applying the principles of his approach in his context, but it was one of the aspects of his methodology that we felt it was important to translate, as closely as possible, into our context. We often found that people were talking about the same theme but expressing it in different words—often the jargon specific to their professional context. Through dialogue and the problem-posing, or problematization, that takes place within it, it was possible to enable the group to realize that they were actually expressing the same concern and thus referring to one in the same theme.

A curriculum based on generative themes and this process of selecting them is often confused with progressive ideas, such as "issue-based" curricula and negotiated curricula. In fact, during the first two years of the course, I tended to think that they were very similar. Issue-based work is not that far removed, except that issues tend to be component parts of generative themes or sometimes what Freire calls "hinged themes" (Freire, 1972, p. 92). Given the particular interest of a group, one way to arrive at a generative theme is to begin with a particular issue, but since our groups rarely shared one single issue that was of central concern to them, we tended not to approach the generative themes in this way. Negotiated curricula, on the other hand, are something entirely different from the selection process that we used. We were not simply trying to put together a syllabus that would hold some element of interest to everyone involved or working out some sort of compromise that would be relevant to a particular group. We were trying to "read the world" critically and thus trying to come to a collective consensus about the themes that would lead us to this critical understanding. And we did not choose the themes all at once but, instead, in a developmental manner such that each theme was selected because our need to investigate it developed from our investigation of the preceding theme.

In other courses offering the same or similar academic awards, students normally study adult and community education from a variety of disciplinary perspectives, including psychology, philosophy, sociology, history and sometimes, but not often, political economy. We tried to make sure that the resources we selected to enhance our investigation of a theme reflected as far as possible these different disciplines. If there was nothing available in a particular area, or if we could not find anything related to it, then John, I, or some other member of the group, or a member of our academic staff with expertise in the discipline would fill in the gaps. However, we only did this when we felt that the perspective offered by that discipline would deepen our understanding of the theme as well as the role of adult and community education with respect to the theme. Since any form of extant knowledge or exposition—whether written or oral—was always an "object focus" or the "knowledge-object" from which our learning began rather than the final objective of the learning process, this enabled John, myself, or any other member of the group to offer this knowledge without contradicting our role as co-investigators, equally and mutually trying to deepen our understanding and increase our criticality with respect to the object-focus or extant knowledge that we were sharing with the group.

Selecting and sequencing the materials that are intended to support the groups' co-investigation of the theme is a responsibility that the Freirean educator must assume. It would be impossible to ensure coherence if this task were undertaken by everyone—that is, each person contributing resources. Someone has to have an overall view of the resources and be able to sequence them in terms of how they might best unfold so as to enable the development of the groups' understanding of the theme. The teacher–learner who takes on this responsibility should, of course, be open to suggestions and take any suggestion seriously, but in the final analysis that person must decide whether or not to include the suggested resources. However, the teacher–learner who takes on this responsibility also has another very important and related responsibility. Whenever resources are distributed to the group, this person should explain briefly what each resource is about and why it was chosen. Sharing one's reasoning with the group is important in Freirean education. It helps to build trust and is also highly educational for everyone. It offers learning colleagues valuable insights into the process and also a general overview of the types of evidence the group will be investigating; and it serves as a critical check on the teacher–learner. By this I mean that if the teacher–learner is unable to offer a good justification for choosing a resource, then it might not have been an appropriate choice.

Because of the constraint of working in an award-granting institution, we had to try (as far as possible) to co-investigate one theme each term (10- to 12-week period). However, since generative themes are integrally and inherently related and thus tend to lead on, one from the other, we could always continue our investigation of a theme with which we felt we had not had time to deal sufficiently by integrating it with the following theme. Therefore, there were no definitive ruptures in our learning from term to term, but if someone had to take a leave of absence from the course for a term or longer, they would be assured of having reached at least some level of understanding of the theme they had been investigating during the previous term.[3] In addition, we also tried to make sure that during each term everyone in the group had developed a certain level of understanding of Freirean critical education. It is important to emphasize that we were not only engaged in trying to "read the world" more critically but also, and in a related way, to furthering the professional education and development of adult and community educators and thereby preparing them to work more effectively and critically. Therefore, as I mentioned before, it was our intention that by the end of the course, if they chose to do so, all members of the group would be able to begin using a Freirean approach in their own contexts.

Before beginning the second term and, conveniently, at the end of our Christmas break, we always held a residential weekend. The object focus of the weekend was Freire's philosophy of education—his "educational approach," as I often refer to it in order to distinguish it from the exact methodology he used in literacy teaching. During the last session before the Christmas break, we gave everyone a booklet that we had prepared specifically for the residential weekend. It contained all the details about the schedule, venues, accommodation and, most importantly, a selection of key readings, from Freire's *Pedagogy of the Oppressed* (1972) and *The Politics of Education* (1985).This selection of readings was extracted from these sources and then carefully sequenced in order to enhance learning colleagues' understanding of his ideas.[4] Learning colleagues had been informed in both the course publicity and again during the interview that the residential weekend was a required part of the course. Of course, this was an extra expense for them, but in comparison to other University courses the diploma was very inexpensive, and as a result participants always seemed to accept this extra expense without reservations. This was the case for even people who were unemployed while they were on the course. However, we also tried to minimize the costs in every way possible so that the residential weekend—that is, accommodation and meals, the only costs that were impossible to ignore—never amounted to more than £50.00 (about $75.00). If a learning colleague had not been able to meet this expense, John and I would have been willing to cover the cost for them, but the situation never arose.

We delayed an explicit and focused study of Freire until the residential week-end because we thought that people would be able to grasp his ideas more fully once they had experienced an approach to education that was trying to translate these ideas into a specific context. This residential period of study was a very rigorous, concentrated and exhausting experience; yet, it never failed to be high-ly evaluated and thus appreciated by the learning colleagues with whom we worked. In fact, part-time students often wanted to have another residential experience in their second year. On one occasion we tried to include the second-year part-timers in the residential weekend, but we found that the time was really insufficient to integrate the two groups effectively. We witnessed the benefits of the residential experience in the second term, when our learning colleagues began to join us truly as learner–teachers. They had finally begun to experience authentically the "rebirth" of which Freire (1974) speaks, and this enabled us, also, to begin to function more fully, or authentically, as teacher–learners and thus experience the complete process of "rebirth" that Freirean educators must go through with each new group of learning colleagues.

Therefore, not far into the second term, we all began to function more effec-tively as either teacher–learners or learner–teachers mutually engaged in a pro-cess of critical education that would soon develop into an authentic experience of critical/revolutionary praxis. At least, this was our intention and also what nor-mally happened by this point in the course. There were a few years when not everyone in the group had reached this stage by this time. For a few people, it took most of the first year. Whether or not the majority of participants would have reached this stage at this point without the residential weekend, we will never know, nor will we ever know whether they would have reached it more quickly if we had focused on Freire's writings earlier in the course. We will never know because we never altered the pattern. Even though, in many ways, this entire endeavor was an experiment, I never felt that we had the right to try anything that we did not have a very good reason to believe would work effec-tively. Given my continuing critical analysis of the context in which this course took place, I thought that a residential study was essential, and therefore I would not have sacrificed it simply for the purposes of experimentation. And I also had good reason to believe, on the basis of the first few years of experience, that introducing a focused study of Freire any earlier in the course would also have been much less effective and possibly even counterproductive.

As you will know if you have ever used residential study as part of a course, those who participate in the experience grow closer as friends. On a Freirean course, not only does this happen, but participants also become much more effective as learning colleagues. As I mentioned before, full-time students, just like John and I, were members of two learning groups, but they shared the residential experience only with the first year part-timers, not with the second-year group. This might have meant that they would always feel a closer bond with the Tuesday group, thereby cohering and working more effectively with the first-year group. Therefore, with this possible problem in mind, and also because I thought that it was important to foster the further development of collective learning in the second year, we had a group project in the second year.

I managed to persuade our head of department and the external examiner, even in the first year of the course, that one piece of assessed work should be a collective project (i.e., one of the five pieces of course-work rather than either of the extended essays or the dissertation, all of which were written requirements for the course set by university regulations). Among other things, this meant that whatever grade or mark was awarded would pertain to every member of the group. The group project was based on a theme or issue. It did not have to be a generative theme, but it was usually related directly to the theme we had been investigating prior to the project. This was especially the case after the first two years. The project could involve anything that would help the group to develop their intellectual and professional skills, especially skills involving collective and cooperative working with others, and which would equally engage the effort and thinking of every member of the learning group. This idea came from the work I did with the group that initiated me into Freire's ideas. We had continued working together after the course finished, spending one weekend session every month working together writing a monograph on our ideas about adult education.[5]

In the first year of the Freirean course, the group project involved planning, organizing and hosting a one-day (an extended day) national conference on "Adult Education for Social Action." In addition, we also produced a conference report or booklet that contained transcripts of the talks given by our invited speakers and feedback reports from the workshops. The conference began at 10 a.m. and ended at 9 p.m. About 150 people from all over the United Kingdom attended; and Tony Benn, M.P. (Member of Parliament), was our main speaker. Geri Kirkwood from the Freirean-inspired Adult Learning Project in Scotland, Tom Lovett from Northern Ireland and at that time the best-known figure in community education in the United Kingdom, and Jimmy Boyle, author, sculptor, community development and drug rehabilitation worker, exconvict and formerly, by his own admission, the most notorious criminal in Scotland, were our other invited speakers. We arranged a buffet supper for the participants in order to give something of a residential atmosphere to the occasion. The work entailed in this project was enormous and perhaps a bit too ambitious. No one complained, but finishing the booklet meant, once again, working well beyond the end of the academic year and therefore the period of attendance required for the course. I realized how lucky I was to be working with such a dedicated group and also one that was able to continue meeting only by chance. Therefore, even though the conference was a huge success and a very worthwhile and educative group project, rather than risk future disappointment and also because I felt that the project had taxed the students too heavily, making it difficult for some of them to complete the other elements of their assessed work in time for the university's submission dates, I always suggested, thereafter, that we choose a project that could be contained within the second term of the second year—that is, the Wednesday groups' second term.

From then on, the projects were usually group-writing projects on a particular theme. (I will explain what I mean by a group-writing project.) After experimenting with a few different ways of packaging or presenting our writing, one group came up with the idea of producing an annual newsletter for former students and other interested individuals and groups. In part, this was a response to something that I mentioned in chapter 5—the requests from former students for ongoing support and the reconvening of their group—a request that we had, of course, shared with the present group. (The main, but not only, way we responded to this request was by organizing an annual "reunion day"—an extended day of serious dialogue based, normally, on an object-focus supplied by a guest speaker and also a day of social mixing of learning colleagues from past and present groups.) The newsletter was to be a supplement to and not a replacement for these other points of contact.

I cannot emphasize too strongly the value of this joint, or collective, writing project. I think that all those who experienced it would concur with this but also would testify to what hard and exacting intellectual work was involved. Many learning colleagues said that they actually learned to write with greater clarity and coherence as a result of their participation in the collective writing of the group project. We would usually begin the collective writing about three-quarters of the way through the investigation of a theme. We would write during our dialogue sessions, interweaving the writing with our dialogue about the theme. It is difficult to describe the process, but I will try.

Once we had reached a good level of critical understanding with respect to the theme, we would focus our dialogue on how we could share this understanding with others. First, we would devise an outline or plan of how we intended to present our ideas in writing. Then each word, sentence and paragraph was deliberated upon until we finally decided how to express an idea, only committing it to paper either to see how it read or finally when we had all agreed on a particular way of expressing the idea. Although we once tried having just one person record the words on an overhead transparency so that we could all see an enlarged projection of what we had agreed to write, we found that it worked better for everyone to write the sentences as they were constructed by the group. This approach seemed to engage each of us more directly and personally in the writing, and it also meant that everyone had an immediate record of what we had written during the session, which they could reflect on before our next meeting. Because of this, we always began the next writing session by asking whether anyone had come up with suggestions for any revisions of what we had written during the previous week.

As you can probably imagine, group-writing was a very time-consuming process. There were times when we spent an entire afternoon writing just one or two sentences. In trying to find the best way to express something we wanted to say, we sometimes found that either our understanding was not yet entirely clear or that we had not yet reached the common understanding that we thought we shared. When this happened, it meant that we needed to go back over our resources and also spend more time dialoguing until we could move forward with a clearer and more critical understanding that we all shared and could express to others in our writing. Although at times we struggled to keep to this, there was an agreement before we ever started the group-writing project that developing our critical understanding of the theme had to take precedence over writing about it. In fact, however, the two processes tended to work together. Once our understanding was crystal-clear, the writing would proceed much more rapidly; therefore, the time spent in coming to our critical understanding was not only extremely educational but also improved our efficiency as well. I will describe one of these projects in the hope that it might clarify this type of highly unusual but valuable learning experience.

In our co-investigations we had run into conflicting uses of the term "ideology"; we therefore decided to base the group project on *ideology*. I had begun studying Marx's and Gramsci's works and was far enough along with my study to be able to provide the group with important resources. (Here, I am referring to the personal study project that I had found necessary in order to implement Freire's ideas more authentically and effectively—a project that I discuss in greater detail later.) After a great deal of reading and dialogue, we decided to use the term "ideology" as a critical concept, in the way that Marx does and also, as I have argued elsewhere, Freire and Gramsci do (Allman, 1999). By this time, we were using the newsletter format for presenting our project; so we decided to write a concise exposition, explaining the critical, or negative, concept of ideology and how it could be used to critique dominant discourses. We also decided to devise and include some shorter sections that would demonstrate how ideology operates in various aspects of our lives in a way that justifies and normalizes various types of oppression or forms of domination. The whole group wrote the main section that explained the negative concept of ideology, and the other sections were written by subgroups that had been formed according to the particular issues that interested us. The subgroups decided how they would present their demonstration or critique of ideology and then collectively devised their presentation; however, all subgroup decisions and submissions were subject to the editorial comments and approval of the whole group.

The group I was in had chosen education as our issue; another group looked at race and gender oppression and thus racist and sexist/ homophobic ideology, and a third group looked at how ideology functioned with reference to unemployment. The group I was in devised a cartoon based on a character we had dreamed up called "Hermione the Hegemonic Hedgehog," and the other groups presented their demonstrations or critiques of ideology using prose, poetry and/or graphics. The main portion of the newsletter and focus of the project was the serious piece of academic writing on ideology, but we also tried to inject some humor. This was not unusual for the group project and tended to unfold quite naturally in the process of working on it. Although this form of critical education is rigorous and exacting, it also fosters a high level of camaraderie and optimistic playfulness that lightens what might otherwise be a very serious and heavy atmosphere, where, drawing on Gramsci's words, "pessimism of the intellect" could drown out "optimism of the will." This also relates to my own personal philosophy of education. I started teaching in my teenage years as a swimming instructor (I had been a competitive swimmer since the age of 9). I always taught people to swim by first encouraging them to play in the water—to play so freely and with such abandon that water on their faces soon became as natural and acceptable as a warm summer's breeze. Serious learning, whether intellectual, physical or both, demands rigor, and rigor demands release; therefore, it is hard for me to imagine an effective experience of critical education—or, for that matter, critical revolutionary praxis—that does not include a mixture of arduous study, thought and reflection with laughter, joy, humor or, in short, light-heartedness. This mixture should arise from the hope and critical, realistic utopianism that this approach to education is intended to foster. It also arises quite naturally from something else that Freire attributes to both critical or problem-posing educators and authentic revolutionaries. People who initiate these activities have a "love" for humanity— in other words, they care deeply about the well-being and future of those with whom they are working. This is not a possessive love but one that "generates acts of freedom" (Freire, 1972, p. 62). In fact, he says that true dialogue cannot happen in the absence of a profound love for others—a faith in their "power to make and remake, to create and recreate, faith in [their] vocation to be more fully human" (p. 63). As I always try to stress, Freire's most fervently held objective or vision of the future was "the creation of a world in which it will be easier to love" (p. 19).

As I mentioned before, evaluation of our learning and whether or not we had engaged in critical praxis, or the degree to which we were developing in that direction, was an integral part of each course day. Usually we set aside the last 40–60 minutes of the day for this. After a brief period of silent reflection, during which we all looked back over any notes we had made pertaining to the principles and aims of the course and a checklist of the features that characterize authentic dialogue,[6] we began another dialogue in which our focus was the learning experience in which we had just engaged. At the end of this evaluation dialogue we would then "forward plan" the session for the following week. Study circles usually planned their next sessions during the time allocated for them to meet, but final adjustments could also be made during this whole group-planning session once all decisions had been taken and individual requirements—especially requests for tutorial time—had been taken into account. Most people made a note of the agreed schedule, but copies were also available first thing in the morning of the following week and were always mailed before then to anyone

who had been absent from the session. Absences were rare, partly because
everyone realized the importance of continuity for their learning and the development of their critical thinking.

We also held a summary evaluation at the end of each term, in which we
reflected on our learning during the whole period. And at the end of each
academic year an entire day was devoted to evaluating the course. The final
evaluation was planned and conducted by our learning colleagues, and proved to
be extremely helpful for our ongoing development of this approach to critical
education.

For me, the first two or three years of the course—or what, with hindsight, I
would call Phase 1—was a period of intense and rewarding learning. When I
began the Freirean trial, my politics were left-of-center–Left. Even then, I was
well aware of the political implications of this approach to learning and also
enthusiastic about the possibilities for political awareness that could be fostered
by engaging in it. However, I never anticipated that my own political awareness
would be so radically altered, or that I would soon become an ardent advocate of
revolutionary social transformation. Despite my growing radicalization, I maintained then, as I do now, that if Freirean education is handled correctly, or in a
way that is a sympathetic or authentic expression of the principles embodied in
the approach, then participants would always feel free to choose their own
political directions and would in no way be pressured to follow the left-wing
implications that invariably arise from critically "reading the world." It has
always been satisfaction enough for me if participants come to a point where they
are critically in charge of their own decision-making—for them to know the
alternatives and to understand why they are choosing one direction rather than
another at a particular time in their lives. I have found that very often when
people choose a more moderate position, it is because their current personal
circumstances make it impossible, or at least extremely risky, to choose a more
radical direction at that particular point in time. I also have been satisfied with
this type of outcome because I contend that Freirean learning is a better approach
to the development of adult cognitive abilities than any other that I have been
involved in and therefore can be extremely valuable to all adults, regardless of
their initial or end-of-course political positions. Having said all this, I must also
admit that there were few people who participated in this approach to critical
education who did not move to the left in their political thinking either during or
soon after completing the course. Nevertheless, I honestly feel that those who did
not share our own or Freire's politics were comfortable with our differences. We
genuinely respected anyone who had made a critical decision about their political
beliefs, and I always felt that their respect for us was mutual.

As I said before, this first phase was a period of concentrated learning for me.
Because of my initial political leanings and also my expectation that Freirean
education would develop a greater degree of criticality in the participants' thinking, I was constantly reflecting upon and questioning what was happening during

this phase of the course's development. Of course, this type of continuous critique is indispensable for Freirean educators, but during the first three years I was totally preoccupied by it and also my search to understand Freire more fully and comprehensively. I knew that both I myself and the original group who had campaigned to get the Freirean course established had come from backgrounds in progressive education, which at that time was heavily influenced by humanistic psychology—the writings of Carl Rogers, Abraham Maslow, and so on. Soon after beginning the course I began to wonder whether I was interpreting Freire too squarely within the parameters of that framework and, as a result, engaging in a domesticated version of Freire as opposed to one that truly embodied his philosophy and radical intentions. For example, according to the progressive framework, teachers are supposed to facilitate the students' learning in a nondirective and nonprescriptive manner. I was well aware that Freire never used such terms, but during the first year or so of the Freirean course I did not understand that his approach to education demanded both epistemological and ontological transformations in students' and teachers' relations. I thought that the main priority was to relate differently to the students—to bring about an ontological transformation in the student–teacher relationship—and as a consequence I was not aware that this was impossible to do authentically in the absence of the necessary epistemological transformations, or the transformation of both students' and teachers' relations to knowledge. Therefore, initially, I saw no danger in integrating the progressive ideas of facilitation, nonprescription and nondirection into the Freirean approach.

However, I quite rapidly realized that this was a mistake and that Freirean education was incompatible with these "progressive" notions—in much the same way and for the same reasons that a negotiated curriculum was incompatible. As I have since stressed in various publications, Freirean education is prescriptive, and Freirean educators are directive. It is prescriptive to say that we should "read the world critically" in order to transform it in way that will foster humanization rather than the dehumanization that is the norm. In fact, it is prescriptive to say that the world needs transforming and that education should play a role in this. And Freirean educators must use the authority that comes from their own critical "reading of the world" and their understanding of Freire's philosophy of education if they are to enable (and sometimes this involves direction) others also to engage in critical/revolutionary praxis. Of course, Freirean educators, because of their transformed relation to knowledge—their epistemological position—prescribe and direct with humility and with a spirit of mutuality that would be impossible to convey had they not undergone the necessary transformations. Therefore, when they prescribe and direct, they are doing so from the basis of an alternative philosophical position, and thus what they are doing cannot be equated with traditional or conventional modes of direction and prescription.

It also became clear to me that nonprescription and nondirection are impossible. They are even present, despite their purveyor's intent, in the most facilitative,

myths of freaks

nonprescriptive, nondirective forms of progressive teaching because any form of laissez-faire or for that matter, relativism is just another form of uncritical/ reproductive praxis. No matter how unintentional, this is a prescription for domestication—that is educating people to accept and adapt successfully to capitalist reality. Understanding all of this, however, comes with fully understanding what Freire means when he says that all education is political—it either has the potential and the intent to liberate all those involved in it or it domesticates both teachers and learners.

Moreover, I realized that notions such as nonprescription, nondirection and facilitation were incompatible with Freirean education because they are tied to the epistemological relations that we are seeking to transform in Feirean education. When teachers actually transform their relation to their own knowledge so that they treat it not as possession but as something they want to co-investigate with others, either with a view to critically transforming it or to knowing it more deeply and thus critically—realizing that it is never finished and complete—then the problem of directiveness or authoritarianism vanishes. If the teacher's knowledge—or, for that matter any other person's knowledge—is to be co-investigated by the group, it must be shared and thus some form of exposition must take place. But this is an exposition that is subjected to the critical scrutiny of the learning group. For me, this understanding developed slowly over the first phase of the course. It was derived primarily from listening, over and over again, and reflecting, together with learning colleagues, upon what Freire says on the audiotapes that were made during his speaking tour of Australia—the tapes I always reference in my writings on Freire. The Chilean student whom I mentioned earlier gave these tapes to me as a gift. They were one of the most important gifts I have ever received, and I, together with the many learning colleagues who benefited from them over the years, shall be forever indebted to our Chilean friend.

In addition to my political interests, another interest that I brought with me when I embarked on the Freirean course was an interest in the development of dialectical thinking. As naïve as it may sound, I must admit that at that time I was not fully aware that dialectical thinking was related to my political position. I had come to this interest in dialectical thinking through my interest in Piagetian developmental psychology and through my attempts to extend Piaget's theory of cognitive development into a psychological study of adult learning and development that also drew on Lawrence Kohlberg's theory of moral development and Eric Erikson's theory of identity development. Primarily, I was following the same lines as the American psychologist Klaus Reigel, who had formulated a theory of the development of dialectical operational thinking during adulthood. Freire speaks of the dialectic in his writings, and this was one of the first things that drew me to him; however, his meaning is not explicitly defined. Nevertheless, it is fairly clear that his points of reference are Hegel and Marx. During the first phase of the course, I began to realize that I could not fully understand his use of the term and, in a related sense, his important concept of the contradiction between the oppressed and the oppressor, unless I traced his usage of dialectic and contradiction back to these sources. Therefore, I began a personal study project—the one I mentioned before—that was to prove extremely helpful and also exciting.

It was also during this first phase that we first came up against conflicting uses of the term "ideology." As a result, we were becoming increasingly confused as to whether we should be trying to embrace an ideology that could counter the dominant ideology or perhaps even construct one of our own, or whether our task was to critique ideological thinking. Freire also refers to ideology, especially in an interview published in *The Politics of Education*, where he opposes ideological thinking with scientific or dialectical thinking (Freire, 1985, p. 163).[7] In pursuing this question of ideology, we came across the writings of Jorge Larrain. It was Larrain's two books on ideology (Larrain, 1979, 1983), together with the many questions that were beginning to arise from my attempt to apply Freire's ideas, that finally made it clear to me that I not only needed to read Marx but also study his writings in depth. The questions surrounding the uses of the term "ideology" had also led us to the writings of Stuart Hall and various publications by the CCCS[8] and via them to the writings of Antonio Gramsci. And thus my own personal study program expanded tremendously. In addition to Marx, who was the main focus of this project, and for the sake of comparison also Hegel, I realized that I also needed to develop my understanding of Gramsci's writings, as well as concepts that had become crucial to our work, such as ideology, the dialectic and many others as well. This study project provided the necessary background I needed in order to apply Freire in a way that was coherent and consistent with his philosophy of education and thus the aims and principles of Freirean education, which I was beginning to understand more deeply and authentically through the initial attempts to apply it in my context. I was learning to "read" Freire's philosophy more critically as I analyzed it in operation.

Enrollments for the course had increased substantially by the end of the first two academic years. My job was becoming increasingly difficult, not just because the course was running at full capacity, but also because the more I understood what Freirean education entailed, the more complex my work became. This did not deter me because the time and effort was more than compensated for by the fact that this was the most exciting, interesting and, importantly, the most educationally effective form of education that I had ever experienced in twenty years of teaching at various levels and in many different contexts. However, I knew that both I and learning colleagues would benefit if another member of full-time staff joined us. John Wallis was the member of staff who had shown the greatest interest in the course, and so I asked him to consider joining me on an apprenticeship basis. He enthusiastically accepted the invitation. During the apprenticeship period, I acted as a mentor, or partner in reflection, so that we could be sure that we were working to and expressing the same aims and principles. This situation also meant that I needed to explain to John my reasoning with respect to every feature of the course—that is, why I thought that each element was an expression of Freirean principles, as well as why I had decided to do something one way rather than another. Of course, as I said before, I also shared my reasoning with learning colleagues, but since John and I were working together throughout the entire week, there was time to go into greater detail and there was also more time to explore alternatives critically. When we came up with a feasible and appropriate idea, we would then share it with our learning colleagues and collectively decide whether or not to implement it. Very soon the apprenticeship arrangement became a mutual learning process that we continued to employ during the entire period we worked together.

After a few terms, this team or co-teacher–learner approach began to work very well, and it was at this point, I think, that the Freirean trial entered its second phase of development. By the beginning of this phase I had completed most of the in-depth study that I mentioned before, and soon John and I began working on several joint writing projects. This joint writing was extremely valuable to us because it added a new dimension to our critical reflection on what we were doing and also increased the precision with which we were able to apply Freire's ideas. An important part of this was that we also began to integrate important elements of Marx and Gramsci into our interpretation of Freire. My reading and study of Marx's and Gramsci's writings had not only deepened my critical "reading of the world" but had also given me a much better understanding of Freire's philosophy. I think that applying Freire's ideas in concert with Marx and Gramsci greatly enhanced our application of Freire's philosophical approach to critical education.

In 1988 we also took over the M.Ed. course and based it on a Freirean approach. For a few years, enrollment was good for both courses. However, running two separate Freirean courses and thus working with learning colleagues from 10:30 to 5:00 four days a week would have been extremely taxing and would have left hardly any time to fulfill our other departmental duties. More-over, learning colleagues had difficulty obtaining a full day-release for the M.Ed. At that time, employers tended to equate master's degrees with personal aca-demic development rather than with professional or vocational improvement; they were therefore not as willing to release people from work for the M.Ed. as they were for the Diploma, which was considered to be a more vocationally orientated course. As a result, we ran the M.Ed. on a half-day basis on two days per week. At first the M.Ed. was filled almost entirely with part-time students. We had only a few full-time students, and we asked them to participate in both the M.Ed. and the diploma programs so that they would have a more comprehen-sive full-time experience.

By 1993, the external environment had begun to change considerably. In addition to a general loss of hope (by potential applicants) for a radical transfor-mation of society (other than on the terms that had been laid down by Margaret Thatcher), people's jobs were becoming much less secure as the cutbacks in educational spending as well as restructuring began to be felt in many areas of postcompulsory education. We continued to recruit sufficient numbers, but by the beginning of the academic year we started experiencing precourse dropout. People always gave very understandable reasons for these last-minute withdrawals. Some felt that they might be putting their jobs in jeopardy if they were absent from work for any length of time. In other cases, attendance had become impossible because one or more of their colleagues had been made redundant, and therefore their work-loads had increased to a point that made their own continuing education impossible, or they, themselves, had been made redundant and thus were in no position to pursue anything other than trying to find alternative employment. Even for some of those who did manage to take part there seemed to be an increasing mood of uncertainty and confusion, often accompanied by high levels of stress and anxiety, especially from 1993 onwards. Although the initial reactions to these changes in the external environment had been an increased criticality toward what was happening in education and a general enthusiasm for resisting and challenging it, by 1993 what we called the "postmodern condition"—skepticism, uncertainty, fragmentation, nihilism and incoherence—had enveloped at least a few of our learning colleagues, and for the first time this negativity of a few members of the group began to have a knock-on effect on the rest of us, even though we remained committed to critical/revolutionary praxis. Even though I doubt that I was acutely aware of this at the time, when I look back over these years I can detect that, at least to some degree, this negativity was having an effect on all of us.

When student numbers began to decline, we were able to keep the courses going by integrating the M.Ed. with the diploma course to form one good-sized learning group. There was no problem justifying this, because the two courses were virtually the same, the only difference being different requirements for the assessed work. There had never been a difference in the intellectual standard of the courses or the rigor that was required from all those involved, and our external examiners had often remarked that the top level of assessed work submitted by diploma students was of a high-grade master's standard. It was possible to fulfill the diploma written requirements at a lower standard, but this was rarely the case. In fact, as far as I can recall, the only time work of a lower-than-average standard was submitted was when, in a few cases, someone from abroad had difficulty mastering the command of written English required for academic work. Most students who came to us with little or no academic experience developed dramatically while on the course; and this was the main reason why a succession of external examiners not only made extremely favorable assessments of the course but also supported its continuation. (I should also mention, while talking about this type of evaluation of the course, that many diploma students continued on with the master's course either immediately or after a short absence, and others encouraged their partners or close friends to undertake the course.) Nevertheless, even with the integration of the two courses

working well and the favorable evaluations of the course, there was no way that
we could combat what was happening in the external environment—at least no
way that was compatible with what we were trying to do.

By 1994, departments of adult education throughout the United Kingdom were
struggling to survive. Many had already become departments of continuing
education in an attempt to present a more vocationally oriented face or one that
was primarily geared to modular accreditation of continuing professional or
vocationally useful development. However, despite these attempts at "modernization," several diploma and M.Ed. courses throughout the United Kingdom
ceased functioning. We were also struggling, and by 1995 we found it increasingly difficult to justify two full-time staff devoting so much time to the course—
even though a great deal of what our jobs entailed pertained regardless of
whether we had large or small groups. As a result, John decided to take over the
running of the department's flagging research center, and I was left struggling to
keep the course alive for another year, with an ever-diminishing number of
students.

Finally, I decided to take a two-semester sabbatical in 1996–1997—the first
sabbatical leave I had ever been able to take in over twenty years of university
teaching. By that time, plans were well underway, in compliance with new
university regulations, for other members of the department to restructure the
course into a series of credit-based modules; and I saw little hope of being able to
adapt the type of Freirean education that we had been involved in to that structure—at least, not with in any way the same coherence and intensity. I am sure
that someone else could employ a Freirean approach to some extent within such
a limited structure, but having become accustomed to an extensive and intensive
application of this approach to critical education, it would have been tortuous for
me. Although I can now, with the advantage of hindsight, draw this conclusion,
at first I made some extremely frustrating and, as it turned out, futile attempts to
argue for a series of integrated Freirean modules within the new course structure.
However, it soon became obvious that this was not what other members of the
department wanted, and the two professors who had originally supported the
Freirean course were no longer there to offer the kind of support that would have
been necessary for me to win the argument.

Needless to say, after having experienced such an exciting and stimulating
alternative form of education, this was an extremely depressing outcome. And
since I was beginning to suffer a bit more from a long-standing disability that
makes it difficult for me to travel abroad as frequently as contemporary academics are expected to do, I decided to take ill-health early retirement when the
opportunity arose in 1997. The university was into its second phase of purging
academic staff and was offering very attractive retirement packages that were
difficult for someone in my position to refuse. Nevertheless, even given these
circumstances, I still left reluctantly. It has only been with a great deal of critical
reflection and, once again, the advantage of hindsight that I have realized how
impossible and soul-destroying it would have been for me to have returned to a

more conventionally structured framework of teaching after my sabbatical. In the years since, I have had time to reflect critically upon and assess what we tried to do. I conclude this chapter with a summary of the conclusions I have reached thus far.

Thinking back about how limited my understanding of Freire was when I first began the trial sends chills down my spine, and at first I felt quite guilty about having subjected others to the approach when my own thinking was still at such a formative stage. However, I know that I would never have developed the understanding I now have if I had not tried to apply his ideas in terms of those original limitations. Perhaps other people can understand and apply Freire without going through a similar process, but, given my previous background and especially my formation within progressive theory and practice, there was no other way for me to come to this understanding. Of course, I regret that during the first two years of the course learning colleagues did not experience the full benefits of what I think was the much more authentic application of his ideas that developed after that initial teething period. Thankfully, according to their evaluations, they were happy with what they did experience: they said that they had experienced a much more egalitarian and critical approach to education than previously; and I know that, without their help, I would never have come to a more critical understanding of Freirean education. This would seem to vindicate the conclusion that working toward Freirean education is preferable to conventional approaches.

Furthermore, being able to share, with subsequent groups, the problems of trying to implement Freirean education with a limited understanding has enabled me to clarify what is and what is not an authentic Freirean approach—or, at least, an authentic attempt to apply this approach. It has also enabled me to encourage others to try to apply the approach when they are less than confident about their own level of understanding. Another important outcome is that I have realized that learning to engage in Freirean education is an open and ongoing experience. I don't think anyone ever becomes, or should become, a "polished" Freirean educator. This is one of the reasons why I always stress that this is a philosophical approach to education and not a method. It is an approach that improves with experience and the heightened criticality and understanding that this experience fosters. However, most importantly, it is an approach in which the teacher's authority depends upon the degree to which he or she "lives" the principles of the approach and especially upon a genuine expression of humility and thus a continuing willingness and also enthusiasm to question one's own knowledge and current understandings and to continue learning in concert with each new group of learning colleagues.

Another conclusion I have reached is that Freirean education will always be somewhat limited within any formal educational context because at least some of the participants will, quite naturally, be more interested in the academic credentials that can be gained by participating in the course than they are interested in and thus committed to social transformation. This is true no matter how much applicants profess a commitment to the course aims and principles; and I think it would be naïve to expect otherwise. Nevertheless, in my experience the commitment of those who were truly seeking to engage in this type of abbreviated experience of social transformation acted a bit like a magnet, thus raising the level of enthusiasm and energy among the entire group—at least, this was the case until what I previously referred to as the "postmodern condition" descended on us, and even then the magnetism was still partially effective. Furthermore, most people I have encountered seem to become energized when their critical faculties are stimulated and enhanced, and this, in itself, tends to increase the level of commitment in the group. And as I said before, I have never been involved in an approach to education that is even half as effective as the Freirean approach in developing critical thinking.

Peter Mayo (1999) offers an excellent analysis of the various contexts within which Freirean and/or Freirean/Gramscian education have been implemented. He identifies several external factors that constrain the approach and that can lead to its domestication. In my experience I also found that the internal constraints—the constraints within individual members of the learning group—could be just as onerous as any external factors existing within the institution or even the socioeconomic and political contexts. I cannot recall a single year in which there was not at least one individual who initially resisted engaging in liberation and thus refused to struggle for the necessary transformations. Such refusals were never overt—in fact, usually just the opposite, with the individual professing commitment at every opportunity. However, in my experience, the vast majority of those who initially resisted and engaged in various methods of challenging our authenticity finally came around and often, thereafter, became some of the most seriously involved and committed members of the group. Again, it would be naïve to expect an absence of resistance; and, in fact, I think it should be welcomed. The challenges made by any member of the group can help critical educators to reflect critically on their praxis—to examine in depth and to question continually what they are doing and whether or not they are expressing Freirean philosophy as fully as is humanly possible within their particular context.

Mayo (1999) also contends that an approach based on Freire or a Freire/Gramsci synthesis is more likely to succeed, on some levels, in nonformal or informal educational contexts than in formal education. I cannot deny that applying a Freirean approach to critical education within the context of formal education is difficult—in fact, the most arduous and time-consuming approach that one could choose. Nevertheless, the rewards one experiences more than compensate for this and even for the various, and I presume obvious, risks one takes in adopting this approach. Although I agree with Mayo's analysis of the difficulties involved, I also contend that there is a far greater potential for applying Freire within formal contexts than most critical educators seem to accept.

I think that our experience stands as proof that Freirean education—or what, in fact, was a synthesis of Freire, Gramsci and Marx—can work in a formal context.

It may not constitute a specific point on a continuum of revolutionary political struggle or function as a direct connection with a more comprehensive movement for prefigurative revolutionary social transformation, but it certainly is one way of preparing people to engage in or to initiate that type of prefigurative challenge to capitalism. We made several attempts to form alliances with various social movements and community groups external to the course, in particular the education subgroup within the Socialist Movement, which is, itself, an alliance of socialists from various organizations and political parties that was set up in Britain in the late 1980s. However, such alliances proved difficult, mainly because our own group was so transient. Few of our learning colleagues came from the immediate Nottingham area, and John and I were, of course, the only permanent members of the group. And since it took a certain amount of time for each new group to develop to a point where they were interested in taking part in activities external to the course, we could not offer the type of consistent contact and support—in other words the continuity—that other groups were seeking. However, if the course had continued, we had planned to try to initiate the type of international alliance of critical educators that, as I mentioned before, Peter McLaren has recently suggested.

One reason why I decided to write about our experience is to try to encourage and support the formation of such an alliance—to demonstrate that there is a great deal we could be doing even now and to persuade others to engage in this type of work in every possible context rather than assuming that it will only be possible after revolutionary social transformation has succeeded on a national or even global scale. I contend that we will never experience that type of transformation unless we begin, now, to prepare people authentically to engage in it—to transform ourselves as far as possible in order to engage in a struggle for the type of revolutionary social transformation that holds the promise of a better future for humankind.

The very least we should be doing is to challenge the current direction that capitalist education is taking.[9] In our praxis, we had the luxury of being able to spend a considerable amount of time with learning colleagues. We inherited a course structure that in Britain is called a day-release (from work) course, which is very conducive to Freirean education. Freirean critical education does not necessarily demand the amount of time we devoted to it, but we felt that we needed this amount of time in our situation[10] because our participants came from such varying local contexts and also because their level of initial commitment, despite our effort to combat this problem, often varied considerably. I realize that many people teaching in universities have much less time to spend with students, sometimes because of their other duties and sometimes because of the limited time allocated to a course sessions within the overall university structure. However, I contend that effective critical education, partly because of its developmental nature, takes time—perhaps not as much as we spent, but to be truly effective, it takes more than the norm; and I think that this is one of the things that critical educators should be campaigning for within their institutions.[11] Clearly an international alliance of critical educators would add much greater force to such campaigns. At every level of education, we need to be challenging the slippage of education into training and also the incorporation of education into the market paradigm—that is, the general marketization and commodification of education, a slow but sure and unrelenting process that is taking place in concert with the increasing globalization of capitalism.

In reading back over this chapter, I fear I may not have conveyed the depth of feeling that I have about Freirean critical education, or what I also call revolutionary critical education—the sheer joy I experienced by engaging in it as well as the sense of excitement and fulfillment we all experienced each time our critical "reading of the world" grew deeper and more complex, and, of course, the many wonderful and lasting friendships that were forged. I have found it difficult to write about because, quite simply, it brings out mixed emotions—the joy, excitement and hope for the future I felt while engaged in the course, but also a certain sense of sadness that comes from the knowledge that I will probably never again be in a situation where I can take part in such a comprehensive experience of Freirean education. Nevertheless, I will be quite satisfied if I can experience it vicariously through reading or listening to other people's accounts—accounts that I hope will be forthcoming if I have managed to encourage others to try this approach to critical education.

NOTES

1. Racism, sexism, homophobia, ageism, etc. were constant issues of concern in our co-investigation of generative themes. We tried to make sure that with respect to almost every theme we investigated, we considered how it was cross-cut by issues of class, race, gender and other oppressions. The two learning colleagues to whom I refer to in the diary extract greatly enhanced my own understanding of their specific oppressions, and they also managed in the end to harmoniously cross-fertilize each other's understandings.

2. To avoid any conflict with copyright laws, we secured permission for each student to make a single copy for themselves of any material needed and thus requested for their own individual research purposes. We made the copies for them because with only one original available, which was normally the case, it would have taken hours—if not days or even weeks—for each person to get hold of the original and make their own copy from it. When this entailed extracts from a book, I can sincerely assure authors that by doing this, we helped to sell many more copies of their books than would have been sold otherwise. In those cases where we felt a particular book—that is, the whole of it—was important for everyone to read, it became a recommended text for the course. This meant that either every person or else each study circle bought a copy. *Pedagogy of the Oppressed* and *The Politics of Education* were, of course, required texts, which everyone was asked to purchase.

3. I can only recall one instance of someone needing to take a leave of absence. This was a leave of two terms after completing the first term of the first year. Because of the need for coherence, not just in what we were learning, but also in the development of the thinking within the group, we asked the person in question to begin the course again with a new group, and this proposal was readily accepted. Of course the fees for the first term were waived. This was not a course that people could drop into and out of casually; therefore, it would have contravened one of the objectives of contemporary modular programmes. During the twelve

years of the course, there were only a few people who left the course, usually because of changes in their professional or personal circumstances.

4. Being able to select the appropriate sequence for the reading that the group undertakes, is an important intellectual skill for Freirean educators. It involves making an informed professional judgement regarding the difficulty of the readings and also a judgment as to the way in which the sequence of the readings can best foster the conceptual development of individuals in the group. Being able to problematize one's own and learning-colleagues' thinking is another important skill. In fact, Freire often refers to his approach as problem-posing education. Problematization, or problem-posing, is a complex skill—or set of skills—that involves the continuous interpretation of the way in which each person's thinking is developing—and by each person I mean the thinking of the educator as well. While I am making this note on skills, I should also point out that Freirean educators need to understand learning as a developmental process. By this, I mean that they need to realize that people only hear things when they are ready, cognitively and affectively ready, to hear them—that is, hear them in a way that allows them to integrate what they have heard into their thinking or overall conceptualization of something they are seeking to understand. And this means that teacher-learners, and hopefully learner-teachers as well, must always be ready to repeat what they have said as many times and on as many occasions as necessary. Obviously in our context, or any other teacher-education context, these skills and understandings must be made explicit and then developed, as far as possible, within the learning process. However, I also think that these skills and understandings should be developed in almost every conceivable context where this approach to critical education is being used. In a socialist society, many of them would be integral to the life-processes of every member of society and would, thus, be a part of everyone's education.

5. This monograph was published by my Department in 1983. It was entitled: *Towards a Developmental Theory of Andragogy,* and was written by The Nottingham Andragogy Group. At that time, I thought that adult educators needed to develop an alternative to pedagogy. I also thought that the "andragogy" being promoted by Malcolm Knowles was not the answer. Our learning group, which we later called the Nottingham Andragogy Group, felt we had found the answer in Freire, and this is why we decided to write about our interpretation of his ideas. Shortly after the beginning of the Freirean course, I ceased thinking that there should be a distinction between andragogy and pedagogy. In my opinion, once one has undergone the epistemological and ontological transformations that are integral to Freirean learning, the distinction between andragogy and pedagogy becomes unnecessary.

6. This list was originally devised for a workshop session during the residential weekend. It was then revised over the next few years in accord with feedback that we received from subsequent groups. My discussion of dialogue, in chapter 5, indicates the features that we thought were important to effective dialogue. The check-list was nothing more than an aide memoir to these features.

7. Freire's ideas about ideology and his use of the term are explained in greater detail in Freire and Macedo, *Ideology Matters* (2001).

8. CCCS or the Centre for Contemporary Cultural Studies, at the University of Birmingham in the UK, once under the directorship of Stuart Hall, produced a range of valuable publications during the 1970s and 1980s.

9. In Britain, Glenn Rikowski, Dave Hill, Mike Cole and other members of the Hillcole Group, a left-wing educational "think-tank," have been challenging these shifts in educational policy and practice for a number of years through their various publications both as members of the Hillcole Group and as individuals.

10. It is perhaps important to mention that we always felt that it was a good idea to share lunch together—as a whole group—on various occasions throughout the course. At least once

per term, we therefore had a slightly extended lunch break during which we all brought a special dish to share with the group. This was simply another way of creating an atmosphere of harmony and solidarity in the group—and a very satisfying one at that.

11. Ample time is particularly crucial when it comes to assessing, or evaluating/marking, students' written work—an inescapable task that must be undertaken by critical educators working in formal contexts. There is insufficient space here to do the topic justice, but, in essence, we used a type of formative evaluation. We asked our learning colleagues to tell us what mark they were aiming to achieve, and then we agreed to read, and extensively comment on, as many rough drafts as necessary to help the person reach the desired standard. This often involved a great deal of person-to-person and written tuition—and thus time. In some cases, people would choose not to submit drafts, or the necessary number of drafts, but most people did. This process, together with a system of automatic second marking (every piece of work assessed "blind" by two members of academic staff) plus external examination of students' work, was the best we could do in our context. In the final analysis, all assessment is really summative, so there is no ideal solution for critical educators; the best approach, however, is to be honest and open about the problems and to focus on them collectively within dialogue. (For further information, contact the author [p.d.allman@ntlworld.com].)

REFERENCES

Allman, P. (1999). *Revolutionary Social Transformation: Democratic Hopes, Political Possibilities and Critical Education.* Westport, CT: Bergin & Garvey.

Freire, P. (1972). *Pedagogy of the Oppressed.* Harmondsworth, U.K.: Penguin.

Freire, P. (1974). "Authority versus Authoritarianism." Audiotape, in series: *Thinking with Paulo Freire.* Sydney, Australia: Australian Council of Churches.

Freire, P. (1985). *The Politics of Education.* London: Macmillan.

Freire, P., and Macedo, D. (1999). *Ideology Matters.* London: Rowman and Littlefield.

Larrain, J. (1979). *The Concept of Ideology.* London: Hutchinson.

Larrain, J. (1983). *Marxism and Ideology.* London: Macmillan.

Mayo, P. (1999). *Gramsci, Freire and Adult Education: Possibilities for Transformative Action.* London: Zed.

Nottingham Andragogy Group (1983). *Towards a Developmental Theory of Andragogy.* Monograph No. 9 in P. Allman and K. J. Mackie (Eds.), *Adults: Psychological and Educational Perspectives Series.* Nottingham, U.K.: Department of Adult Education, University of Nottingham.

Williams, R. (1983). *Keywords: A Vocabulary of Culture and Society.* London: Fontana.

7

Toward the Abolition of Absurdity: Saying "NO" to Capitalism

Neoliberalism has been and continues to be an effective and efficient pedagogue of capitalist truths. This most recent and, to date, most devastating regime of capitalist accumulation has left capitalism exposed, at least to those with the courage to look and to see. If we have been attentive to this oppressor's pedagogy—its ineptly hidden as well as its overt curriculum—we will have learned that when we try to control and manage capitalism in a way that allows for the modicum of social justice we associate with the welfare state, we end up with sluggish and complacent corporations, plagued by insufficient gains in productivity and falling profit rates—moreover, insufficient productivity not just in terms of profitability but also, and crucially, in terms of promoting the degree of competition necessary to sustain the health of capitalist economies. We could have avoided the punitive lessons and this tyrannical schoolmaster, but only if we had listened to Marx and understood the truths of capitalism that he exposed over a century ago.

One of the most important conclusions that can be drawn from Marx's dialectical explanation of capitalism is that the law that makes capitalism work—the Law of Value and all the attendant contradictory tendencies it sets in motion—only functions in fully developed capitalist societies, under competitive conditions; and, of course, without value—that is, surplus-value—there is no capital. In other words, when capitalism becomes a fully developed form of socioeconomic organization, "the inner law [Law of Value] operates only by way of their [capitalist commodity producers] competition, their reciprocal pressure on one another . . ." (Marx, 1865, p. 1020). Neoliberalism is an attempt to address the problem of competition—an attempt to reenergize that reciprocal pressure, to stimulate competition. What we should now understand, if not from Marx, then at least from the neoliberal solutions to capitalist crisis—solutions that effectively disrobe the contradictions of capitalism—is that periods of relative prosperity for both labor and capital, together with relative harmony in class relations and progress toward greater social justice and equality, are nothing more than "blips" in an otherwise crisis-prone system, where class conflict is the reality, and other forms of social division and injustice serve useful functions.

The valedictorians of neoliberalism are the "Third-Way" politicians. Having learned their lessons well by never deviating from capital's syllabus or the required texts, in which they have a great deal invested and therefore see no reason to question, they are now hell-bent on helping their citizens to adjust and to adapt—to be flexible responsible risk-takers and to accept without flinching the new watered-down meanings of fairness, social justice and human rights. They are convinced and thus want to convince us that globalization means that we must embrace the new realism—the one that redefines fair distribution in terms of "possibilities" (Giddens, 1998, p. 101) rather than, or at least as more important than, the redistribution of material wealth. These very intelligent and reasonable people are masters at uncritical/reproductive praxis (nearly as accomplished as some postmodern intellectuals); and unselfishly and with the utmost sincerity they want their citizens to become equally adept. Without a dialectical conceptualization and understanding of capitalism, this is really the only form of praxis that is possible; and "Third-Way" solutions are arguably the most progressive or liberal responses on offer. For those who have not grasped the dialectical truth of capitalism, it is entirely reasonable to think that there is no alternative to it and thus to formulate the most feasible way forward within the parameters—the boundaries and barriers—that are defined by capitalist social relations. However, once capitalism is grasped dialectically, it is possible to see that the "Third Way" is nothing other than the velvet version of neoliberalism—business as usual but clothed in the regressively transmuted language of social democracy.

In this book I have tried to provide the basis for the type of understanding that can enable us to see beyond the capitalist horizon—not only to imagine and hope that an alternative is possible, but also to know that it is possible, and, equally, to know that it is up to us to create this alternative. Moreover, this understanding should enable us to realize that if we fail to act, then humanity and the human project will be permanently propelled into the globalization of misery and the total demise of human dignity. For those who believe in humanity, the project for humanity—the possibility and necessity of humanizing the world and thus the abolition of dehumanization—the only option is the struggle to create a socially and economically just alternative to capitalism.

It is from this premise that I begin my final discussion in this book. I focus not on the question—what *can* be done?—but instead on what *should* and *must* be done, in order to emphasize that I am speaking about choices that are both political and ethical. My discussion focuses on critical education and what, I think, critical educators should do, suggesting what could be done once educators make the political and ethical choice to act. As always, my suggestions are offered as a basis for and as a stimulus to dialogue, and I hope that they will be received in that spirit. Critical education—that is, revolutionary critical education—both without and within various organizations, social movements and political parties can and must serve as the necessary basis for and catalyst to the establishment of an international social movement capable of challenging capitalism. With respect to more general strategies for the present conjuncture, I endorse, with one qualification, what Ellen Meiksins Wood proposes when she says:

The best [?—this is my one qualification] that socialists can do is to aim as much as possible to detach social life from market-dependence. That means striving for the decommodification of as many spheres of life as possible and their democratization—not just their subjection to the political rule of "formal" democracy but their removal from the direct control of capital and from the "impersonal" control of market imperatives, which subordinate every human need and practice to the requirements of accumulation and profit-maximization. If that seems utopian, just consider how unrealistic it is to adopt a strategy of export-oriented competitiveness in a crisis-ridden global economy with an irreducible structural tendency to overcapacity. [September, 1999, www.monthlyreview.org]

Whether or not this is the "best" we can do will only be decided through the international dialogue and subsequent praxis of those who are committed to human dignity and the revolutionary social transformation that is necessary to ensure it. Nevertheless, it is a strategy that could contribute to the establishment of that dialogue.

A STRATEGY FOR REVOLUTIONARY CRITICAL EDUCATION: CRITICAL EDUCATION "RENEWED" AND "REVIVIFIED"

To begin with, we must be explicit that critical education is not about making capitalist education more palatable. We must make it clear that we, as individuals and hopefully in the near future as a global movement (more about this in a moment), are saying "NO" to capitalism and that we are engaging with others in a prefigurative struggle to prepare ourselves to transform our societies. Tony Benn once said that "no" was the most powerful word in the English language (Benn, 1984). But living the "no" is even more powerful; and this is what I think we should be striving to do through our critical/revolutionary praxis, or revolutionary critical education. The approach to critical education that I discussed in chapters 5 and 6 is an approach aimed at enabling people to engage in an abbreviated experience of pro-alternative, counterhegemonic social relations within which they can learn to "read" the world critically and glimpse humanity's possible future beyond the horizon of capitalism (see also Allman, 1999). There may be even more effective approaches that we could devise from a critique of capitalist social relations, ontologies and epistemologies, but they should always aim at enabling people to "live the no" by struggling to transform it into an affirmation of humanization, an affirmation of our faith in human beings' ability and need to "make and remake, create and recreate" their world (Freire, 1972, p. 63). We "must not fear being ridiculed for our critical utopianism or for trying to ignite the fire of hope in people's hearts and minds" (Allman, 2001). For some that fire may have been irrevocably extinguished and, instead, they profess or acquiesce to a truly ludicrous utopia—the belief that liberal democracy can continue to buffer us from the worst excesses of capitalism and that it can enable us to continue to live as civilized beings, regardless of the deepening and expanding of capital's contradictions and the attendant crisis in capitalist social relations. However, I think that this type of risible utopianism is only lodged indelibly in a small minority and that a dialectical understanding of capitalism can rekindle the light—our hope for humanity's future. This is a light that always burns in some hearts, somewhere; the task is to enable it to burn more brightly and widely until it obliterates the horizon of capitalism.

Furthermore, we must also be clear that in saying "NO" to *capitalism*, we are saying "no" to the habituated structure of human social relations that we are all involved in reproducing and sustaining, rather than some representative or manifestation of it. In other words, our struggle is not against evil individuals and corporations, although at times it may be this as well, but against the totality of interlocking internal relations—dialectical contradictions—or the capitalist social relations into which people enter each day and within which they live their lives and understand their world through uncritical/reproductive praxis. These are the relations that foster the greed, bigotry and hypocrisy we find despicable in the individual representatives of capital and their corporations. With a dialectical understanding of capitalism, we can see that these dispositions arise from following the "logic" of the system; they do not preexist the social relations of capitalism, or oppressive relations more generally.

We can also understand, in relation to this, that trying to persuade individual capitalists and corporations to be fairer or more just or, alternatively, using legislation to force their hand (although sometimes useful as a short-term tactic) really leads nowhere except, perhaps, teaching them to become more adept at portraying their public image in a favorable light, often by incorporating our language of protest and totally disfiguring its meaning. Equally, we should be able to understand that neoliberalism, as I said before, is not the main enemy. It is only a particular form or manifestation of the enemy—capitalism in its latest garb—one that has become necessary to overcome or attenuate the present crisis of national capitalism as nations are jettisoned more forcibly than ever before into the vortex of globalization—capital's most recent and universalizing attempt to displace its contradictions. Moreover, we should be able to understand that most attempts to present alternatives to neoliberalism—alternatives that remain within the horizon of capitalism—will turn out to be neoliberalism disguised by the rhetoric of social democracy—neoliberalism in a more palatable, or "velvet," form that attempts to veil at least the harsher "truths" of capitalist reality.

It follows from what I have suggested thus far that we must do everything we can to promote a dialectical understanding of capitalism and, more generally, a dialectical conceptualization of all aspects of our material reality. In other words, we must work educationally with other people of all ages to help them and ourselves to develop the ability to think in terms of internal relations—to think dialectically—and thus to understand the material basis for the binary or dichotomized thinking that critics rail against and mistake as some culturally induced deficiency of Western thought. [To reiterate by material basis, I mean our fragmented experiencing of capital's dialectical contradictions—our experience of the opposites at different times and in different places, an experience that inhibits our ability to grasp their internally related nature (Marx, 1858, p. 148).] And as part of our efforts to enable people to think dialectically, or in terms of internal relations, we must work toward establishing a countercapitalist, pro-humanity form of worldwide togetherness, or universality, as an alternative and a challenge to capital's pseudo-universalism. This would be a universality that recognizes and embraces the necessity of creating an internal relation between *diversity* and *unity*, and equally an internal relation between our *individuality* and our *collectivity*. These internally related concepts are discussed in greater detail later in this chapter. At this point, I want to stress that as individuals, we can all find ways, even when working within severe constraints, to work toward all of these general strategies; however, no matter how much we manage to accomplish through our individual efforts as critical educators, we will never begin to affect the drive for revolutionary social transformation until we join forces.

As I urged in chapter 5, we need an international movement of revolutionary critical educators—that is, critical educators passionate about working with others, so that together we all might become prepared to engage in the struggle for revolutionary social transformation. This movement must be an authentic alliance, or the type of alliance that Gramsci advocated—that is, one with an internal coherence rather than a network of casually or loosely linked individuals and groups, which, as Gramsci warned (borrowing one of the metaphors Marx used to refer to the same problem), would have no greater affinity than "a sack of potatoes" (Gramsci, 1971, p. 190). Since the beginning of the twentieth century, and particularly in the wake of globalization, there has been a proliferation of both governmental and nongovernmental international alliances or networks. And several commentators have noted that not only do we already have various forms of global governance but a global civil society has also begun to form. In 1900 there were only 180 nongovernmental organizations with a transnational scope, whereas by the end of the twentieth century there were around 5,000 (Giddens, 1998, p. 140). The type of movement or alliance I am suggesting would aim to politicize both this rapidly growing global civil society and also the many diverse sites of civil society throughout the world. But first it would need to develop and cement an internal cohesion that would enable it to move forward with an unswerving allegiance to an agreed upon moral–ethical position and an irrevocable solidarity and commitment to a consensually devised set of principles and aims for revolutionary critical education. In other words, I am suggesting that, at least initially, this alliance might begin as a relatively small grouping, so long as it was as international as possible in composition.

This alliance would focus attention not just on the impossibility of economic justice within capitalist relations, but also, given these relations, the impossibility of resolving various other problems that plague humanity—for example, racial and ethnic divisiveness, conflict and oppression, homophobia and gender oppression, monocultural determinism, environmental destruction, unemployment, the intractability of military conflict and perpetual rearmament, malfunctioning democracies, socially disabling practices and conditions, as well as various other assaults on human dignity—in other words, the impossibility of capitalism and also liberal democracy delivering any semblance of authentic social justice. The last thing it should be, however, is an alliance that gratuitously juxtaposes voices supporting various issues in a way that ends up in a collage of highly compromised, albeit represented, images (Allman and Wallis, 1995a). Those forming the alliance must be deeply committed to the resolution of all of these problems but also aware that their *ultimate* resolution is inextricably linked to and thus will only begin in earnest with the abolition of capitalism. And they must express this commitment by continuously and courageously explaining why the aspirations arising from these ostensibly disparate issues will never be fulfilled within capitalist relations (Allman and Wallis, 1995a).

The alliance I am advocating would initially be the embryo or seed of a much larger movement, a movement that, given a catalytic kick-start, would then grow primarily from local or grass-root organizations or groups. The "seed" alliance would in no way function as a vanguard of Marxist intellectuals. Although many of its members may be Marxist intellectuals—that is, people with a dialectical understanding of capitalism—their main function as an alliance would be to pool their resources to inspire and then support the efforts of others who wanted to engage in or who were already engaged in critical education for revolutionary social transformation. More specifically, they would focus their energies on the strategies I detailed previously (as well as one further strategy I discuss later) and also on promoting the concept as well as the theory, principles and aims of critical education for revolutionary social transformation, and then they would work to inspire, support and serve those who choose to engage in this form of critical/revolutionary praxis. And their primary resources would be their solidarity, commitment and "an intellectual base [a common dialectical conception of the world] so well rooted, assimilated and experienced that it becomes passion" (Gramsci, 1971, p. 349), together with their own ongoing experience of critical/ revolutionary educational praxis. They would also provide the grass-roots groups with an overview of what was going on elsewhere and facilitate contact among groups; and when invited, they could also provide assistance and advice to groups on matters related to various aspects of revolutionary critical education, such as participatory research, the principles of dialogue, how to gain access to resources that might inform a thematic investigation, and so on.

With the aid of email and the Internet, all of these services could be provided on a fairly wide-scale basis, and members of the "seed" alliance might also act as email reflection partners or mentors to those who felt they were initially working in relative isolation. However, it is important that the "seed alliance" and the larger movement do not become too Internet-focused and dependent. This would be self-defeating for an alliance that potentially will have many members who, at present, have no access to the Internet. With this factor in mind as well as other considerations pertaining to the acquisition of resources or the facilitation of communication, the "seed alliance" could also initiate worldwide fund-raising activities and support grass-roots-initiated ones, but as far as possible the *services* provided by this alliance would be purely use-values, with no exchange-value attached. In other words, as far as possible, the alliance would function outside market relations. Nevertheless, while we exist in a capitalist world, there will be a need for fund-raising. In the first instance, for example, fund-raising could help to facilitate the two-way communication between members, especially those without access to modern telecommunications and, if possible, to even provide these members and their communities with the type of technology that could facilitate certain aspects of their participation in the alliance and also enhance their own local educational and organizational efforts. I want to emphasize that this latter type of participation would be the main criterion for participating in the alliance. In other words, participation via the Internet is only a secondary form of participation and in no way should it become a substitute for collective critical/ revolutionary praxis aimed at social transformation.

Once the larger movement takes off, the original members of the "seed" alliance, along with every other member of the movement, would be able to stand for election to a coordinating committee, which would then take over the functions of the original "seed" alliance. These functions, however, would need to be reviewed by all the members of the movement and revamped as necessary on a regular basis. It perhaps goes without saying that all those elected to serve as members of this international coordinating committee would be subject to immediate recall by some, yet to be determined, percentage of the movement's membership. To suggest further detail than this would be counterproductive. I have only offered my ideas about an alliance in order to get the ball rolling—to move that one step beyond simply suggesting that such an alliance is needed—and to suggest some Gramscian-inspired fundamentals on alliance formation (see also Allman and Wallis, 1995a).

The idea of beginning with a relatively small (in global terms) but extremely cohesive and coherent "seed" alliance is based on practicality and urgency. If we had the luxury of time—say another century or so—to rescue the project for humanity, to halt the degradation and destruction of human dignity and restore the health of the planet, it would be better for the movement to grow from the bottom upwards. However, capitalism has robbed us of this luxury. In fact, as I explained in chapter 2, it has turned time into a compulsive aspect of social domination. Experience has also suggested to me that moral–ethical considerations, which I see as being fundamental to cementing the commitment and forging the solidarity of the "seed" alliance, may be the only factor that might override the doctrinal and theoretical differences that have so effectively and ridiculously kept the Left divided and thus ineffectual in mounting a concerted challenge to capitalism. A strongly united and explicit "seed" alliance would function in the way that Freire did individually and urged others to do collectively. He felt that it was possible to be straightforward about your own beliefs without imposing them on others; this was what it meant to be both committed and ethical. And he stressed this on several occasions, for example:

I cannot deny or hide my posture, but also cannot deny others the right to reject it. In the name of respect I should have toward my students, I do not see why I should omit or hide my political stance by proclaiming a neutral stance that does not exist. On the contrary, my role as teacher is to assent the students' right to compare, to choose, to rupture, to decide. [Freire, 1998, p. 68]

In other words, the position, or stance, of the "seed" alliance would become an "object focus" for other individuals and groups. It would enable them to clarify their own thinking, feelings and desires so that they would know whether the position advocated by the "seed" alliance was also the one they were committed to or at least one to which they could become committed. In this way the larger movement would from the very beginning have a centrality of purpose—a coherence and shared vision—that would continuously nourish it with an energy and dynamism that would radiate outwards toward the hearts and minds of educators throughout the world.

At this point, I would like to consider one further strategy for saying "NO" to capitalism—a strategy to which critical educators, either as individual or as members of a group or a larger movement, should devote considerable time and energy. The representatives of capital are engaged in a very obvious struggle to maintain capitalist hegemony and also the hegemony of liberal democratic governance—the form of abstract, alienated, illusory, pseudodemocratic government that serves capital so well. As part of this, they must use or promote various ideological explanations of our reality in order to persuade us that what is happening is natural, inevitable and ultimately for our own well-being. And they must weave all of these ideological explanations into a dominant ideological discourse that is expressed not just in words but also in the symbols and practices that form the material fabric of our lives. Although it may sound as if I am suggesting that this is an intentional project to deceive, it is important to note that, in most cases, it does not require any intentional plan or deliberation. When we understand that ideological explanations arise from the actual conditions they serve to justify, it is possible to see that planned deception is unnecessary. I am quite sure that for the most part those who weave together the dominant discourse do so because they actually believe they are explaining the truth of capitalist reality. In recognition of this and of the powerful role that ideology plays in sustaining domination, Freire (1985) stresses that in order to prepare people capable of challenging capitalism, we should not only engage in a dialectical "reading" of reality but should also analyze and "clarify the process of ideologiz-ing" (p. 163). In other words, we should engage in critiquing ideology and all aspects of our reality—both the verbal and the nonverbal aspects—that perform ideological functions, or the functions of manipulating and adapting us to accept the conditions of an oppressive reality.

Many critical educators recognize the importance of ideology critique and are already adept in engaging their students in this type of critical analysis. I simply want to suggest certain aspects of the dominant ideology that I think it would be wise to prioritize within an overall strategy of ideology critique. I see them as the Achilles' heel of capitalist hegemony—that is, some of the most vulnerable aspects of the dominant ideology, the cement of that hegemony. Before discuss-ing each of these aspects, I would like to emphasize that one of the most effective ways to critique ideology is to "show it up"—to expose it—by expressing through our counterfactual actions how it distorts the truth. This is part of the larger project of "living" the "NO" to capitalism, of offering others a glimpse of our alternative vision of "being" and thus relating to one another. Drawing on Giroux (1989), it means that our praxis is one of "possibility" as well as "cri-tique."

The ideology of progress is a fundamental component of the dominant ideol-ogy; however, as I have suggested throughout this book, capitalism itself has begun to expose the mythical nature of its notion of progress. As a consequence, there have never been more propitious conditions for prioritizing our challenge to it. The ideology of progress is used to assure us that capitalism is a positive force; therefore, capitalism's legitimacy hangs, to a large extent, on the idea that it provides the best possible and most advanced arrangement for human beings— that capitalism is, in fact, the embodiment of the fullest development of human reason, capacity and skill. To challenge this aspect of capitalist ideology effec-tively, we must understand how it works, especially how it is used, whenever necessary, to actually readjust or reformulate our ideas of what is and what is not "real" progress. Postmodernists eschew this idea of progress and equate it with modernist thinking, thus implying that it is not historically specific to capitalism per se but more of a culturally determined way of thinking. This may be because it appears also to have been the idea of progress promoted in the former socialist countries and moreover because the emphasis on the power of rational thought places it more widely within the Enlightenment project.[1] However, regardless of its origins or the expansiveness of its influence, this idea of progress is extremely important for capitalism. It is also pervasive—in fact so much so that even postmodernists, despite their dismissal of this idea, tend to buy into its basic tenets or concepts. I will return to this idea, but first we need to look more carefully at what actually constitutes the ideology of progress. If we consider some of its most important conceptual components, we can see that this idea of progress is always linked with whatever is the most recent and equally with whatever results in more rather than less, and these concepts are crucial for capitalist legitimacy. Drawing on Marx's theory of consciousness/praxis, I want to suggest that they are related directly—or, more precisely, internally—to the material reality of capitalist production, especially the processes of competition between productive capitalists that I explained in chapter 3.

As I stressed before, ideology, in that it is part of our consciousness, initially arises from our material practices, and its relation or linkage to these material conditions is what gives ideology the power to persuade us to think in a particular way. The ideology of progress also conveys the notion that advances are permanent moves forward or irreversible improvements, and this, together with the other two concepts that are central to this notion of progress, bears an amazing resemblance to various aspects of how the Law of Value operates, in particular to the movements and developments within the social labor hour, which I discussed in chapter 2. When greater productivity (in this case, the production of *more* in the same time) is brought about by the intensification of labor, the labor hour becomes a denser or less porous hour—that is, one that contains *more* minutes of value-creating labor—and whatever is the most *recent* degree of density in a labor hour eventually becomes the standard that is reflected in the "socially necessary labor-time" that determines the value of a particular commodity. In capitalist terms, this is real progress. Furthermore, within capitalist relations, these increases in the density of the labor hour are *irreversible* advances for capital, so long as competition holds them in place. In other words, our idea of progress is inextricably related to the way the Law of Value works in a fully developed capitalist society. I would argue that this is one of the factors—probably the main one that makes it such a pervasive and persistent idea and also an idea that was accepted virtually without question until fairly recently. This questioning, however, has led, in turn, to some rather frantic attempts to readjust our thinking about what constitutes "real" progress—attempts that seek to preserve the idea that "real" progress is irreversible.

For a number of years now, we have witnessed one progressive gain after another in our social conditions being reversed; and yet we are told that these are not reversals. In fact, we are told that these policy changes are necessary to progress—necessary to the "modernization" of the welfare state and also our idea of social democracy—and that what we had before has proven to be a mistaken notion of progress. And we are also told that it is other mistaken notions of progress (rather than capitalism per se) that have inflicted catastrophes on both the environment and various human groups, especially indigenous peoples. In other words, a necessary requirement for the ideology of progress is the idea that real progress is irreversible; therefore, if we think we are witnessing a reversal, it is because we previously had a mistaken idea of progress. As I suggested earlier, even the postmodernists, who are extremely critical—or so they seem to think—of the modernist notion of progress, promote an implicit idea of progress, which is remarkably similar in certain respects to the modernist concept they reject. Postmodernism, and in Britain its political variant, first "New Times" and now the "Third Way," which is perhaps a more cosmopolitan, or at least Anglo-American, rendition of "New Times," are all ideological responses directly linked to the most *recent* changes in the material reality of capitalism—a material reality that is constantly being shaped and reshaped by the pursuit of surplus-value. When "the most recent" brings into question the postmodernists' previous ideas of what constitutes progress, rather than questioning this latest development, they either renegotiate or totally disavow their former ideas. And this, of course, makes it possible for them to champion and promote the new development, while still holding on to the idea that real progress is irreversible.

The pursuit of surplus-value—that is, the contemporary crisis-driven pursuit—has also brought about readjustments in the concept of *more* when it is used in association with progress—readjustments that are also reflected in postmodern thought. For most of human history, the concept of more has been linked to progress because it was associated with the eradication of scarcity and thus more usually referred to more of specific, necessary items, such as bread or cabbage or whatever. At present, there is a subtle move to readjust or realign the association so that more has to do with variety and choice; in other words, progress means that consumers with purchasing power have more from which to choose and more to choose as their needs grow in magnitude. This realignment, therefore, effectively shifts the ground away from any notion of eliminating scarcity, as the presence of millions with little or no purchasing power actually having less in the world of global capital is totally ignored. Decoupling *more* from its association with the eradication of scarcity and recoupling it with variety and choice and clinging tenaciously to the equation of progress with whatever is new or most *recent* and also to the notion of its *irreversibility* creates several problems, especially when capitalism is in crisis. These are problems we can pick up on and use as the basis for ideology critique. One of these can be seen in the postmodern turn toward relativism, a mode of thinking capable of offering philosophical justification, or cover, for all sorts of contemporary mayhem and confusion.

As I have tried to demonstrate, it is value that mediates our social relations, and thus it is value that provides the type of coherence necessary for sustaining capitalism and its quasi-abstract form of social domination, which I discussed in chapter 2. However, since the early 1970s, the ongoing production of value—that is, surplus-value—has been riddled with problems, and as a consequence capitalists have been constantly, sometimes frenetically, searching for new ways of promoting the creation of surplus-value and the accumulation of capital. Value in its money form has also spun off, or away, from the cycle of reproduction and has thus become separated or fragmented from its source. Unaware of how their system actually works, capitalists think that any way of making profit is just as good as any other—there is no single or "true" way to profitability—and thus it is irrelevant where they invest their money. This is relativism *writ large* in the world of capital; and this is the relativism that postmodern theorizing seems bent on emulating. However, this apparent relativism in the world of capital is not the result of a critically chosen approach; it is the result of confusion and often desperation—a helter-skelter approach to keeping the ship afloat. I would suggest that this is the real origin of the cultural relativism, or the relativism that is reflected in postmodern consciousness, including its political manifestations, a relativism that is equally indicative of confusion and desperation rather than the progressive disposition or intellectual sophistication it pretends to be. Nevertheless, as I discuss later, this cultural relativism is providing a useful service to capital, or more precisely, the maintenance of capitalist hegemony.

Although it would take much more space than I have left in this book to fully argue this point, I am actually suggesting that every major facet in postmodernist thought and its political variants is related to some fundamental aspect of the way that capital has to move and develop in order to displace and thus temporarily resolve its internal contradictions. Whether these movements in consciousness and ideology simply mimic the surface movements or are more deeply and intimately related to the crisis that exists within capitalism's dialectical "essence" is something that Marxists need to investigate. For now, I would venture the hypothesis that it is probably a mixture of both of these. Whatever the depth of the relation, these forms of consciousness—and this is what moves them into the realm of ideology—actually act back on and facilitate these movements and developments in capital by legitimating them: that is, by persuading or convincing us that what is happening is perfectly normal, natural, inevitable, or even "cool," "hot" or whatever and, of course, in the long-term interest of human progress.

In other words, these forms of consciousness not only move with the "grain of new times," as their political purveyors stress we all must do, but they also reinforce this grain, thereby helping to sustain its development (Allman and Wallis, 1995a). In fact, postmodernism has picked up so strongly and accurately on these material trends that it appears that instead of economic determinism, we now have cultural determinism, a kind of neoidealism, or a new rendition of the older form of idealism that Marx's revolutionary theory of consciousness was challenging more than 150 years ago. Both types of determinism are equally misguided. My interpretation is not a reductionist or correspondence "reading" of the situation, any more than it is an argument for relative autonomy. I am proposing, in accord with Marx's revolutionary theory of consciousness—that is, praxis—a dialectical "reading," or one that grasps the internal relation between thought and human practice, or consciousness and material reality. By grasping this internal relation, we can more readily and effectively problematize the various ideological understandings that arise from it.

Many of these attempts to readjust our thinking about progress draw on a misunderstanding, and thus the misuse, of Gramsci's thinking on progress or the progressive. I will be brief about the misuse, which I have explained more fully elsewhere (Allman and Wallis, 1995a), because I want to focus primarily on his valuable insights regarding what is truly progressive—insights that, I think, we can use to challenge the capitalist ideology of progress. The misuse stems from an inaccurate reading of the essay on "Americanism and Fordism" in Gramsci's (1971) prison notebooks. What he actually says (and whether he is right or not is another matter) is that "Fordism" is only potentially progressive. It would only be a progressive method of production if it were used within noncapitalist social relations in order to eliminate scarcity and thus fulfill human needs, as opposed to being used to increase the exploitation of labor and thus the profitability of capital. A number of writers on the Left interpret this essay differently; and as a result, they conclude that the new modes of "flexible" accumulation, which include "flexible" working practices and conditions as well as "flexible," or varied, product styles, are progressive and thus preferable to "Fordist" mass production, which (according to their reading of Gramsci) was progressive in its own time but is no longer progressive in our "new times."

This type of misinterpretation is a reflection of people's thinking being influenced by the ideology of progress, but it is also bolstered by certain problems I discussed previously. When people fail to realize that Marx, or in this case Gramsci, is explaining the historical specificity of capitalism, they also tend to think that the difference between capitalism and socialism is simply one of private versus collective ownership, and, therefore, for them it follows that capitalism can be abolished by simply "expropriating the expropriators"—that is, transferring capitalist production processes and the means of production, preferably the most advanced or recent ones, into social ownership. Furthermore, they do not realize that when Marx or Gramsci describes something as being advanced within capitalist terms, or relations, it is just that: namely, in the case of Fordism, it is the most advanced way of exploiting labor and producing surplus-value. These misunderstandings work together with the ideology of progress. Therefore, they also assume that since postmodern forms of "flexible" production and accumulation are more recent developments than Fordist mass production and accumulation strategies, they must be more advanced—as if there were some sort of teleological force pulling history forward toward some inevitable progressive end. And, of course, not only do they fail to recognize that Gramsci was referring to a potential, they also miss the point that this potential had to do with the elimination of scarcity, not the potential for "niche" production and the constant expansion of product variation and consumer choice. For Gramsci, the latter would only ever be progressive once scarcity, and thus poverty and hunger, had been relegated to the "dust bin" of history.

The main criticism the British Left made of "Thatcherism" was that it was a regressive form of modernization. In their manifesto for "New Times," which they published in the journal, *Marxism Today* in September 1989, they suggested that the Left should promote a "progressive" modernization, and by this they meant that they would make the necessary restructuring of capitalism take place on their terms. Unfortunately, they seem to be totally unaware that capitalist restructuring is a reactive response to crisis, and a rather frenetic one at that. Instead, they treat it as if it were a response to developments within capitalism that are inherently progressive. The best rebuttal that can be made to this type of muddled left-wing thinking is to echo, once again, Ellen Meiksins Wood (1999), who stresses emphatically that "[m]anaging capitalism is not the job of socialists, but more particularly, it's not a job that can be done at all." As I said before, despite these rather persistent misinterpretations of Gramsci, it is important to consider his important insights about what was truly progressive and how we might use these insights to challenge the capitalist ideology of progress.

Gramsci distinguished between change that was epochal and change that was conjunctural, but he also dialectically related these different types of change, and in so doing he formulated a distinctive idea of what was truly progressive (1971, p. 223). Epochal changes were those having to do with revolutionary social transformation, or the abolition of capitalism, and thus with the culmination of the epoch during which capitalist social relations dominated humanity. Some conjunctural changes, forces and aspirations are related, or can come to be related through revolutionary praxis, to epochal change, but others are irrevocably secondary issues. Secondary issues, or what Gramsci also called "marginal forces," were not capable, on their own, of epochal change, and thus they were not truly progressive (p. 223). They were only relatively progressive in so far as they exposed the opposition's inability to construct a situation of equilibrium between conflicting groups or positions. For Gramsci, the truly progressive force at any conjuncture of the capitalist epoch was the working class, or the proletariat, and all others who could potentially be drawn into the labor–capital relation; this was the only force capable—or, rather, potentially capable—of creating a new form of society and thus bringing about the abolition of capitalism.

Nevertheless, the "secondary issues" were not to be ignored. Gramsci's idea of working with the ostensibly "progressive" forces at any conjuncture was to demonstrate the limitations of what could actually be achieved within capitalist relations and thus to win over or persuade representatives of these forces that their interests would be best served by joining the working class in their "war of position" and eventually their "war of movement" against capitalism (for a much more detailed explanation of this, see Allman and Wallis, 1995a). Only in an authentic alliance led by the proletariat could any of these "marginal forces" become truly progressive—that is, part of a force that was truly progressive because it was the only force capable of bringing about epochal change. Gramsci's project was to educate people and also to organize them into a philosophically and politically cohesive social and "historic bloc." His project was clearly at odds with contemporary post-Marxist and postmodernist projects that claim Gramsci as their inspiration—projects that simply respond to and reflect popular aspirations that are thwarted within capitalist relations. Even though the fulfillment of some of these aspirations may be theoretically possible within capitalist relations (e.g., gender equality) and others are not (e.g., greater and more authentic democracy), none of them is practically feasible, at least in terms of being totally fulfilled, as long as it serves a useful function in maintaining the domination of capital. As for Gramsci's idea of the truly progressive—that is, the proletariat, or the working class—I return to this at the end of the chapter.

In order to challenge some of the other vulnerable elements of the dominant ideology, we need to be critically aware that the substance of this ideology is undergoing dramatic changes, in particular changes that involve its transformation from a relatively coherent system of ideas into one that is riddled with logical contradictions.

A concept that is rapidly becoming a central component of the dominant ideology and that signals these changes—and which should, therefore, be a priority for ideology critique—is difference and/or diversity—in other words, the "knee-jerk" reaction to and also the "flip side" of the capitalist notion of universalism, or what I referred to earlier as capitalism's pseudo-universalism. The capitalist idea of universalism is one that promotes those aspects of Western civilization—such as values, life-styles and other aspects of culture, including habituated social practices—that favorably serve the interest of capitalism. It is actually a process of homogenization that creates "universal equivalents" in various realms of our existence, equivalencies operating much like the money form of value and that therefore also enable capital (value) to move more freely and rapidly around the globe, thereby greatly facilitating the recent intensification of capital's globalizing processes. As I explained in chapter 3, these processes are inherent in capitalism; therefore, in one form or another capital's totalizing, or monolithic, pseudo-universalism must endure as part of the dominant ideology, and it must continue to be one of our priorities for ideology critique. However, we must also challenge the equally abstract and artificial notions of diversity and difference that have recently been incorporated within the dominant ideology. And we must try to come to a critical understanding of how and why contradictory uses of these ideas have come to coexist within the dominant ideological discourse of capitalism. Once again, I think we can begin to form that understanding by looking at the changes and developments that are taking place within global capital.

The greater the forces of centralization and homogenization have become with capital's mad-dash, frenetic attempts to displace its contradictions into the global arena, the greater has been the reaction to it—a reaction that in its most extreme forms is expressed as religious fundamentalism or ethnic hatred and conflict. In a milder form—the form that has rapidly been absorbed within the dominant ideology—it has been less a matter of reacting to globalization, especially the insecurities it creates in people's lives and identities, and more one of mimicking the dialectically opposite processes, processes that are every bit as real, or material, as the homogenizing forces of globalization and that have also arisen from conjunctural adaptations in capitalism. These are the processes that concentrate capital in and tie it to specific regions or pockets of cultural differentiation—the processes I discussed earlier that begin to take place in unison with the outward thrust of globalization, once the ground has been prepared, processes through which capital, or some of it, returns to, or moves back toward, specific national, regional and local thus differentiated bases of accumulation. Some of the mimicry of these processes comes over as either a gratuitous or an obligatory celebration of pastiched differences and diversity—a celebration that invariably leads to the incorporation, adulteration and eventual commodification of the diversity that might have enriched humanity. As a result, we end up with little more than a shopping mall or consumer-led version of our multicultural diversity and differences. However, this should not be surprising if we consider that the dominant ideology has to accommodate the contradictory movements and developments that are taking place.

As I said before, capital's attempt to relocate its contradictions on a global scale are eventually accompanied by a dialectical reworking and relocation of the contradictions back into specific national, regional and local contexts, albeit not always the same contexts from which they originated. These reverse processes do not replace the homogenizing processes of globalization but occur simultaneously, and they also take place unevenly, only moving away from the global arena toward more local venues when the local ground has been prepared for new or renewed efforts at successful capitalist accumulation—when, for example, unemployment or the threat of a jobless future has effectively undermined working-class strength and militancy and thus guaranteed greater docility and "flexibility" within the local labor force. These reverse processes are not indicative of a return to some prior state of affairs; they, too, are part of globalization.

In other words, capital's accumulation strategy has become flexible, moving at one moment into the global arena and at another time and in other places moving back into a more localized context, but all of these strategies are a part of the world of global capital. These movements, together with all the other flexible readjustments in capitalists' accumulation strategies, result in disjointed, fragmented and incoherent material conditions, the sum total of which David Harvey (1989) refers to as the "condition of postmodernity"—the material condition that is reproduced, or appears to be mimicked, in various cultural and political practices and which, in turn, is sustained and supported by this mimicry. In other words, this two-directional, outward and inward, seemingly incoherent movement of value—capital—is mirrored in people's consciousness, that is, in their uncritical/reproductive praxis. As a consequence, it is also embraced by and eventually reflected in the dominant ideology.

When the dominant ideology has to accommodate such contradictory movements in reality, it will draw on and incorporate, as necessary, any ideas that have a basis in the material world. For example, postmodern relativism, especially the relativity of truth, has been ushered in as a legitimizing mechanism within the dominant ideological discourse. Interestingly, it is entirely in keeping with previous periods of capitalist crisis and subsequent, conjunctural restructuring that relativism becomes the predominant characteristic of contemporary thought (Hughes, 1959). This is why I said in an earlier chapter that postmodernism did not arise by chance. The notion that there is no truth, no universal values, has become the new "truth" promulgated in celebration of human diversity (Allman, 1999; Allman and Wallis, 1995b); and this has proved to be a very useful idea when it comes to dealing with the exceedingly contradictory tendencies of our contemporary world. For instance, in politics it has offered an apposite rationalization for the state to devolve responsibility to local decision-making, thereby relinquishing its claim that it can determine what is best (the truth) for the diverse communities that exist within its borders. However, this is a far cry from being the progressive move it claims to be. To devolve decision-making and responsibility while retaining power over disbursing financial resources and also power over judging whether they have been used wisely and, even more importantly, accountably is a very subtle and clever way of maintaining control and thus exercising power while simultaneously being able to devolve the blame when things go wrong. In many ways it is similar to what we now call "neocolonialism" or "neoimperialism"—that is, forms of external economic and financial "postcolonial" control that have been found to be much more effective and cost-efficient than political domination and that are thus exercised routinely, at the international level, by trans- and multinational corporations, foreign banks, national governments (for example, through foreign aid and loans) and likewise by institutions such as the International Monetary Fund (IMF) and the World Bank, which link their offers of financial assistance with certain "conditionalities." The state has utilized the contemporary passion for relativism and the vacuous celebration of difference to pull off this sleight of hand—that is, the application of a neocolonial or neoimperial form of control within its own borders, a form of control that works efficiently and also insidiously not just internationally but at the intranational level as well.

It is important to bear in mind, as I suggested before, that what I am describing may only have a generalized affect on people's consciousness. (And this includes *our* consciousness too, as there are certain forms of habituated, reproductive praxis in which no one can avoid being involved.) Individuals relate to their material conditions differently due to their previous experiences, and they also have varied experiences of these conditions—for example, some people are much more directly involved in the current movements and developments associated with capitalist restructuring than are other people. Therefore the impact or degree of influence that these material conditions will have on consciousness will vary and for many may be more of a general tendency or pattern rather than something more all-encompassing. Nevertheless, at the very least, general patterns of thought emerge from people's continuous engagement in uncritical/reproductive praxis, and this makes their consciousness (and ours, too, whenever our critical guard is down or not working at full capacity) very susceptible to ideological explanations. This is why it is so important for critical educators to grasp critically how the reemergence of capitalist crisis during the last quarter of the twentieth century has affected, and continues to affect, the dominant ideology. In general, therefore, it is crucial to understand that this crisis has brought the contradictions of capitalism bubbling up to the surface of our existence, and as a result the dominant ideology, if is to maintain the legitimacy of the system, has to embrace and neutralize or obscure the absurdity of these contradictions—having it this way and that way and, if possible, all ways that serve the interest of capitalist accumulation. Challenging this chameleon type of dominant ideology is not an easy task. It requires vigilance from critical educators.

Among other things, vigilance means that we need to be clear in our own thinking about what we mean by expressions such as "unity in diversity," and it requires us to articulate our concepts of truth, coherence, universality, difference/diversity and humanity. Moreover, it requires us to be clear about *how* we are using them in a radical context as well as *why* they are fundamental to the human project and the struggle for social and economic justice. And vigilance also means that we must have a good idea of how we might use our concepts and expressions, especially those that convey our values or principles, to challenge the dominant ideology through our critical/revolutionary praxis. Although I already have touched on all of these concepts at one point or another in this book, I want to make a few further comments on what I think is happening to them as well as a few other important concepts in our contemporary experience of capitalism—that is, the way, within the dominant ideological discourse, that their use, which often amounts to either denigration or dismissal, helps to maintain the legitimacy of capitalism and obliterates any hope of an alternative form of existence. These comments are intended to highlight further areas of vulnerability in the dominant ideology—areas that should be priorities for ideology critique not just because of their vulnerability, but also because they are barriers to revolutionary social transformation. My comments are also intended to demarcate a critical stance with respect to each of these concepts—a stance from which we might be better able to critique the dominant ideological discourse that arises from capitalist social relations and that serves to maintain capitalist hegemony, and thus a stance from which we might also begin to engage in a truly effective challenge to global capitalism. I begin with a brief résumé of some of the worst barriers we face in mounting this challenge.

The idea that certain values, experiences and knowledge have a potential resonance for all members of humanity is being decisively discredited. As a consequence, ideas, such as "truth" and even "humanity" and many of the values associated with them are losing all but a very particularistic or localized significance (Allman, 1999; Allman and Wallis, 1995b). As I said before, the idea that there are no truths or universal values to which all human being might subscribe is becoming the new "truth" promulgated in celebration of human diversity. And this so-called celebration of human diversity ends up as little more than a glib artifice—a disingenuous recognition of the other—that forestalls genuine attempts to come together to work through our differences and diverse experiences in order to discover the ideas, values and experiences that might truly mediate the social relations of human beings, thus establishing our human identity—our humanity.

I would argue, and have done elsewhere (e.g., Allman, 1999), that coherence is one of the values that must be rescued for our struggle for social transformation. Coherence has come under concerted attack, but it is persistently ridiculed in a way that may betray a significant misunderstanding of why coherence was once something that people valued. If not a misunderstanding, then it certainly betrays an ignorance of the critical importance of the human quest to create a coherent self (Gramsci, 1971; Lovibond, 1989). Thwarting this quest could mean the end of any possibility of critically transforming our society or of envisioning a better future for the whole of humanity. The coherent self was never a given, but rather a self or an identity that individuals had to struggle to create—an identity based on developing ideas, values and beliefs that were logically and ethically consistent and which could help us to make sense of our diverse experiences. This was a struggle with no finality, or discontinuous points of arrival, but one that involved ongoing critical reflection and development—in other words, a life-long process of becoming more fully human. This struggle also entailed working through the contradictions in our multilayered identities, not just accepting them and embracing the resulting incongruities. Moreover, the ideas, values and beliefs that one eventually chose in striving to establish coherence were not chosen because of some trivial aim or individual whim; they were social ideas, values and beliefs that developed their significance within our social relations and often through social struggle (Taylor, 1991). Choosing or deciding on the basis of socially derived significance was, therefore, an important aspect in the individual's struggle for coherence and also the key to establishing the ethical core of one's individuality. In fact, the idea of being able to freely choose one thing rather than another—that is "freedom of choice" itself—only became a value of significance because people had to struggle within their societies for this freedom, and it retained its significance because individuals could choose and then embrace values that were significant in terms of the social good as well as their own individual fulfillment (Allman, 1999; Allman and Wallis, 1995b; Taylor, 1991).

All of these aspects of the coherent self are interrelated; therefore, the ridicule or flagrant dismissal of the coherent self poses a threat that strikes at the very heart of the radical project for revolutionary social transformation—that is, the transformation of ourselves and the development of our individuality that must go hand-in-hand with the transformation of our socioeconomic conditions of existence. Individuals—that is, the postmodern version—may still value "freedom of choice" in the creation of their identities, but the choice is made from a potpourri of fragments. Other than diversity, there is no other value with any agreed social significance that can provide coherence to the identity that is created. Those who promote the idea of this kaleidoscopic self express no sense of loss, but surely a great deal has been lost. The whole notion of human agency or the idea of "subjects"—sensual human beings—who can envision their future and take part in the creation of their own destinies hangs on the possibility of the coherent self—a possibility that is extinguished with the "death of the subject" or, in other words, the "death of the coherent self," a self capable of critical agency. And with that loss, what reason could we possibly have for promoting revolutionary critical education or, for that matter, revolutionary social transformation? In fact, there is little reason to promote any kind of critical education.

People do not need to be critical or even nominally intelligent to live in and adapt to a fragmented world—the world of commodities where our social relations are mediated by commodities. They can easily adapt to such a world with fragmented identities, where the only task is to satisfy their wants and desires and establish their "rights" to do so. All anyone needs to do is to succumb to the intoxication of the marketplace, the world emporium of capitalist commodities, and create life-styles and "Disneyfied" cultures from these already processed and commodified raw materials (Allman, 1999; Allman and Wallis, 1995b). Global capitalism increasingly separates humanity into rich and poor—the haves and the have-nothings—and accordingly capital needs consumers, or those with purchasing power, who are ever needy, multineedy and ever ready to shop. As a consequence, capital's ideology of progress also needs a concept of "more" that is linked to consumer choice rather than the elimination of scarcity. The fragmented and insatiable self is capital's ideal consumer. Clearly there is more at stake here than critical education or even revolutionary social transformation, although what this is may well depend on our engagement in both of these. The very meaning of being human or of realizing our potential as human beings is also at stake, but, then, of course, it always has been. Throughout the history of humankind there has always been the possibility that human beings might uncritically, and thus unwittingly, choose to become less human rather than critically choosing the ultimately more difficult task of becoming more fully human (Allman, 1999; Allman and Wallis, 1995b).

Hopefully, it is clear that we must challenge the dismissal of coherence and do everything we can not only to struggle for our own coherence but also to support others in their struggles—in other words, to do everything we can to reinsert coherence into the radical agenda. There are also many other challenges we could be making to the aspects of the dominant ideology I have commented on thus far, but, as I suggested before, the most crucial aspect of any challenge is our own clarity with respect to the concepts we are challenging. For example, critical educators should never have bought into a positivistic or static idea of truth. Critical, dialectical thinking enables us to understand the historical specificity of truth and to also be able to distinguish between various categories or levels of truth. I have explained throughout this book as well as elsewhere (e.g., Allman, 1999), that certain truths are historically specific to capitalism, just as there were truths historically specific to feudalism. There are also some truths, usually highly generalized ones, which seem to pertain thus far in human history. Due to their highly generalized nature, these transhistorical truths are usually only of use in critical analysis, when they are used in conjunction with historically specific truths (Sayer, 1987), and it is important to remember that they might not hold in the future. For example, thus far in human history one class or group of people has always exploited the labor of another group, but this need not be true and would not be if we take our destinies into our own hands. There are other truths that come into being at a particular conjuncture of capitalist history—in other words, conjuncturally specific truths that first come into existence at a particular conjuncture but that may endure beyond it as well. And there may be some truths that are eternal verities, or we may like to think of them as such because it is almost impossible for us to envision that it could be otherwise; however, we must be cautious of these, never becoming closed in what Freire refers to as "circles of certainty." I call these "metatranshistorical truths." Together, these categories or levels of truth constitute what I have called previously a dialectical concept of truth (Allman, 1999). This is the concept of truth that can, I think, be used to challenge either the modernist, positivistic concept of static, irrevocable truth or the postmodernist idea of the "impossibility of truth," both of which are embraced and used as needed within the dominant ideological discourse of capitalism.

As I said before, we also need to be clear about our ideas of unity and diversity as well as, in relation to these, our concept of humanity. It works entirely to capital's benefit that we devote so much time and energy focusing on our differences—e.g., cultural, ethnic, gender, racial, physical, intellectual, religious, sexual, age and status. It is advantageous to capital because it keeps us divided and struggling against one another rather than against capital—the grand puppet-master of all oppressions. When we are not focused on one of these significant differences, then we are encouraged to be autonomous individuals and to assert our individualism. (I think that there is a subtle difference between autonomy and individualism, and I will come to this in a moment.) Somewhere in all of this the fact that we are all members of the same species gets lost. We also forget the very significant fact that we are social beings—that is, beings who come into this world needing other human beings in order actually to survive and not just because we need what other human beings can do for us or provide for us but because we cannot survive if we are isolated from other human beings and deprived of their touch.

Individualism, autonomy, diversity and difference can all perform an ideological service to capital when they are forcibly separated or, as Marx would say, "violently abstracted" from their dialectical opposite (Marx, 1863; 1865, p. 268). Just as both the experience and the concept of leisure lose their true significance in the absence of work, so, too, does diversity, or difference, in the absence of unity. Likewise, without diversity and difference, unity becomes an empty, vacuous concept. This dialectical basis of meaning also pertains to autonomy. Individuals or groups seek to establish their autonomy or distinctiveness as part of something that is bigger or more encompassing, but without that "something" bigger or more encompassing, of which they are also an integral part, autonomy would have no meaning. Understood as internally related opposites—as part of a unity of opposites—difference, diversity and autonomy are radical and liberating concepts, but when conceptualized outside their unity, they become ideological weapons of capital, weapons that serve as one of the most useful forms of conquest: namely, divide and rule (Freire, 1972). Therefore, one of the most effective ways to challenge the ideological use of these concepts is to stress their dialectical unity—a unity that, in this case, is nonantagonistic and that provides for the full and authentic development, fulfillment or expression of each of the opposites. But to stress this unity authentically, we must also try to live the truth of their unity. This is the only way we can provide real substance and thus material strength to our challenge—our ideology critique.

Individualism, as I intimated before, is something entirely different. It is a concept embedded with capitalist sentiment and antisocial connotations that takes us beyond ideology and into the realm of mythology. Ideology may distort our understanding by not revealing the whole truth, but at least it is based on something tangible or something that exists. Individualism, on the other hand, is a myth that simply serves to legitimate selfishness, conceit and often greed. However, it works very much like ideology. We only profess our own or admire other people's individualism by leaving out or forgetting the others who are involved in any individualistic achievement—a bit like imagining one's self or another to be like Robinson Crusoe and forgetting all about his man, Friday, to say nothing of all the others who were significant to his self-formation. In other words, I am arguing that individualism is a thoroughly capitalist concept, one that has been violently and irretrievable extracted from any notion of the "other"— and one, therefore, that we should be challenging at every opportunity. And one way to do this is to stress an alternative concept that is not only more radical and more creative but also the dialectical opposite of our collectivity—the cooperative, interdependent spirit of our humanity. Individuality is a concept that encompasses all the aspects of our individual uniqueness, both those that we bring with us as we enter the world and also those that we consciously choose to incorporate into our identities from the social, political, moral–ethical and cultural realms of our existence. It is the sum total of our expressive being, a highly integrated composite of our individual uniqueness and the inner needs that constitute us as social beings. It is our internal link with our humanity. In other words, individuality and our collectivity, or humanity, are an internally related "unity of opposites" wherein the existence and full development of one depends upon the existence and the full development of the other.

Humanity is one of the most important concepts of all in our challenge to capitalist ideology. Humanity, as conceived within critical/revolutionary praxis, like coherence, is also not a given but, rather, something that is constantly in the "making" within a process that involves our constant striving to reach out to and become internally related to every other man, woman and child who inhabits this globe. It is a critically conscious process that involves not just a mere recognition of ourselves as social beings but that is motivated and energized by our need for one another—the idea that Freire (1974) expresses so well when he says: "I cannot be unless you are; for me to know [or to be], I need another subject of knowing [or being]." As I indicated before, this is a dialectical concept that embraces the unity—the internal relation—between our individuality and our humanity but one that involves, or depends on, a process of working through our differences in order to discover the ideas, values, experiences and knowledge that have a potential resonance for all human beings and that would thus enable us to establish our human identity—an identity, just as with our individual identities and individuality, that is always open to further growth and development. It is also a process that involves challenging and ultimately abolishing value, or more precisely value in its commodity and money forms, as the mediation of our social relations—a revolutionary process that then becomes a project for establishing a thoroughly human way of mediating our relations with one another (Postone, 1996).

This critical/revolutionary, dialectical concept of humanity can be developed through our critical/revolutionary praxis and then be used to underpin our challenge to many other vulnerable aspects of capitalist ideology. By recognizing our own individuality as being internally related to our humanity, we also recognize the impossibility of our own attainment or exercise of freedom, justice, equity, rights and responsibilities when these are not yet integral and universal aspects of the human condition. And this recognition should furnish us with further ammunition to expose the vacuous and "violently abstract" nature of the concepts that form the core aims or principles of liberal democracy—a nature that makes them compatible with capitalism and thus indispensable components of capitalist ideology. It should also enable us to challenge more effectively the way in which, once abstracted from the human condition, these concepts become located entirely within the experience of individuals, thus atomizing, or individuating, them from our collective or communal experiences. For example, the dominant ideological discourse on rights and responsibilities assigns responsibilities, together with rights, to the individual; therefore, any failures or shortcomings in exercising one's rights or assuming responsibility is pathologized—that is, attributed to an individual's pathology, an individual totally abstracted from his or her social context. To orchestrate this challenge, we can begin to develop and then struggle for the acceptance of "a communal and collective concept of rights and responsibilities" (Allman, 1999, p. 132). This concept would not neglect our individuality, but it could strike at the heart of capitalist individualism, and it could also encourage and foster dialogue and a much more democratic approach to decision-making as part of our preparation for social transformation.

In confronting the abstract and ideological nature of liberal democracy, we must also make it clear that its inherent ideas of freedom of choice and democratic decision-making are very specific ideas based on a market model of choosing or deciding by exit rather than voice (Bowles and Gintis, 1986). In our own efforts to democratize various aspects of our lives, we can develop an approach to democracy that involves people in voicing—that is, expressing and explaining—their ideas, hopes and desires in dialogue with others and (as far as possible within capitalist societies) in transforming their concrete reality in accord with these. It is especially important that we challenge any attempt to use the new communication technologies as a means of spreading exit rather than voice forms of decision-making, wherein the "click" of the mouse, as a form of virtual participation, becomes a substitute for real participation (Hellman, 2000). For example, the use of opinion polls or polling more generally could become substitutes for public debate and dialogue, substitutes that are likely to be employed increasingly as people gain access to the new technologies and which could then be used to convince us that we are engaging more fully in democratic governance or, for that matter, any type of high-tech encounter, even those initiated by the Left. Of course, the new technologies could be used alternatively to increase an authentic engagement of voices in our democratic governance, but this is unlikely to happen so long as that decision-making has to remain within the horizon of capitalism, the horizon that can be easily incorporated into questionnaires, opinion polls or any preset agenda framework.

Finally and perhaps most crucially, if we are to effectively critique and challenge capitalist ideology, we need to develop a clear concept of class. However, our task is complicated by the fact that the concept of class conveyed by capitalist ideology is actually drawn from traditional socialism. As I noted in chapters 2 and 4, Marx's concept of class—especially his concept of the working class—is bedeviled by various confusions. Some Marxists and also non-Marxists have accused him of not leaving a clear concept or definition of class. Others have narrowly defined the working class as those engaged in manual labor who have to sell their labor-power for a wage to the capitalists who privately own the means of production. I began to challenge these ideas in chapter 2 by explaining that Marx had left a very clear definition of class, at least a clear definition that could be easily discerned if we followed the leitmotiv that runs throughout his explanation of capitalism. To reiterate, for Marx the dialectical opposite—the negative and antagonistic opposite—of capital is productive labor. Productive labor is not only, or even necessarily foremost, the labor that produces tangible, or corporeal, commodities but, instead, any and all labor that produces surplus-value within the labor–capital relation. Marx predicted that there would be a continuous expansion of the working class—that is, the proletariat, a class that included all those who were as well as all those who were potentially productive laborers; and given this definition, a definition that is integral to his dialectical explanation of capitalism, his prediction could not have been more accurate.

Marx's concept of class could be revivifying and strengthening the Left, but instead we find a considerable number of socialists unwittingly supporting capitalist ideology because, holding fast to their undialectical concept of class, they are equally convinced that the working class is shrinking. As a result, some of these diehards urge us to refocus our revolutionary aspirations on what they consider to be the only remaining concentrations of the industrial working class, which, they argue, are now located primarily in developing countries; while others urge us to join forces with the new social movements and to consider the working class as no more important in the struggle against capital than any other group. Ironically and sadly, these are the ideas with the widest currency at the very moment in capitalist history when with daily regularity millions of people are having their labor incorporated into the labor–capital relation. And this involves not just the millions across the globe whose farming and handicrafts have been commodified for the world market and who now sell their labor-power as a commodity to the owners of capital, but also millions of others, working in a myriad of services and also professions, who are going through the same process of incorporation or, in Marx's words, the "subsumption" of their labor within the labor–capital relation. Never in the history of capitalism have there been so many people whose work now involves not only a labor process but also a process of creating value, a twofold value-creating process that includes the process of valorization and thus the impregnation of commodities—tangible or intangible—with surplus-value. Therefore, never have there been so many of us who could potentially join forces in opposition to capital. And in Gramscian terms, never have the truly progressive forces for epochal change been greater.

We must do everything we can to help others to understand that class has finally become, just as Marx predicted it would, the one factor that the vast majority of the world's population shares in common. This is why Gramsci stresses that the working class, or the proletariat, is the "truly progressive force," the only force capable of bringing about epochal change. Although it was always potentially the case, the world is now basically divided between those who produce surplus-value (or whose work is being transformed so that it will in the near future be productive of surplus-value) and those who extort it. Those who fall outside this divide have the same interests (theoretically but not necessarily) as one or the other of the two main classes. For a great number of these people, either their labor is equally exploited in order to enable some capitalists to claim a bigger share of the surplus-value that has been directly extorted (e.g., those who are employed by commercial capitalists) or they make their living by using their assets to claim some portion of the total surplus-value that is extorted by the commodity producing sector of their class (e.g., landlords and those who live off of interest-bearing capital). And, of course, disastrously, these are the millions who have become superfluous to capital's needs and whose interests coincide with those of the proletariat. Class is the one factor that runs across all social movements and issue groups and which also, of course, has the potential to divide them from within, but equally the potential to instigate a regrouping of forces that could stand together solidly in opposition to capital. In other words, Marx's definition of class has the potential to renew people's hope for a socialist future and to also renew and reenergize their solidarity and commitment to struggle for that future with a greater strength in numbers than they have ever had in the past. Clearly, disseminating and promoting this concept of class, through ideology critique and by other means as well, are important and crucial tasks for revolutionary critical education. And it should go without saying that Marx's dialectical concept of class also has tremendous implications for our organizational strategies.

One of the most gratifying aspects of Marx's explanation of capital is that it is truly one imbued with both a "language of critique and a language of possibility"—the dialectical potential of language, which is something Henry Giroux continuously argues all critical education should embrace (e.g. Giroux, 1989). Faced with the despair and destruction that follows in the wake of capitalism, it can sometimes seem difficult to sustain this type of more hopeful language; however, I would argue that when we dialectically conceptualize the reality of capitalism, hope becomes infectious for a number of reasons, two of which I will mention as I bring this discussion to a close. I said before that this is a propitious time for critical education because the contradictions of capital have become more transparent. That transparency should breathe the fresh air of hope and optimism into our hearts and minds because as we witness the dark and dismal truth of capital, we can also glimpse the promise of a brighter future for human-ity—a future in which we can collectively choose, and then make certain, that human dignity will be restored, scarcity eliminated and the planet restored and also a future in which the diverse communities of the world will establish a universality based on our need for and commitment to one another's well-being. A dialectical understanding of capitalism also enables us to imagine the real possibility of all those, whom C. L. R. James (1980)[2] calls the "restless nega-tives"—that is, all of the millions of human beings on the face of the earth who exist in an internal and antagonistic relation to capital—coming together with one voice to say "NO" to capital and "NO" to the relation that makes it possible and then joining together in solidarity to abolish that antagonistic relation and all its consequent absurdities so that we might become internally related to one another in the project for humanity. From this hope and imagination we might, just at last, begin the making of human history—a history created through the collective, critical/revolutionary praxis of human beings.

NOTES

1. Enlightenment philosophy accompanied the awakening of modernity in the eighteenth century, the century during which capitalism finally emerged as the dominant form of socioeconomic organization in Britain and in a few other Western countries. Enlightenment thought, and what has been called the Enlightenment Project, was the mode of thinking appropriate for those "New Times"; it moved, in the language of today's "New Times" thinkers, with the "grain" of its time. It stressed the power of rational thought, and by the nineteenth century, it was embraced by many of the most critical thinkers of the time, including Marx (although Marx expanded the idea of rational thought, thus considerably improving it, by his inclusion of dialectical conceptualization). This emphasis on rationality tended to exclude other forms of thinking and led to the dichotomization, or dualistic separa-tion, of rationality and objectivity from spirituality and subjectivity. As I have argued in the text, dichotomized thinking, or the tendency to think in terms of dichotomies, arises from the material conditions of capitalism.

2. I owe an apology and a debt of gratitude to C. L. R. James. For a number of years I have used his expression, the "restless negative" (e.g., Allman, 1999) believing it to be my own rendition of Marx's concept of internal movement or restlessness within the negative, which he refers to in both *The Holy Family* (Marx and Engels, 1844)and his *Economic and Philo-sophical Manuscripts* (1844a), but I was always plagued by a niggling memory that I had

come across it in another text—one of the many—I had read when I was trying to come to grips with dialectical thinking. Recently, when I was having dinner at a dear friend's house, I noticed a stack of books on her sideboard, a rather large stack that could not help but draw my attention. When I asked why she had a stack of books sitting on the sideboard, she said that it was books she had borrowed from various people, but she could not remember when or from whom she had borrowed them. Of course, I asked to take a look and proceeded to find three of my books that I thought were lost forever. One of them, in particular, was like finding a long-lost friend, and that was James's *Notes on Dialectics*, a book I remembered fondly for its wit but also because it had given me a real feel for dialectical movement. I could not wait to reread it; and when I did, I found, of course, his wonderful expression, the "restless negative," one that I had for so long wanted to claim as my own. So all I can say is "thank you" C. L. R. James; and I'm truly sorry for the plagiarism. I should note, in case any reader is fortunate enough to come across this book, which I believe is out of print, that James uses Marx's concept of "negativity" in a slightly deterministic or teleological manner that is indicative of a Hegelian dialectic rather than Marx's open and nonteleological dialectic; therefore this use of the expression is something that I did not borrow.

REFERENCES

Allman, P. (1999). *Revolutionary Social Transformation: Democratic Hopes, Political Possibilities and Critical Education.* Westport, CT : Bergin & Garvey.

Allman, P. (2001). "Education on Fire!" Foreword in M. Cole, D. Hill and G. Rikowski in discussion with P. McLaren, *Red Chalk: On Schooling, Capitalism and Politics.* Brighton, U.K.: Institute for Educational Policy Studies.

Allman, P., and Wallis, J. (1995a). "Gramsci's Challenge to the Politics of the Left in 'Our Times.'" *International Journal of Lifelong Education*, 14 (No. 2, March/April), 120–143.

Allman, P., and Wallis, J. (1995b). "Challenging the Post Modern Condition: Radical Adult Education for Critical Intelligence." In M. Mayo and J. Thompson (Eds.), *Adult Learning, Critical Intelligence and Social Change* (pp. 18–33). Leicester, U.K.: National Institute for Adult and Continuing Education.

Benn, T. (1984). "Discussion as an Instrument for Social Change." Presentation at a one-day conference on "Adult Education for Social Action," The University of Nottingham, 30 June.

Bowles, S., and Gintis, H. (1986). *Democracy and Capitalism.* London: Routledge and Kegan Paul.

Freire, P. (1972). *Pedagogy of the Oppressed.* Harmondsworth, U.K.: Penguin.

Freire, P. (1974). "Authority versus Authoritarianism." Audiotape, in series: *Thinking with Paulo Freire.* Sydney, Australia: Australian Council of Churches.

Freire, P. (1985). *The Politics of Education.* London: Macmillan.

Freire, P. (1998). *Pedagogy of Freedom: Ethics, Democracy and Civic Courage,* translated by Patrick Clarke. Oxford: Rowman & Littlefield.

Giddens, A. (1998). *The Third Way: The Renewal of Social Democracy.* Cambridge: Polity Press.

Giroux, H. A. (1989). *Schooling for Democracy, Critical Pedagogy in the Modern Age.* London: Routledge.

Gramsci, A. (1971). *Selections from the Prison Notebooks of Antonio Gramsci,* edited and translated by Quinton Hoare and Geoffrey Nowell Smith. London: Lawrence & Wishart.

Harvey, D. (1989). *The Condition of Postmodernity.* Oxford: Basil Blackwell.

Hellman, J. A. (2000). "Real and Virtual Chiapas: Magic Realism and the Left." In L. Panitch and C. Leys (Eds.), *Socialist Register 2000, Necessary and Unnecessary Utopias* (pp. 161–186). Rendlesham, U.K.: Merlin.

Hughes, H. S. (1959). *Consciousness and Society.* London: MacGibbon and Kee.

James, C. L. R. (1980). *Notes on Dialectics: Hegel, Marx, Lenin.* London: Allison & Busby.

Lovibond, S. (1989). "Feminism and postmodernism." *New Left Review,* 178 (November/December), 5–28.

Marx, K. (1844). *Economic and Philosophical Manuscripts.* In K. Marx and F. Engels, *Collected Works,* Vol. 4 (pp. 229–346). London: Lawrence & Wishart, 1972.

Marx, K. (1858). *Grundrisse,* translated and with a Foreword by Martin Nicolaus. Harmondsworth, U.K.: Penguin, 1973.

Marx, K. (1863). *Theories of Surplus Value,* Part 3. London: Lawrence & Wishart, 1972.

Marx, K. (1865). *Capital,* Vol. 3, translated by David Fernbach, Introduction by Ernest Mandel. Harmondsworth, U.K.: Penguin, 1981.

Marx, K., and Engels, F. (1844). *The Holy Family.* In K. Marx and F. Engels, *Collected Works*, Vol. 4 (pp. 5–211). London: Lawrence & Wishart, 1975.

Postone, M. (1996). *Time, Labor, and Social Domination: A Reinterpretation of Marx's Critical Theory.* Cambridge: Cambridge University Press.

Sayer, D. (1987). *The Violence of Abstraction: The Analytical Foundations of Historical Materialism.* Oxford: Basil Blackwell.

Taylor, C. (1991). *The Ethics of Authenticity.* Cambridge, MA: Harvard University Press.

Wood, E. M. (1999). "Unhappy Families: Global Capitalism in a World of Nation-States." *Monthly Review*, 51 (No. 3) [www.monthlyreview.org].

Brosio, R. A. (1997). "The Complexly Constructed Citizen-Worker: His/Her Centrality to the Struggle for Democratic Politics and Education." *Journal of Thought* (Autumn), 9–26.

Brosio, R. A. (2000). *Philosophical Scaffolding for the Construction of Critical Democratic Education.* New York: Peter Lang.

Brown, T. (1999). "Challenging Globalization as Discourse and Phenomenon." *International Journal of Lifelong Education,* 18 (No. 1, January/February), 3–17.

Buttigieg, J. A., and Mayo, P. (2000). *Gramsci and Education.* Lanham, MD/Oxford: Rowman & Littlefield.

Callinicos, A. (1983). *Marxism and Philosophy.* Oxford: Oxford University Press.

Callinicos, A. (1998). "World Capitalism at the Abyss." *International Socialism.* 81 (Winter), 3–43.

Callinicos, A. (1998). "The Secret of the Dialectic." *International Socialism,* 82 (Summer), 93–103.

Callinicos, A. (1999). "Social Theory Put to the Test: Pierre Bordieu and Anthony Giddens." *New Left Review,* 236 (July/August), 77–102.

Carnoy, M., Castells, M., Cohen, S., and Cardosa, F. A. (1993). *The New Global Economy in the Information Age.* London: Macmillan.

Castells, M. (1996). *The Rise of the Network Society.* Oxford: Basil Blackwell.

Chomsky, N. (1998). "Power in the Global Arena." *New Left Review,* 230 (July/August), 3–27.

Cole, M. (1998). "Globalisation, Modernisation and Competitiveness: A Critique of the New Labour Project in Education." *International Studies in Sociology of Education,* 8 (No. 3), 315–332.

Cole, M., Hill, D., and Rikowski, G. (1997). "Between Postmodernism and Nowhere: The Predicament of the Postmodernist." *British Journal of Educational Studies,* 45 (No. 2, June), 187–200.

Colletti, L. (1975). "Marxism and the Dialectic." *New Left Review,* 93 (September/October), 3–29.

Connell, D. (1997). "After the Shooting Stops: Revolution in Postwar Eritrea." *Race & Class,* 38 (No. 4, June), 57–78.

Craig, G., and Mayo, M. (Eds.) (1995). *Community Empowerment: A Reader in Participation and Development.* London: Zed.

Dunayevskaya, R. (1964). *Marxism and Freedom . . . from 1776 until Today.* New York: Twayne.

Dunayevskaya, R. (1973). *Philosophy and Revolution.* New York: Delta.

Eagleton, T. (1996). *The Illusions of Postmodernism.* Oxford: Basil Blackwell.

Einstein, A. (1998). "Why Socialism?" *Monthly Review,* 50 (No. 1), 1–10.

Foley, G. (1999). *Learning and Social Action: A Contribution to Understanding Informal Education.* London: Zed.

Foley, G. (1999). "Back to Basics: A Political Economy of Workplace Change And Learning." *Studies in the Education of Adults,* 31 (No. 2), 181–196.

Freire, A. M. A., and Macedo, D. (Eds.)(1998). *The Paulo Freire Reader.* New York: Continuum.

Freire, P. (1978). *Pedagogy in Process: Letters from Guinea-Bissau,* translated by C. St. John Hunter. New York: Continuum/Seabury Press.

Freire, P. (1994). *Pedagogy of Hope.* New York: Continuum.

Further Readings

Allman, P. (1994). "Paulo Freire's Contributions to Radical Adult Education." *St_ ies in the Education of Adults,* 26 (No. 2), 144–161.

Allman, P., and Wallis, J. (1990). "Praxis: Implications for 'Really' Radical Ed_ tion." *Studies in the Education of Adults,* 22 (No. 1), 14–30.

Bauman, Z. (1990). *Globalization. The Human Consequences.* New York: Col University Press.

Benn, T. (1989). "Obstacles to Reform in Britain." In R. Miliband, L. Panitc Saville (Eds.), *Socialist Register 1989* (pp. 130–145) London: Me_

Bloch, B. (1971). *On Karl Marx.* New York: Herder and Herder.

Bonefeld, W., Gunn, R., and Psychopedis, K. (Eds.)(1992). *Open Marxis_ I: Dialectics and History.* London: Pluto Press.

Bonefeld, W., Gunn, R., and Psychopedis, K. (Eds.) (1992). *Open Marxi_ II. Theory and Practice.* London: Pluto Press.

Bonefeld, W., Gunn, R., Holloway, J., and Psychopedis, K. (Eds.) (*Marxism, Volume III: Emancipating Marx.* London: Pluto Pr_

Bonefeld, W., and Holloway, J. (Eds.) (1996). *Global Capital, Nation_ Politics of Money.* London: Macmillan.

Bordieu, P. (1998). "A Reasoned Utopia and Economic Fatalism." *N_ 227 (January/February), 125–130.

Borg, C., Mayo, P., and Sultana, R. (1997). "Revolution and Real with Peter McLaren." In W. Pinar (Ed.), *Curriculum _ York: Garland.

Brosio, R. A. (1990). "Teaching and Learning for Democratic Critical Evaluation." *Educational Theory,* 40 (No. 1),

Brosio, R. A. (1994). *A Radical Democratic Critique of Capit_ York: Peter Lang.

Freire, P. (1996). *Letters to Christina. Reflections on My Life and Work.* New York: Routledge.

Freire, P. (1997). *Pedagogy of the Heart.* New York: Continuum.

Gadotti, M. (1994). *Reading Paolo Freire: His Life and Work.* Albany, NY: SUNY.

Giroux, H. A. (1999). "Rethinking Cultural Politics and Radical Pedagogy in the Work of Antonio Gramsci." *Educational Theory,* 49 (No. 1, Autumn), 1–19.

Gramsci, A. (1977). *Selections from Political Writings 1910–1920,* edited by Q. Hoare, translated by J. Mathews. London: Lawrence & Wishart.

Gramsci, A. (1978). *Selections from Political Writings 1921–1926,* edited and translated by Q. Hoare. London: Lawrence & Wishart.

Gramsci, A. (1979). *Letters from Prison,* translated and with an Introduction by L. Lawner. London: Quartet Books.

Gramsci, A. (1994). *Pre-Prison Writings,* edited by R. Bellamy, translated by V. Cox. Cambridge: Cambridge University Press.

Green, A. (1994). "Postmodernism and State Education." *Journal of Educational Policy,* 9 (No. 1), 67–83.

Green, A. (1997). *Education, Globalization and the Nation State.* London: Macmillan.

Harman, C. (1999). *Explaining the Crisis: A Marxist Re-Appraisal.* London: Bookmarks.

Harstock, N. (1998). "Marxist Feminist Dialectic for the 21st Century." *Science & Society,* 62 (No. 3), 400–413.

Harvey, D. (1998). "The Geography of Class Power." In L. Panitch and C. Leys (Eds.), *Socialist Register 1998, The Communist Manifesto Now* (pp. 49–74). Rendlesham, U.K.: Merlin.

Hatcher, R. (1998). "Social Justice and the Politics of School Effectiveness and Improvement." *Race, Ethnicity and Education,* 1 (No. 2), 267–289.

Hayter, T., and Harvey, D. (Eds.)(1993). *The Factory and the City: The Story of Cowley Automobile Workers in Oxford.* London: Mansell.

Hill, D. (1998). "Neo-liberalism and Hegemony Revisited." *Educational Philosophy and Theory,* 30 (No. 1), 69–83.

Hill, D. (Ed.) (2001). *Education, Education, Education: Capitalism, Socialism and "The Third Way".* London: Tufnell Press.

Hill, D., and Cole, M. (Eds.) (1999). *Schooling and Equality: Factual and Conceptual Issues.* London: Tufnell Press.

Hill, D., McLaren, P., Cole, M., and Rikowski, G. (1999). *Postmodernism in Educational Theory: Education and the Politics of Human Resistance.* London: Tufnell Press.

Hillcole Group (1997). *Rethinking Education and Democracy.* London: Tufnell Press.

Hirsch, J. (1999). "Globalization, Class and the Question of Democracy." In L. Panitch and C. Leys (Eds.), *Socialist Register 1999, Global Capitalism Versus Democracy* (pp. 278–293). Rendlesham, U.K.: Merlin.

Hodgkinson, P. (1991). "Educational Change: A Model for Its Analysis." *British Journal of the Sociology of Education,* 12 (No. 2), 203–222.

Holst, J. (1999). "The Affinities of Lenin and Gramsci: Implications for Radical Adult Education Theory and Practice." *International Journal of Lifelong Education* 18 (No. 5, September/October), 407–421.

Hudis, P. (2000). "The Dialectical Structure of Marx's *Revolution in Permanence.*" *Capital & Class,* 70 (Spring), 127–143.

Huws, U. (1999). "The Material World: The Myth of the Weightless Economy." In L. Panitch and C. Leys (Eds.), *Socialist Register 1999, Global Capitalism Versus Democracy* (pp. 29–55). Rendlesham, U.K.: Merlin.

Itoh, M., and Lapavitsas, C. (1999). *Political Economy of Money and Finance.* Basingstoke, U.K.: Macmillan.

Jameson, F. (1998). "Persistencies of the Dialectic: Three Sites." *Science & Society,* 62 (No. 3, Autumn), 358–372.

Johnston, R. (1999). "Adult Learning for Citizenship: Towards a Reconstruction of the Social Purpose Tradition." *International Journal of Lifelong Education,* 18 (No. 3, May–June), 175–190.

Kelly, J. (2000). "Gender and Equality: One Hand Tied Behind Us." In Cole, M. (Ed.), *Education, Equality and Human Rights.* London: Routledge/Falmer.

Kincheloe, J. (1999). *How Do We Tell the Workers?* Boulder, CO: Westview.

Kincheloe, J., and Steinberg, S. (1997). *Changing Multiculturalism.* Buckingham: Open University Press.

King, A. (Ed.) (1991). *Culture, Globalization and the World-System: Contemporary Conditions for the Presentation of Identity.* New York: Macmillan.

Lasch, C. (1995). *The Revolt of the Elites and the Betrayal of Democracy.* London: W. W. Norton.

Ledwith, M. (1997). *Participating in Transformation: Towards a Working Model of Community Empowerment.* Birmingham, U.K.: Venture.

Livingstone, D. W. (1995). "Searching for the Missing Links: Neo-Marxist Theories of Education." *British Journal of the Sociology of Education,* 61 (No. 1), 53–73.

Livingstone, D. W. (1999). The Education–Jobs Gap: Underemployment or Economic Democracy. Boulder, CO: Westview.

Lukács, G. (1971). *History of Class Consciousness: Studies in Marxist Dialectics,* translated by R. Livingstone. London: Merlin.

Luxemburg, R. (1961). *The Accumulation of Capital,* introduced by Joan Robinson, translated by A. Schwartzschild. London: Routledge and Kegan Paul.

Luxemburg, R. (1972). *Selected Political Writings,* edited and introduced by R. Locker, translated by W. D. Graf. London: Cape.

Luxemburg, R. (1989). *Reform and Revolution,* introduced by D. Gluckstein. London: Bookmarks.

Martin, I. (1999). "Lifelong Learning for Democracy: Stretching the Discourse of Citizenship." *Scottish Journal of Adult and Continuing Education,* 5 (No. 2), 89–105.

Martin, R. (1999). "Rereading Marx: A Critique of Recent Criticisms." *Science & Society,* 62 (No. 4), 513–536.

Mayo, M. (1997). *Imagining Tomorrow: Adult Education for Transformation.* Leicester: National Institute for Adult and Continuing Education.

Mayo, M., and Thompson, J. L. (Eds.). *Adult Learning, Critical Intelligence and Social Change.* Leicester, U.K.: National Institute for Adult and Continuing Education.

Mayo, P. (1997). "Workers' Education and Democracy." In G. Baldacchino and P. Mayo (Eds.), *Beyond Schooling: Adult Education in Malta.* Malta: Mireva.

McLaren, P. (1995). *Critical Pedagogy and Predatory Culture: Oppositional Politics in a Postmodern Era.* London: Routledge.

McLaren, P. (1997). *Revolutionary Multiculturalism: Pedagogies of Dissent for the New Millennium.* Boulder, CO: Westview.

McLaren, P. (1999). "The Educational Researcher as Critical Social Agent." In C. A. Grant (Ed.), *Multicultural Research. A Reflective Engagement with Race, Class, Gender and Sexual Orientation.* Philadelphia: Falmer.

McLaren, P. (2000). *Che Guevara, Paulo Freire, and The Pedagogy of Revolution.* Lanham, MD: Rowman & Littlefield.

McLaren, P., and Farahmandpar, R. (2000). "Reconsidering Marx in Post-Marxist Times: A Requiem for Postmodernism?" *Education Researcher,* 29 (No. 3), 25–33.

McLellan, D. (1979). *Marxism After Marx.* London: Macmillan.

McLellan, D., and Sayer, S. (1991). *Socialism and Democracy.* London: Macmillan.

Morley, D., and Chen, K. H. (Eds.) (1996). *Stuart Hall. Critical Dialogues in Cultural Studies.* London: Routledge.

Morrow, R. A., and Torres, C.A. (1995). *Social Theory and Education. A Critique of Theories of Social and Cultural Reproduction.* Albany, NY: SUNY Press.

Neary, M., and Taylor, G. (1998). *Money and the Human Condition.* London: Macmillan.

Ollman, B. (1993). *Dialectic Investigations.* New York: Routledge.

Ollman, B. (1998). *Market Socialism: The Debate Among Socialists.* New York: Routledge.

Ollman, B. (1998). "Why Dialectics? Why Now?" *Science & Society,* 62 (No. 3, Autumn), 338–357.

Panitch, L., Wood, E. M., and Saville, J. (1995). *Socialist Register 1995, Why Not Capitalism.* Rendlesham, U.K.: Merlin.

Radice, H. (1999). "Taking Globalisation Seriously." In L. Panitch and C. Leys (Eds.), *Socialist Register 1999, Global Capitalism versus Democracy.* Rendlesham, U.K.: Merlin.

Ransome, P. (1992). *Antonio Gramsci. A New Introduction.* London: Harvester Wheatsheaf.

Rikowski, G. (1996). "Left Alone: End Time for Marxist Educational Theory?" *British Journal of Sociology of Education,* 17 (No. 4), 415–451.

Rikowski, G. (1997). "Scorched Earth: Prelude to Rebuilding Marxist Educational Theory." *British Journal of Sociology of Education,* 18 (No. 4), 55, 1–574.

Rikowski, G. (1998). "Nietzsche, Marx and Mastery." In H. Rainbird and P. Ainley (Eds.), *Apprenticeship: Towards a New Paradigm for Learning.* London: Kogan Page.

Rikowski, G. (2001). *The Battle in Seattle: Its Significance for Education.* London: Tufnell Press.

Rikowski, G., and Neary, M. (1997). "Working School Children in Britain Today." *Capital & Class,* 63, 25–35.

Robertson, R. (1992). *Globalization: Social Theory and Global Culture.* London: Sage.

Sassoon, S. A. (Ed.)(1982). *Approaches to Gramsci.* London: Writers and Readers Publishing Cooperative Society.

Scheuerman, W. E. (1999). "Globalisation and Exceptional Powers: The Erosion of Liberal Democracy." *Radical Philosophy,* 93 (January/February), 14–23.

Schugurensky, D. (1998). "The Legacy of Paulo Freire: A Critical Review of His Contributions." *Convergence,* 31 (Nos. 1 and 2), 17–38.

Simon, B. (Ed.) (1990). *The Search for Enlightenment: The Working Class and Adult Education in the Twentieth Century.* London: Lawrence & Wishart.

Spring, J. (1998). *Education and The Rise of the Global Economy.* Mahwah, NJ: Lawrence Erlbaum.

Taylor, C. (1989). *Sources of Self: The Making of the Modern Identity.* Cambridge: Cambridge University Press.

Walters, S. (Ed.)(1997). *Globalization, Adult Education and Training: Impacts and Issues.* London: Zed.

Waters, M. (1995). *Globalization.* London: Routledge.

Welton, M. (1993). "Social Revolutionary Learning: The New Social Movements as Learning Sites." *Adult Education Quarterly,* 43 (No. 3), 152–164.

Wood, E. M. (1998). "The Communist Manifesto 150 Years Later." *Monthly Review,* 50 (No. 1), 27–37.

Index

ABOUT THE AUTHOR

Paula Allman is an Honorary Research Fellow in the School of Continuing Education at the University of Nottingham, England. She is the author of *Revolutionary Social Transformation: Democratic Hopes, Political Possibilities and Critical Education* (Bergin & Garvey, 1999).